MATILDA OF SCOTLAND:
A STUDY IN MEDIEVAL QUEENSHIP

MATILDA OF SCOTLAND: A STUDY IN MEDIEVAL QUEENSHIP

Lois L. Huneycutt

THE BOYDELL PRESS

© Lois L. Huneycutt 2003

All Rights Reserved. Except as permitted under current legislation
no part of this work may be photocopied, stored in a retrieval system,
published, performed in public, adapted, broadcast,
transmitted, recorded or reproduced in any form or by any means,
without the prior permission of the copyright owner

First published 2003
The Boydell Press, Woodbridge

The Boydell Press is an imprint of Boydell & Brewer Ltd
PO Box 9, Woodbridge, Suffolk IP12 3DF, UK
and of Boydell & Brewer Inc.
PO Box 41026, Rochester, NY 14604–4126, USA
website: www.boydell.co.uk

ISBN 0 85115 994 X

A catalogue record for this book is available
from the British Library

Library of Congress Cataloging-in-Publication Data
Huneycutt, Lois L.
 Matilda of Scotland : a study in medieval queenship / Lois L.
Huneycutt.
  p. cm.
 Includes bibliographical references and index.
  ISBN 085115994X (hardback : alk. paper)
 1 Matilda, Queen, consort of Henry I, King of England, 1080–1118.
2. Henry I, King of England, 1068–1135 – Marriage. 3. Monarchy –
Great Britain – History – To 1500. 4. Great Britain – History –
Henry I, 1100–1135. 5. Queens – Great Britain – Biography. I. Title.
DA199.M38H86 2003
942.02′3′092 – dc21   2002154563

This publication is printed on acid-free paper

Typeset by Joshua Associates Ltd, Oxford
Printed in Great Britain by
St Edmundsbury Press Ltd, Bury St Edmunds, Suffolk

Contents

Acknowledgments	vii
Abbreviations	ix
Introduction	1
1 Edith, Princess of Scotland	9
2 Strategies for Success: English Queenship before 1100	31
3 The Queen's Demesne: The Lands and Revenues of Queen Matilda II	55
4 'Godric and Goddiva': Queen Matilda's Political Role	73
5 'Mater, Nutrix, Domina et Regina': Queen Matilda and the Church	103
6 Queen Matilda and the Arts	125
Conclusion	145
Appendix I A Handlist of Matilda of Scotland's Acta	151
Appendix II A Translation of the *Life of St Margaret*	161
Bibliography	179
Index	201

To my mother, Carol Marie Sime Huneycutt,
and my husband, A. Mark Smith

Acknowledgments

No one can write a book without incurring debts of gratitude along the way. My list of those who have helped in various ways is long, and starts with my graduate days at the University of California, Santa Barbara, where I began working on Matilda and medieval queenship under the direction of Jeffrey Burton Russell, Sharon A. Farmer, and, most directly, the late C. Warren Hollister. Warren would have loved to see the book in print, and if I had not had longer-standing debts to my mother and husband, I would have dedicated this book to his memory. My graduate professors were incredibly supportive and generous with time, expertise, and encouragement. They also ran wonderfully stimulating seminars. Thanks are due to fellow seminarians and friends Robert S. Babcock, Heather Tanner, Cassandra Potts, J. Michael Burger, Marylou Ruud, Donald Fleming, Janet Pope, Lauren Jared, Jan Ryder, Penelope Ann Adair, Miriam Davis, Fiona Harris Stoertz, Angus MacDonald, Deborah McBride, and Richard Barton. Deborah Gerish, Robert Helmerichs, David Spear, Marc Meyer, Sally N. Vaughn, and Karen Jolly, fellow Santa Barbarians but who matriculated before or after I did, also offered their perspectives and encouragement at crucial moments during the development of this text. Other graduate friends, not from Santa Barbara but working in similar fields, also stimulated my thinking, and to Elizabeth McCartney, Miriam Shadis, and Kimberly LoPrete more thanks are due. A research trip to England brought me into contact with many people who read parts or all of my manuscript, and whose comments have been invaluable. Special thanks are due to Elisabeth M. C. van Houts, Marjorie Chibnall, Janet Nelson, David Crouch, Chris Lewis, Robert Bartlett, and the late W. L. Warren, who among many others heard my fledgling presentations and lent their expertise in one way or another. I was able to spend parts of two summers researching in London, and access to the collections of the University of London's Institute for Historical Research allowed me to get done in weeks what would have taken several months otherwise. My colleagues at the University of Missouri, Columbia, have been supportive all along; special thanks go to Larry Okamura, Charles Nauert, Anne Stanton, Steve Watts, and John Bullion. The staff of the history department, including Marie Sloan, Nancy Taube, Melinda Lockwood, and Patty Eggleston, have made my life easier in many ways. My own graduate students, in particular Kristi B. Keuhn, Robyn Kehoe Ramsey, and Jason W. Evans, have read or heard parts of this book, and their critiques and insightful questions have sharpened my prose. I have also received institutional grants from the University of Missouri Research Board and Research Council. Chapter Three was written during a summer when I was supported with a grant from the National Endowment for the Humanities.

Finally, there are those people without whose constant support and encouragement the book would never have been written. My mother, Carol Marie Huneycutt, is everything a daughter could ask for and more; my husband, A. Mark Smith, shares the perils of combining a career and the raising of two rambunctious boys, and usually manages to do it cheerfully. Caroline Palmer and the other editorial staff at Boydell & Brewer have been prompt, tactful, and helpful beyond the call of duty. Finally, John Carmi Parsons has been a friend, a mentor, and a model of meticulous scholarship and personal integrity. His comments on many of my articles and an earlier version of this manuscript made the book much better than it would have been without him; that it is not better still remains no one's fault but my own.

Abbreviations

Abingdon Chronicle	*Chronicon monasterii de Abingdon.* Ed. Joseph Stevenson. 2 vols. London, 1858.
Anselmi opera omnia	*S. Anselmi Cantuariensis archiepiscopi opera omnia.* Ed. Francis S. Schmitt. 6 vols. Stuttgart, 1946–61, repr. 1968.
Cartulary HTA	*The Cartulary of Holy Trinity Aldgate.* Ed. Gerald Hodgett. London, 1971.
Gesta regum	William of Malmesbury. *Gesta regum anglorum: The History of the English Kings.* Ed. and trans. R. A. B. Mynors, R. M. Thomson, and M. Winterbottom. Oxford, 1998.
MGH	*Monumenta Germaniae Historica.* Ed. Georg H. Pertz, Georg Waitz and others; Hanover, Berlin, Weimar, etc., 1876– .
Orderic	Orderic Vitalis. *The Ecclesiastical History of Orderic Vitalis.* Ed. and trans. Marjorie Chibnall. 6 vols. Oxford, 1969–80.
PL	*Patrologiae cursus completus, series latina.* Ed. J. P. Migne. 221 vols. Paris, 1844–64.
RRAN	*Regesta regum Anglo-Normannorum.* Vol. 1 ed. David Bates, Vol. 2 ed. C. Johnson and H. A. Cronne, Vol. 3 ed. H. A. Cronne and R. H. C. Davis. Oxford, 1956–98.
RS	Rolls Series
Rolls Series	*Rerum Brittanicarum mediiaevi scriptores.* London: Her Majesty's Stationers Office, 1858–96. Reprints (in progress), Kraus Reprint House, New York.
S	P. H. Sawyer, ed., *Anglo-Saxon Charters: An Annotated List and Bibliography.* London Offices of the Royal Historical Society, 1968.
TRE	*Tempore regis Eadwardis: Domesday* abbreviation for 'in time of King Edward' (1042–1066).
TRW	Tempore regis Wilhelmi: Domesday abbreviation for 'in the time of King William I' (1066–1087).
VCH	*Victoria County Histories of England.*

Introduction:
Another Esther in our Times

Matilda, princess of Scotland and consort to Henry I of England from 1100 to 1118, was one of the most powerful and influential women of the twelfth century. As queen, she controlled a substantial demesne that allowed her to exercise both lay and ecclesiastical patronage. She helped to introduce the new Augustinian canons into England by founding Holy Trinity, Aldgate, and she continued to be a patron of its daughter houses. Matilda was also responsible for works of practical importance, particularly in London and the surrounding area. She built hospitals, bridges and a public bathhouse. In addition, the personal relationship between Henry and Matilda was evidently one of mutual respect, and contemporaries throughout Europe corresponded with her, knowing that she was in a position to influence the king's actions. She was a trusted partner in administering Henry's cross-channel realm, served as a member of his *curia regis*, and, on occasion, acted with what amounted to vice-regal authority in England while Henry was in Normandy. Furthermore, Matilda enjoyed music, the visual arts, and literature, and under her guidance the Anglo-Norman court became a focus for these cultural activities. She earned the devotion of the realm through her numerous charities as well as her reputation for personal piety. Chroniclers of the twelfth and thirteenth centuries invariably refer to her as 'Mathilda bona regina' or 'Matildis beatae memoriae' and, after her death, contemporaries commented that signs and miracles were occurring at her tomb, although she has never been officially canonized.

Yet, despite her obvious influence in her own time and beyond, she remains little known to modern historians. The reign of Queen Victoria inspired several series of collective biographies of England's queens and queen-consorts, and Agnes Strickland's chapters on Matilda in her multi-volume study of England's queen-consorts have up until now formed the most complete account of Matilda's career.[1] But Strickland, not an academically-trained historian, took much of her information from antiquarian sources of the sixteenth through eighteenth centuries and made little effort to separate fact from colorful legend; nor was she much interested in anything other than the character and good works of her subjects. The twentieth century did not serve Matilda much better. Even Anglo-Norman scholars have only mentioned Matilda in contexts peripheral to other subjects. In some cases, she is seen only as the daughter of her

---

[1] Agnes Strickland, *Lives of the Queens of England from the Norman Conquest from the Official Records and other Private and Public Documents* (12 vols, London, 1840–8). This series has been reprinted many times, and I have quoted from the 1902 edition, published in Philadelphia, throughout this book. Matilda is covered in Volume 1, 72–111.

better-known mother, St Margaret of Scotland.[2] Others have touched upon one aspect or another of Matilda's career, often acknowledging her importance or influence but seldom treating the queen at any length.[3] A full account of the career of Henry I's queen, an important patron and politician of the first quarter of the twelfth century, is therefore clearly in order, and this biographical study forms the focus of this work. My investigation has shown that Queen Matilda wielded a great deal of power and enjoyed a great deal of prestige among contemporaries.

This book is divided into seven chapters, the first of which introduces Matilda by her original name, Edith, as daughter of King Malcolm of Scotland and his consort Margaret. I explore Edith's ancestry and childhood, education, and her marriage to Henry I. This chapter relies heavily on narrative sources and so includes a discussion of the problems inherent in those sources, particularly the text known to us as the *Life of St Margaret*. I conclude that Edith grew up with a strong sense of her exalted ancestry and that she retained close ties to members of her natal family. In Chapter Two, I discuss the institutional nature of English queenship, introducing some traditions of insular queenship and providing the necessary background for understanding Matilda's career. I discuss the traditions and structures of queenship and explore the ways Matilda's predecessors learned to manipulate them to their advantage. The third chapter looks at the records from several centuries to try to piece together the household, resources, and patronage of Matilda of Scotland. With the marriage came a large dower, and the possession of and control over her substantial dower gave Matilda the means to exercise political influence. I provide a reconstruction of the queen's holdings and place Matilda's holdings in the framework of what is known about other medieval English queens. Chapter Four opens the detailed analysis of Matilda's career, covering her public and governmental role, including not only her political actions within the *curia regis* but also the births of her children and the structure of her household. Many of her *acta* can be dated only to within a

---

[2] For instance, R. L. G. Ritchie, *The Normans in Scotland* (Edinburgh, 1954) and Derek Baker, 'A Nursery of Saints: St Margaret of Scotland Reconsidered', in Baker, ed., *Medieval Women* (Oxford, 1978): 119–142.

[3] Sir Richard Southern, in his studies of Anselm of Canterbury, has discussed Matilda's relationship to the saintly archbishop. See especially Southern, *St Anselm and his Biographer: A Study of Monastic Life and Thought, 1059–c.1130* (Cambridge, 1963). Her relationship to the city of London forms a part of one chapter of Brooke's and Keir's study of medieval London. See Christopher N. L. Brooke and Gillian Keir, *London 800–1216: The Shaping of a City* (Berkeley, 1975). Edward Kealey, in separate studies, has acknowledged Matilda's role in shaping the political life of the kingdom and has discussed her as a founder of hospitals. See Kealey, *Roger of Salisbury: Viceroy of England* (Berkeley, 1972), for Matilda's political role, and *Medieval Medicus: A Social History of Anglo-Norman Medicine* (Baltimore, 1981), for her charitable activities. Matilda's sponsorship of the Augustinian canons figures heavily in John C. Dickinson's *The Origins of the Austin Canons and their Introduction into England* (London, 1950). Her impact on the art and architecture of twelfth-century England has only been discussed in passing, but her literary patronage has been well explored by such writers as Reto R. Bezzola, in *Les origines et la formation de la littérature courtoise en occident 500–1200* (3 vols, Paris, 1944–63), and M. Dominica Legge, in her studies of Anglo-Norman literature. See especially *Anglo-Norman Literature and its Background* (Oxford, 1963), 7–26. Marcelle Thiébaux included a chapter on Matilda and a translation of her letters to Anselm and Pope Paschal II in her *The Writing of Medieval Women* (New York, 1987), 165–79. Pauline Stafford discusses the chroniclers' view of royal women, including Matilda, in 'The Portrayal of Royal Women in England, Mid-Tenth to Mid-Twelfth Centuries', *in Medieval Queenship*, ed. John Carmi Parsons (New York, 1993), 143–67. I have published several articles analysing aspects of Matilda's career, which will be cited in the relevant chapters of this book.

range of years, making it somewhat difficult to construct an entirely accurate chronology of her reign but we do always find the queen acting within the broad outlines of the important political developments of the first two decades of the twelfth century. The next two chapters are devoted to Matilda's various patronage projects. Chapter Five concerns her relationship to the Anglo-Norman church, in terms of both her institutional patronage and what can be discerned about her own spiritual awareness. The sixth chapter concentrates on her literary and artistic interests. While the division of Matilda's activities topically into the political, the religious, and the artistic reflects a division that may be more meaningful in the minds of modern readers than it would have been in reality, this division allows a departure from a purely chronological account, which permits exploration of some of the issues and trends of the period and puts Matilda's activities and interests more firmly into context. Chapter Four concentrates on the 'official' side of queenship while Five and Six cover more personal issues. In the concluding chapter, I look at Matilda's posthumous reputation and the growth of the legend of 'Good Queen Maud'. The book ends with a discussion of Matilda's place in the history of medieval queenship.

The primary sources available for this study have proven much richer than I had imagined when Professor C. Warren Hollister suggested I begin looking at Matilda in a graduate seminar I was privileged to take under his direction. As has often been noted, the twelfth century saw a virtual explosion in the production of historical literature in England and Normandy, and it is not surprising that almost all of the chroniclers long familiar to students of Anglo-Norman history included comments about Queen Matilda. Orderic Vitalis, William of Malmesbury, and Eadmer of Canterbury provide the fullest and most reliable accounts.[4] William of Malmesbury is particularly useful since he knew the queen personally and probably began the *Gesta regum anglorum* at her bidding. The 'Hyde Chronicler' provides details on Matilda's patronage and funeral; Hermann of Tournai gives an inventive account of Matilda's girlhood that just might contain some reliable details.[5] Aelred of Rievaulx's *Genealogia regum anglorum* provides vivid details most likely supplied by Matilda's younger brother David.[6] Other chronicle accounts have also proven useful and will be introduced as appropriate in later chapters.

Literature as well as history flourished in the early twelfth-century Anglo-Norman realm. Matilda was known as a patron of poetry and song, and the

---

[4] Orderic Vitalis, *The Ecclesiastical History of Orderic Vitalis*, ed./trans. Marjorie Chibnall (6 vols, Oxford, 1969–80); William of Malmesbury, *Gesta regum anglorum*, ed./trans. R. A. B. Mynors, R. M. Thomson, and M. Winterbottom (Oxford, 1998); and Eadmer of Canterbury, *Historia novorum in Anglia*, ed. Martin Rule (London, 1866, repr. 1964). Portions of Eadmer have been translated and appear in Geoffrey Bosanquet, trans., *Eadmer's History of Recent Events in England* (London, 1964).

[5] Edward Edwards, ed., *Liber monasterii de Hyda* (London, 1866, repr. 1964). The chronicle was once believed to have been produced at Hyde Abbey but more recently has been associated with the monastery of Lewes. See C. Warren Hollister, *Henry I* (New Haven, 2001), 15. Hermann of Tournai included a discussion of Matilda's marriage and the controversy surrounding it in his 'Liber de restauratione S. Martini Tornacensis', *MGH Scriptores* 14 (1956). The chronicle has been translated by Lynn H. Nelson, *The Restoration of the Monastery of St Martin of Tournai* (Washington, DC, 1996).

[6] Aelred of Rievaulx, 'Genealogia regum anglorum', in J. P. Migne, ed., *Patrologia cursus completus, series latina* (221 vols, Paris, 1844–64), 195: cols 711–58.

content of the poetry addressed to her or commissioned by her tells us much about current conceptions of queenship as well as providing glimpses into the queen's personality, tastes, and abilities. Saints' lives and miracle stories were once shunned by serious historians but have recently been embraced as rich sources of social history. Political historians have been only a little slower to mine them for what they can tell us about public power and its uses in the medieval period. Matilda and members of her natal family often figure in hagiographical accounts. The *Life of St Margaret* forms one of the richest sources for understanding Matilda and her view of the world in which she lived. Thus, a portion of the first chapter is dedicated to the texts that shaped Matilda's own ideas about what it meant to be England's queen. I argue that much of Matilda's conception of her own office grew out of the example, both real and literary, of her mother, Margaret of Scotland. To show this relationship I have devoted part of this section to a study of Margaret's background in England, her career in Scotland, and an analysis of that sometimes troubling text, Margaret's biography. This biography, while a source of rich detail about the everyday life of the royal family, has been controversial because it has often been labeled as merely hagiographic, an interpretation I reject. A main tenet of my thesis is that literary representations of both Margaret and Matilda helped to create an ideal of queenly behavior that contributed to the development of queenship into the later twelfth century and beyond. Other saints' lives and miracle stories have been used to add depth to the study here. These sources include the lives of old English saints such as Lawrence and Ebba, a few texts, such as the Anglo-Norman *Voyage of St Brendan*, that I argue were commissioned by Matilda herself, and accounts of miracles occurring during Matilda's lifetime and shortly afterwards.

Despite the incorporation of non-traditional sources such as hagiography, historians as a whole are still often most comfortable with record sources, and documents such as letters, financial accounts, and charters figure prominently in the material used to reconstruct the life and activities of Queen Matilda II. I have located references to thirty-two charters Matilda issued, some with full texts and witness lists. They are calendared in Appendix One and discussed in detail in Chapters Three through Five. In addition, Matilda witnessed about sixty-five of King Henry's charters issued during the first eighteen years of his reign. After factoring out the Norman charters issued when Henry and Matilda were apart as well as obviously spurious acts, this leaves Matilda as a documented witness to about fifteen per cent of the king's *acta*, placing hers among the top ten names appearing in witness lists on Henry's charters. Financial accounts such as the *Domesday Book*, the *Dialogus de Scaccario*, and the *Pipe Roll* of 1131 have been useful in reconstructing Matilda's holdings, and in the case of the *Pipe Roll*, the value of some of the lands she gave away and privileges she extended during her reign. Letters to and from the queen form another rich source of information, for correspondence with the queen is preserved in the records of many of the influential churchmen of the age, including Pope Paschal II, Anselm of Canterbury, Hildebert of Le Mans, and Marbod of Rennes.

Finally, I have used evidence from the visual arts in an attempt to understand Matilda and her world. She was interested in building projects of various kinds, and she also patronized artists who specialized in needlework and metalwork. These projects are discussed in some detail in Chapter Six.

A few words about Matilda's name are in order here. She was named Edith originally, and thus some modern historians have referred to her as Edith–Matilda or by the toponym Matilda of Scotland in order to distinguish her from the numerous other women of the same name during the era. I found the use of the hyphenated 'Edith–Matilda' to be clumsy and unnecessary in this study, which focuses quite closely on only one of the many Matildas. I have preferred to call her as she would have been known at the time, referring to her as Edith before her marriage, and thereafter as Matilda. When it becomes necessary to be more specific, I refer to her either as 'Matilda of Scotland', or sometimes, especially when discussing documentary sources, as Matilda II, the formula she used on her seal. I do not use the diminutive 'Maud' unless I am quoting from another source.

Throughout the book, I have tried not to fall into the trap of calling Matilda an 'exception' to the rules and norms that governed the lives of other medieval noblewomen. However, it is next to impossible to understand Matilda or evaluate her impact on the ecclesiastical, political, and cultural development of the Anglo-Norman realm without knowing whether her actions were innovative or standard, unusual or expected, bold or routine. By looking at Matilda in comparison to her contemporaries and immediate successors on the English throne, it is possible to speculate about why she was able to succeed in her role as queen to the degree that she did. Thus, in order to establish these 'norms' for medieval queenship, the focus of this study sometimes broadens into a comparative exploration of Matilda's predecessors and successors on the throne of England. A little more than a decade ago, 'queenship' was a rarely used term, and the idea of studying any medieval queen in other than purely biographical terms was almost inconceivable. For the most part, scholarship was limited to biographies of a few exceptional women who managed to affect the course of political history. Even biography was problematic, for the sources for even the best known of medieval women allow for only sketchy reconstructions of their lives, and it is rare to hear them speaking in their own voices. This lack of interest in medieval queenship is clearly no longer the case. In addition to studies of individual queens, there are now analyses of the rituals and ceremonial duties of the queen, monographs on the queen's political role, the cultural aspects of queenship, the religious duties and facets of queenship, the administrative problems of queenship, and on and on.[7] Although the field is

---

[7] The field has burgeoned to the extent that a complete list of relevant publications is too long for inclusion here. For a general introduction, readers should consult Janet L. Nelson, 'Medieval Queenship', in Linda E. Mitchell, ed., *Women in Medieval Western European Culture* (New York and London, 1999), 179–207. Recent essay collections include Parsons, ed., *Medieval Queenship*, and Anne Duggan, ed., *Queens and Queenship in Medieval Europe* (Woodbridge, 1997). Pauline Stafford's work has also been of the utmost importance. Her book on early medieval queenship, *Queens, Concubines, and Dowagers: The King's Wife in the Early Middle Ages* (Athens, Ga, 1983), is superb, as is her latest work on eleventh-century English queenship, *Queen Emma and Queen Edith: Queenship and Women's Power in Eleventh-Century England* (Oxford, 1997). John Carmi Parsons and Bonnie Wheeler, ed., *Eleanor of Acquitaine: Lord and Lady* (New York, 2003), focuses on Eleanor's career in France, but also contains several essays on queenship in England. Ann Trinidade's *Berengaria: In Search of Richard the Lionheart's Queen* (Dublin, 1999) provides an example of a fruitful study of very limited sources. The

fairly new, queenship studies have contributed much to our understanding of medieval Europe. The medieval queen has been firmly identified as a subject worthy of scrutiny, and her story is becoming an integral part of the political, social, and cultural history of the Middle Ages. Although there is still much to be learned, scholars are in the process, I think, of uncovering a 'history of queenship' that will show how the role of the queen-consort developed and changed throughout the medieval period, and how the queen's role varied in the different regions of Europe.

In Matilda's case, favorable historical circumstances such as control of lands and other forms of wealth, generally good relations with Henry, the legitimacy of being crowned, and the flexible, not-quite-institutionalized nature of the eleventh- and twelfth-century state, combined to allow her, like the other Anglo-Norman queens, to enjoy a privileged position. This position allowed them to act with wider latitude than either their Anglo-Saxon predecessors or their Angevin successors.

I am far from being the first person to see a need for a scholarly study of Matilda of Scotland. Toward the end of the twelfth century, King Henry II asked the Cistercian monk Ælred of Rievaulx to provide him a genealogy of Henry's ancestors, the kings of England. Ælred, whose lifelong friendship with Henry's great-uncle David of Scotland (who was also Matilda's younger brother) put him in a unique position to write about Henry's maternal ancestors, hesitated to include a biographical sketch of Matilda of Scotland. 'For', he wrote, 'the magnitude of the matter', as well as his own ignorance, made him unfit to tackle the task. He hoped then that some future writer would take it on, and declared that whoever did so would certainly declare Queen Matilda to be 'another Esther in our own time'.[8] Ælred's allusion referred to the biblical Queen Esther's role in marrying a foreign king, and then interceding with him to save her oppressed people from extinction. I am not sure that many Anglo-Saxons believed that they were that badly oppressed because of their ethnicity by the time of King Henry I, but Matilda did much to help bring about a reconciliation between the children of the conquered and those of the conquering people, as these pages will show. The privileged position of the Anglo-Norman queens, particularly of William the Conqueror's wife Matilda of Flanders and Matilda of Scotland, is generally recognized by historians of queenship. But it was not just historical circumstance that was at work in twelfth-century England. In a study of this kind, it is neither possible nor wise to ignore the impact of personality. All four Anglo-Norman queens, but especially the three Matildas, were intelligent, capable women with a strong interest in doing their jobs and doing them well. In addition, all seemed to have good working relations with their royal spouses and were able to project the idea that the king and the queen worked in unison.

---

thirteenth century in England has been explored by Margaret Howell, *Eleanor of Provence: Queenship in Thirteenth-Century England* (Oxford, 1998) and John Carmi Parsons, *Eleanor of Castile: Queen and Society in Thirteenth-Century England* (New York, 1995). Finally, Robert Bartlett's volume for the New Oxford History of England, *England under the Norman and Angevin Kings, 1075–1225* (Oxford, 2000) shows how thoroughly queenship studies have been integrated into general political history.

[8] Aelred of Rievaulx, 'Genealogia regum anglorum', col. 736.

Early on, the study of women's history was plagued by the effort to find a golden age, that is, a time in history when women's contributions to both the public and the private spheres were valued on a par with those of men. That age has not yet been found and probably never will be, and those who are still looking will not find it in Anglo-Norman England. Indeed, many historians have argued that, after the conquest, economic and political status declined for the vast majority of William's female subjects. However, for the few women at the top of the feudal pyramid, the queens, princesses, duchesses, and countesses, this era was one that allowed them, if they had the desire and the ability, to act meaningfully and influentially in the economic, ecclesiastical, political, and cultural life of the Anglo-Norman realm. What I hope to show here is that Matilda of Scotland succeeded at queenship to an extraordinary degree because the political structures of her day allowed her the opportunity to do so and because she was herself skilled at manipulating those structures.

1

Edith, Princess of Scotland

Sometime in the late summer or very early autumn of 1080, a daughter was born to the Scottish king Malcolm Canmore and his second wife, the Anglo-Saxon princess Margaret.[1] This little girl, like her four elder brothers, carried the blood of the kings of England as well as those of Scotland. Her mother, later recognized as the only Scottish saint to be officially venerated by the Catholic church, was the granddaughter of Edmund Ironside and thus a kinswoman of King Edward the Confessor. Both Malcolm and Margaret had lived for long periods at the Confessor's court. After having spent his youth in exile on the continent of Europe, Margaret's father had returned to England with his Hungarian wife and their three children, intending to take his place as Edward's heir. But he died under mysterious circumstances shortly after his arrival, and the status of his children in relation to the throne of England remained unclear. When the Normans captured the English throne, Margaret's family, realizing their tenuous position in the new regime, left England by about 1068, announcing that they were returning to Hungary. They were driven by a storm onto the eastern coast of Scotland. Whether they landed in Lothian by chance or by design will never be known. The chroniclers believed that they had intended to return to Hungary, but it is worth remembering that the Norman Conquest was a new and uncertain event in 1068, and the court of Malcolm III had drawn many others who were disenchanted with life under the rule of William the Bastard.[2] Within a short time of the family's arrival in Scotland, Margaret abandoned her professed desire to enter the cloister, and by 1070 or 1071, when she first appears in the sources as queen, had married the king of the Scots.[3] The princess born in 1080 was their fifth child and first daughter in about ten years of marriage. Sons were usually more desired than daughters in the medieval period, but daughters were also useful for alliances, and since she

---

[1] Her birth date is calculated from correlation of Robert of Curthose's sponsorship of the infant with the date of his only known visit to Scotland, reported by Simeon of Durham, 'Historia regum' (in Thomas Arnold, ed., *Symonis Dunelmensis opera et collectanea* (Surtees Society 51), 1868, 100, and Joseph Stevenson, ed., *Chronicon Monasterii de Abingdon* (2 vols, RS, London, 1858 repr., n.d.), 2: 9–10. The date is corroborated by testimony taken in 1100 that stated that Edith was 'about twelve years old' in August of 1093. See Hermann of Tournai, 'Liber de restauratione', 281–2.
[2] Simeon of Durham, 'Historia regum', 2: 190–1.
[3] The fullest account of the life, works, influence, and cult of Margaret of Scotland remains W. Moir Bruce, 'Saint Margaret and her Chapel in the Castle of Edinburgh', *The Book of the Old Edinburgh Club* 5 (1913): 1–66.

came after many sons, this daughter was likely to have been welcomed.[4] When the time came for her to be baptized, usually within a month of birth, her godparents were chosen from the very family that Margaret and her siblings had fled. Robert Curthose, eldest son of William the Conqueror and well known to the members of the Scottish royal family, was serving as a diplomatic envoy to Malcolm's court and agreed to sponsor the princess. His mother, Queen Matilda of Flanders, served as a godmother. During the ceremony the infant princess reached up and grabbed at the royal headdress Queen Matilda was wearing, pulling the garment over her own head. This action of the baby's was later remembered as an omen that she would grow up to be a queen herself.[5] Margaret and Malcolm liked to stress their children's relationship to the old English line of kings, and the child, like her elder brothers Edward, Edmund, Æthelred, and Edgar, was given a name drawn from the House of Wessex. She was named Edith, after the wife of Edward the Confessor, or possibly in honor of the tenth-century saint Edith of Wilton, who had been the daughter of King Edgar by his concubine Wulfthryth.[6] In hindsight, the name chosen for the princess proved especially apt, since, like two of her royal predecessors who had borne that name, she was to be fatefully associated with the convent at Wilton dedicated to St Edith.

Spent at the increasingly Normanized Scottish court, Edith's early childhood years were evidently happy ones. In her later years, she tended to idealize both of her parents but showed a particular attachment to her mother, Margaret. Both Margaret and the domestic life of the Scottish court are presented in laudatory terms in the *Life of St Margaret*, a text written in the early part of the twelfth century as a teaching tool for Edith after she had become queen of England. Historians have differed in the amount of trust they are willing to place in the historical value of this text. Written some ten years after her death at Matilda's commission, and making its way into hagiography when Margaret was canonized in the middle of the thirteenth century, the biography has plagued students of Scottish history because of its numerous ambiguities.

Since the *Life of St Margaret* is so problematic, and since we must rely so heavily upon it as a source for Edith's childhood, it is worth a digression here to discuss and resolve some of the questions which have so troubled scholars.[7]

---

[4] For gender preferences in the medieval period, see Shulamith Shahar, *Childhood in the Middle Ages* (London, 1990), 71, and John Boswell, *The Kindness of Strangers: The Abandonment of Children in Western Europe from Late Antiquity to the Renaissance* (New York, 1988), 258–9 and 262–4.

[5] *The Letters and Charters of Gilbert Foliot*, ed. Z. N. Brooke, A. Morey, and C. N. L. Brooke (Cambridge, 1967), 60–6, at p. 66. Discussed in Elisabeth van Houts, *Memory and Gender in Medieval Europe, 900–1200* (Toronto, 1999), 73.

[6] The claim of Orderic Vitalis (*Orderic* 4: 272) that Queen Matilda 'was first named Edith' is corroborated by an entry in Joseph Stevenson, ed., *Liber vitae Ecclesie Dunelmensis* (Surtees Society 13, 1841), 54, which includes the list of names 'Eadwardus, Eadgarus, Eadmundus, Æilredus, Alexander, David, Eadgith, Maria'. See R. L. G. Ritchie, *The Normans in Scotland* (Edinburgh, 1954), 99 and Appendix D, 393–4.

[7] The discussion of the *Life of St Margaret* is summarized from my article 'The Idea of the Perfect Princess: *The Life of St Margaret* in the Reign of Matilda II (1100–1118)', *Anglo-Norman Studies* 12 (1990): 81–97. One question I will not be attempting to resolve here is that of the authorship of the *Life*. Suffice it to say that the commonly-accepted attribution to Turgot, prior of Durham and later bishop of St Andrew's, is problematic. For a discussion of the problem see Antonia Gransden, *Historical Writing in England c.550–c.1307* (2 vols, London, 1974–82), 1: 116, note 71; Ritchie, *Normans in*

Perhaps R. L. Graeme Ritchie most eloquently phrased the exasperation expressed by many as he lamented that the author's 'mental vagueness, further dimmed by the rhetorical, almost meaningless Latin, reduces Scottish historians to despair. Despair, however, takes on different forms, ranging from tears to mirthless ribaldry or a dull, implacable resentment against author and subject alike – a strange fate to have befallen so good a man and so great a queen.'[8] G. W. S. Barrow attributed the author's 'indifference to topographical details of every sort' to the genre of early-medieval hagiography, while Ritchie searched for a recognized category in which to place the troublesome text, pointing out elements of hagiography, the character sketch, and court biography.[9] Derek Baker seemingly solved some of the technical problems inherent in the text by re-dating the extant versions of the *Life*, a solution that ultimately created more problems than it solved in light of the evidence from the manuscripts. Baker believed the short version of the *Life*, which now survives in a fourteenth-century manuscript, to be closer to the original text than the surviving manuscript of the longer version of the *Life* known to exist at the time Baker wrote. Until that time, the longer version had been assumed to be the earlier of the two. Many of the most troubling passages of the longer version do not appear in the shorter, and Baker's argument that those passages were later accretions is at first glance attractive. However, there are also problems in accepting Baker's thesis that the shorter version represents an earlier, independent text.[10] It appears in manuscript only within a collection of abbreviated saints lives made by John of Tynemouth in the fourteenth century. There is no reason to believe that the *Life* of Margaret represents an exception to John's practice of collecting and abbreviating from existing collections or individual *vitae*.[11] Some of John's abridgement has created awkward transitions in the shorter version, awkwardness that is easily rectified by reference to the

---

Scotland, Appendix E (395–9); *Symeonis Dunelmensis opera et collectanea*, ed. Hogdson Hinde (Durham, 1868 [Surtees Society 51]), lvii–lx; and Daniel Papenbroch's introduction to the *Vita Margaretae* appearing in the *Acta sanctorum quotquot tote orbe colunter vel a catholicis scriptoribus*, ed. Jean Bolland, Daniel Papebroch *et ali*.(Brussels and Antwerp, 1643, Volume 1 for June (Antwerp, 1658, rep Brussels, 1966), 289–94, 10 June.

[8] Ritchie, *Normans in Scotland*, 397–8.

[9] G. W. S. Barrow, *The Kingdom of the Scots: Government, Church, and Society from the Eleventh to the Fourteenth Century* (London, 1973), 190 and Ritchie, *Normans in Scotland*, 398. With the exception of one miracle story, for which the author is apologetic, the text seems to be similar to the secular biographies Frank Barlow described in his introduction to the *Vita Ædwardi regis: The Life of King Edward who Rests at Westminster* (London, 1962), xx–xxiii.

[10] See Baker, 'A Nursery of Saints'. At the time Baker wrote, scholars knew only one version of the surviving medieval manuscript of the longer version of the *Life*. It appears in a collection of saints' lives from the thirteenth century, now BL MS Cotton Tiberius Diii. The text of the *Life* as it appears in the *Acta sanctorum* for 10 June, ed. Daniel Papenbroch, came from a manuscript in the Bollandist monastery at Hainault. The Bollandist text, which has since been lost, differed only slightly from the British Library manuscript. Since Baker wrote, another version of the *Life* along with the *Miracles of St Margaret*, has been located in Madrid (Madrid, Biblioteca del Palacio Real, II. 2097, fols 26–41v). Professor Robert Bartlett of the University of St Andrews is in the process of editing the miracle collection. He kindly shared a photostatic copy of the Madrid version of the *Life* just as this book was going to press. The Madrid *Life* is both longer and later than the British Library version and will certainly repay further scholarly investigation.

[11] Carl Horstmann, ed., *Nova legenda angliae* (2 vols, Oxford, 1901), 1: ix–xi, and Huneycutt, 'Idea of a Perfect Princess', 82. The shorter version that Horstmann printed has also survived only in one medieval manuscript, BL Cotton Tiberius Ei.

longer version but is otherwise inexplicable.[12] The problematic passages in the longer version occur in sections entirely eliminated in the process of abridging, and the manuscript of the shorter life is much closer to the longer *Life* than is the printed version Baker used for his study.[13] Baker argued that the longer version was probably created for the canonization procedures in the mid-thirteenth century, but in fact it lays less stress on Margaret's saintliness than does the shorter. One of Baker's points was that the author of the longer version clearly considered Margaret already to be a saint, which would argue against a twelfth-century date of composition since Margaret was not canonized until the mid-thirteenth century.[14] But there is some evidence that the author of the *Life* was not alone in numbering Margaret among the saints long before the queen's official canonization. Indeed, before the Fourth Lateran Council of 1215 regularized the process of formal canonization, the word 'sanctus' was routinely used for people popularly considered holy. Reginald of Durham, writing well before the end of the twelfth century, spoke of 'Queen Margaret, whose virtue of sanctity is worshiped and venerated by the entire kingdom of the Scots' and told of processions taking place in Scotland on her anniversary date.[15] Simeon of Durham, who also wrote in the twelfth century, referred to 'Sancta Margareta regina'.[16] Yet another indication that the cult of Margaret was flourishing during the twelfth century comes from the chronicler Roger of Hovedon, who reported that King William the Lion of Scotland spent a night at the tomb of his ancestress, 'Saint Margaret, the former queen of Scotland', before invading England in 1199. While there, he had a dream that warned him of the futility of his ambitions, so he allowed his army to return home.[17] Finally, further evidence of the early development of the cult of the Scottish queen is to be found in the final leaves of a copy of the Gospels that she owned, where a poem describing a miracle that had benefited the queen is inscribed. The hand appears to be that of the late eleventh or early twelfth century. Margaret, like many others in the period before Lateran IV, was popularly acclaimed a saint long before her case was brought to the papacy for formal approval.[18]

In addition to the problems of understanding the *Life* that Baker pointed out,

---

[12] Huneycutt, 'Idea of a Perfect Princess', 84–7.
[13] Baker used the printed text in John Pinkerton, *Vitae antiquae sanctorum qui habitaverunt in ea parte Britannia nunc vocata Scotia vel in ejus insulis* (London, 1789), 303–70, which was itself taken from Surius, who included or paraphrased several sections of John of Tynemouth. See Huneycutt, 'Idea of a Perfect Princess', 82, 97.
[14] Baker, 'Nursery of Saints', 130; see also Ritchie, *Normans in Scotland*, 396.
[15] Reginald of Durham, *Libellus de admirandis beati Cuthberti quae novelis patratae sunt temporibus*, ed. James Raine (Surtees Society 1, 1835), 218.
[16] Simeon of Durham, 'Historia regum', 330.
[17] Roger of Hovedon, *Chronica magistri Rogeri de Houedene*, ed. William Stubbs (4 vols, RS, London, 1868–71), 4: 100.
[18] The book itself is now in the Bodleian Library, Oxford, MS. Latin liturgical f5. For a discussion of the hand and its dating, see the introduction to the facsimile edition, W. Forbes-Leith, ed., *The Gospel Book of St Margaret: Being a Facsimile Reproduction of St Margaret's Copy of the Gospels Preserved in the Bodleian Library, Oxford* (Edinburgh, 1896), also Falconer Madan, F. E. Warren, and I. O. Westwood, 'The Evangelistarium of St Margaret, Queen of Scotland', *The Academy: A Weekly Review of Literature, Science, and Art* 32, Issue 796 (Saturday, 6 August 1887), 88–9; Issue 798 (Saturday, 20 August 1887), and Issue 800 (Saturday, 3 September 1887), 151.

historians have also objected to the author's description of the Scottish queen's presiding over a church council, an unusual role for even a sovereign female. Others have understandably bristled at the chauvinistic portrayal of the Scottish court as backward and rustic in comparison with that of the English.[19] However, all of these problems are easily overcome when it is realized that the author was not creating a saint's life, a history of the era, or even a secular biography of the queen. My own interpretation of the purpose of the text is that it is exactly what the author states it is in his preface: a 'mirror' or didactic tool for the new queen of England, presenting the virtues of an ideal or perfect princess. Thus, we can understand that the author idealized the historical Margaret in order to reflect a pattern of a perfect princess. He may well have exaggerated Margaret's virtues or her activities and their effectiveness in order to encourage the daughter to imitate her already-legendary mother. For the purposes of understanding Edith's early childhood, the question is how much trust we can place in the author's anecdotes about the everyday life of the palace and the private lives of the Scottish royal family.

Much of the charm of the text comes from passages describing the physical setting of the palace or narrating interactions among the royal family. If the *vita* were indeed written for Margaret's daughter, we can assume that it would also have been read by her brothers and sister and that, although the domestic scenes would certainly have been idealized, they would also have had some general conformance with the memories of the royal children. Nor would the descriptions of the palace itself be too distorted, for there would have been many who could and would have objected to a completely outlandish portrayal. Thus, although we can be skeptical of the author's objectivity about Margaret's virtues, there is no reason to doubt the accuracy of the incidental details about the domestic life of the family. For instance, we may reject the claim that the eight children never fought among themselves but accept that the family customarily attended church services together and that the children took the Eucharist in order of their age.[20] Recent work on the court of eleventh-century Scotland suggests a more political sophistication than is portrayed in the *Life*, and it is no doubt the case that the author exaggerated the rusticity of the Scottish court and downplayed King Malcolm's accomplishments in order to stress the effectiveness of his heroine.

Margaret's biographer paints a rosy picture of the circumstances in which the princess Edith spent her first six years. The internal political strife of the early years of Malcolm's reign was largely over by the time he married Margaret, and Scotland was gradually turning away from its Scandinavian neighbors and becoming integrated into the realms dominated by the Anglo-Norman monarchs. Both Malcolm and Margaret had passed their youths at the court of the

---

[19] Baker, 'Nursery of Saints', 128–9, and Archibald A. M. Duncan, *Scotland: The Making of the Kingdom* (Edinburgh, 1975), 117. Ritchie, *Normans in Scotland*, dismissed Margaret's chairing of the council as 'unprecedented in all Christendom' (397, n. 5). Early Scottish culture and identity have been explored well by Dauvit Broun, *The Irish Identity of the Kingdom of the Scots in the Twelfth and Thirteenth Centuries* (Woodbridge, 1999).

[20] Turgot (?), *Life of St Margaret*, paragraph 13. A translation of the British Library version of the *Life* appears in Appendix Two. The British Library manuscript of the *Life* supplies the name 'Theodericus' for the author, the Bollandist text just 'T', and the Madrid manuscript identifies him as Turgot.

Confessor, where they imbibed French as well as English styles and values. Malcolm is said to have known 'the language of the Angles equally with his own', and both of Edith's parents must have had at least a smattering of French. Margaret, although educated enough to read Latin, apparently never learned the Scottish tongue, at least not to the point where she felt comfortable enough to use it when leading theological discussions.[21] Unless their nurses were strictly Gaelic-speaking, the children's first language was likely to have been English. The author of the *Life* portrays the palace as richly furnished, hung with brightly-colored tapestries, and 'glittering with silver and gold'. Under Margaret's influence, the Scots began to acquire a taste for foreign goods and even to dress more gaily (though the suggestion that Margaret introduced the tartan into Scotland can be easily discounted).[22] Malcolm also acquired an impressive retinue of retainers who accompanied him whenever he appeared in public.[23]

However, according to Margaret's biographer, the Scottish monarchs did not get caught up in worldly pomp and so neglect their religious duties. Again, the biographer's portrayal is likely to have been distorted by his purpose in writing as well as by his obvious affection for Margaret, but charter and independent chronicle evidence confirm the general outline of his narrative. Margaret, evidently born and reared in the newly-Christian Hungarian kingdom, brought some of the Hungarian zeal and piety to her new home in the north.[24] She was particularly attracted to the suffering Saviour, as evidenced in her own ascetic practices as well as in her personal devotion to the Holy Cross. She donated jewelled crosses to St Andrews, Durham, and Dunfermline.[25] She also owned a gilt or gold reliquary containing a piece of the True Cross, which she venerated on her deathbed and bequeathed to her sons. This object of devotion, known as the 'Black Rood of Scotland', which Margaret may have brought with her from Hungary, later formed part of the treasury of Scotland and was usually carried into battle by the Scottish kings.

Margaret also may have been attracted to local saints. The miracle collection of St Ebba of Coldingham includes the story of a woman whose speech and hearing were restored by Ebba after Queen Margaret advised the woman to visit the abbess' tomb.[26] Like other members of the European aristocracy, Malcolm and Margaret were monastic patrons. Among her other projects, Margaret rebuilt the shrine on the island of Iona, established a free ferry service

---

[21] *Life of St Margaret*, paragraph 13.
[22] See T. Radcliffe Barnett, *Margaret of Scotland, Queen and Saint: Her Influence on the Early Church of Scotland* (Edinburgh, 1926), 62, n. 12.
[23] *Life of St Margaret*, paragraph 11.
[24] For a succinct discussion of Margaret's likely roots, see Nicholas Hooper, 'Edgar Ætheling: Anglo-Saxon Prince, Rebel and Crusader', *Anglo-Saxon England* 14 (1985): 197–214. See also Ritchie, *Normans in Scotland*, 389–92.
[25] The Durham cross was described in the *Libellus Cuthberti* (218) as 'crucem praemirifice unionibus et margaritis expolientibus radiatam'. The crosses given to Dunfermline and St Andrew's are mentioned in the *Life of St Margaret*, paragraph 7.
[26] See *Acta sanctorum*, 25 August (Vol. 5 for August, 198). Ebba, a princess of Northumbria, was the foundress and first abbess of the nunnery at Coldingham. She died in 683, and her relics were discovered in the late eleventh century. The miracle collection contains two miracles in which Margaret played a part.

on the Firth of Forth that carried pilgrims going to worship at St Andrews, and built the great monastery at Dunfermline, which was colonized with monks sent by Lanfranc from Canterbury.[27] Margaret also requested continental clerks to join her in reforming the Scottish church. One of these, Theobald of Étampes, chose not to join the queen, citing fear of the channel crossing. But, during the reign of Henry I, Theobald did come to England to serve as a lecturer in liberal arts at Oxford. Known to Bishop Robert Bloet of Lincoln and Abbot Faritius of Abingdon, both members of the inner circle at the English court of Henry I, Theobald may even have met Margaret's daughter.[28] Margaret and Malcolm also patronized local holy men, including the hermits on Loch Leven as well as the congregations at Dunfermline, St Andrews and Durham.[29] Margaret gave a jewelled cross, a book written in silver letters, and a 'precious cap of linen' to the monks of St Cuthbert.[30] It is possible that this linen headdress came from the workshop maintained in the queen's chambers, where the queen and her ladies produced 'caps for singers, chasubles, stoles, altar cloths and other sacred vestments'.[31] Reginald of Durham wrote that the queen had always held St Cuthbert in special veneration, a claim that gains credence in light of the confraternity agreement between the Scottish royal family and the servants of St Cuthbert contained in Durham's *Liber vitae*. The monks promised to feed one pauper daily and two on Sundays during the lifetime of the king and queen as well as to say collects and masses for the royal couple and their sons and daughters 'both in this life and after'.[32] Malcolm and Margaret, hearing of the holy reputation of Bishop Wulfstan of Worcester, also requested that he remember them in his prayers.[33] The charters, confraternity agreement, and hagiographic and chronicle evidence confirm the evidence from the biography that presents Margaret as a truly pious woman, whose religious devotion and ecclesiastical concerns influenced her children in their later lives.

Margaret's biographer convincingly portrays Malcolm and Margaret as a genuinely loving couple. He also makes clear that Margaret's contributions to the kingdom were not negligible. Malcolm, although illiterate, used to cherish the books that Margaret loved, simply 'for love of her love'. He delighted in surprising the queen by having her favorite volumes sent out to be ornately bound.[34] In a revealing passage, the author recounts that the queen used to pilfer

---

[27] *Life of St Margaret*, paragraph 7, which refers to the priory (later abbey) of Dunfermline. See Lanfranc of Bec, *The Letters of Lanfranc, Archbishop of Canterbury*, ed. Helen Clover and Margaret Gibson (Oxford, 1979), 160. For the ferry service to and from St Andrews, see *Life of St Margaret*, paragraph 20. Orderic Vitalis (*Orderic* 4: 272) is the source for the queen's patronage of Iona.

[28] See 'Lettere Theobaldi Stampiensis', *PL* 163: col. 765.

[29] Archibald C. Lawrie, ed., *Early Scottish Charters (Prior to A.D. 1153)* (Glasgow, 1905). For the Culdees, see 7, entry VIII. No original charter survives to record the gifts to Dunfermline, though a spurious charter (9, entry X) may contain reliable information about an original grant (see Lawrie's note on p. 238). David I's pancarta confirm gifts of his parents to the abbey (entry LXXIV, 61–4; entry CCIX, 167–71).

[30] *Libellus Cuthberti*, 218.

[31] *Life of St Margaret*, paragraph 7.

[32] *Libellus Cuthberti*, 217–18, and *Liber vitae ecclesiae Dunelmensis*, 73.

[33] William of Malmesbury, *Vita Wulfstani* (ed. R. R. Darlington, Camden Society, 1928), 59–60.

[34] *Life of St Margaret*, paragraph 11.

coins from the royal treasury so that she could use them for charitable purposes. Knowing that she did so, the king nevertheless pretended not to know, in order to catch her with the coins still in her fist, 'infangtheof', so to speak. 'He greatly loved this sort of jest', writes the biographer. 'Sometimes he would seize her hand full of the coins, and lead her to me for justice, joking that he wanted to accuse her in court.'[35] In large part because she was trusted as a true partner in the marriage, Margaret was also able to take an active role in ruling the Scottish kingdom. Her biographer claims that she had an interest in furthering commerce and providing a better set of laws for Scotland, as well as in improving the domestic life within the palace. King Malcolm was usually sage enough to profit from her advice, although, according to the *Life*, he discounted her foreboding about his final raid into England.[36]

As well as being a strong queen and a cherished wife, Margaret was a loving mother concerned about both her children's spiritual education and their outward behavior. The biography provides a rare glimpse into parent–child relations in the late eleventh century. Margaret, according to her panegyrist, 'poured out care to her children not less than to herself, seeing that they were nourished with all diligence and introduced to honest manners as much as possible'.[37] She seems genuinely to have enjoyed the company of children. One of her Lenten charities was to bring orphaned children into the palace, where she held them on her knees and fed them 'soft foods, the kind infants love', with the same spoons she herself used.[38] She may have been harsh by modern standards, believing in the proverb that 'he who spares the rod spoils the child', but the author leaves no doubt that Margaret was motivated by true concern for her children's characters. And her methods were perceived to be successful. As the author proudly writes, 'because of the religious zeal of their mother, the children's manners were far better than those of other children who were much older than they were'. The queen had her children brought to her 'very often' and taught them the precepts of the Christian faith 'using words suitable to their age and understanding' – a statement that argues against modern writers who have claimed that the Middle Ages lacked a concept of childhood or child-development.[39] In one episode where Margaret is quoted talking with her children, she speaks tenderly, addressing them as 'mea viscera' – 'my flesh', or more literally, 'my guts'.[40] It is reasonable to assume that Edith's first experience of queenship as well as of family life was positive, and that these early impressions affected her choices and expectations later in life. Her earliest experiences also presented her with a female role model who was passionately devoted to the Christian faith as represented by the Roman church and who was also intelligent, literate, articulate, and strong-minded. Moreover, the author of the biography indicated that Margaret was respected within the palace for

[35] *Life of St Margaret*, paragraph 18.
[36] *Life of St Margaret*, paragraph 29.
[37] *Life of St Margaret*, paragraph 9.
[38] *Life of St Margaret*, paragraph 22.
[39] For more on Margaret's maternal role, see my 'Public Lives, Private Ties: Royal Mothers in England and Scotland, 1070–1204', in John Carmi Parsons and Bonnie Wheeler, ed., *Medieval Mothering* (New York, 1996), 295–311.
[40] *Life of St Margaret*, paragraph 9.

possessing and exercising those qualities. It is no wonder that Margaret's daughter would consciously emulate her mother's virtues when she herself became queen of England.

Although rarely the 'nightmare' conjured up by theorists, medieval childhood was short by modern standards.[41] Edith, like most of her aristocratic peers, left her natal household early, possibly in 1086, a year that brought several changes to the Scottish royal household. Margaret's younger brother, the ill-starred Edgar Ætheling, decided to leave Scotland to seek his fortune among the Normans in Apulia.[42] The royal nursery had experienced something of a population boom with the addition of three more children, Mary, Alexander, and David, all born between c.1082 and c.1085. Margaret's sister, Christina, also left Scotland in 1086 to become a nun of Romsey. We know that the two princesses were sent south for their education, and it is probable that they accompanied Christina to Romsey. The pre-conquest foundation was one of England's wealthiest nunneries and had long been favored by Margaret's forebears, the royal house of Wessex.[43] Shortly after the Conquest, Romsey had served as a place of refuge for many Saxon women who had fled their homes in fear of the lust of the Normans. But, within twenty years, the wealthy pre-Conquest nunneries of England had begun to attract the daughters of the new Norman aristocracy. Indeed, as Ritchie has pointed out, it would have been difficult for the nuns of Romsey to avoid Normans even if they had wished to do so. Romsey was located in the heart of the royal demesne, less than ten miles from the seat of the treasury at Winchester, about halfway between it and what he termed the 'not-very-happy-hunting-ground' of the New Forest.[44]

Edith's later description of life under her aunt's tutelage made it appear that Romsey had not been a particularly happy training ground for her. Certainly Christina seemed determined that her eldest niece would follow in her footsteps, and she dressed the child accordingly, making her wear a nun's habit, complete with the black veil. Edith outwardly conformed but later claimed that she had spent her childhood 'in fear of the rod of my Aunt Christina', who 'would often make me smart with a good slapping and the most horrible scolding, as well as treating me as being in disgrace'. But Edith clearly developed no sense of vocation and later related her dislike of Christina's choice of apparel. 'That hood I did indeed wear in her presence, chafing and fearful', she confessed, 'but as soon as I was able to escape out of her sight, I tore it off and threw it in the dirt, and trampled on it. That was my only way of venting my rage and the

---

[41] The description of pre-modern childhood as a 'nightmare' comes from Lloyd DeMause, in DeMause, ed., *The History of Childhood* (New York, 1974), 1–2.

[42] *Anglo-Saxon Chronicle*, s.a. 1086. All citations to the *Anglo-Saxon Chronicle* are from Michael Swanton, ed./trans., *The Anglo-Saxon Chronicle* (New York, 1998 [originally published London, 1996]). Florence of Worcester supplies the information that Edgar left King William's service and went to Apulia. See B. Thorpe, ed., Florence of Worcester, *Chronicon ex chronicis* (2 vols, London, 1848; repr. Vaduz, 1964), 2: 19.

[43] See Marc Anthony Meyer, 'Patronage of the West Saxon Royal Nunneries in Late Anglo-Saxon England', *Revue Bénédictine* 91 (1981): 332–58. Ritchie, *Normans in Scotland*, 47, n. 2, discussed the late and unreliable tradition that claims that Margaret's mother, Agatha, entered an English convent, sometimes said to be Romsey, just before her death.

[44] Ritchie, *Normans in Scotland*, 76.

hatred of it that boiled up in me. In that manner, and no other, as my conscience is witness, was I veiled!'[45] It has been suggested, not implausibly, that Edith's later devotion to the memory of her mother resulted from idealizing her earliest memories of the Scottish court and contrasting those memories with her later childhood in the convent.[46] Certainly she retained a sense of identification with her natal family. In later life she commissioned the biography of her mother, made religious donations in the names of her parents and siblings, and did all she could to further the careers of her brothers and sister.

Sometime before 1093, Edith and Mary moved from Romsey to the nearby monastery at Wilton. Whether Christina accompanied them is uncertain but unlikely. William of Malmesbury, who informs us that Edith was educated 'from infancy among the nuns of Romsey and Wilton', also indicates that Christina 'grew old at Romsey'.[47] Edith's move from one monastery to the other has created some confusion about whether the events of her adolescence took place at Romsey or Wilton. Historical discussion that promotes Christina to the abbacy of Romsey is dependent upon identifying Christina with the abbess who dressed the young princess in a veil during the summer of 1093 to protect her from the eyes of William Rufus.[48] The action certainly sounds as if Christina could have instigated it. But many women had dressed as nuns to protect themselves from the eyes of the Normans, and according to Edith's testimony, the events of her early adolescence took place at Wilton.[49] Apparently, when the two princesses reached a suitable age, they left Christina at Romsey and moved to Wilton for their education 'both in letters and good morals', as Orderic Vitalis describes it.[50] While at Wilton, Edith seems to have continued to don monastic apparel when the occasion warranted, for on two separate occasions in the late summer of 1093, chance visitors found her veiled.

Wilton, another pre-Conquest foundation, long retained its reputation as a center of learning and literary culture. About 1080, the famed hagiographer Goscelin of Canterbury produced lives of the local royal saints, Edith and Wulfhilde, at the nuns' request.[51] In his *Life of Wulfhilde*, Goscelin mentions a school at Wilton for girls who were not necessarily intended for

---

[45] Eadmer, *Historia novorum*, 122.
[46] Baker, 'Nursery of Saints', 124.
[47] *Gesta regum*, 755. Concerning Christina, see *Gesta regum*, 417 and the *Anglo-Saxon Chronicle*, s.a. 1086. Modern historians have tended to assume that Edith had to have been at either Romsey or Wilton, and have argued for one or the other. Barlow, *William Rufus* (Berkeley, 1983), surmised that the convent in question was 'probably Wilton', while David Knowles, C. N. L. Brooke, and Vera London, in *Heads of Religious Houses in England and Wales 942–1216* (Cambridge, 1972), 219, believe that Edith went to Wilton without Christina. Eleanor Searle took a similarly cautious position by accepting Eadmer's account that puts Edith at Wilton in 1093, adding that 'whether she had previously been at Romsey is unclear'. See Searle, 'Women and the Legitimization of Succession at the Norman Conquest', *Proceedings of the Battle Conference on Anglo-Norman Studies* 3 (1980): 159–61. Anselm's letter of February–March 1094 requesting that Matilda be returned to the convent is written to the bishop of Salisbury, the diocesan for Wilton, but not Romsey. See F. S. Schmitt, ed., *S. Anselmi Cantuariensis archiepiscopi opera omnia* (6 vols, Stuttgart, 1946–61). Eadmer's eye-witness account of the hearing to determine Edith's eligibility for marriage mentions Wilton exclusively. See *Historia novorum*, 121–6.
[48] Hermann of Tournai, 'Liber de restauratione', 281.
[49] Eadmer, *Historia novorum*, 124.
[50] Orderic 4: 272–3.
[51] See André Wilmart, 'Eve et Goscelin', *Revue Bénédictine* 46 (1934): 414–38.

the cloister.[52] Goscelin did not indicate whether the school still existed but took for granted that his audience would accept that one had been there in the middle of the tenth century. Indeed, because Goscelin was writing of a woman whom Edgar had made his mistress, he could not very well portray her as a consecrated virgin. He may even have used the school as a literary device, projecting the conditions of his own day back onto the tenth century in order to gloss over Edgar's crime. The clerk who composed the *Vita Ædwardi* for Queen Edith had also passed some time at Wilton.[53] After the Conquest, both Romsey and Wilton remained centers of female learning and literary culture, a place where the worship of the Anglo-Saxon saints flourished and where the memory of the Old English kings was fresh. Toward the end of the eleventh century, Archbishop Anselm had to send an archdeacon of Winchester to Romsey to root out worship of the executed Anglo-Saxon rebel Waltheof, whom some were beginning to venerate as a saint.[54] William of Malmesbury described both Wilton and Romsey as places where 'letters were trained into the female heart'. David Knowles and R. N. Hadcock estimated that Wilton housed between eighty and ninety women by the beginning of the twelfth century.[55] These nuns possessed numerous relics, including part of a nail from the True Cross and part of the body of the Venerable Bede as well as that of its own patron saint, Edith, which made it something of an attraction for pilgrims.[56] Wilton had also been the home of the Confessor's queen, who had spent a period of exile in the convent she herself rebuilt in stone, as well as having retired there before her death in 1075.[57] Memories of the Anglo-Saxon queen would have been quite fresh during the Scottish Edith's girlhood. During Edith of Scotland's schoolgirl days, Wilton was also the home of the poetess Muriel, who died sometime before 1113. Muriel enjoyed a widespread reputation and cultivated a circle of literary correspondents. One of her admirers, the poet Serlo of Bayeaux, wrote that he hesitated to address a poem to her because he feared the derision of 'the poetic congregation where you dwell'.[58] Among its other celebrated residents, Wilton had for a time housed the literary recluse, Eve, who had received her education after entering the convent as a child oblate. Wilton was also a favorite stopping-off place for Goscelin, who reports that he quizzed the abbess and inhabitants of the monastery before producing his account of the life of St Edith. Goscelin evidently respected the training that his protégé had received, for in his *Liber comfortarius*, written for Eve after she left the communal life to pursue greater holiness as a recluse in France, he recommended that she read

---

[52] Goscelin of Canterbury, 'La vie de Sainte Vulfhilde', ed. Mario Esposito, *Analecta Bollandiana* 32 (1913): 10–26. See especially p. 17.

[53] David Knowles, *The Monastic Order in England, 973–1216* (second edition, Cambridge, 1966), 136.

[54] *Anselmi opera omnia* 4: 144–5. Letter #236 is to Stephen, archdeacon of Winchester, letter #237 to the abbess of Romsey, ordering that Waltheof's worship cease. See also William of Malmesbury, *Gesta pontificum*, 322; Francisque Michel, ed., 'Vita et passio Waldevi comitis', in *Chroniques Anglo-normandes* (3 vols in one, Rouen, 1836), 2: 111–23.

[55] Knowles and Hadcock, *Medieval Religious Houses: England and Wales* (London, 1953), 221.

[56] See Wilmart, ed., 'La légende de Saint Edith', 73; Carl Horstmann, ed., *S. Editha sive chronicon Vilodunense* (Heilbronn, 1883), lines 1377–407.

[57] *Vita Ædwardi*, 217–21.

[58] See J. S. P. Tatlock, 'Muriel: The Earliest English Poetess', *Publications of the Modern Language Association of America* 48 (1933): 318.

the church fathers as well as the Bible.[59] Goscelin may have been thinking of the Wilton of his own day when he described the inhabitants of the tenth-century convent as 'drawn, as is customary, from the most illustrious daughters of the princes, thegns, and magnates of the realm'.[60]

If Goscelin met with the members of the Scottish royal family, he may have heard from them a story about Queen Margaret that he included in his 1091 report in the translation of the relics of St Augustine of Canterbury. He expanded on the story in the *Life and Miracles of St Lawrence*, written about 1095. According to the latter account, Margaret had recently *(nuper)* traveled to the church of St Lawrence (who had been an early disciple of Augustine of Canterbury) near East Fortune in East Lothian, where she intended to worship at his shrine. But the site was considered so holy that no women were allowed to enter, a fact that was explained to the queen by the local priests. Margaret must have perceived the ban on women as simply another aberrant Scottish custom, for she informed the community that she intended to lay her gifts on the altar. But no sooner had she entered the porch of the church, Goscelin asserted, than she was overcome by excruciating pains and called to her retainers to save her, exclaiming that she was about to die. Margaret was eventually revived by the prayers of St Lawrence's priests and, chastened, delivered her gifts to the custody of the community.[61] If stories of this kind were known to the young Edith, it argues for the fact that the mother continued to influence her daughter despite their physical separation.

Wilton remained a center of literary culture into the early twelfth century as is evidenced by the 1118 entry on the mortuary roll of abbot Vitalis of Savigny, where it is one of only four houses in England and France which contributed a verse in his memory.[62] The literary climate at Wilton provided Edith with what must have been an outstanding education for her day. In her later writings, she displayed familiarity with the Old and New Testaments and the Church Fathers as well as at least a passing familiarity with some of the major Latin authors. Edith probably learned, or perfected, her French in the convent. The monasteries of Romsey and Wilton were also places in which the Scottish princesses could learn of their maternal heritage and also associate with other aristocratic girls, both French and English. Just twenty years after the Conquest, both monasteries had become places where, as Ritchie wrote, 'the daughters of the conquered and conquerors met on equal terms'.[63] The daughter of William the Conqueror's naval captain became a nun at Romsey, and it may have been through her stories that details of the invasion were preserved in the oral tradition of the nuns.[64] Gunnhildr, the daughter of King Harold by his mistress

---

[59] For Eve, see Wilmart, 'Eve et Goscelin' and Sharon Elkins, *Holy Women of Twelfth-Century England* (Chapel Hill, 1988), 21–7.
[60] Wilmart, ed., 'La légende de Ste Edith', 61–2.
[61] *Acta sanctorum*, 1 February, Volume One for February, 296–7. The identification of 'Fortuna' as East Fortune follows Ritchie, *Normans in Scotland*, 77, n. 1.
[62] Leopold Delisle, ed., *Rouleau mortuaire du B. Vital, Abbé de Savigni, contenant 207 titres, écretis en 1122–23 dans différents églises de France et d'Angleterre* (Paris, 1909), Plate 38, entry #153.
[63] Ritchie, *Normans in Scotland*, 76.
[64] Elisabeth van Houts, 'Medieval Historiography and Oral Tradition: The Norman Conquest of England in 1066', paper presented to the Medieval Group, University of Cambridge, October 1990.

Eadgyth Swan-Neck, was also a resident at Wilton, although she had never taken vows.[65] Malcolm and Margaret must have been aware of the society in which their daughters would be educated and may have chosen Romsey and Wilton specifically to prepare their daughters for their future role as Norman ladies. While eventual marriage into the Norman royal family was probably not envisioned in 1086, Malcolm may have hoped to marry one or both girls into prominent Anglo-Norman families, particularly into those families where a marriage alliance could be helpful in securing (or extending southward) the border between England and Scotland.

By 1093, Malcolm had evidently found just such a family. He agreed to marry Edith to the Breton Alan the Red, count of Richmond and one of the greatest landholders in the north of England. The marriage never came about, for reasons not entirely clear. Orderic Vitalis' cryptic remark that Alan was 'prevented by death' from obtaining the hand of the princess conceals six months of frenetic activity that ended with Edith out of the convent, Malcolm and Margaret dead, Gunnhildr kidnapped from Wilton, romantically involved with Alan the Red but finally married to his brother, and, in a rare display of harmony, both William Rufus and Anselm expressing outrage over the turn of events.[66] Constructing a narrative for the period between August 1093 and March 1094, involves sorting through several annals and chronicles, none wholly reliable, as well as conflicting charter and epistolary evidence. Each of the sources has something to say of the events but none tells the whole story. Because we have no precise chronology of the events of that busy autumn, it is difficult to determine their sequence and even more difficult to interpret them. Any reconstruction is therefore bound to be speculative, and several persuasive but contradictory interpretations already exist. We know Malcolm Canmore was present at the dedication of Durham Cathedral on 11 August 1093, one of the few secure dates in the entire chain of events.[67] According to the 1093 entry in the *Anglo-Saxon Chronicle*, Malcolm asked William Rufus to ensure that terms of an earlier agreement be fulfilled, and William Rufus summoned Malcolm to Gloucester for discussions. On his way to Gloucester, Rufus stopped over at a convent (authors disagree over whether it was Romsey or Wilton) where, after seeing Edith veiled, he immediately left.[68] Malcolm arrived at Gloucester in late August, possibly on 24 August, but for reasons that remain unclear, the English king refused to see him, a refusal that Malcolm interpreted as an insult to his royal dignity.[69] He immediately rode to the convent, arriving within the same week as Rufus. When Malcolm saw his daughter veiled, he ripped off the offensive headdress in a great burst of anger and tore it to shreds. Hermann of Tournai reports that he threw the shredded garment onto the

---

[65] *Anselmi opera omnia* 4: 43–50 (letter #168–9). See André Wilmart, 'La destinaire de la lettre de Saint Anselm sur l'état et le voeux de religion', *Revue Bénédictine* 38 (1926): 331–4.
[66] *Orderic* 4: 273.
[67] Simeon of Durham, 'Historia Regum', 220–1.
[68] Hermann of Tournai, 'Liber de restauratione', 281.
[69] *Anglo-Saxon Chronicle*, s.a. 1093. Simeon of Durham provides the date of 24 August. Frank Barlow provides an excellent chronology of events and cogent discussion of them in *William Rufus*, 309–17. See also Valerie Wall, 'Malcolm III and the Foundation of Durham Cathedral', in David Rollason *et al.*, edd., *Anglo-Norman Durham, 1093–1193* (Woodbridge, 1994), 325–7.

ground and trampled on it.[70] The Scottish king pronounced that he would rather have had his daughter marry Alan the Red than become a nun, and he rode off in great haste, taking the girl with him.[71] Sometime during the summer, Alan also came to the convent, but whether he arrived before or after Rufus and Malcolm or saw Edith at all is not known. When Alan left, he took with him Harold's daughter Gunnhildr, despite Gunnhildr's having professed her intention to take the veil to Anselm, the newly-nominated archbishop of Canterbury.[72] Alan died shortly after abducting Gunnhildr, and his bride married his brother, Alan the Black.[73] Malcolm returned to Scotland, presumably with his daughter, who would have found her mother confined to bed in what proved to be her last illness. Within a few months, Malcolm and his heir-designate, Edward, mounted a particularly fierce raid into Northumbria where they were killed by a band led by Robert de Mowbray, the earl of Northumbria. Although the sources name Robert and his kinsman Morel as Malcolm's killers, they disagree over whether Malcolm and his son received their fatal blows during a siege of Alnwick Castle or by ambush when they were returning north. Margaret outlived her husband by only three days, dying on 16 November. Margaret's brother, Edgar Ætheling, having returned to Scotland after wearing out his welcome nearly everywhere else in Europe, knew that the Scottish succession would not be smooth and so gathered up the younger children and took them south for protection. There is a later romantic description of Edgar taking advantage of a foggy night to smuggle Margaret's body out of the besieged castle. This may be an invention of the storytellers, but it remains the case that Edgar has received singularly little historical credit for his familial loyalty. Whatever the case with Margaret's body, it is clear that Malcolm and Margaret's children were not safe in Scotland, and it may have been they that Edgar smuggled from the castle precincts.[74] The children's immediate fate is not known, but all survived the succession crisis. William Rufus eventually lent his assistance to one of their sons, also named Edgar, who gained the Scottish throne in 1097.

Obviously the tangled skein of events of the summer of 1093 is of great significance for the history of Scottish–English relations, and Edith's role is a crucial one. The narrative accounts make clear that the disagreement between the two kings somehow involved Edith but offer no explanation of her role. If she was not intended for the cloister, why was she dressed in a habit when the Red King visited? Why did he leave so suddenly after seeing her so dressed? Hermann of Tournai, whose garbled account is the only twelfth-century source for Rufus' visit to the convent, says that his visit was unexpected. The king,

---

[70] Hermann of Tournai, 'Liber de restauratione', 281–2.

[71] Hermann of Tournai, 'Liber de restauratione', 281, and more reliably, Eadmer's eyewitness account of Matilda's testimony at the ecclesiastical council of 1100. See *Historia novorum*, 121–6.

[72] Searle, 'Women and the Legitimization of Succession', and Southern, *St Anselm and his Biographer*, also *Anselmi opera omnia* 4: 60–1 (letter #177).

[73] Southern, arguing from an entry in York's *Liber vitae*, made a case in favor of Alan Rufus being dead by 4 August 1093. See *St Anselm and his Biographer*, 187, n. 2.

[74] See Alan Orr Anderson, ed., *Early Sources of Scottish History AD 500–1286* (2 vols, Edinburgh, 1922), 2: 86, n. 1, citing the tale of Edgar's rescue of Margaret's body from John of Fordun, *Chronica gentis Scottorum* 5: 21.

accompanied by a band of knights, arrived at the gates, demanding to see the daughter of the king of Scotland.[75] The alarmed abbess, wishing to protect the girl from the lust of the 'young, fierce king who always wished to carry out without delay whatever popped into his head', disguised her as a nun to hide her beauty and protect her from violence. The king managed to get a furtive look at Edith while pretending to admire the abbess' roses. When the king abruptly turned and rode away just moments after seeing her in the habit, the abbess' suspicion that the king had wished to harm the princess was confirmed.[76] But why was Rufus, who normally had no interest in females, so interested in this particular maiden? Edward Augustus Freeman, Rufus' nineteenth-century biographer, speculated that Rufus himself was a reluctant candidate for the hand of the Scottish princess. On seeing her veiled, the king had a perfectly legitimate excuse not to meet Malcolm or to go through with the proposed marriage.[77] Or perhaps Rufus was genuinely angered, thinking that Malcolm intended to involve him with a daughter who had worn the veil. Rufus was on fairly good terms with the church in the autumn of 1093, and if he wished to preserve that rare harmony, the last thing he needed was to scandalize the church with an irregular marriage. Recent students of the reign of Rufus have tended to accept Freeman's suggestions, and certainly no other persuasive interpretation of Hermann's tale has been proffered.[78] However, no contemporary writer provides more than a hint that a marriage was being considered, and, although the suggestion is not impossible, insisting upon Rufus as an intended bridegroom for the daughter of Malcolm and Margaret is reading a great deal into one brief visit.

If William Rufus' role in the drama is problematic, that of Alan is even more so. Had Malcolm intended to marry Edith to Alan, as Orderic Vitalis reports, or was Malcolm's comment that he would rather have his daughter 'married to Alan than a nun' intended as sarcasm? André Wilmart suggested that Alan's visit to Wilton occurred before that of either king. If that is so, Malcolm's comment was intended to convey that he was so incensed upon seeing his daughter, the valuable marriage-pawn, veiled, that he would rather have had her marry a scoundrel like Alan (the kidnapper of nuns) than become a nun.[79] The possibility also exists that William Rufus suggested Alan as a suitable substitute bridegroom when he himself declined to marry Edith, an offer the Scottish king saw as insulting to his dignity and that of his daughter. If Malcolm did not favor

---

[75] Hermann of Tournai, 'Liber de restauratione', 281–2. Hermann's account, written about 1140, is full of factual errors and is colored by his knowledge of the death of Henry's and Matilda's only son and of the accession of King Stephen. Nevertheless, most modern historians have accepted the story as essentially reliable.

[76] Hermann of Tournai, 'Liber de restauratione', 281.

[77] Freeman, *William Rufus*, 2: 282–3, 598–603.

[78] See Barlow, *William Rufus*, 314–15, who accepts Freeman's suggestion after some discussion, and Emma Mason, who accepts it uncritically in 'William Rufus: Myth and Reality', *Journal of Medieval History* 3 (1977): 1–20. Richard Southern proposed that it may have been Rufus himself who prompted the abbess to dress Edith as a nun in order to prevent the marriage between Alan Rufus and the Scottish princess. See R. W. Southern, *Saint Anselm: A Portrait in a Landscape* (Cambridge, 1990), 260–2.

[79] Wilmart, 'Alain le Roux et Alain le Noir, Comptes de Bretagne', *Annales de Bretagne* 38 (1929): 578–602. Also, Wilmart, 'Une lettre inedité de S. Anselme a une moniale inconstante', *Revue Bénédictine* 40 (1928): 328–32.

Alan's suit, perhaps he took his daughter out of the convent before Alan arrived, leaving Alan to kidnap King Harold's daughter in lieu of King Malcolm's. Sir Richard Southern rejected Wilmart's reading in favor of a literal interpretation of Malcolm's outburst. According to Southern, the proposed marriage between Edith and Alan was cancelled when Alan arrived at the convent and 'saw a young woman whom he liked better'.[80]

To complete the range of suggestions for the sequence and meaning of the events of 1093-4, Eleanor Searle offered a persuasive 'possible history', which has the merit of accounting for all the events while requiring far fewer assumptions than any previous interpretation. She argues that Malcolm did indeed intend his daughter as a bride to Alan the Red. A marriage between Edith and Alan would have created an alliance between Malcolm and Alan to resist the encroachment of Robert de Mowbray, the earl of Northumbria, whose property lay between those of Malcolm and Alan. The earl's presence in the region after 1080 had checked Scottish ambitions south of Lothian as well as Count Alan's activities north of Richmond. Thus, an alliance between Malcolm and Alan would constitute a 'pincer movement' against Northumbria, checking any expansionist ambitions harbored by Robert de Mowbray. As Searle noted, 'a marriage that would give Alan claims to Lothian and Malcolm a grandson in Richmond would suit them both very well'.[81] But, she speculated, the king's vassals protected each other's interests to the extent that, if William Rufus had even considered a marriage that would provide such a disturbing alliance, Rufus' vassals, rallied by Robert, would have vehemently objected. When Rufus refused to see Malcolm at Gloucester, it was because Rufus refused to deal with the Scottish king except in Rufus' own court according to the judgement of the English king's vassals, exercising 'flamboyantly' good feudal lordship. However, the king of Scotland resented being treated as just another of Rufus' vassals, and his outrage stemmed from the notion that his daughter's marriage was subject to the approval of the English. Positing that Gunnhildr must have been abducted within a few days of the quarrel between the two kings, Searle objected to Southern's romantic interpretation as one that fails to see that property and succession claims inhered strongly in women. As the heiress of Eadgyth Swan-Neck, Gunnhildr was not simply a young woman whom Alan liked better than he did Edith but was instead a 'second-best' replacement for the Scottish bride who had been denied him. Especially relevant were Gunnhildr's connections in the Danelaw that added legitimacy to Alan's claims to property in five counties of the old Danelaw.[82] When Alan the Red died, his younger brother and heir, Alan the Black, understanding his brother's reasons, married Gunnhildr himself.

Searle's case is attractive and highly plausible, but given the gaps in the existing evidence, ultimately not provable. However, Malcolm's vehemence in attacking the Northumbrian lands of Robert de Mowbray in the autumn of 1093 argues for the possibility of personal animosity in the Scottish king's actions,

---

[80] Southern, *St Anselm and his Biographer*, 185, n. 1.
[81] Searle, 'Women and Succession', 161.
[82] Searle, 'Women and Succession', 168-9.

which ultimately proved fatal.[83] Malcolm, along with Edward, his oldest son by Margaret, was killed on 13 November. Most sources agree that he was killed while besieging Alnwick Castle, but Orderic Vitalis reports that Malcolm and Edward were ambushed by de Mowbray and his kinsman, Archil Morel, while the royal party was returning to Scotland.[84] Edith herself may have believed Morel to have been Malcolm's murderer, for, many years later, when she was queen of England, she granted 'the land of Archil Morel' to Tynemouth Priory on behalf of the soul of her father. While donations on behalf of the parents were commonplace in the medieval world, this is the only surviving grant of the queen's where she named her father specifically as the spiritual beneficiary of her action.[85] Normally her grants were much more formulaic, naming for the benefit of herself, the king, and 'antecessorum meorum' (or 'nostrorum').

Edith's whereabouts between August 1093, when Malcolm took her away from Wilton, and the autumn of 1100, when she met with Anselm in Salisbury prior to her marriage to King Henry, are not known. She may have gone back to Wilton, although it is not likely that she continued to wear the veil. Several chroniclers reporting the marriage of the Scottish princess to King Henry I in 1100 hint of a long courtship. William of Malmesbury says that Henry's friends, chiefly the bishops of the kingdom, persuaded him to marry and that he chose the daughter of the king of the Scots, 'to whom he had long been attached'. Orderic reports that Henry, 'appreciating the high birth of the maiden whose perfection of character he had long adored, chose her as his bride'. Eadmer's account, not surprisingly, emphasizes that Edith was free to marry by declaring that 'long after she discarded the veil, the king fell in love with her'.[86] But in 1093–4, Anselm exercised his pastoral duties with great zeal in the matter of what he perceived to be two runaway nuns. To Gunnhildr he wrote two stinging letters, warning her that she faced damnation unless she returned to the monastery. He argued that, even though she had never taken vows, she had worn the veil both publicly and privately, 'so that all seeing you said that you were [dedicated] to God, no less than if you had affirmed [your] profession legally'.[87] When Alan the Red died, Anselm graphically compared the transitory joys of the flesh with the eternal joys of the heavenly life she had forsaken.[88] Anselm approached the case of Edith through administrative

---

[83] Simeon of Durham, 'Historia regum', 221–2. See also Judith Green, 'Anglo-Scottish Relations, 1066–1174', in Michael Jones and Malcolm Vale, edd., *England and her Neighbours, 1066–1453: Essays in Honour of Pierre Chaplais* (London, 1989), 57.

[84] Marjorie Chibnall rejects Orderic's story, which is nevertheless accepted by many Scottish historians. See Chibnall's note to *Orderic* 4: 270, and G. W. S. Barrow, *Kingship and Unity, Scotland 1000–1306* (Edinburgh, 1981), 31. For the near-contemporary notices of Malcolm's death, see Florence of Worcester, *Chronicon ex chronicis*, 2: 31–2; Simeon of Durham, 'Historia regum', 221–2; *Anglo-Saxon Chronicle s.a.* 1093; and the *Waverly Annals, s.a.* 1093 in Henry Richards Luard, ed., *Annales Monastici* (5 vols, RS, London, 1864), 2: 202. The Anglo-Saxon chronicler, *s.a.* 1070, pointed out that the death was shameful because Archil Morel was Malcolm's 'sworn companion' *(godsib)*.

[85] See David Bates, H. W. C. Davis, Charles Johnson, H. A. Cronne and R. H. C. Davis, edd., *Regesta regum Anglo-Normannorum* (4 vols, Oxford 1913–98) 2: 624, and Judith Green, 'Aristocratic Loyalties on the Northern Frontier of England, c.1100–1174', *England in the Twelfth Century: Proceedings of the 1988 Harlaxton Symposium* (Woodbridge, 1990), 87.

[86] See *Gesta regum* 2: 495, *Orderic* 5: 300–1, and Eadmer, *Historia novorum*, 127.

[87] *Anselmi opera omnia* 4: 44–5 (letter 168).

[88] *Anselmi opera omnia* 4: 44–5 (letter 169).

channels, urging Osmund, the saintly bishop of Salisbury, to see that this 'prodigal daughter *(filia perdita)* of the king of Scots, whom the devil made to cast off the veil' was returned to Wilton. The archbishop added that he had suspected that the king had aided and abetted the girl but after conferring with him, was heartened to discover that Rufus, 'as is fitting for a good king', had no interest in the princess other to ensure that she was provided with food.[89] Edith, financially supported by the English king, may even have visited the court along with her brothers, who also lived under Rufus' protection. At some point before 1100 William II of Warenne, earl of Surrey, made application for her hand, but, as Orderic interprets the matter, 'she was destined by Heaven for a more illustrious marriage'.[90]

The earl of Surrey's proposal marks the last time that we hear of the princess Edith. When she emerges in the sources some six years later, she appears as Matilda. The reasons for the name change are not known. It has been suggested that Robert Curthose, Edith's godfather, may have given the child his own mother's name at the time of her baptism. Given the close relationship between Robert and his mother, this scenario seems plausible. But the entry in the Durham *Liber vitae* calendar listing the names of the children of Malcolm and Margaret affirms that the child had been called Edith while she was in Scotland. Whether she continued to be called Edith after going to England is a matter of speculation. The only evidence that she was ever called Edith in England comes from the Winchecombe annalist, writing in the latter part of the twelfth century. He twice referred to her as 'Edith' but corrected himself by scratching out 'Edith' and inserting the name 'Matilda'. This particular annalist made several mistakes when writing of events and personalities of the eleventh and early twelfth centuries, and it could be that he was thinking of the Confessor's queen rather than the Scottish princess when he used the name Edith.[91] For whatever reason the change occurred, it was probably fortunate that contemporaries knew King Malcolm's daughter only as 'Matilda'. Given the climate of opinion surrounding her proposed marriage to Henry I, it is just as well that there were no popular associations with that other Edith of Wilton. St Edith's aunt had been kidnapped from the convent by King Edgar, her mother had been Edgar's concubine, and she, when offered the choice between the crown of England and the religious life, piously chose to remain in the convent.[92]

When William Rufus fell victim to a stray arrow while hunting in the New Forest in August 1100, Henry seized the throne with what would prove to be his characteristic efficiency. With the newly married and now wealthy Curthose returning from the Crusade, Henry took immediate steps to secure his hold on the kingdom. He issued his famous coronation charter, recalled Anselm from his exile on the continent, and proposed marriage to the daughter of the king of

---

[89] *Anselmi opera omnia* 4: 60–1 (letter 177).
[90] *Orderic* 4: 272.
[91] See R. R. Darlington, ed., 'The Winchcombe Annals, 1049–1181', in Patricia M. Barnes and C. F. Slade, edd., *A Medieval Miscellany for Doris Mary Stenton* (London, 1962), *s.a.* 1100, 1118. The name 'Edith' appears in only one of the two manuscripts of the annals, which are both riddled with errors.
[92] Wilmart, ed. 'La légende de Ste Edith', 84.

the Scots.[93] Contemporary commentators stressed that Henry was making a love-match. Warren Hollister speculated that Henry might have spent part of his youth at Salisbury being educated by Bishop Osmund. If so, Osmund may also have been responsible for bringing the girl to Henry's attention after he was made aware of her plight in Anselm's 1093 letter.[94] William of Malmesbury claimed that Henry loved Matilda so much that he 'barely considered the marriage portion'.[95] We know little of the physical appearance of the Scottish princess. According to Hermann of Tournai, the abbess in 1093 had feared that William Rufus, aroused by the girl's beauty, might do her some harm. But Hermann had never seen the queen, and the best that William of Malmesbury could do was to describe her as 'not entirely to be despised regarding beauty'.[96] It is true that Henry and Matilda could have been acquainted, particularly if she did visit Rufus' court after 1093. But even if Matilda had been both poverty-stricken and plain, a variety of advantages could be expected from the marriage. If they were fond of one another, as the chroniclers insisted, it was a undeniably conveniently placed affection, or, to paraphrase Freeman, a case where policy and inclination argued for the same conclusion.[97] Modern historians have discounted the personal element and argued over whether Henry's marriage was aimed at appeasing his English subjects and strengthening his claims to the throne by marrying a daughter of the House of Wessex, or whether his aim was to pacify the north.[98] But Henry I was wise enough to perceive all the possibilities inherent in the union, and there is no reason for anyone to insist upon a monocausal explanation of Henry's motives. Matilda, as the daughter of a crowned king, carried the advantage of having been 'born to the purple', an intangible but highly prestigious benefit in medieval Europe. As the daughter of an Anglo-Saxon princess, she also represented the House of Wessex. Matilda's royal bloodline proved a constant source of inspiration to the poets and chroniclers of the age. The annalist of the *Anglo-Saxon Chronicle, s.a.* 1100, spoke for many when he described Matilda as 'of the rightful kingly line of England'. An alliance between the son of the Conqueror and a relative of Edward the Confessor would indeed provide some much-needed legitimacy for Henry's tenuous claims to the throne. In addition, such a marriage would be

---

[93] For the coronation charter, see David Douglas and George Greenaway, edd., *English Historical Documents, 1042–1189* (second edition, London, 1981), 432–5. The letter to Anselm is printed in *Anselmi opera omnia* 4: 109–10 (letter 212). The best discussion of the events between Rufus' death and Henry's coronation is Hollister, *Henry I*, 102–117.

[94] Hollister, *Henry I*, 36–7.

[95] *Gesta regum*, 715. See also *Orderic* 5: 300–1; Eadmer, *Historia novorum*, 127.

[96] Hermann of Tournai, *'Liber de restauratione'*, 281, and *Gesta regum*, 756.

[97] Edward A. Freeman, *The Reign of William Rufus and the Accession of Henry I* (2 vols, Oxford, 1882; repr. New York, 1970), 2: 330.

[98] Southern, for instance *(St Anselm and his Biographer*, 188), insisted that the Scottish alliance was the reason Henry pushed the marriage, even over Anselm's objections, perhaps inspiring the comment by Brooke and Keir that 'modern historians have dreamt of a Scottish alliance' *(London 800–1216*, 32). Brooke and Keir, along with Frank Barlow, favor the traditional explanation that Henry's marriage was made to woo his English subjects. See Barlow, *William Rufus*, 265–6. Marjorie Chibnall notes the advantages of the Scottish union but believes Henry was motivated most of all by the link to Edmund Ironside and the Confessor. See Chibnall, *The Empress Matilda: Queen Consort, Queen Mother, and Lady of the English* (Oxford, 1991), 7. Hollister, *Henry I*, 126, recognizes other advantages but argues that Matilda's lineage provided the chief motive for the marriage.

tremendously popular among Henry's English subjects. The Normans could not be expected to object, for, as Ritchie has pointed out, they had also claimed Edward for their own and based their right to rule on Edward's designation of William the Bastard as his heir.[99] With Curthose about to return from his enormously successful adventure in the Holy Land, legitimacy was probably foremost in the mind of the king. In addition, the alliance between England and Scotland did secure the northern border and allowed Henry to concentrate his military resources on Normandy and Wales.

However advantageous the marriage might appear to be, there was, in the fall of 1100, a large obstacle to be overcome before it could take place. The king's proposed bride was known to have worn the veil, and there may even have been a general belief that she had actually been a nun. Eadmer, in his defense of Anselm's role in allowing the marriage, goes so far as to say that rumors to that effect had prevented Henry from marrying Matilda earlier.[100] Anselm's letter to Osmund of Salisbury demonstrates that he believed that she had left the monastery unlawfully, and even if he were persuaded of the advantages of the marriage, he would not allow a marriage between Henry and a runaway nun. Foreseeing his objections to the match, Matilda took the initiative. Shortly after he returned to England from his continental exile, she requested a personal hearing with the archbishop. Anselm warned her that he could not be 'induced by any pleading to take from God his bride and join her to any earthly husband'. During their meeting, which took place in the city of Salisbury, Matilda explained that she had lived in the monastery only for education, claiming that her father and mother had never intended for her to take vows, nor had she done so. Matilda's story included her memories of the indignities she had had to endure under Christina's authority, her loathing of the monastic headdress, and her narrative of her father's anger at finding her wearing it. Anselm, who had been so positive about the correct path when chastising Gunnhildr, was now reluctant to rule on the matter of the king's marriage. Rather than decide so weighty a matter on his own, he called an ecclesiastical council to hear and decide the case.[101]

After Anselm's death, criticism arose over his part in the decision to allow the marriage. This criticism prompted Eadmer, Anselm's secretary and disciple, to write a detailed defense of Anselm's actions in order to counter allegations that he had acted improperly. According to Eadmer's eye-witness account of the council, Matilda's claims that she had never been intended for the cloister and her account of her father's anger at finding her in a nun's headdress were supported by 'credible witnesses summoned from diverse places'. Anselm sent archdeacons from Canterbury and Salisbury to Wilton to make inquiries. They returned to tell the members of the council that they had not been able to discover anything that contradicted the girl's story. The archbishop then addressed the council, admonishing the members not to let 'fear or favor' pervert their judgement, and then, as Eadmer relates, withdrew to allow the

---

[99] Ritchie, *Normans in Scotland*, 116.
[100] Eadmer, *Historia novorum*, 121.
[101] Eadmer, *Historia novorum*, 121–5.

assembled bishops and nobles to decide the case on their own. After the evidence was discussed, the churchmen concluded that, 'under the circumstances of the matter, the girl could not rightly be bound by any decision to prevent her from being free to dispose of her person in whatever way she legally wished'.[102] They reported to Anselm that, although they could have reached the same decision through simple logic, they had preferred to rely on the precedent of Lanfranc's judgement in a similar case. Lanfranc had ruled that Saxon women who fled to monasteries and adopted monastic dress during the disruption following the arrival of the Normans were free to leave once the threat to their virtue had subsided. Anselm pronounced himself satisfied with the judgement of his suffragans, especially, he added, since Lanfranc's authority supported it. Matilda was called back into the room, where she 'received the news with a happy expression on her face'. She then earnestly offered to prove the truth of her testimony by an 'oath or any other process of ecclesiastical law', an act which the council deemed not to be necessary.[103] A few days later, on the feast of St Martin, Sunday, 11 November 1100, on the steps of the Confessor's church in Westminster, Anselm married the couple and crowned the new queen of England. Before doing so, however, Anselm addressed the crowd that had gathered to witness the royal marriage. He related the full story of his investigation into Matilda's status, and requested that anyone who was aware of anything contrary to the verdict that had been reached come forward and openly declare his or her knowledge. Eadmer, no doubt influenced by allegations current in the late 1120s and early 1130s, reported that 'the crowd cried out in one voice that the affair had been rightly decided, and that there was no ground on which anyone, unless possibly led by malice, could properly raise any scandal'.

Both of the twelfth-century chroniclers who describe the events leading up to the marriage betray an uneasiness over whether Anselm had done the correct thing. Eadmer's account was purposely written to clear the archbishop of charges of wrongdoing. He portrayed Anselm as uncharacteristically passive throughout the proceedings. Anselm allowed Matilda to take the first initiative but refused to accept her story without an inquiry. After the witnesses had testified, Anselm withdrew to allow the bishops to make the ruling, and his relief at discovering that Lanfranc had allowed women in similar circumstances to shed their veils is almost palpable. Eadmer stressed the very public nature of the proceedings, carefully detailing that the crowd assembled to witness the marriage understood why the wedding had been allowed to proceed. Both at the beginning and at the end of his narrative, Anselm's encomiast interrupts the flow of the story to assure the reader that he is telling the whole truth and that he is a credible witness to what had happened.

A second account of the events leading up to the royal marriage came from the pen of Hermann of Tournai, who wrote toward the middle of the twelfth century. Hermann was even more negative about the wisdom of the marriage than was Eadmer. He claimed that he personally questioned Anselm about why

---

[102] Eadmer, *Historia novorum*, 123.
[103] Eadmer, *Historia novorum*, 124–5.

the marriage was allowed to proceed. Hermann related that Anselm had filled him in on the facts of the matter, confiding that he himself had continued to believe that the marriage should never have taken place. According to Hermann, although Anselm was convinced after the hearing that the marriage was legal, he still felt it prudent that the king choose another bride. 'For', as he asserted, 'however it came about, still she has carried the veil upon her head.' Anselm approached the king with his doubts, begging that he cancel his wedding plans. 'England will not long rejoice in the children she will bear', he is supposed to have forecast. As Hermann saw it, the tragic fate of William Ætheling and the failure of Matilda's daughter to gain the crown of England provided proof of Anselm's prophetic powers.[104] But, since both Eadmer and Hermann were influenced by later events when writing about Anselm's role in the marriage, it is impossible to know whether Anselm shared their misgivings. Richard Southern has argued that Anselm's letters to Matilda show a stiffness and formality which indicate that the archbishop remained uneasy about the queen, but this stiffness occurs mainly in letters dealing with the delicate political situation. In other circumstances, Anselm was capable of expressing what appears to be genuine warmth in his correspondence with Matilda.

Whatever his private reservations, Anselm officiated at the wedding and coronation of the new queen. In describing Anselm's role in the ceremony, Eadmer mentions that the new queen was presented to 'totam regni nobilitatem populumque' to be acclaimed.[105] The acclamation by the people, first mentioned as taking place during the ceremonies for the Conqueror's accession, may have become a necessary part of the English coronation ceremony. Unfortunately, Eadmer stops short of describing the exact ritual used to consecrate the new queen. It is entirely possible that Matilda of Scotland, like Matilda of Flanders, was anointed and crowned with the new rite. This rite portrayed the queen as placed by God among the people to share in the royal power, all for the benefit of the English nation, who could rejoice in both the power of the ruler and the ability and virtue of the queen. While it cannot be shown that this was the *ordo* used at either coronation, this new articulation of the queen's right to participate in public affairs echoed resoundingly in her influence on Henry's government. Before turning to the queen as political actor, I will interrupt the narrative to consider the structure of English queenship as Matilda of Scotland might have perceived it. In the next chapter, I look at the development of queenship during the Anglo-Saxon era and, briefly, at the changes wrought by the Norman Conquest of 1066. The third chapter examines the queen's dower, the gift of lands and monies given to her at marriage, for it was ultimately these holdings that allowed her to function as a political figure and a source of patronage. The aim of the following two chapters is to discover the kinds of traditions Matilda inherited and the resources over which she exercised control. The nature of the evidence requires that we range both backward and forward in time, trying to understand just what comprised the Anglo-Norman experience of queenship.

---

[104] Hermann of Tournai, 281–2.
[105] Eadmer, *Historia novorum*, 125.

2

Strategies for Success: English Queenship before 1100

When Matilda of Scotland became queen of England in 1100, she was taking on a role that already had developed rich and complex traditions. Over the course of the early Middle Ages, queenship in England had been influenced by the cultural shifts that accompanied renewed contact with continental Europe, Christianization and the creation of the centralized monarchy that characterized the last century of the Anglo-Saxon state.

Despite recent interest in women's history and in the early Middle Ages, few studies have systematically investigated the role of royal or noble women in the British Isles before the tenth century. What little we know of early-medieval queens and queenship tends to be anecdotal, and chronicle and documentary sources for the period before the tenth-century reform show that, on the whole, marriage patterns among the royalty and aristocracy in the British Isles corresponded to those of the Germanic peoples on the continent. In common with the latter, unions in the British lands were freely formed and easily dissolved, and serial monogamy and partible inheritance were common familial patterns.[1] Under these conditions, royal women were forced to engage in vigorous, often colorful power-struggles within the court and kingdom, lining up both noble and clerical factions in order to secure the throne for their sons. Because of their access to wealth and their perceived influence over their husbands and sons, successful women could wield a great deal of power. Medieval chroniclers and annalists were well aware of the potential for royal women to participate in the exercise of public authority, and many individual women are prominent in the pages of early sources such as Bede's *Historia* or the *Anglo-Saxon Chronicle*. Some queens, such as Æthelbert's wife Bertha or Æthelflæd, Lady of the Mercians, made lasting contributions and were recognized by the chroniclers as having done so.

Used carefully, literary sources can also provide a window into the role of the

---

[1] See, for example, Suzanne Fonay Wemple, *Women in Frankish Society: Marriage and the Cloister 500–900* (Philadelphia, 1981), and Margaret Clunies Ross, 'Concubinage in Anglo-Saxon England', *Past and Present* 108 (1985): 3–34, which demonstrate similar patterns and offer similar conclusions about cross-channel marital patterns in early medieval society. Pauline Stafford's 'Sons and Mothers: Family Politics in the Early Middle Ages', in Baker, ed., *Medieval Women*, pp. 79–100, demonstrates that English succession politics under these conditions paralleled those Wemple found among the Franks.

queen in pre-Christian society. One of the most important of these sources for understanding insular society is, of course, the epic poem *Beowulf*. Although the date of the poem remains in dispute among literary scholars, even those who would push the poem into the later tenth century agree that the society it depicts dates from a much earlier era. In the poem, Hrothgar's queen Wealhtheow is virtually the only female visible within the royal hall. The poet goes into great detail describing the ritual of the king and his warriors drinking together from the great golden goblet bestowed by the queen. Michael J. Enright recognized the importance of the drinking ceremony and linked the familiar role of the treaty-bride, or peaceweaver, with that of the queen in the hall:

> Just as women in the wider world were used to bind families in alliances, so did the queen act to help achieve cohesion and unity of purpose between lord and follower in the royal hall ... The queen, acting as her husband's delegate, exercised a number of important functions which ... have noteworthy implications for the study of early European political organization and its ritual affirmation.[2]

Among the queen's important functions was her role in regulating the ceremonial gatherings of the king and his 'comitatus'. In the *Beowulf* poem, it is the queen, Wealhtheow, who greets Beowulf, evaluates his prowess, and assigns him his proper status within the hall. The *Beowulf* author lays particular stress on the words heard and spoken by the queen. Wealhtheow offers the cup first to the king, bidding him to 'be happy' at the 'beer-assembly'. Then, 'careful of noble usage', she offers the cup to groups of old and young men, until at last she comes to Beowulf. Here she is described as greeting him, 'wise in her words', giving thanks to God for sending the noble warrior. When Beowulf offers his vow to slay the monster who was terrorizing the hall, the poet tells us that Wealhtheow 'well liked those words'.[3] After Beowulf is served, Wealhtheow takes her place next to the king where, presumably, she reports what had been said and perhaps even offers her own assessment of the warrior and his boasts.

Wealhtheow's role as a mediator and intercessor reflects a long tradition in Germanic society. As early as the first century, the Roman historian Tacitus represented Germanic society as one in which women's advice was not scorned or lightly disregarded.[4] Sedulius Scottus, whose ninth-century *Liber de rectoribus christianis* provides one of the few early theoretical treatises mentioning queenship, acknowledged the tradition of the 'wise counsel' given by upright wives. Sedulius reminded his readers that 'not only unbelieving, but also pious and orthodox princes often ponder and give heed to the marvelous prudence in their wives, not reflecting on their fragile sex, but rather, plucking the fruit of their good counsels'. The wife's duty to give good advice was strengthened by biblical examples and exhortations. Like many churchmen both before and after him, Sedulius encouraged royal wives by

---

[2] Michael J. Enright, 'Lady with a Mead-Cup: Ritual, Group Cohesion and Hierarchy in the Germanic Warband', *Frühmittelalterliche Studien* 22 (1988): 170–203, at 171.
[3] *Beowulf*, trans. Michael Alexander (London, 1973), lines 617, 613, 625-6, and 639.
[4] Tacitus, *The Agricola, Germania and Dialogus*, trans. M. Hutton, M. Ogilvie, H. Warmington, W. Peterson and M. Winterbottom (Cambridge, Mass., 1930), 142.

quoting St Paul's epistle to the Corinthians, noting that 'the unbelieving husband is sanctified by the wife'.[5]

The early-medieval queen's appearance and reputation for wisdom reflected and enhanced the status of her husband. It was important, especially on ceremonial occasions, that she wear gold, jewels, and sumptuous clothing, both to proclaim her own importance and to reflect the status and wealth of her husband. It was no mere literary convention that led the *Beowulf* poet to describe Wealhtheow as 'gold-adorned' ('goldhroden') and 'ring-adorned' ('beaghroden').[6] In addition to her duty to serve as a loyal counselor to the king, the early-medieval queen also presided over the royal household. The first group of maxims in the *Exeter Book*, believed to have been compiled in the second half of the tenth century, includes a commentary on the proper role of the queen that emphasizes her wisdom and her generosity:

> A king has to procure a queen with a payment, with goblets and with rings. Both must be pre-eminently liberal with gifts. . . . The woman must excel as one cherished among her people, and be buoyant of mood, keep confidences, be open-heartedly generous with horses and with treasures; in deliberation over the mead, in the presence of the troop of companions, she must always and everywhere greet first the chief of those princes and instantly offer the chalice to her lord's hand, and she must know what is prudent for them both as rulers of the hall.[7]

Continental sources confirm that the queen had charge over the palace, including the royal treasury. Because she managed the treasury, the early-medieval queen participated in and sometimes even presided over the distribution of gifts to the king's retainers. Charlemagne's instructions in the *Capitulare de villis* demonstrate the trust he placed in his queen, for he ordered that anything she instructed a judge to do ought to be 'carried out to the last word'. If the judge failed to do so, he had to abstain from drink until the emperor or the queen granted him absolution.[8] Toward the end of the ninth century, in a treatise on the workings of the ideal palace, Hincmar of Reims was specific about the queen's responsibilities. In order to free the king from the burden of domestic trifles, the queen was to direct the royal servants and maintain control over financial matters.[9]

Although most of the early literary evidence shows the queen acting in the king's hall, scattered clues dropped in both charter and narrative sources show

---

[5] Sedulius Scottus, *Liber de rectoribus christianis*, ed. S. Hellmann (Munich, 1906), Chapter 5. The quotation is from the translation by Edward Gerard Doyle, *On Christian Rulers* (Binghamton NY, 1983), 59–60. See 1 Corinthians 7:14.

[6] *Beowulf*, lines 614 and 623.

[7] The maxims are contained in the compilation known as the 'Exeter Book' (Exeter Cathedral Library 3501, ff. 88b–99b). This translation is taken from S. A. J. Bradley, *Anglo-Saxon Poetry: An Anthology of Old English Poems in Prose Translation with Introduction and Headnotes* (London, 1982), 348, beginning with line 81.

[8] See JoAnn McNamara and Suzanne Wemple, 'The Power of Women through the Family in Medieval Europe, 500–1100', in *Women and Power in the Middle Ages*, ed. Mary Erler and Maryanne Kowaleski (Athens, Georgia, 1988), 90–1.

[9] Hincmar of Reims, 'De ordine palatii', ed. A. Boetius, *Monumenta Germaniae Historica, Capitularia regum francorum* (Hanover, 1883), 2: 590–1.

that, from an early date, the king's wife in the English kingdoms also maintained a separate household. Bede matter-of-factly accepted the fact that Æthelbert's queen, Bertha, was allowed to keep her own bishop after coming to Kent. In another instance, he narrated the story of Owin, a monk who had previously been a household official for an eighth-century Northumbrian queen, calling him the 'chief of her servants and head of her household'. Bede also illustrated the inconvenience of non-uniform celebration of the Easter feast in the king's and queen's households by pointing to the seventh-century Queen Eanflæd, who, although married to the Northumbrian King Oswy, insisted on following the Roman custom which necessitated the expense of two separate feasts, one for the king's household and a second for the queen's.[10]

But despite the important ceremonial role a queen could play or the visibility and effectiveness of a few individuals, it is important to realize that the power of an early-medieval queen was not institutional and therefore tenuous. An aristocratic wife's power was based always on her presence in the royal hall, her relationship to her spouse or male kinsmen, and her control of wealth and political factions. Although the queen might maintain a household and a staff, there was no 'office' of queenship, and indeed, the Anglo-Saxons were late in adopting any kind of formal ritual to mark the status of the queen-consort. As far as historians can discern from surviving sources, installation of the queen was not normally a ritual occasion anywhere in Europe before the ninth century. None of the early Germanic peoples seem to have had anything other than the marriage ceremony itself to distinguish the queen or to recognize her special status. Throughout Europe, however, the queen sometimes shared in the special aura, or charisma, that elevated members of royal families and set them apart from other mortals. In some cases, a queen came to be associated with the right to rule, and at times, early-medieval usurpers married their predecessor's wives in order to gain legitimacy. In several instances, a king's son married his step-mother in order to consolidate his hold on the kingdom and possibly the aristocratic factions to whom the queen was allied. Later, under the Carolingians, Frankish queens and empresses were anointed, often along with their husbands, while the Anglo-Saxons developed an inauguration ceremony focused on the ritual enthronement of a new queen.[11] Asser's *Life of Alfred* reveals that the rulers and aristocracy of ninth-century Wessex were all too aware of the potential power of a queen and, after a bad experience with Eadburgh of Mercia, actually made it illegal to raise a woman to queenly status. Eadburgh had worked against 'her lord and the whole people', earning hatred not only 'for herself, leading to her expulsion from the queen's throne', but also bringing the 'same foul stigma on all the queens who came after her'. As a result, writes Asser, 'all the inhabitants of the land swore that they would never permit any king to rule over them who during his lifetime invited the queen to sit beside him on the royal throne'. Going further, these West Saxons did not allow the

---

[10] Bede, *Opera historica* (2 vols, trans. J. E. King, Cambridge, Mass, 1929) 1: 108–10, 2: 19, and 1: 458.
[11] See Janet Nelson, *Politics and Ritual in Early Medieval Europe* (London, 1986), 133–73, 239–59, 283–309, 341–61.

royal consort to be called 'queen' ('regina') but only 'king's wife' ('regis coniunx').[12] The West Saxon case demonstrates that the king and aristocracy, recognizing that 'queenship' implied something more than just marriage to the king, had tried to formally limit the power of the royal consort.

In the mid-ninth century, when Charles the Bald agreed to allow his daughter Judith to marry King Æthelwulf of Wessex, he insisted that she be crowned and wanted some sort of guarantee that her queenly status would be recognized. The author of the 856 entry into the *Annals of St Bertin* confirmed the exceptional nature of the ceremony, reporting that 'after Hincmar, bishop of Reims, had consecrated her [Judith] and placed a diadem on her head, Æthelwulf formally conferred on her the title of queen, which was not something customary before then to him or to his people'.[13] The process of devising a coronation ceremony for the queen must have impelled the king and bishop who performed the ceremony to articulate the necessary and desirable components of queenly behavior. The rites used for investing a new queen can provide insight into both the queen's duties and contemporary expectations regarding the queen's conduct. Fortunately, a few of the *ordines* from Frankish and Anglo-Saxon coronation ceremonies survive to provide clues to such early-medieval concepts of the queenly office. In the earliest continental *ordines*, including the one composed by Hincmar of Reims for the coronation of Judith, the queen's fertility is a prime concern.[14] The queen's potential influence over the king is also recognized. In the Judith 'ordo', Hincmar compares Judith's sway over the king with that of the Old Testament queen Esther, who persuaded her husband to spare the Jewish people.[15]

Although she was consecrated on the continent, Judith's ceremony established a precedent for queenly consecration and anointment in the Anglo-Saxon kingdoms. The ceremony does not seem to have been performed in England until 973, when Edgar and his queen Ælfthryth were anointed, seemingly at the instigation of Archbishop Dunstan.[16] Although the Judith 'ordo' was available as a model for the new queen's coronation rite, there are more differences than similarities between Judith's rite and the one written for Ælfthryth. In the new Edgar 'ordo', the coronation and anointment of the queen are abbreviated versions of the king's ceremony. Instead of laying stress on the queen's fertility and chastity, as Hincmar did for Judith, the author of the new rite, traditionally said to be Dunstan himself, saw the

---

[12] Simon Keynes and Michael Lapidge, trans., *Asser's Life of Alfred and Other Contemporary Sources* (Middlesex, 1983), 71–2.

[13] Janet Nelson, trans., *The Annals of St Bertin* (Manchester, 1991), 83.

[14] Pauline Stafford, 'Charles the Bald, Judith, and England', in Janet Nelson and Margaret Gibson, edd., *Charles the Bald: Court and Kingdom. Papers based on a colloquium held in London in April, 1979* (Oxford, 1981): 137–151.

[15] See 'Coronatio Iudithae Karoli II filiae', *MGH Capitularia* 2 (1883, repr. 1960): 425–7.

[16] This is not to say that no ceremonies accompanied the installation of a king or queen, but the formality and liturgical significance of the 973 consecration and anointing of Edgar and his queen mark a clear break from the past and caught the imagination of contemporaries to an unprecedented degree. See Adrienne Jones, 'The Significance of the Regal Consecration of Edgar in 973', *Journal of Ecclesiastical History* 33 (1982), 377–8, and Judith Elaine Abbott, 'Queens and Queenship in Anglo-Saxon England, 954–1066: Holy and Unholy Alliances' (unpublished Ph.D. dissertation, University of Connecticut, 1989), 107–12.

queen primarily as a regal protectress of religion rather than as the king's consecrated bed-mate.[17]

The 973 consecration ceremony was one indication of the powerful alliance between the monarchy and the Benedictine reformers, an alliance that helped bring about a new emphasis on the Christ-like qualities of the king. To some extent, the queen and other members of his family shared his special status. Another reflection of the elevated status of the tenth-century queen was the role of protectress of the nunneries accorded her by the author of the *Regularis concordia*. The queen's responsibility for the nunneries mirrored that of the king for the male convents in the kingdom. The *Regularis* also directed the inhabitants of monasteries to offer frequent prayer during public services for the welfare of both the king and the queen. Inclusion of the queen was apparently an English innovation, for none of the continental models upon which the rule was based mention the queen.[18]

During Edgar's reign, Ælfthryth's activities and visibility mirror the theoretical elevation of the queen's status as reflected in the literature of the reformers. Because of the perception that she was involved in the murder of her stepson Edward the Martyr, who was later canonized, Ælfthryth's historical reputation has been largely negative. In her own day, however, she seems to have enjoyed a positive relationship with her husband, and the evidence indicates that she worked closely with Dunstan, Æthelwold, and other reform-minded churchmen during Edgar's lifetime. She may even have supported the reformers before her marriage to Edgar. Tenth-century documents copied into the *Liber Eliensis* credit 'a certain matron, Ælfthryth' with persuading King Edgar to donate land to the abbey, and one manuscript of the *Liber* identifies this Ælfthryth as the widow who later became Edgar's queen.[19] Further evidence of the queen's persuasive power includes the twelfth-century account of the foundation of Peterborough Abbey, which credits Ælfthryth with urging and entreating the king to repair the churches of God.[20] In the city of Winchester, Ælfthryth worked closely with Bishop Æthelwold to reform the monastic community associated with the New Minster, witnessing Edgar's refoundation charter as 'Aelfthryth, legitimate wife of the aforesaid king, with the king's approval having established monks in this place, as my mission'.[21] Ælfthryth's actions as overseer

---

[17] See Abbott, 'Queens and Queenship', 587–602. See also Percy Ernst Schramm, *A History of the English Coronation* (Oxford, 1937), 22,P. L. Ward, 'An Early Version of the Anglo-Saxon Coronation Ceremony', *English Historical Review* 57 (1942): 345–61, and Robert Deshman, 'Christus rex et magi reges: Kingship and Christology in Ottonian and Anglo-Saxon Art', *Frühmitterarterliche Studien* 10 (1976): 367–405.

[18] Thomas Symons, ed., *Regularis concordia angliae nationis monachorum sanctimonialiumque* (London, 1953): xxxii, Chapters 3 and 7.

[19] Ælfthryth was a widow with at least one child upon her marriage to the king. See E. O. Blake, ed., *Liber Eliensis* (Camden, 3rd series, 92; London, 1962), 111–13n. Abbott, 'Queens and Queenship', 119–27 provides a thoughtful analysis of the sources for Ælfthryth's life and reign, distinguishing between contemporary documents and later accretions. See pp. 119–27 and 135–6. Also, Stafford, 'The Portrayal of Royal Women in England, Mid-Tenth to Mid-Twelfth Centuries'.

[20] Hugh Candidus, *The Chronicle of Hugh Candidus, a Monk of Peterborough*, ed. W. T. Mellows (Oxford, 1949), 28–9.

[21] 'Ego Ælfthryth, legitima praefati regis coniunx, mea legatione monachos eidem loco rege annuente constituens, crucem impressi'. See John M. Kemble, ed., *Codex diplomaticus ævi Saxonici* (6 vols, London, 1839–48; repr. Vaduz, 1964), charter #527.

of Barking Abbey suggest that she carried out the duties assigned to her as the protectress of England's nunneries. After Edgar's death, certain nuns at Barking laid complaints against their abbess Wulfhilda, and Ælfthryth deposed her, only to reinstate her twenty years later. The story, recorded by the hagiographer Goscelin of St Bertin a century after the events took place, was told to him by nuns at Barking who were still hostile to the queen. These nuns believed Aelfthryth's actions to have been unjust and Wulfhilda's reinstatement due to a miracle. It is difficult to deduce the facts of the situation other than to point out that Wulfhilda had at one time been the object of Edgar's amorous intentions, so perhaps personal animosity did play a part in the queen-mother's actions.[22]

Contemporaries perceived Ælfthryth's influence over Edgar and saw her as a means of access to the king. When Bishop Æthelwold sought the freedom of Taunton in 968, it was recorded that he gave the king two hundred mancuses in gold and a silver cup worth five pounds, along with fifty mancuses of gold for the queen 'in return for her help in his just mission'. Four extant tenth-century wills include gifts to Ælfthryth, and in one of them the testators were specific about the reason for their bequest. The queen was to receive an armlet worth thirty gold mancuses in return 'for her advocacy that the will might stand'.[23]

Judith Abbott suggested that Ælfthryth served as a formal counselor to the king, sitting in on at least some meetings of the witan, witnessing charters, and even acting as Edgar's deputy by adjudicating cases involving disputed land tenure. It may be true that Ælfthryth did have at least a quasi-official role in Edgar's curia, but I would hesitate to push the evidence as far as Abbott did. Members of the king's family often witnessed charters, even in their infancy. The presence of the child aethelings probably served to imprint the proceedings firmly on the minds of the participants, but children obviously could not be called upon to testify about what they had observed.[24] The queen's presence carried greater weight, and on at least one occasion Ælfthryth was later summoned to testify about events she had witnessed years before the dispute arose.[25] Abbott's assertion that Ælfthryth acted as Edgar's 'deputy' is more problematic. All the cases she cites involve the monastic community in Winchester, a city that may have been assigned to the queen in dower. But whatever the basis for Ælfthryth's actions concerning Winchester, it is clear that

---

[22] Esposito, ed., 'La vie de sainte Vulfhilde', 21, and Susan Ridyard, *Royal Saints of Anglo-Saxon England* (Cambridge, 1988), 43. See also Marc A. Meyer, 'Women and the Tenth-Century Monastic Reform', *Revue Bénédictine* 87 (1977), 54–61.

[23] A. J. Robertson, ed./trans., *Anglo-Saxon Charters* (Cambridge, 1939), 94–5. I owe this reference to Dr Janet M. Pope, who also generously guided me through several thorny problems with Anglo-Saxon sources. Also, Dorothy Whitelock, ed./trans., *Anglo-Saxon Wills* (Cambridge, 1930), 26.

[24] See Abbott, 'Queens and Queenship', 140–1, 155–8. For use of the æthelings as witnesses in Edgar's reign, see Walter de Gray Birch, *Cartularium Saxonicum: A Collection of Charters Relating to Anglo-Saxon History* (3 vols, London, 1885–93, repr. New York, 1964), charter #1190. Edward the Confessor is first listed as a witness in one of his father's charters in 1005, probably the year of Edward's birth (Kemble, *Codex diplomaticus ævi Saxonici*, #714).

[25] Abbott, 'Queens and Queenship', 179–81; Ælfthryth's writ appears in F. E. Harmer, ed., *Anglo-Saxon Writs* (Manchester, 1952), #108, pages 396–7.

she was a visible, active part of the monarchy, during both Edgar's reign and that of her son, Æthelred II.[26]

Modern historians have come to varying conclusions about the significance of Aelfthryth's reign. For Abbott and, to a lesser extent, H. G. Richardson and G. O. Sayles, Ælfthryth represents a turning-point in that she is the first true English 'regina consecrata', and these historians argue that the consecration itself is what allowed Ælfthryth to act in such a public and official manner. Abbott attached such importance to the consecration and its effects that she posited that the ceremony actually 'provided for a more peaceful succession and it also encouraged a becoming gratitude [toward the church] in the new king; it was the church's consecration of his mother that made him king'.[27] Others have been less willing to accord such importance to Ælfthryth and her reign. Documentation is scarce for the period before the reform, and it may be that other women acted in the same capacities as did Ælfthryth. Janet Nelson has suggested that Aelfflaed, wife of Edward the Elder, may have been consecrated. Although Marc Meyer has not addressed the question directly, evidence from a series of his articles suggests that Ælfthryth is best seen within a continuum of a developing 'office' of queenship in late Anglo-Saxon England.[28] It is not my intention to resolve any questions of tenth-century historiography in this chapter, other than to introduce the element of personality into the equation. Ælfthryth's position as one of several women who had borne children to the reigning king was quite common in early-medieval Europe. Meyer described her as 'an ambitious woman of great ability whose political maneuvers helped secure her own position and that of her son'.[29] Accordingly, her alliance with the reformers is neither revolutionary nor unexpected, for the pages of early-medieval chroniclers such as Gregory of Tours are full of stories of women who used both familial and episcopal allies to further their own interests and those of their children. Is it not possible that Ælfthryth's visibility did not arise out of her consecration but rather that Edgar and Dunstan arranged for her to be publicly acknowledged because she was already a valuable political asset?

Acceptance of Abbot's views on the importance of the consecration ceremony itself as the constituent element in the elevation of the queen's role requires belief that the reformers' views of both canonical marriage and the sacral nature of king- and queenship were widely shared by the English public. The frequency with which sons of unconsecrated mothers (and, indeed, fathers) were accepted

[26] Geoffrey Gaimar, writing in the middle of the twelfth century, says that Ælfthryth held property in Winchester, Rockingham, and Rutland. See Gaimar, *L'estoire des Engleis*, ed. Alexander Bell (Oxford, 1960, repr. NY, 1971), lines 4138–40; also Abbott, 'Queens and Queenship', 139–41. Also, 'The Queen's Demesne in Anglo-Saxon England', in Meyer, ed., *The Culture of Christendom: Essays in Medieval History in Commemoration of Denis L. T. Bethell* [London, 1993], 75–114. For Queen Edith's control of Winchester, see Catherine Morton and Hope Muntz, edd./trans., *The Carmen de Hastingae proelio of Bishop Guy of Amiens* (Oxford, 1972), 40, lines 625–34, and Edward A. Freeman, *The History of the Norman Conquest of England: Its Causes and Results* (3rd edition, Oxford, 1877–9), 3: Appendix K. For Queen Emma, see *Encomium Emmae reginae*, ed. Alistair Campbell (London, 1949), xliv.
[27] See Richardson and Sayles, *The Governance of Mediaeval England from the Conquest to Magna Carta* (Edinburgh, 1963), 301–4 and Abbott, 'Queens and Queenship', 29, 588.
[28] Nelson, *Politics and Ritual*, 300, n. 10, speculated that Ælfflæd may have been consecrated in 900. See also Meyer, 'Women and the Tenth Century Reform', 37–51, along with 'Patronage of West-Saxon Royal Nunneries in Late Anglo-Saxon England', 332–58.
[29] Meyer, 'Women and the Tenth-Century Reform', 51.

as king in the tenth and eleventh centuries suggests otherwise. Of the nine kings who claimed the English throne between the death of Edgar and the accession of William Rufus, only three were born of women who we can even posit were consecrated.[30] It is true that both the queen and some leading reformers stressed the legitimacy of Ælfthryth's and Edgar's marriage. This emphasis may result from the queen's realization that canonical legitimacy would be a potent argument in favor of her son and for the exclusion of Edgar's other children when Edgar died. Certainly the importance of legitimate birth and the need for consecration and coronation grew over the course of the century, but the elements of access to wealth, control of political factions, and familial connections continued to be crucial to the success of the later Anglo-Saxon queens, consecrated or not.

As a final caution against attaching too much importance to the concept of 'sacred queenship' in the Anglo-Saxon era, historians have no idea how quickly the queen's consecration became a matter of course at the beginning of a new reign. Records for the queen's installation in the later tenth and eleventh centuries are sparse and inconclusive, although most modern authors would agree that eleventh-century Anglo-Saxon queens were consecrated. But, as Lawrence M. Larson pointed out, a passage from Ælfric's translation (c.1000) of verse eleven of the first chapter of the Book of Esther seems to indicate that the queen's coronation had not yet become usual in Anglo-Saxon England. In his translation, Ælfric included an excursus explaining the Persian king's commandment to his queen, Vashti, to appear before him wearing her crown ('posito super caput ejus diademate'). The Anglo-Saxon word for crown was 'cynehelm', or 'king's helmet', and Ælfric glossed the passage by noting that 'such was their custom, that the queen ('cwen') wore a "king's helmet" on her head'. This gloss certainly seems to indicate that crown-wearing was not among the routine perquisites of tenth-century English queens.[31]

The question of coronation or consecration is almost irrelevant for the careers of England's eleventh-century queens. Whether or not she usually wore a crown, an Anglo-Saxon queen could find the means to act in an effective manner to further her goals. Emma, sister of the Norman Count Richard II, remains one of the most controversial women ever to reign as queen of England. She shares with Eleanor of Aquitaine the distinction of having been the wife of two kings and the mother of two others. As the 'treaty bride' to King Æthelred II, Emma bore a daughter and two sons. After Æthelred's death, Emma married his

---

[30] Edgar was immediately succeeded by his son Edward the Martyr, born out of a possibly illegitimate union. Ælfthryth's son, Æthelred II, succeeded his half-brother. Edmund Ironside, Cnut, Harold Harefoot, and Harold Godwinson were all born to unconsecrated mothers. Although no surviving source specifically mentions the ceremony, Queen Emma witnessed one of Æthelred's charters as 'thoro consecrata regio', indicating that Edward the Confessor and Hardacnut were born of a consecrated mother. See Peter Sawyer, ed., *Anglo-Saxon Charters: An Annotated List and Bibliography* (London, 1968), 281, charter #909. William the Conqueror was, of course, born out of wedlock to a non-noble mother.

[31] Ælfric, 'Be Hester', in Bruno Assmann, ed., *Angelsächsische Homilien und Heiligenleben* (3 vols, Kassel, 1889; repr. Darmstadt, 1964): 92–116, 'swa swa heora seodu waes, ðat seo cwen werode cynehelm on heafode' (93, lines 36–7). Discussed by Larson, *King's Household*, 117–18.

successor, Cnut, bearing him a son whom she favored over her children by Æthelred. After Cnut's death, Emma was active as queen mother during the reigns of her sons Hardacnut and Edward. Over the course of her life, Emma's fortunes fluctuated. Three times she was driven out of the kingdom. Toward the end of her life, King Edward deprived her of her possessions. Emma survived all these ups and downs with remarkable fortitude. At one point, she commissioned a written account of her life, an account that has survived in the document known to historians as the *Encomium Emmae reginae*. The document, completed during the reign of Hardacnut, the son of Emma and Cnut, suppresses many of the events in Emma's life and distorts others. In view of its peculiar slant, the *Encomium* is nearly useless as a factual biography, but nevertheless it presents a valuable account of the queen as she wished to be seen and remembered. Because the *Encomium* is such a powerful source, it has often been used as a starting-point in understanding Emma and her reign. Here I will take the opposite tack and look at the documentary evidence of Emma's role before turning to the literary record.[32]

When Emma left her native Normandy in 1002 to become Æthelred's queen, she became the first non-native king's wife in England in nearly a century and a half. In marrying Emma, Æthelred forged a kinship link with the counts of Normandy, a connection which he believed would assist him in fighting off the Danish invaders, who posed a constant threat to his throne. To the Normans, Emma's marriage was one more in a series of alliances designed to spread their influence and further their power. The literary evidence suggests that Emma knew her own worth and always considered herself part of the 'conquering family'. During Æthelred's reign, Emma appears in surviving records as both a witness to the king's charters and a landholder in her own right. References to the queen's household and her officials occur both in charter attestations and in the narrative sources. One infamous example of a queen's official comes from the 1003 entry in the *Anglo-Saxon Chronicle*, claiming that Emma's 'French' reeve betrayed the city of Exeter, allowing it to be sacked. Although she was no doubt given a generous dower as part of her marriage settlement, Emma's relationship with Æthelred does not seem to have been as personally felicitous as that of Edgar and his queen. Æthelred had fathered many sons by the time he married Emma, and there is some indication that a rift had developed among the sons of the king's first family, perhaps involving the queen and her sons. The extent to which Emma ever had a hand in public affairs during Æthelred's reign is difficult to gauge. Nowhere in the genuine surviving acta does Emma act

---

[32] Emma has certainly been the subject of more historical inquiry than perhaps any other Anglo-Saxon woman. Pauline Stafford's work should be the starting place. See Stafford, *Queen Emma and Queen Edith* and 'Emma: The Powers of the Queen in the Eleventh Century', in Duggan, ed., *Queens and Queenship in Medieval Europe*, 3–27. See also Miles Campbell, 'Queen Emma and Ælgifu of Northampton' and 'Emma, reine d'Angleterre, mère dénaturée ou femme vindicative?', *Annales de Normandie* 23 (1973): 97–114; and 'The *Encomium Emmae reginae*: Personal Panegyric or Political Propaganda?', *Annuale Mediaevale* 19 (1979): 27–45; Abbott, 'Queens and Queenship', 332–4, 336–7, 376–82; Eric John, 'The *Encomium Emmae reginae*: A Riddle and a Solution', *Bulletin of the John Rylands Library* 63 (1980): 58–94; Felice Lifshitz, 'The *Encomium Emmae reginae*: A Political Pamphlet of the Eleventh Century?', *The Haskins Society Journal: Studies in Medieval History* 1 (1989): 39–50; Eleanor Searle, 'Emma the Conqueror', in Christopher Harper-Bill, Christopher Holdsworth, and Janet Nelson, edd., *Studies in Medieval History Presented to R. Allen Brown* (Woodbridge, 1989), 281–8.

jointly with her royal husband, and her name usually appears further down on witness lists than did Ælfthryth's. References to Emma's independent actions during her first marriage seem always to describe private deeds concerning her own property. Gaimar indicates that Emma received Ælfthryth's property in Winchester, Rockingham, and Rutland as dower, and other sources show that she controlled the town of Exeter and possibly all of Devonshire. She also seems to have held extensive property in Oxfordshire and Suffolk. A charter that probably contains authentic information shows that Emma commemorated the birth of her son Edward by setting aside the revenues of one of her estates, Islip in Oxfordshire, as a gift to the infant prince. A second estate in the shire was given to the monks of Christchurch, Canterbury.[33]

It is probably the case, as others have suggested, that Emma, raised with the heroic values of her Scandinavian forebears, never found much to admire in Aethelred. Her tie to her natal family remained strong enough to make it possible for her to flee to Normandy in 1013–14, even as her brother provided aid to her husband's enemies. When Æthelred died in 1016, Emma's position and that of her sons became even more precarious, and Emma seems to have given her allegiance to her step-son Edmund Ironside, perhaps even sending Edward to serve in his household.[34] Emma's acceptance of Edmund's rule and her later marriage to Cnut were actions that obscured the claims of her sons, and because historians have perceived that she had personal ambitions that went beyond furthering the claims of her children, she has been called an 'unnatural mother'.[35] Although Emma has drawn criticism from both medieval and modern commentators for marrying Cnut and abandoning the cause of her sons Alfred and Edward, her motives and goals in the period between Æthelred's death and her second marriage are far from clear. If her actions are seen within the context of Cnut's seeming determination to rid himself of all rival claimants to the English throne, the fact that the aethelings' lives were spared seems remarkable. Emma must have had a hand in the decision to spare her two sons from death by sending them to her relatives in Normandy. In 1016–17, Emma was faced with the prospect that no son of hers would ever inherit the English throne, for Cnut had fathered sons by another woman, Ælfgifu of Northampton, who remained alive to fight for her sons' rights to succeed their father. Emma's Norman relatives, eager to extend their influence and connections, were aiming to have one of Emma's sons as king of England, and the new marriage, with the hope of an heir for Cnut by Emma, probably seemed to them to provide the best possible means of securing the throne. As a condition of her marriage to Cnut, Emma and her kin required the new king to promise that he would not name as his successor any of his sons born outside of his marriage with Emma. Although it is generally assumed that this vow excluded Emma's sons by Aethelred, Felice Lifshitz has observed that the form of the vow recorded

---

[33] For a thorough discussion of Emma's holdings, see Stafford, *Queen Emma and Queen Edith*, Chapter Five.
[34] Frank Barlow, *Edward the Confessor* (Berkeley, 1970), 35–6.
[35] The oft-quoted phrase originated with Edward A. Freeman in his *History of the Norman Conquest*, 1: 454.

in the *Encomium Emmae reginae* excluded only Cnut's other sons, saying nothing of Emma's offspring by other men.[36]

Despite her success in extracting the promise of succession rights for her offspring, Emma must have had a difficult time earning her new husband's confidence. At the beginning of his reign she rarely appeared as a witness to or participant in his *acta*. But after about 1020, a date that may coincide with the birth of her son by Cnut, Emma became more active in public affairs. During Cnut's reign, she was addressed jointly with Cnut in several extant writs and pleas. Testators looked to Emma as a guarantor of their wills as others had with her predecessor Aelfthyrth.[37] Charters confirm Emma's rise in authority, for at about this time the queen's name moved to the top of the witness list in many of Cnut's extant charters, indicating her prestige and standing among the bishops and nobles of the realm.[38]

Emma, like other royal figures, used the church as an ally in her political strategies. Abbot Ælfsige of Peterborough was one of her closest advisors and even accompanied her when she fled to Normandy in 1013, where they remained for three years.[39] Emma was the lay lord over Evesham and Wilton abbeys and a patron of many others, including Abingdon, Ely, Bury St Edmunds, Westminster, Sherbourne, and both St Augustine's and Christ Church, Canterbury.[40] William of Malmesbury claims that Cnut's generosity to Winchester, which was such that 'strangers are alarmed by the masses of precious metal', was prompted by Emma's 'holy prodigality'.[41] The influential churchmen of the age welcomed Emma as a benefactress and as a 'persuasive voice' who helped to direct Cnut's patronage. Cnut's rise to favor with ecclesiastical authorities may have been in part due to the gifts he lavished upon monastic establishments after the first years of his reign. Many accounts of these gifts indicate that they were prompted by the intercession of Queen Emma. Some of the accounts of Emma's patronage and intercession claim that Emma shared the goals of the Benedictine reformers, but these claims may be wishful thinking on the part of their authors. Just as Edgar and Ælfthryth had adopted the language of the church reform movement as a way of elevating kingship and queenship, so Cnut and Emma used church patronage as a way to legitimize their reign. The degree to which they succeeded can be seen in words of the various chroniclers who went from distrust of the new king to total acceptance. One of the most strikingly honest articulations of that sentiment appears in a letter from Fulbert of Chartres. In gratitude for the gifts Cnut and Emma sent toward the rebuilding of Chartres cathedral, Fulbert addressed the

---

[36] Lifshitz, 'The *Encomium Emmae reginae*', 41.
[37] Whitelock, *Anglo-Saxon Wills*, 66–7 and the *Liber Eliensis*, 157.
[38] *Encomium Emmae reginae*, Appendix II, 62–5.
[39] *Chronicle of Hugh Candidus*, 48–9; *Anglo-Saxon Chronicle s.a.* 1013.
[40] Emma's patronage has been discussed in detail in T. A. Heslop, 'The Production of De Luxe Manuscripts and the Patronage of King Cnut and Queen Emma', *Anglo-Saxon England* 19 (1990): Appendix II, 182–8, and by Richard Gem, 'A Recession in English Architecture during the Early Eleventh Century and its Effect on the Development of the Romanesque Style', *Journal of the British Archaeological Association*, 3rd series, 38 (1975): 28–49. Also, Stafford, *Queen Emma and Queen Edith*, 143–55.
[41] *Gesta regum*, 323.

king as 'you whom we had heard to be a prince of pagans', acknowledging that he found the king 'not only to be a Christian, but a most generous benefactor to churches and to the servants of God'.[42] There are also indications that Emma was involved in filling episcopal vacancies and that she relied on her candidates for support in her many struggles. The wording of a letter from Archbishop Wulfstan of York to the royal couple strongly suggests that Emma had a hand in choosing Æthelnoth to be the new archbishop of Canterbury in 1020. If Aethelnoth did owe his position to the support of the queen, it lends credence to the later claim of her encomiast that the archbishop refused to crown Harold Harefoot, the son of Emma's rival Ælfgifu, as king in 1035.[43]

Much has rightly been made of the pattern of patronage and political alliances between the queen and ecclesiastical figures in medieval Europe, yet political or economic advantage was not the only reason for churchmen and highly placed laywomen to form friendships. Because of their monastic educations, it was sometimes the case that laywomen, particularly before the twelfth century, were educated as well as or better than their brothers and husbands. These women often shared cultural interests with male ecclesiastics. Emma's gifts indicate that she had an interest in books, and although there is no reason to believe that she was highly educated or even literate, she certainly understood the power of the written word. The intended audience and purpose of the *Encomium Emmae reginae* have been the subject of much debate. It is clear, however, that the queen commissioned the panegyric and that the facts of her life were manipulated in order to present her and her son Hardacnut in the best possible light. The author, whose possible purpose was to establish the queen's ability to transmit throne-worthiness to her sons, stressed Emma's heroic origins, describing her as 'a most noble wife', one who 'derived her origin from a victorious people, who had appropriated for themselves part of Gaul'. Emma herself was 'the most distinguished woman of her time', a 'famous queen', who, in addition to an impressive bloodline, possessed all the qualities desirable in a consort: nobility, wealth, beauty, wisdom, and fame. She was also, in literature if not in fact, a 'peaceweaver'. The encomiast contended that the marriage of 'so great a lady bound to so great a man' would bring an end to the disturbances of war.[44] Perhaps the most striking characterizations in the work are those of the rival claimants to Cnut's throne, Harold and Hardacnut. The author makes no mention of Emma's being a consecrated queen or even the legitimate wife of Cnut, instead contending that Harold had no royal blood but was rather the offspring of a low-born servant-girl whom Ælfgifu had tried to pass off as her son.[45] No one reading the *Encomium* has failed to see it as intended to further Hardacnut's ambitions, and both Lifshitz and Miles Campbell have pointed out that the work does nothing to obscure Edward's claims should Hardacnut fail to leave a direct heir. Since none of the Anglo-Norman queens lived to become queen-mother, that role is beyond the scope of this study. But it has become a historical commonplace to note that it was in widowhood that royal and

---

[42] In F. Behrends, ed., *The Letters and Poems of Fulbert of Chartres* (Oxford, 1976), 66–9.
[43] See Harmer, *Anglo-Saxon Writs*, 182–3. Also, the *Encomium Emmae reginae*, 40–1.
[44] *Encomium Emmae reginae*, 32–3.
[45] *Encomium Emmae reginae*, 39–41.

noblewomen often enjoyed the greatest freedom of movement and economic independence, and undoubtedly Emma would have done whatever she could to procure the role of queen-mother for herself. She was initially successful, for even as Harold Harefoot was elected king, she managed to hold Wessex as regent for Hardacnut until he arrived in England, and she may have been custodian of the treasury during Hardacnut's reign. Emma was visible in her son's court and often acted jointly with him in issuing writs and judgements. Her status was perhaps never higher. During Edward's reign, however, the always-strained relationship between mother and son finally erupted into an open rift, and Edward seized Emma's possessions, thus depriving her of her sources of power. Although the pair were outwardly reconciled, and Emma was treated honorably until her death in 1052, she never regained the influence she had enjoyed either as Cnut's wife or as Hardacnut's mother.

Emma, like Ælfthryth, had a long career as England's queen, and throughout their careers, both women used a variety of advantages in order to secure their political and dynastic ends. Emma had powerful relatives to whom she could and did turn for support when the need arose. Both queens seem to have enjoyed control over substantial property and resources with which they could support households and reward members of their own political factions. Emma and Ælfthryth were astute patrons of the church, and both enjoyed the legitimacy of being the crowned and consecrated queen of England. Emma used the written word as a tool and worked hard at presenting her life and reign in the way it would benefit her and her offspring most. It worked to everyone's advantage when the king and queen enjoyed a harmonious relationship. Perhaps most important, both women produced at least one son through whom they could channel their ambitions and secure their power. Using these measures, Ælfthryth and Emma were both 'successful' as queens, although Emma's career was so tumultuous that the historian must be careful to balance her successes and failures. In Ælfthryth's case, her historical reputation has suffered because of the suspicion that she was involved in the murder of her stepson. The last great queen of Anglo-Saxon England, Edith, did not share the general good fortune of her predecessors. She and her husband, Edward the Confessor, were married for political reasons and seem never to have learned to work together easily. Edith had no children, and as a member of the powerful clan headed by Earl Godwin, she saw her fortune rise and fall with that of her natal family. The relatively unhappy career of Queen Edith stands in contrast to that of most of the other queen-consorts of late Anglo-Saxon and Anglo-Norman England.[46]

Edward the Confessor came to the throne in 1042 as a bachelor who had spent most of his life in Normandy. As the son of Æthelred II and Emma, he was

---

[46] Outside of the work of Pauline Stafford, Queen Edith has received surprisingly little attention. In addition to *Queen Emma and Queen Edith*, see Stafford, 'Women and the Norman Conquest', *Transactions of the Royal Historical Society*, series 6, vol. 4 (1994): 221–49. See Barlow, ed., *Vita Ædwardi regis*, especially pp. 15, 22–3, 41–2, 46–8, 59, 76, and 79, and Kenneth E. Cutler, 'Edith, Queen of England 1045–1066', *Medieval Studies* 35 (1973): 222–31.

undeniably throne-worthy, but as Kenneth Cutler pointed out, the Anglo-Danish nobility that had come to power during the reigns of Cnut and his sons had little respect or affection for the descendants of Alfred the Great.[47] Edward was forced to rely on the family of earl Godwin for support in his bid for the throne, so much so that he agreed to marry the earl's eldest daughter, Edith. The marriage, which did not take place until 1045, can only have worsened relations between Edward and his mother, for the sources make clear that Emma considered Earl Godwin a traitor who was responsible for the murder of her middle son, Alfred.[48] That Edward was never comfortable with the power and influence of Godwin and his children is clear from the events of 1051, when Edward finally had the ability to exile Godwin's sons. During that year he sent his childless wife to live in a monastery, perhaps hoping to divorce her and marry a woman who could provide him with heirs. But Edward was not strong enough to hold off the Godwinists for long, and they were back in power – and Edith was back in court – by the end of 1052.[49]

Because so much of the history of the Confessor's reign comes to us via Norman-influenced pens, it is difficult to reconstruct the climate of Edward's court. The twelfth-century view of Edith is colored by Edward's growing cult and by the Norman insistence that William was Edward's true and designated heir. This insistence forced the Normans to associate Edith with her husband's sanctity rather than her brothers' perfidy. On the other hand, it is tempting for modern historians to see Edith as the ultimate advocate for the Godwinist cause, and, as Edward's wife, perhaps she was. Certainly she was much attached to her brothers, especially Tostig. The anonymous author of the *Vita Ædwardi* said that she helped persuade the king to name Tostig Earl of Northumbria, and she stands accused of ordering the murder of a Northumbrian thegn who was Tostig's enemy.[50] But historians have been willing to suggest that Edith urged Edward toward certain actions and policies, ascribing to her more sympathy for her family's goals than can be supported by the contemporary sources. Edith the woman is impossible to know, but, like Emma before her, she commissioned a piece of literature that presents an idealized portrait of Edith the queen. This discussion of Edith is therefore by necessity more a study of the texts presenting an ideal queen than it is a biographical account. I have tried to indicate the possible biases of the authors and chroniclers in order to gain better insight into the personality, loyalties, and strategies of the Confessor's queen.

One new element in the panegyric literature is the stress placed on Edith's education and accomplishments. In addition to praising the queen's beauty and bloodline, authors point out her vast learning and skill at feminine accomplishments such as embroidery and weaving. William of Malmesbury indicated that

---

[47] Cutler, 'Edith, Queen of England', 223.
[48] *Encomium Emmae reginae*, 40–7.
[49] See the *Vita Ædwardi regis*, 20–3. The 'E' version of the *Anglo-Saxon Chronicle* entry for 1051 states that the queen was deprived of 'all that she owned in land and gold and silver and all things', while Florence of Worcester (*The Chronicle of Florence of Worcester with Two Continuations*, ed./trans. Thomas Forester [London, 1854], p. 152) wrote that she was 'sent away in disgrace with only a single handmaid'. See also Stafford, *Queen Emma and Queen Edith*, Chapter 9.
[50] *Vita Ædwardi regis*, 31. The story of Edith's involvement in Cospatric's murder occurs only in a late source, Florence of Worcester's *Chronicle*, 167.

she was beautiful and modest as well as 'a woman whose breast was a school of all the liberal arts'.[51] According to Osbert of Clare, Edith was outstanding for 'the distinction of her family' in addition to being a gifted writer, both of verse and prose and 'another Minerva' in her command of textile arts.[52] Although panegyric literature is by nature exaggerated, Edith may indeed have been literate and even somewhat learned. We know that Earl Godwin and his wife had trained their children in 'the arts necessary for ruling' and that Edith had been sent to the convent at Wilton for her schooling. The author of the *Vita Ædwardi regis* called Wilton 'the place which had taken pains with her education and where above all she had learned those virtues which made her seem suitable to become queen of the English'.[53] Godfrey the Prior, who wrote about several of England's royal women, credited Edith alone with being learned. He claimed that she had knowledge of all seven liberal arts and was able to speak several languages.[54] The *Vita Ædwardi* shows Edith as a wise counselor to the king, whose advice was sought by all at court, and who guaranteed peace in the kingdom. Edward's *vita* is at least as difficult a source as the *Encomium*, but like the earlier work, it finds its chief value in the preservation of the patron's vision of herself as queen. In describing the personal relationship between the king and his consort, the author of Edward's *vita* managed to present the couple as a loving pair and at the same time preserve rumors of Edward's chastity by portraying Edith as a dutiful daughter to the king.[55] The biographer also claimed that Edith had some influence over Edward's domestic habits, persuading him to dress more formally and lavishly than he would have preferred and urging him to be more systematic in his charitable activities.[56] The biographer, who obviously had to overcome difficulties in presenting Edith as the ideal queen of a flawed but holy monarch, did a remarkable job in preserving the ideal of the queen-consort as an influential and respected counselor. Edith's real degree of participation in public affairs is more difficult to discern. Like her predecessors, Edith sometimes witnessed the king's charters but more rarely than other eleventh-century consorts. Frank Barlow noted that her signature is absent from all of Edward's *acta* that can be dated to the years between 1048 and 1060.[57] But contemporaries seem to have perceived that she had some sway over the king, for in at least one case she was given a monetary gift to guarantee Edward's verdict in a lawsuit.[58]

Edith is well known to have had at least nominal control over vast dower lands in 1066. Because of the popularity of her given name in Anglo-Saxon England, it is difficult to make an exact assessment of her wealth from

---

[51] *Gesta regum* 1: 333–4.
[52] Quoted in *Vita Ædwardi regis*, 14.
[53] *Vita Aedwardi regis*, 14.
[54] See Thomas Wright, ed., *The Anglo-Latin Satirical Poets of the Twelfth Century* (2 vols, RS, London, 1872; repr. 1964), 2: 148–50.
[55] *Vita Ædwardi regis*, 60.
[56] *Vita Ædwardi regis*, 41–2.
[57] Barlow, *Edward the Confessor*, 93.
[58] Macray, ed., *Chronicon Abbatiae Rameseiensis* (RS, London, 1886), 169–70. In another, similar instance, King Edward granted an estate to the abbot of Evesham in return for '6 marks of gold to the king and one to the queen'. See *S* 1026; discussed in Barlow, *Edward the Confessor*, 142, n. 4.

Domesday Book, but estimates of the value of her lands have ranged from a low of just over £400 to a high of £1,500. Even the lowest of those figures would have made the queen a very wealthy woman.[59] The degree of personal control she exercised over her wealth is not known. Since several members of Edith's household and their relatives held land of the queen at the time of the Domesday survey, it can be assumed that she did use gifts of land as a means of patronage. In fact, one estate in Buckinghamshire was recorded as being a betrothal gift from Edith to the daughter of her chamberlain.[60] An anecdotal reference from the *Abingdon Chronicle* also suggests that Edith had some knowledge of and interest in the sources of her income. The chronicle relates that once, when the king, Edith, and Emma were visiting the abbey, Edith became dismayed because the abbey's youngsters were being served nothing but bread at their noon meal. When told that poverty usually prevented the monks from feeding the boys anything more substantial, the queen called Edward over and 'vigorously entreated' him to donate something to the abbey so that the children might receive better meals in future. Edward is said to have responded 'with a smile' that he would love to help, if only he had some lands or other possessions to give away. Edith replied that she had recently been given a manor in the area which, with the king's permission, she would turn over to the monks. Edward consented, and so, the chronicler related, the abbey of St Mary received the manor of Lewknor, the proceeds of which were to provide daily meals for the boys of the abbey.[61]

Edith seems to have had enough influence at court to be able to manipulate church appointments as another means of rewarding members of her household. Edith's chaplain Walter the Lotharingian was appointed to the see of Hereford in 1060; and in 1058, when the bishopric of Sherborne fell vacant, it was claimed by the bishop of Wiltshire and joined to his see 'because of the former promise of Queen Edith'. Edith also took part in the ceremonies that sealed the creation of the see of Exeter. An extant charter, possibly the original, describes the queen's part in the ceremony installing the new bishop: 'I King Edward, put this *privilegium* on St Peter's altar with my hand, and leading Bishop Leofric by the right arm, with my queen, Edith, leading him by the left, place him in this cathedral.'[62] Edith's promotion of Walter may have been sealed by a gift of an

---

[59] The most widely accepted figure of about nine hundred pounds comes from the research of R. H. Davies, whose unpublished MA thesis, 'The Land and Rights of Harold, Son of Godwine, and their Distribution by William I' (University College, Cardiff, 1967) has been widely quoted and is accepted by Barlow. See *Edward the Confessor*, 74. The low figure comes from Robin Fleming, 'Domesday Estates of the King and the Godwines: A Study in Late Saxon Politics', *Speculum* 58 (1983): 987–1007; the high estimate from Marc Meyer, 'The "Queen's Demesne" in Later Anglo-Saxon England'. As a basis for comparison, William John Corbett used a figure of £750 as the low cut-off point for the wealthiest group of magnates in his classification of England's Domesday landholders according to wealth. See Corbett, 'The Development of the Duchy of Normandy and the Norman Conquest of England', *Cambridge Medieval History* 5 (1926; repr. 1968), 505–13.

[60] Marc Meyer, 'The Politics of Possession: Women's Estates in Later Anglo-Saxon England', *The Haskins Society Journal: Studies in Medieval History* 3 (1992): 111–29.

[61] *Abingdon Chronicle* 1: 460–1.

[62] 'Antiquis Edgithae reginae promissis', according to William of Malmesbury in *Gesta pontificum anglorum*, 183. For the Exeter charter, see Kemble, ed., *Codex diplomaticus ævi Saxonici*, charter #791 (S 1021), discussed by Pierre Chaplais, 'The Authenticity of the Royal Anglo-Saxon Diplomas of Exeter', *Bulletin of the Institute of Historical Research* 39 (1966): 1–34.

estate from his see. Frank Barlow points out that 'at least two royal clerks who received bishoprics "lost" an episcopal estate to Queen Edith'.[63]

Edith depended on her brothers and their faction rather than members of the church as political allies, and it is perhaps because she did not need to court ecclesiastical factions that she did not make as many gifts as her predecessors Emma and Ælfthryth. Although Edward's biographer praised Edith for being more systematic than her husband in her charitable activities, little survives to document his claim. She shared in several of Edward's gifts, but in most cases it cannot be determined that her role exceeded that of being named in the charters as a co-benefactor. There are many notices of small gifts to various churches in the kingdom, but her greatest work was to finance the complete rebuilding of Wilton Abbey, where she had spent her girlhood.[64] The author of Edward's *vita* described himself as a humble monk who had been expelled from his house because of political intrigue. He was grateful to Queen Edith for taking him into her household and naturally praised her Christian compassion and charity. Other accounts of contacts between the queen and members of the clergy show Edith to have been both rapacious and keenly aware of her royal dignity. The *Peterborough Chronicle* contains several complaints about disputed property being seized by Edward and Edith, and in one case she took away 'a book of the Evangelists richly adorned with gold, and the villa of Tinewell, and ornaments which were worth £300', that had been bequeathed to the abbey.[65] When Gervin, the abbot of St Riquier in Ponthieu, visited the Confessor's court, the queen became incensed when he refused her kiss of greeting, and she demanded that he return the gifts that had been bestowed on him. But when Edith understood that the rebuff was not personal, but part of Gervin's policy of avoiding all women, she relented and even suggested to native churchmen that they might consider adopting the abbot's holy mode of life. The queen also placated Gervin by sending him an embroidered amice so valuable that it was later traded for two churches for St Riquier.[66] The picture of the outraged and avaricious queen contrasts sharply with the portrait painted by Edward's biographer, who illustrated the humility he claimed for the queen with the fact that, although a throne was available to her, she preferred to sit at the king's feet rather than at his side. A final example of Edith's imperious behavior comes out of the pages of the *Abingdon Chronicle*. According to the monks' records, the queen appeared at the abbey after the Battle of Hastings, demanding to see their treasure collection so that she might choose some things for herself. The monks tried to deceive the queen by presenting a selection of their less-valuable treasures, but Edith was not to be put off. She eventually took a preciously-bound gospel-book and several of the monks' vestments which had been decorated with gold and precious jewels.[67]

[63] Barlow, *Edward the Confessor*, 149, n. 4.
[64] *Vita Ædwardi regis*, 46–7.
[65] Hugh Candidus, *Peterborough Chronicle*, 67 and 73. See also Kemble, *Codex diplomaticus ævi Saxonici*, #808.
[66] Hariulf, *Chronique de l'abbaye de Saint-Riquier*, ed. Ferdinand Lot (Paris, 1894), 237–8.
[67] *Abingdon Chronicle* 1: 485. W. D. Macray discusses a second story with similar elements in his introduction to the *Evesham Chronicle*. See Macray, ed., *Chronicon Abbatiae de Evesham* (London, RS, 1863), xi–xii, 317–18.

Edith's career as England's queen both mirrors and diverges from those of her two predecessors discussed here. Like Emma, Edith was a treaty-bride whose marriage was intended to seal a political alliance. Like Emma, Edith had powerful relatives from her natal family who served as her chief support in helping her gain and hold her position as queen. But unlike Emma and Ælfthryth, Edith does not seem to have been able to win her husband's confidence to the extent that she became a real partner in ruling the kingdom. Perhaps most tellingly for her 'success' or 'failure' as a queen-consort, Edith failed to produce the essential heir to the kingdom, and, although she outlived her husband for nearly a decade, she never had the chance to bask in the role of queen-mother. When the coming of the Normans finally destroyed the power of the House of Godwin, Edith fared better than might have been expected under the new regime. William, who claimed the throne as the true heir of Edward the Confessor, could hardly further his cause by mistreating Edward's widow. Edith was also astute enough to realize the hopelessness of further opposition to William after the battle that killed three of her brothers. The Norman author of the *Carmen de Hastingae proelio* claims that Edith remained in Winchester until William sent a messenger to the city to accept her surrender. She was allowed to live quietly with all the honors due her.[68] Little is known of Edith after 1066. Domesday Book records that 'after King William arrived', she gave one of her Buckinghamshire manors to a member of her household. She attended the consecration of the new bishop of Winchester in 1071. When she died in December 1075, William allowed her to be buried 'with great pomp' beside Edward in Westminster Abbey. Altogether, what emerges from the sources that describe Edith is a portrait of a woman who knew quite well how to manipulate the roles of daughter, sister, wife, and widow to her own advantage.[69]

Harold Godwinson married Ealdgyth, the widow of the Welsh king Gruffydd, and sister of Edwin and Morcar, the brother earls of Northumbria, in early 1066. She bore Harold a posthumous son, named after his father, but Harold's reign was so short that his wife is scarcely mentioned in surviving sources, and for all intents and purposes, Anglo-Saxon queenship came to an end with Edith. The careers of the Norman queens of England are strikingly similar to those of their Anglo-Saxon counterparts, with one important difference. Because the kings of England after 1066 were usually responsible for continental domains as well as the island kingdom, the king was forced to rely more heavily on deputies than ever before. He usually turned to trusted family members to assist in the administrative and ceremonial duties that he could not carry out in person. Matilda II served Henry I in a capacity that, I will argue, could very well be seen as vice-regal. Although she was unusually active in a public and political capacity, her activities were hardly novel or unexpected. A brief look at the career of the Conqueror's queen, Matilda of

---

[68] *Carmen de Hastingae proelio*, lines 625–34.
[69] *Gesta pontificum*, 272. The fullest account of Edith's fate is in Florence of Worcester's *Chronicle*, 177–8, elaborating on the *Anglo-Saxon Chronicle* entry for 1075. My insight into Edith's ability to refashion herself according to need owes much to my reading of the work of Kristi Keuhn in graduate seminars at the University of Missouri, Columbia.

Flanders, will finish the survey of Matilda II's predecessors and allow her career to be judged in context.

Daughter of Count Baldwin V of Flanders and grand-daughter of King Robert II of France, Matilda was an able and astute woman who had assisted William for many years as he sought to tame the rebellious barons of Normandy.[70] Like her Anglo-Saxon predecessors, Matilda owed much of her effectiveness to the fact that she and her husband worked well together, and contemporaries perceived her as a true partner to William. Their marriage had been politically advantageous, but there may also have been personal attraction involved. For reasons that are not totally understood, Pope Leo IX had prohibited the proposed marriage in 1049, but the prohibition was ignored. As penance, William and Matilda endowed separate male and female abbeys in the city of Caen.[71] Whatever the reason for the Pope's disapproval, most contemporary chroniclers considered Matilda eminently suited for queenship. One enumerated her good qualities as 'fairness of face, noble birth, learning, beauty of character, and strong faith and fervent love of Christ'. In perhaps the most important of her duties, that of providing an heir, Matilda was extremely successful, for she bore William four sons and as many as five daughters.[72]

Generously endowed with lands in England after 1066, Matilda also commanded significant resources before the Conquest. When William embarked upon his campaign to conquer England, his wife is said to have provided his flagship. Although the authenticity of the 'ship list' has been questioned, it has more recently been strongly defended, and at the very least it must have been believable to contemporaries that the duchess *could* have donated the ship.[73] Matilda's control over her own lands is beyond doubt, for she was able to provide funds to aid her son Robert Curthose even when he was in disgrace with the king.[74] She kept a separate household with her own staff, several of whom we know by name.[75]

It was well over a year after the Battle of Hastings before Matilda even visited William's new realm. She was crowned queen on Whitsunday 1068, in an

---

[70] There has been surprisingly little work in either English or French on the Conqueror's queen, a lacuna which is being filled by Laura Gathagan's dissertation, 'Embodying Power: Gender and Authority in the Queenship of Mathilda of Flanders' (City University of New York, 2002), and 'The Trappings of Power: The Coronation of Mathilda of Flanders', forthcoming in *The Haskins Society Journal: Studies in Medieval History*.

[71] But see Lucien Mussett, 'La reine Mathilde et la fondation de la Trinité de Caen (abbaye aux dames)', *Mémoires de l'Académie des Sciences, Arts et Belles-Lettres*, Caen, n.s. 21 (1984): 191–210.

[72] David C. Douglas, *William the Conqueror: The Norman Impact upon England* (Berkeley, 1964), 75–80 and Appendix C: The Marriage of William and Matilda, 391–5, discusses the events surrounding the marriage and historiographical speculation about the reasons for the papal prohibition.

[73] Elisabeth van Houts, 'The Ship List of William the Conqueror', *Anglo-Norman Studies* 10 (1987): 159–83, and C. Warren Hollister, 'The Greater Domesday Tenants-in-Chief', in *Domesday Studies*, ed. J. C. Holt (Woodbridge, 1987): 219–48, especially 221–6 and 240–3. Marc Meyer, 'Queen's Demesne', provides an enumeration of Matilda's known holdings in England.

[74] *Orderic* 3: 102–3.

[75] Orderic mentions a Breton messenger named Samson who entered the monastery at St Evroul in order to escape William's wrath after he was caught taking messages and money to Robert Curthose. See *Orderic* 3: 104. Aiulf, sheriff of Dorset and Somerset at various times between 1084 and 1123, may have been Queen Matilda's chamberlain. See Judith A. Green, 'The Sheriffs of William the Conqueror', *Anglo-Norman Studies* 5 (1982): 135.

elaborate ceremony at Westminster presided over by the archbishop of York. There is considerable scholarly debate surrounding the ordines of the Anglo-Norman monarchs and their consorts. It is known that the *laudes regiae* were sung during Matilda's coronation. In addition, there exists now a revised version of the old Anglo-Saxon *ordo*, which was perhaps first used for this ceremony. The new *ordo* adds three significant phrases to the ceremonial for installing the queen. She is now conceived of as being placed by God among the people ('constituit reginam in populo'), and she shares in the royal power ('regalis imperii ... esse participem'). According to the rite, the English people are fortunate in being ruled by the power of the ruler and the ability and virtue of the queen ('laetatur gens Anglica domini imperio regenda et reginae virtutis providentia gubernanda').[76]

The tone of the coronation ritual certainly reflects the role Matilda assumed in William's government. Like the Anglo-Saxon queens, Matilda may have played an unofficial role in many major decisions affecting public policy in both England and Normandy. For instance, Orderic Vitalis believed that Matilda urged Lanfranc to accept the appointment as archbishop of Canterbury.[77] But, because of the geographic and political structure of the new Anglo-Norman realm, Matilda had a much more visible and official role in public affairs than did any of her predecessors on the English throne. From the time William first left the duchy, bent on assuming the English monarchy, until she died in 1083, Matilda served at the head of his Norman administration during his absence, chairing a group of advisors who were responsible for the day-to-day workings of the duchy. Matilda's name often appeared as a witness to judicial decisions and her presence was noted when charters were drawn up, permissions granted, or private charters confirmed.[78]

Despite her coronation and new title after 1068 and occasional appearances in a judicial capacity in England, Matilda's interest lay in the duchy of Normandy rather than the kingdom of England. After her visit to England in 1068–9, where she gave birth to her youngest son, Henry, she continued to live mainly on the continent. David Bates speculated that she never left the duchy at all between 1072 and the early 1080s.[79] Her ecclesiastical benefactions were overwhelmingly

---

[76] Discussed in Schramm, *English Coronation*, 29–30, and printed in J. Wickham Legg, *Three Coronation Orders* (London, 1900), 54–64. See also H. G. Richardson, 'The Coronation in Medieval England: The Evolution of the Office and the Oath', *Traditio* 16 (1960): 111–202; J. Brückmann, 'The *Ordines* of the Third Recension of the Medieval English Coronation Order', in T. A. Sandquist and M. R. Powicke, edd., *Essays in Medieval History Presented to Bertie Wilkinson* (Toronto, 1969), 99–115; H. W. C. Cowdrey, 'The Anglo-Norman *Laudes Regiae*', *Viator* 12 (1981): 38–78; Raymonde Foreville, 'Le sacre des rois anglo-normands et angevins et le serment du sacre (XIe–XIIe siècles)', *Anglo-Norman Studies* 1 (1978): 49–62; Nelson, 'Rites of the Conqueror', in *Politics and Ritual*, 371–402. See also Douglas, *William the Conqueror*, 249–50 and Judith Elaine Abbott, 'Political Strategies in the Coronation of Matilda I (1068)', paper presented at the annual meeting of the Charles Homer Haskins Society, Houston, Texas, November 1990.

[77] *Orderic* 2: 252.

[78] Orderic Vitalis several times casually assumes Matilda's control of the duchy and a few times explicitly mentions that Matilda was left to head the government. See *Orderic* 2: 208, 210, 222, 280. See also William of Poitiers, *Histoire de Guillaume le Conquérant*, ed. Raymonde Foreville (Paris, 1952), 260.

[79] Douglas, *William the Conqueror*, 218, n. 1, concludes that Matilda left England sometime after the 1069 Easter court but before the rising of the north in the autumn of that year. Matilda's judicial role in England is described in the *Abingdon Chronicle*, and discussed by Gathagan, 'Embodying Power', pp. 145–73. See David Bates, 'The Origins of the Justiciarship', *Anglo-Norman Studies* 4 (1981): 7.

continental, and upon her death she willed her crown and other royal regalia to the monastery at Caen, where she was buried.[80]

When examining the course of the two centuries from the coronation of Ælfthryth to the death of Matilda I, historians of queenship have discerned patterns in the activities and literary portrayals of England's queen consorts. A queen could bring a valuable alliance into her marriage, and it gradually became important that the king's wife be specifically chosen with political goals rather than personal preference as the primary criterion. Although kings continued to practice concubinage throughout the period under consideration, the tenth-century reform gradually served to elevate both the importance of canonical marriage and the role of the consecrated queen. The tenth- and eleventh-century women under discussion here were generously dowered so that they could maintain their own households and use patronage as a way of rewarding political allies, both lay and ecclesiastical. The numerous payments made to these women so that they might use their influence over their husbands shows two things about the way the Anglo-Saxon queens were perceived. First, contemporaries clearly believed that their queens had knowledge of the day-to-day workings of the king and his council. Evidence of the queen's participation in public affairs is attested to by charter-witnessing and narrative evidence. Secondly, those with access to the queen must have believed that her word carried weight within the royal administration. The church played an important part in royal administration and thus in the careers of all the women under consideration here. Judith Abbott posited that the alliances between the queen and influential churchmen were essentially political in nature. Churchmen promoted the ideals of sacral queenship that served to elevate the power and status of the queen, while the queen provided economic support for the activities of the church, particularly the reforming monasteries. For Abbott, the proof of the strength of the alliance shows in the reign of Edward and Edith. 'By the reign of Edith', Abbott contended, 'reginal patterns and expectations had the force of custom. Edith did not need the church alliance to establish her position; she was known, nevertheless, for her benefactions and influence on church appointments.'[81] Edith did make benefactions to the church, but so did nearly every other wealthy woman in medieval Europe, whether or not she was crowned. In tenth- and eleventh-century England, philanthropy was as expected as beauty, wisdom, lineage, and serving as a 'peaceweaver', and these qualities showed up in panegyric literature regardless of whether they reflected reality. In Edith's case, her liberality to the church was tempered by her tendency to seize

---

[80] Matilda's ecclesiastical benefactions have not been the subject of systematic inquiry, and such a study is beyond the scope of this chapter. She gave monies, liturgical objects, and lands to favored continental institutions such as St Evroul and Cluny, but despoiled the English abbey of Abingdon. See the *Abingdon Chronicle* 1: 485, 491. Her name appears with William's in many of the charters calendared in David Bates, *Regesta Regum Anglo-Normannorum: The Acta of William I (1066–1087)* (Oxford, 1999). Bates' volume largely supersedes that of the first volume of the old series. Matilda's will is printed in Lucien Musset, ed., 'Les actes de Guillaume le Conquérant et de la Reine Mathilde pour les abbayes caennaises', *Mémoires de la société des antiquaires de Normandie* 37 (1967): entry 16, pp. 112–13.

[81] Abbott, 'Queens and Queenship', abstract preceding p. i.

property or valuables from it. The relationship of royal women to the church is far too complex to be dismissed as a mere alliance for political convenience. Simple piety and the desire to make amends for previous errors cannot be dismissed as motives for ecclesiastical benefaction. Some of the women studied here formed sincere friendships with members of the church hierarchy, with whom they apparently shared cultural interests. Several queens perceived the written word as a vehicle for dynastic ends, and they naturally turned to literate churchmen to shape their words and thus, to a large extent, their historical images. In Anglo-Saxon England, royal patronage of poets, authors, and artists was beginning to turn the court into something of a cultural center well before the 'official beginning' of the twelfth-century renaissance.

In looking at the career of Matilda of Scotland, it is evident that she too used familial connections, political alliances, and patronage of the church to further her goals. She did not invent any of the elements of queenship, yet she was skilled in manipulating them to her own advantage. Keenly aware of the privileges of birth and the prerogatives of queenship, and even something of a student of history, she used all the means at her disposal to create and further her own image. Having set forth the elements of successful queenship present in the careers of her predecessors, let us now turn to another element in the structure of English queenship, the resources over which royal consorts exercised control. Her lands and monies gave the queen the ability to function as both a political actor and a source of patronage, and the next chapter is dedicated to reconstructing both the sources and the extent of queenly income during the queenship of Matilda of Scotland. In order to do so, I will again be ranging both backward and forward from the time of Matilda's tenure, as the nature of the sources require us to make inferences from patterns of landholding and revenues that stretch over several centuries.

3

The Queen's Demesne: The Lands and Revenues of Queen Matilda II

When Agnes Strickland, the best of the nineteenth-century biographers of England's queens, wrote about the extensive building works of Queen Matilda, she concluded that they 'were in all probability the fruits of her regency during the absence of her royal husband in Normandy; for it is scarcely to be supposed that such stupendous undertakings could have been effected by the limited power and revenues of a mere queen-consort'.[1] In another passage, however, she contradicted her earlier conclusion, writing that 'she was so nobly dowered, withal, that in after reigns the highest demand ever made on the part of a queen-consort was that she should be endowed with a dower equal to that of Matilda of Scotland'.[2] Unfortunately there is little evidence to support either statement. Although it is certainly true that Queen Matilda acted with wide authority concerning sizable properties, the extent of her dower and the basis of her exercise of control over wealth are very much matters of conjecture. Indeed, marital practices are so unevenly documented as to make it impossible to draw firm conclusions about what kind of property arrangements were usual in the period under scrutiny. Although some evidence from the early medieval period indicates that dower lands may often have been administered by a wife during her husband's lifetime, there is little to tell us whether, in royal marriages, lands and revenues usually fell under the queen's personal control. Royal charters are the logical place to begin a survey of this nature, but vital facts about the nature of land transactions are often concealed in the formulaic phrasing of the charters. For instance, charters that record the queen's granting away or exercising control over specific properties rarely reveal whether she is giving land of her own or acting in a vice-regal capacity. There are even a few investigated instances in which what looks like a donation from the queen turns out to be merely a royal confirmation of someone else's gift. The fact that some charters can be shown to be confirmations is troubling in cases where no supplementary documentation exists. If the text of a charter does not specify that the gift is of personally-held lands, it is rarely safe to assume that it records

[1] Strickland, *Lives of the Queens of England*, 1: 138.
[2] Strickland, *Lives of the Queens of England*, 1: 153.

a gift from the queen's resources rather than a confirmation of someone else's act. Another problem with relying on charters to reconstruct holdings is that charters normally record alienations of land, and while it is helpful to know what a queen granted away, the record of a grant rarely specifies anything about properties or privileges that the queen retained. Finally, it is dangerous to assume that a charter represents a decision made by the queen herself. There is always the possibility that a charter issued in the queen's name could have been drawn up, sealed, and witnessed by the king's officers without the queen ever becoming personally involved in the transaction. Fortunately, the surviving charters from Queen Matilda make this last possibility unlikely, for her grants sometimes specify when she was acting at the king's request. In other cases, her charters clearly state that a gift came from someone else at her instigation or out of her own demesne land.

Literary sources are sometimes helpful in fleshing out the skeletal outlines reconstructed from the charters. For instance, William of Malmesbury claimed that Matilda came to Henry without much of a marriage portion.[3] But, within months of the marriage, the new queen was engaged in large-scale patronage projects. If we accept William's statement, Matilda's wealth can only be explained by assuming that Henry recognized the importance of the queen-consort's position and provided Matilda with extensive dower lands. Access to wealth gave her the means to live in an appropriate fashion and to dispense the all-important patronage necessary to allow her to consolidate her position at court. If this is the case, such a generous marriage gift suggests that Henry placed a large amount of trust and confidence in his bride and does not accord with the portrait some historians have drawn of Henry as avaricious, suspicious, cruel, and generally unpleasant. If only to put paid to that older view, it would be helpful to have some picture of just what lands and revenues Matilda controlled. But there is a much more important motive for the attempt to reconstruct her holdings. In tracing the history of the lands and customary revenues of England's queen consorts, I shall be looking for continuities and precedents that will allow for some conclusions as to how Matilda fits into the pattern of English queenship. The sources do not allow for more than an outline of her income and possessions. Since there are no fiscal records extant from the queen's household until the thirteenth century, this survey remains highly conjectural, extrapolated from the records of Matilda's reign and supplemented by those of other reigns. For the most part, I am limited to suggesting possibilities rather than offering any firm conclusions. However, even with the limitations imposed by the sources, some patterns in landholding emerge that suggest that Matilda played a pivotal role in the history of English queenship. I shall begin this study by surveying the possibilities for any queen to acquire and control wealth in medieval England and then attempt to place Matilda's income and holdings within that survey. Here, I am concerned only with enumerating the queen's wealth. What Matilda did with her resources, and why, will be explored in later chapters.

[3] *Gesta regum*, 717.

There were at least four possible sources of revenue available for the use of a medieval English queen.[4] The first of these was the marriage portion that the bride brought with her into her marriage. Referred to in England as the dowry or 'maritagium', this portion could be in the form of lands and/or movable goods. This marriage portion could be sizable and was often a factor in the choice of a royal bride. The second possible source of income was 'aurum reginae', or Queen's Gold. This tax, instituted at some point during the twelfth century, was owed at the exchequer as a surtax on certain fines collected by the king. The third category of gifts, or perhaps bribes, offered to the queen by those seeking access to the king, probably formed a significant part of the income of certain queens, but it is, by its very nature, not quantifiable. We do know of many cases where petitioners offered the queen something to ease their path, and in some reigns a gift may have become a usual component in the process of securing royal justice. Finally, the 'dos', or dower, the portion in lands and revenues assigned to a bride by her husband at the time of marriage forms a fourth source of revenue which could and sometimes did provide income for England's queen. Some have speculated that there was, in late Anglo-Saxon England, a group of lands that traditionally formed part of the queen's holdings. The phrase 'queen's demesne' is sometimes used, usually in reference to estates in Rutland and surrounding counties that were associated with at least Queens Æthelthyrth and Emma in the late tenth and early eleventh centuries. Later, Matilda II and some of the Angevin queens appear in the records administering these lands. No one has claimed that every queen held the lands; that would be impossible if a widowed queen lived into succeeding reigns and retained as dower those lands assigned her as queen-consort. Marc Meyer has argued that, although most later Anglo-Saxon queens held properties of nearly equivalent value, there was little or no true continuity in queenly landholding patterns before 1066.[5] In Edward the Confessor's reign, for instance, the Godwin family held enormous amounts of land, and his queen Edith's holdings reflect her status as a member of that clan at least as much as they do her status as Edward's queen. Edith lived into the Conqueror's reign, retaining most of her holdings, so William I assigned new lands to his queen, Matilda I. After Matilda died in 1083, William I granted most of her English property to the baron Robert FitzHamon. By the time Henry I became king in 1100 and married Matilda II, the lands held by the Confessor's widow were again part of the royal demesne, and it was largely from these estates that Matilda II's dower was assigned. Pauline Stafford, who has pointed to the need for a more detailed history of royal lands in the later Anglo-Saxon era before the queen's landholding patterns or lack thereof can be discerned, has challenged Meyer's conclusions as premature.[6] There may not have been a group of traditional queenly holdings

---

[4] For a discussion of the revenues of England's queens in the later medieval period, with some reference to the Anglo-Norman situation, see Anne Crawford, 'The Queen's Council in the Middle Ages', *The English Historical Review* 116 (2001): 1193–211.

[5] Marc Meyer, 'The "Queen's Demesne" in Later Anglo-Saxon England'. See also B. P. Wolffe, *The Royal Demesne in English History: The Crown Estate in the Governance of the Realm from the Conquest to 1509* (Athens, Ohio, 1971), 52–8.

[6] Stafford, *Queen Emma and Queen Edith*, 126–30. Stafford argued that Henry I chose the lands of former queens to endow Reading Abbey about the time of his second marriage to Adeliza of Louvain.

in the Anglo-Saxon era, but it seems the Normans thought so, and that Henry I went out of his way to associate these lands with his own Anglo-Saxon queen. In addition, Matilda received lands and revenues that were not, as far as can be ascertained, part of the Anglo-Saxon queen's demesne. These holdings formed a precedent for later reigns when Matilda's holdings regularly appeared as part of the queen's demesne.

The first three categories of queenly income are almost impossible to reconstruct for Matilda's reign. William of Malmesbury seems to indicate that, unlike most royal brides, Henry's bride brought little or nothing in the way of a *maritagium*. According to William, 'a rich dowry was of no account' to Henry as long as he could 'secure the affections of one whom he had long desired'. Matilda, though of noble lineage, was 'mistress of only a modest fortune, being an orphan without either parent'.[7] Orderic Vitalis' comments on the royal bride seem to back up William, for he wrote that the daughters of Malcolm and Margaret, orphaned and deprived of the support of brothers and friends, looked to God for aid. Certainly the two girls were precariously placed between 1093 and 1097, but Edgar's accession to the Scottish throne restored their positions. It is difficult to believe that the sister of a reigning king would not have brought at least some form of movable wealth into her marriage. Edith had at least two marriage proposals before Henry acceded to the throne, and Mary was married two years after her sister to the Count of Boulogne. At the time, she would have been twenty years old at most, assuming that she was the first sibling born after Edith, within a year of her sister. Orderic sees the girls' fortuitous marriages as rewards for their earlier pious behavior and casts the story in the form of a moral tale that probably should not be taken entirely literally.[8] As a further caution, we may consider the case of Matilda's mother. Margaret was also cast as a penniless Saxon refugee, yet Ritchie noted that she had acquired a veritable treasure-trove of precious art objects from the Anglo-Saxon court, which she brought with her into Scotland, and which were held in the Scottish royal treasury for generations.[9] Matilda may have inherited some of her mother's personal goods, such as books and liturgical objects, as well as jewelry and other forms of personal adornment that she would have brought with her into marriage. Also, historians have noted that intensive settlement by the Normans of the northern areas of England began only during the reign of Henry I, presumably because the pacification of Scotland made living conditions more attractive.[10] It is possible, although not documented, that the marriage of Henry I and Matilda was the occasion for Scotland's renunciation of claims to certain lands that were in dispute before 1100. It is tempting to speculate that some of this property was given to Matilda as dowry. Matilda's

---

See 'Cherchez la femme: Queens, Queens' Lands, and Nunneries: Missing Links in the Foundation of Reading Abbey', *History: The Journal of the Historical Association* 85: 277 (January 2000): 4–27.

[7] *Gesta regum*, 715–17.
[8] See *Orderic* 4: 273.
[9] Ritchie, *Normans in Scotland*, 9, n. 1.
[10] See, for example, William E. Kapelle, *The Norman Conquest of the North: The Region and its Transformation 1100–1135* (Chapel Hill, NC, 1979), 193–210, especially 199.

charters show that she certainly exercised some form of lordship over northern lands, some of which were significant in Scottish history and may have been given her because of her status as a Scottish princess. One charter records her alienation of the church of Carham in favor of Durham Cathedral, giving the monks rights 'as far as they pertain to me'.[11] Carham, on the Tweed, had been the site of an important battle in 1018, a battle which established the Scottish claim to land south of the Tweed. Matilda gave land in Northumbria which had belonged to Archil Morel to Tynemouth Priory, a cell dependent on St Albans Abbey.[12] Although Matilda's control of northern land does nothing other than suggest possibilities, it is difficult to believe that her brother Edgar, who has been described as a 'client-king' of the Normans, did not provide some portion to mark the happy occasion of his sister's marriage to the king of the English.[13]

Turning to the gifts given to the queen in order to ensure or reward her intercession, surviving records from Henry's reign mention these gifts in an offhand way which suggests that they were routine. The practice of rewarding the queen for her influence did not, of course, either originate or end in the Anglo-Norman era. We have seen several cases of Anglo-Saxon consorts being rewarded for their timely intercession on behalf of a petitioner at court. There is evidence that Matilda, too, received (or perhaps extracted) these gifts, at least once in the form of lands, from members of the Anglo-Norman aristocracy. Two of the queen's gifts to Abingdon Abbey were of land that had belonged to Robert Gernon at the time of the Domesday survey. The first gift was of land near Colnbrook, which the queen says was given to her by Robert Gernon. The narrative account in the *Abingdon Chronicle* makes it clear that the queen had actively solicited this so-called gift.[14] The queen's second gift, the manor of Langley Marish in Buckinghamshire, was contested by Gernon's successor William de Montfichet, indicating that this gift, too, might have been solicited from a man who would not have been in a position easily to say no to the queen's request.[15]

Another chronicle account of a gift offered to Matilda may in fact refer to an early form of Queen's Gold. Hugh the Chanter, York's champion in the Canterbury/York disputes, included an account of an action by Durham's bishop, Ranulf Flambard, that describes a bribe to be offered to encourage the queen to use her influence in the required direction. Hugh, writing about 1130, reports that Flambard offered the king a thousand marks of silver and the queen a hundred for a favorable verdict in the dispute over whether York's archbishop should profess obedience to Canterbury. According to the highly partisan narrative, Henry refused to listen to the northern bishop, 'knowing full well which side could make the better offer'.[16] Flambard, who had been Rufus'

[11] *RRAN* 2: 1143.
[12] *RRAN* 2: 624.
[13] Barrow, *Kingdom of the Scots*, 144.
[14] *Abingdon Chronicle* 2: 98–9.
[15] *RRAN* 2: 1402; *Abingdon Chronicle* 2: 77.
[16] Hugh the Chanter, *The History of the Church of York, 1066–1127*, ed./trans. Charles Johnson (second ed., revised by M. Brett, C. N. L. Brooke, and M. Winterbottom, Oxford, 1990), 46–7.

chief financial officer, undoubtedly knew his way around the court better than most, but offers such as his may not have been unusual, and it may not be a coincidence that he offered the queen ten per cent of the amount promised to the king. According to the *Dialogus de scaccario*, written during the reign of Henry II, Queen's Gold was a surtax on monies proffered to the king: 'those who voluntarily engage to pay coined money to the King, must know that they are likewise bound to the Queen, although that was not stated'. Queen's Gold was also due on amercements of the Jews and the ransom of the moneyers. The *Dialogus* explains that whoever offered a sum of one or two hundred marks to the king owed the queen 'one mark of gold for one hundred marks of silver, two for two hundred, and so on'. A queen's clerk who was appointed to be present at the twice-yearly accounting at the Exchequer collected the money. Furthermore, even if monies owed to the king were remitted, 'it will be for the queen to decide about her share, and without her consent, nothing can be remitted or respited'.[17] The author of the *Dialogus* expressed confusion over whether Queen's Gold was due on sums of less than a hundred marks, indicating that the question was in litigation and not yet resolved. This confusion may indicate that Henry II's exchequer officials were trying to resurrect an earlier practice that had lapsed under Stephen or perhaps that they were in the process of creating a new practice. Recent work on thirteenth-century queens has shown that Queen's Gold formed a significant source of revenue, but surviving sources do not permit us to know when sustained and systematic collection of Queen's Gold began, or how long it continued.[18] An 1167 gift to King Henry II included 'one hundred marks of gold to the king and one to the queen', which H. G. Richardson saw as evidence that the gold was being collected for Eleanor of Aquitaine before her 1173 disgrace.[19] It is not even clear at what point Queen's Gold became associated with only the current queen-consort. Eleanor seems to have possessed rights to Queen's Gold as part of her dower revenues, which she retained until her death, despite the presence of Richard's and John's queens. Indeed, the earliest direct evidence of the collection of Queen's Gold comes from the reign of Richard I, in a chronicle recording a settlement reached on Queen's Gold owed to Eleanor by the monks of Bury St Edmunds. But even at that early date, the chronicler referred to the tax as a 'custom of the kingdom'.[20] About the same time, the canons of Waltham Holy Cross, who had been providing a clerk to collect the money, received assurance from the Queen Mother that their service was voluntary and

---

[17] Richard FitzNigel, *Dialogus de Scaccario*, edd./trans. Charles Johnson, F. E. L. Carter, and D. E. Greenway (Oxford, 1983), 121–2.

[18] See Hilda Johnstone, 'The Queen's Household', in T. F. Tout, *Chapters in the Administrative History of Mediaeval England*, (6 vols, Manchester, 1930): 5: 231–89 along with the important correctives in Margaret Howell, 'The Resources of Eleanor of Provence as Queen Consort', *The English Historical Review* 102 (1987): 373–93, and *Eleanor of Provence*, especially Chapter 11, 'Queenship: Images, Practice, and Resources'. Also, John Carmi Parsons, *Eleanor of Castile*, 75–86. See also H.G. Richardson, 'The Letters and Charters of Eleanor of Aquitaine', *The English Historical Review* 74 (1959): 209–11.

[19] Richardson, 'Letters and Charters of Eleanor of Aquitaine', 210–11.

[20] Jocelin of Brakelond, 'Jocelin de Brakelonda Chronica', in Thomas Arnold, ed., *Memorials of St Edmund's Abbey* (3 vols, RS, London, 1890–6), 1: 250–1.

constituted no precedent.[21] John's queen, Isabella, received her mother-in-law's dower rights, presumably including the right to collect Queen's Gold, only after Eleanor died in 1204.[22] Since so little is known about the early history of Queen's Gold, it would be foolhardy to conclude that Matilda II regularly received any form of the revenue, although the tax was clearly customary by the second half of the twelfth century. Furthermore, although Hugh the Chanter has made clear that Queen Matilda could profit from the exercise of royal justice, she may not have done so systematically. Nevertheless, gifts such as that offered by Ranulf Flambard could and probably did occasionally enrich her coffers.

Turning to the final possible source of income for the queen, the queen's *dos*, an investigation of the sources reveals that Matilda exercised jurisdiction over some of the lands that were also associated with her predecessors, the Anglo-Saxon queens of the tenth and eleventh centuries.[23] After Matilda II died, Henry's second wife, Adeliza of Louvain, continued to exercise jurisdiction over some of the properties Matilda had previously held, but she was also granted lands in areas where there is no evidence that Matilda held jurisdiction. The accession of Stephen and his queen, Matilda of Boulogne (Matilda III), complicated the picture in several ways. Adeliza retained some of her property until at least 1150, when she retired to a continental nunnery. Both Adeliza and Matilda III were dead by 1154, when Eleanor of Aquitaine became England's queen. It appears that Eleanor also received control of some of the customary properties. However, Eleanor's lands were confiscated, and the right to control them was seized by Henry II during the 1170s. When Henry II died in 1189, one of Richard's first acts was to restore his mother to the position of power she had lost because of her part in the rebellion of 1173. According to Roger of Hovedon, Richard gave Eleanor 'all the dower that Matilda, wife of the elder Henry had, and all that which Adelicia[24] the wife of king Stephen had, and all the dower that Henry, son of Matilda the Empress and king of England, had given to her'.[25] But after the reorganization of the royal household during the reign of Henry II, fundamental changes took place in the ability of the English

---

[21] Rosalind Ransford, ed., *The Early Charters of the Augustinian Canons of Waltham Abbey, Essex, 1062–1230* (Woodbridge, 1989), entry 36, pp. 26–7.

[22] Richardson, 'Letters and Charters of Eleanor of Aquitaine', 210–11.

[23] Any emerging pattern of queenly landholding was broken at the Conquest, for, although Matilda of Flanders held considerable property in England, little of it was in lands traditionally assigned to the queen, presumably because the Confessor's widow still held her dower. The lands of Matilda of Flanders did not become part of the traditional queen's demesne because they were assigned to the steward Robert fitzHamon after her death. FitzHamon lived until 1107. Hollister places Matilda of Flanders' Domesday income at c.£260–320 per annum (see 'Anglo-Norman Civil War, 1101', 82, n. 1). For the disposition of Matilda I's lands, see *Orderic* 4:95 and Hollister, *Henry I*, 40–1. William Rufus had no queen, and thus when Matilda of Scotland ascended the throne, the holdings of Matilda of Flanders had been largely alienated, but the lands of her Anglo-Saxon predecessors were again part of the royal demesne and available to form her dower. The chart above shows all of Matilda of Scotland's known alienations and indicates whether the land in question is also associated with any other of England's queen consorts.

[24] Clearly an error: Roger either substituted Adelicia for Matilda of Boulogne, or there is a missing phrase which also claims the property of Adelicia, the second wife of King Henry I.

[25] Roger of Hovedon, *Chronica* 3: 27.

Table 1: The Gifts of Matilda of Scotland

The Appendix number here refers to the actum in Appendix I; for those gifts with no surviving actum, refer to the page number in the text itself.

Manor or Gift (Appendix I Number)	Recipient	Date	County and Valuation
Isle of Andresey (VIII, IX)	Abingdon Abbey	1101–1102	Oxfordshire
Robert son of Hervey and his land at Colnbrook (XV)	Abingdon Abbey	1104	Buckinghamshire
Langley Marish (XXXIII)	St Peter's, Gloucester; Abingdon Abbey	1112–1113	Buckinghamshire
Income and produce from Guthery (Lifton Hundred) (XIV)	St Mary's, Tavistock	1103	Devonshire, an ambram of rye and 22d *per annum*
Tolls of Exeter (XXII)	Holy Trinity, Aldgate	c. 1108	Devonshire, £25 *per annum*
Soke of Aldgate, Christ Church within the Walls (XXII)	Holy Trinity, Aldgate	c. 1108	City of London (Christ Church taken from Waltham and given to Holy Trinity, Waltham compensated by gif t of the queen's mills in Essex
Mill/land in West Ham (p. 64)	Barking Abbey	Unknown, 1101–18	City of London
Income from Queenhithe pp. 60–8)	St Giles Hospital	Unknown	City of London; 60s *per annum*
Land on Abbot's Wharf (XXIX)	Westminster Abbey	1116–17	City of London
Waltham Mills And Fair (XXIII, XXVI)	Waltham Abbey	c. 1108	Essex
Two and a half hides of land (XXI)	Waltham Abbey	c. 1108	Essex
Epping and Nazeing (XXVII)	Durham Cathedral	c. 1115	Essex
Manors of Nettleham and Tixover (XI, XVII)	Robert, Bishop of Lincoln	1101–1106	Lincolnshire and Rutland
Belton-in-Axelholme (XII)	St Mary's York	1102	Lincolnshire
Church of Laughton-en-le-Moreton (XVI, XVIII)	St Peter's, York	1100–1106	Yorkshire, West Riding
Stanford-upon-Avon (XX)	St German's of Selby	1107–08	Yorkshire, £6 *per annum* and the service of two knights
Land in Stoke (XXXI)	Church of St Mary's, Northampton	1113–1118	Northhamptonshire
Bewick, Lilburn (XIII)	Tynemouth Priory	1103	Northumbria
Church of Carham (XXVIII)	Durham Cathedral	1107–16	Northumbria
Seaton, Luffenham, Barrowden, Thorpe-by-the-Water (XIX)	Michael de Hanslope	1103 or 1105–07	Rutland
Stretton pp. 71–2.	Aldwin	Unknown, 1100–18	Rutland
Market tolls of Salisbury (XXX)	St Mary's Church	Unknown, 1100–18	Wiltshire
Confirmation of existing Fair (XXIV)	Malmesbury Abbey	Unknown, 1100–18	Wiltshire
Customs of Wood and Income from Fair (XXXI)	Wilton Abbey	Unknown, 1101–18	Wiltshiire

queen consorts to administer their properties. Thereafter, English queens rarely exercised personal control over Queen's Gold, or indeed any of the revenues assigned to them for the maintenance of their households. Nor, it appears, were they usually able to exercise dominion over the lands assigned them in dower while their husbands lived. But even though the queen's household was subsumed into that of the king, the tradition of assigning certain lands as the queen's dower continued. When Henry III was about to marry Eleanor of Provence, he promised to endow her with 'the cities and holdings which were usually given by my predecessors, the kings of England, to the queens of England'.[26] However, Eleanor and her successors exercised dominion over their assigned dower only during widowhood. This lack of control during the husband's lifetime seems not to have been the case in the early part of the twelfth century. The evidence points to the fact that Matilda, like the other three Anglo-Norman queens, exercised control over her own lands and revenues in a way the Angevin queens did not. The ability to control and alienate their own resources led to the ability of the Anglo-Norman queens to form political alliances, control their own households, and exercise public power along with and sometimes independently of their royal husbands.

Most of the lands over which Matilda of Scotland exercised jurisdiction were probably given to her by Henry shortly after their marriage in gifts reminiscent of the earlier Germanic 'Morgengabe'. Only one text describing such a gift survives, an entry in the Waltham Abbey cartulary that shows Henry deeding his queen 'Waltham with all the appurtenances'. This gift was a generous one. Domesday Book records that the bishop of Durham received £63 5s 4d for Waltham in 1086 but that the property was worth £100.[27] Henry's donation charter speaks of the 'queen's court' where all pleas were to be held, and there is no question but that Matilda exercised feudal lordship over Waltham.[28] Waltham's cartulary contains charters concerning inheritance cases, feudal obligations, land exchanges and fairs, all issued by the queen, some confirmed by the king.[29] Waltham continued to form part of the demesne of England's queen consorts throughout the twelfth century. Both Matilda of Scotland and Eleanor of Aquitaine drew royal servants from among the canons.[30] In the following century, Isabella of Angoulême and Eleanor of Castile again drew revenue from Waltham.[31]

Matilda's demesne holdings included several other religious foundations, of which the best documented are the nunnery at Barking and, of course, Holy Trinity, Aldgate, which she established on land that she held in London.[32] She exercised lay jurisdiction over these foundations, receiving rents, tithes, and

---

[26] Pierre Chaplais, ed., *Treaty Rolls Preserved in the Public Record Office* (London, 1955), vol. 1, entry #23, pp. 11–12.
[27] *Waltham Charters*, entry 285, p. 193, n. 1.
[28] *RRAN* 2: 525; *Waltham Charters*, #3, p. 4.
[29] *Waltham Charters*, 4–10, entries #3–#13.
[30] *Waltham Charters*, entry 36, pp. 26–7.
[31] *Victoria History of the Counties of England, Essex* (6 vols, London, 1963), 5: 159. See also *Waltham Charters*, lxiii.
[32] See Winifred Maud Sturman, 'Barking Abbey: A Study of its External and Internal Administration from the Conquest to the Dissolution' (unpublished Ph.D. thesis, University of London, 1961), 382–3.

other tangible benefits, which probably included the right to abbatial revenues at Barking during vacancies. Although none of the original documents survives, later inquests show that Matilda maintained an active overlordship of Barking, trading lands, improving the roads in the area, and assigning customary dues to the demesne tenants. Matilda made the abbey of Barking responsible for the upkeep of a bridge that she built in the community and assigned lands from the manor of West Ham to the abbey to provide the necessary income to pay for the upkeep. Like Waltham, Barking included substantial property. The manor of Barking alone was worth £80 in 1086, and if the total value of the monastery's Domesday holdings is considered, the figure rises to £162 19s 8d. Barking, which had been associated with queens before Matilda II, became a customary holding of queen consorts after the Conquest as well.[33] Stephen granted the nunnery to his queen, to be held in demesne as her aunt Matilda of Scotland had held it.[34] Several Angevin princesses were associated with Barking, and during her widowhood, Eleanor of Provence received the revenues of the abbey during a five-month vacancy in 1275.[35]

Matilda's holdings may also have included some formal lordship over the nunneries of Romsey and Wilton where she grew up. Later in the century, Adeliza of Louvain and Eleanor of Aquitaine certainly held Wilton, but evidence for the jurisdiction of Matilda II is tenuous.[36] Matilda was a benefactress to Wilton, and the editors of the second volume of the *Regesta regum anglo-normannorum* speculated that she received the custom of the borough.[37] Matilda's interest in Romsey is evident from a charter of the king's that includes the queen among the addressees of a grant of a fair to that abbey. Since she was also a witness to the transaction, Henry could not have included her merely to inform her of a decision made in her absence. Rather, she seems to have been addressed as a party interested in the privilege being granted, perhaps as someone who exercised local jurisdiction.[38]

Finally, Matilda seems to have had some formal tie to the abbey of Malmesbury in Wiltshire. Her informal association with the abbey has been acknowledged since the discovery of the Troyes manuscript of the *Gesta regum* (Troyes 294), which is bound with letters from its author, presumably William of Malmesbury. These letters indicate that the project of writing the history was begun at the queen's request but had been delayed because of her death.[39] The contents of these letters suggest that William and the queen had several

---

[33] See Sturman, 'Barking Abbey', 39, and Meyer, 'Women and the Tenth-Century Reform', 54–5.
[34] See *RRAN* 3: 31, a grant of Barking by Stephen to his queen, to be held 'in her custody as her aunt Queen Matilda had held it' ('in custodia sua sicut Matildis regina amita sua unquam illam melius habuit'). Stephen's queen's was the daughter of Mary of Boulogne, the younger sister of Matilda II.
[35] Sturman, 'Barking Abbey', 382–3.
[36] See *RRAN* 3: 793.
[37] For Wilton, see *RRAN* 2: xxiv–v. The Pipe Roll of 1131 also reports gifts from Matilda to Wilton. See Joseph Hunter, ed., *Magnum rotulum scaccarii, vel magnum rotum pipae, de anno trecesimo-primi regni Henrici primi (ut videtur) quem plurimi hactenus laudarunt pro rotolo quinti anni Stephani regis* (London, 1833; repr. 1929), 12–13.
[38] *RRAN* 2: 802.
[39] MS. Troyes 294. See Ewald Könsgen, 'Zwei unbekannte Briefe zu den Gesta regum anglorum de Wilhelm von Malmesbury', *Deutsches Archiv für Erforschung des Mittelalters* 31 (1975): 204–14, and *Gesta regum*, 2–9.

face-to-face meetings. They also claim that the queen directly controlled the abbey. Writing to Matilda's daughter, the monk of Malmesbury pointed to the queen's charitable activities and claimed a special tie because 'she possessed our church in royal dower'. He referred to the abbey as 'the place where she herself ruled' and 'quite closely associated with her household'.[40] Other evidence confirms that the ties between Matilda and Malmesbury were more formal than has previously been recognized. In 1105 or 1106, she wrote to tell Anselm that she had filled the vacant abbacy at Malmesbury. She informed the exiled archbishop that she had appointed Ædulf, the sacristan at Winchester, and invested him 'in the things that are mine by right', although she had reserved the bestowal of the ring and staff for Anselm. Anselm resisted this appointment, claiming simony because Ædulf had sent him a cup.[41] However, the appointment was maintained until 1118, the year of the queen's death.[42] Several years later, Henry issued a precept that formally returned the abbey of Malmesbury to the bishopric of Salisbury.[43] It is difficult to understand why the queen appointed the abbot in the first place, or why the appointment was allowed to stand over the objections of both Anselm and the powerful bishop of Salisbury, unless she did hold formal jurisdiction over the abbey. This inference is further strengthened by a series of charters printed in the *Registrum Malmesburiense*. In the first, issued near the beginning of the reign, Henry confirmed to the monks a fair that had existed since the time of William I. Henry's confirmation is immediately followed by an act of Queen Matilda's. Unfortunately, the compiler of the Malmesbury register chose not to include the text of the queen's charter, simply indicating its existence by writing in red ink 'Carta Matilldis regine: Require ut supra' in the space following the text of the king's charter.[44] Later in the reign, the queen issued a charter extending the fair from five to eight days. Henry's confirmation charter appears below hers in the Malmesbury register.[45] Most students of Henry's reign have considered Matilda's charter granting the augmentation of the fair to have been issued in her vice-regal capacity, and certainly the language of the charter confirms that the queen had the authority to carry out the regal function of granting and augmenting fairs. But Matilda issued a similar charter, with similar wording, to her canons at Waltham.[46] It appears

---

[40] Könsgen, 'Zwei unbekannte Briefe', 213.
[41] *Anselmi opera omnia* 5: 326–8 (letters #384 and #385).
[42] Kealey, *Roger of Salisbury*, 113. Also see W. De G. DeBirch, 'On the Succession of the Abbots of Malmesbury', *Journal of the British Archaeological Association* 27 (1871): 314–43, quoting from an unpublished British Library manuscript (Cotton Vitellius Ax). Roger got the Malmesbury revenues after deposing Ædulf in 1118, presumably after Matilda's death. There are definite gaps in our understanding of the situation. William of Malmesbury scarcely mentions Abbot Ædulf, and the Winchester annals tersely note, under 1118, that 'Edulfus abbatiam Malmesberiae sine causa amisit'. See *Winchester Annals*, 45. William's letters to David of Scotland and the Empress Matilda request that the Empress fill the abbacy, which her blessed mother had left vacant. See *Gesta regum* 5, 7.
[43] W. Rich Jones and W. Dunn Macray, edd., *Charters and Documents Illustrating the History of the Cathedral, Church, City, and Diocese of Salisbury in the Twelfth and Thirteenth Centuries* (RS, London, 1861), 6.
[44] J. S. Brewer and Charles T. Martin, edd., *Registrum Malmesburiense* (2 vols, London, RS, 1879–80), 2: 333.
[45] *RRAN* 2: 971, 1190, and the *Registrum Malmesburiense* 2: 329.
[46] *RRAN* 2: 1090.

that this queen was accustomed to using regal language in her charters, whether or not she was acting as Henry's deputy in any particular case. In weighing the evidence in favor of the queen's holding of the town and/or abbey, we may also consider the fact that the town of Malmesbury was part of the dower of Isabella, the widow of King John. Isabella granted the town to the monks, to be held at a farm of twenty pounds a year.[47]

Matilda also received substantial property in the city of London, which is indicated on the London map on page 67. Brooke and Keir speculated that Matilda's 'substantial rights' in the city could 'hardly be coincidence'. They pointed to the Londoners who had rallied to the cause of Edgar Ætheling during the Conqueror's reign and saw Henry's gift of London properties and the corresponding juridical rights to Matilda as a means of gaining the loyalty of those Londoners who still adhered to the house of Wessex.[48] Whatever the motive for the grant, it is clear that Matilda held a great deal of land in the west end of the city of London, near the 'Old Gate', or Aldgate, in demesne. In 1107 or 1108, she used this land to build a new house of Austin canons and endowed the canons with the soke of the gate and the tithes of seven churches in the area. No details survive as to the ownership of the land outside London upon which she founded the hospital of St Giles, but it is possible that her demesne property stretched all the way from the Old Gate to the west end of London. Matilda also held some land and the soke of the area of the wharf of London known as Ethelred's wharf, or 'hithe'.[49] This area, located on the north side of the Thames at the south-eastern edge of the old city, also became associated with the queens of England, gradually becoming known as 'ripa reginae' or 'Queenhithe', as the ward is still called today. Along with her successors, Matilda received tolls and other fees from users of the docks, which must have been a source of substantial income. She diverted sixty shillings a year from the profits of Queenhithe to her foundation of a leper hospital in London.[50] The queen also held some lands along the wharf, at least some of which was held of her by the sheriff of London and later granted to Westminster Abbey.[51] Later, Adeliza of Louvain endowed Reading Abbey with one hundred shillings a year from the revenues of Queenhithe. Adeliza held on to at least some of the Queenhithe income as Henry's widow, for her gift to Reading was made in 1136, on the first

---

[47] *Registrum Malmesburiense* 1: 430. The text of the charter helpfully relates that the queen 'concessimus et hac carta confirmavimus, Deo et ecclesiae Sancti Aldhelmi de Malmesburia . . . villam de Malmesburia, cum omnibus pertinentibus, quae est dote nostra'.

[48] Brooke and Keir, *London: The Shaping of a City*, 318.

[49] For mention of the queen's soke and its boundaries, see Mary Bateson, 'A London Municipal Collection of the Reign of John (Part One)', *English Historical Review* 17 (1902): 480–511. Matilda's foundation of Holy Trinity is set forth in Hodgett, ed., *Cartulary HTA* (London, 1971), 1–12.

[50] Brooke and Keir, *London, 800–1216*, 334, *VCH Middlesex* 1: 206–10; Marjorie B. Honeybourne, 'The Leper Hospitals of the London Area', *Proceedings of the Middlesex Archaeological Society* (1962), 20. The terms of Matilda's endowment are known through a confirmation charter of Henry II, which lists the existing endowments and their source. See William Dugdale, *Monasticon Anglicanum: A History of the Abbies and other Monasteries, Hospitals, Friaries, and Cathedral and Collegiate Churches* . . . revised edition, edd. John Caley, Henry Ellis, and Bulkeley Bandinel (London, 6 vols in 8, 1821), vol. 6, part two, 635–6.

[51] *RRAN* 2: 1180; discussed in Emma Mason, ed., *Westminster Abbey Charters: 1066–1214* (London, 1988), 59, entry 97.

THE LANDS AND REVENUE OF QUEEN MATILDA II 67

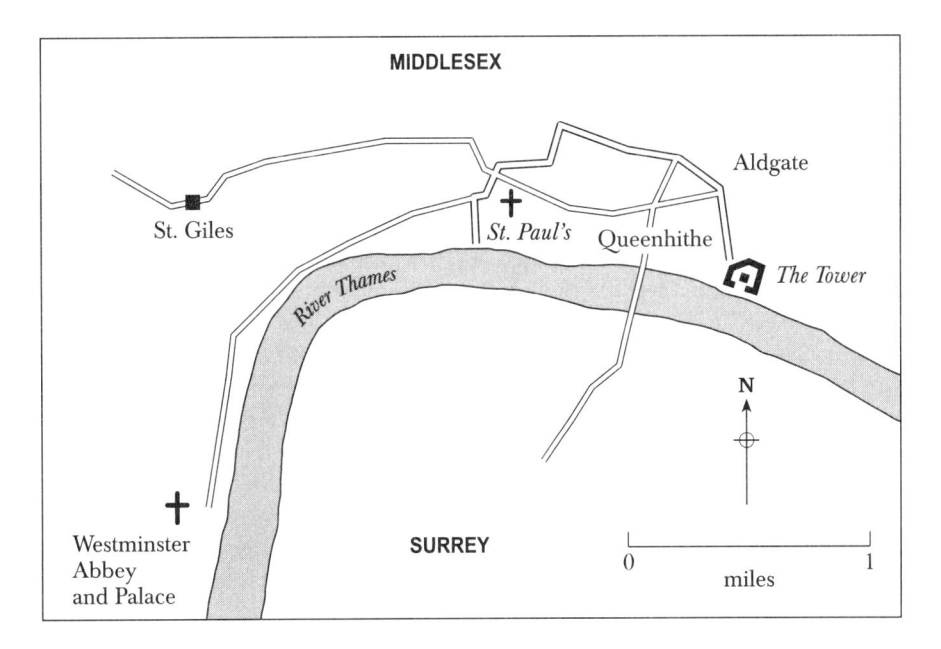

Map 1a

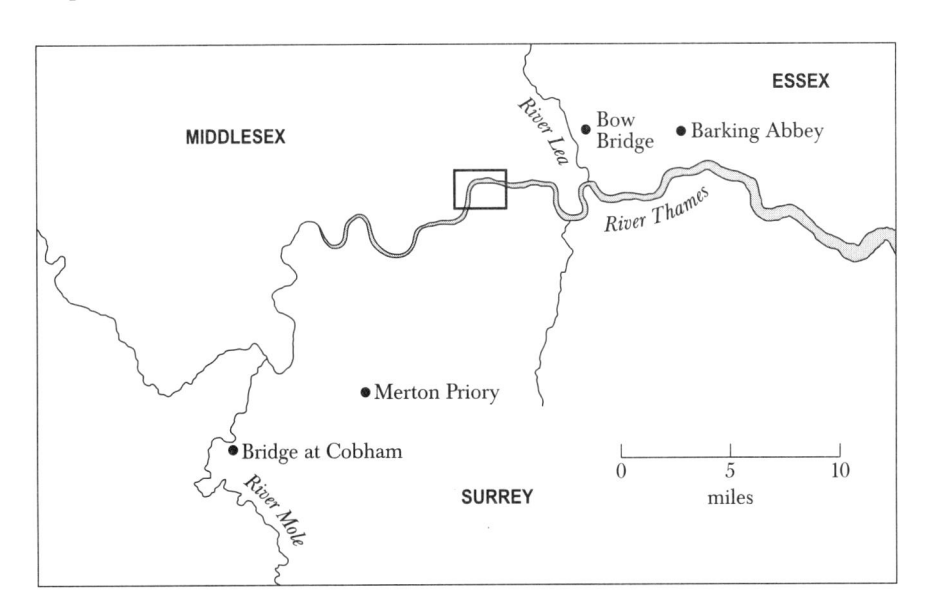

Map 1b

anniversary of the king's death.[52] In the following reign, Matilda of Boulogne founded the hospital of St Catherine's by the Tower and used her income from Queenhithe to form a per centage of the hospital's endowment.[53] The queens of England lost their title to Queenhithe in 1246 when the queen-mother, Isabella of Angoulême, willed the property to her second son, Richard of Cornwall. Richard then turned control of Queenhithe over to the citizens of London in 1246, reserving for himself the reduced farm of £50 per annum'.[54] The possibility remains that the then-current queen, Eleanor of Provence, continued to receive taxes from ships loading and unloading at the wharf.[55]

We know of a few other holdings only because Matilda granted them away. These holdings included the Lincolnshire manor of Nettleham, which, like the Rutland manor of Tixover, Matilda ceded to the bishop of Lincoln at Henry's request. Nettleham, which had a 1086 valuation of £30, had also been among the holdings of Queen Edith.[56] The fact that Matilda is known to have held a cluster of lands in and near Lincolnshire raises questions about other lands in the area previously held by Queen Edith. These Lincolnshire lands had a total value in 1066 of over £200 and may well have been held by Matilda, but since there are no records except for alienations, there is no way to say for sure who held the lands c.1100. One manor, that of Thorpe, which King Henry gave to the bishop of Norwich, was once ascribed to Queen Matilda, but this ascription seems to be erroneous.[57]

John Carmi Parsons has speculated that Matilda ceded at least one Somerset manor to her sister as dower land. The manor in question, Martock, was worth £70 and was held by King William at the time of the Domesday survey but had formerly been held by Queen Edith. Queen Matilda II is not known to have held

---

[52] See Brian Kemp, ed., *Reading Abbey Cartularies* (2 vols, Camden Fourth Series, London, 1986–7), 1: 353. Pope Eugenius' charter of confirmation includes the information that Adeliza's money came from 'a hithe in London which King Henry I gave to his wife Queen Adeliza'. ibid., 1: 130–1.

[53] Catherine Jamison, *The History of the Royal Hospital of St Catherine by the Tower of London* (London, 1952), 1–12 and 177–8.

[54] Gilbert Torry, *The Book of Queenhithe: The History of a Harbour and the City Ward* (Buckingham, 1979), 16–17.

[55] See Martha Biles, 'The Indomitable Belle: Eleanor of Provence, Queen of England', *Seven Studies in Medieval English History and Other Historical Essays*, ed. Richard H. Bowers (Jackson, Miss., 1983), 113–31, especially 116.

[56] *RRAN* 2: 535 and 743. Both grants specifically state that the lands were of the queen's demesne, as does Henry's confirmation charter for Nettleham (*RRAN* 2: 744). See C. W. Foster, ed., *The Registrum Antiquissimum of the Cathedral Church of Lincoln* (Hereford, 1931), 1, p. 18, entry #16. Orderic Vitalis claimed that the Conqueror had given the manor to St Évroul by 1081. There is no mention of the gift in *Domesday Book*. Anthony G. Dyson pointed out that the monks of St Évroul sometimes traded away property too far away to administer effectively and suggested that this might have been the case with this property. See *Orderic* 3: 234, n. 3; and Dyson's review of Chibnall's edition in *The Journal of the Society of Archivists* 4 (1970–3): 667–78. According to the Domesday survey, Nettleham had twelve carucates of land assessed to the geld. The manor was worth 24 pounds TRE, 30 pounds in 1086. See C. W. Foster and Thomas Langley, edd., *The Lincolnshire Domesday and the Lindsey Survey* (Gainsborough, 1976), 19.

[57] See H. W. Saunders, *The First Register of Norwich Cathedral Priory* (Norfolk, 1939), 28–9. Saunders translated 'de Sancte Trinitatis adiutorio confidens dominum regem et reginam Matildem que bona Matildis dicitur confidenter adivit', as 'confident of the help of the Holy Trinity, he acquired it from the King and Queen Matilda (which place belonged to Queen Matilda, so it is said)'. A more straightforward rendering, which I propose as correct, would read 'confident of help from the Holy Trinity, he went to the King and Queen Matilda, who is called Matilda the Good'.

any Somerset property, but the fact that it was held by Eustace of Boulogne by 1125 and was later claimed as part of the dower of Queen Berengaria again suggests more continuity of queenly landholding than can be shown from existing documents.[58]

Along with lands, Matilda's material holdings included the rights to customary dues and taxes from several of England's cities. Exeter, Winchester, the town of Rockingham, and the entire county of Rutland were among the lands that were sometimes assigned to Anglo-Saxon queens. Some of the cities from which Matilda received revenue belonged to these traditional dower lands. The city of Exeter and the surrounding Devonshire countryside provide a clear example of continuity from pre-Conquest practices. Exeter and the English queens were often associated, as we have seen to be the case with Queens Edith and Emma in the eleventh century. Like Edith before her, Matilda received two-thirds of the tolls of Exeter, amounting to £37 10s a year, which she diverted to support the canons at Holy Trinity Aldgate.[59] Later in Matilda's century, the city was named as part of the dower of Berengaria of Navarre. Several queens drew revenues from Devonshire lands outside Exeter. Matilda, along with her predecessor Edith and her successor Eleanor of Aquitaine, took monies and customary dues from Lifton Hundred.[60] Matilda had the right to 22d and an 'ambram' (four bushels) of rye yearly from the Lifton village of Ottery, which she granted to the church of St Mary in Tavistock. Her grant to St Mary's includes her servants in Devonshire among the addressees, indicating a continuing interest in the area.[61] One of the queen's grants speaks of her ministers in Rockingham, which indicates that she held lands in that area as well.[62] However, not all of the Anglo-Saxon customs were continued into the Anglo-Norman era. For instance, although several of Matilda's officers held lands in the city of Winchester, there is no evidence that Queen Matilda had any financial interest there, which had been held in previous centuries by the Confessor's queen and possibly also by Queens Emma and Ælfthryth.[63]

The county of Rutland forms a special case in the history of the queen's demesne. At the time of the Domesday survey, the county was only partially formed. The three northern hundreds, Alstoe North, Alstoe South, and Martinsley, formed the Domesday county of 'Roteland', taxed with Nottinghamshire, while the southern hundred, Witchley, was part of Northamptonshire and was hidated. The administrative unity of Rutland dates from the twelfth century, and Sir Frank Stenton speculated that the county, England's smallest, owed its very identity to its place in the queen's demesne.[64] According

---

[58] *VCH Somerset* 4: 84–5. I owe this reference to Dr John Carmi Parsons.
[59] For the grant to Holy Trinity see *RRAN* 2: 906. For Edith's revenues see John Morris, general editor, *Domesday Book: A Survey of the Counties of England* (Chichester, 1900–), vol. 9, part one, Devon, ed. Caroline Thorn and Frank Thorn (1985), 100a.
[60] See H. Lloyd Parry, 'The Fee Farm of Exeter', *Reports and Transactions of the Devonshire Association* 81 (1949): 197–9. Queen Emma also held an estate near Exeter. See *Encomium Emmae reginae*, xliv.
[61] *RRAN* 2: 632.
[62] *RRAN* 2: 887.
[63] See Martin Biddle, ed., *Winchester in the Early Middle Ages* (Oxford, 1976), 47, entries 83 and 81, entry 128.
[64] See Stenton, 'Introduction to the Rutland Domesday', in *VCH Rutland* (2 vols, ed. William Page, London, 1908–35, repr. Folkestone, 1975), 1: 121–36.

The *Domesday* Holdings of Queen Edith in Rutland

to Geoffrey Gaimar, writing in the second quarter of the twelfth century, English queens as far back as Ælfthryth had been assigned dower lands in 'Roteland', probably in Martinsley Hundred.[65] The Confessor's queen held the lands of her predecessors, and in addition she had the manors of Barrowden and Ketton in Witchley Hundred, as well as seventy *mansiones* in the borough of Stamford just over the border from Lincolnshire.[66] Edward, when granting the lands in Rutland to Queen Edith, had stipulated that they were to pass to Westminster Abbey upon her death. This donation to the abbey is among the few made by the Confessor but not confirmed by the Conqueror. W. L. Warren speculated that William probably retained Edith's dower lands for a hunting preserve rather than out of any sense of their status.[67] However, the memory of the queen's administrative rights in the area continued, as witnessed in place names such as the village of Edith-Weston in Martinsley Hundred. Some historians have speculated that Henry I, in dowering his wife with lands in Rutland, was

---

[65] See Gaimar, *L'estoire des Engleis*, lines 4128–40, a text too lightly dismissed in *Encomium Emmae reginae*, xliv.

[66] The manor of Barrowden consisted of seven members *(membra)* in 1066–86: Seaton, Thorpe by Water, Morcott, Bisbrooke, Glastonn, Luffenham, and Seaton. The value TRE was £3, TRW, £7. See *Rutland Domesday* (vol. 9, ed. Frank Thorn, 1980), 219b [EN1–2]).

[67] Warren, 'The Myth of Norman Administrative Efficiency', *Transactions of the Royal Historical Society*, 5th series, 34 (1984): 113–2.

Rutland and nearby properties alienated by Queen Matilda II

deliberately reviving what he perceived to be the Anglo-Saxon practice.[68] We cannot be sure of how much of Rutland Matilda actually received, but the fact that she granted away the five manors of Tixover, Barrowden, Luffenham, Seaton, and Thorpe in the southeast suggests that she owned at least a large portion of what her predecessors had controlled.[69] In addition, Matilda granted her manor at Stamford (technically in Lincolnshire, but the queen's portion seems to have been in Rutland) with the income of £4 and the service of two knights, to Selby Abbey. The land was that which Queen Edith had owned in 1066 and which had been described in the Domesday survey as '70 residences that lay in Rutland, with all customary dues except the bakers'. The 1066 value of £4 had been re-assessed to £6 by 1086.[70] The inference that Matilda at one time owned much of the county of Rutland is strengthened if we accept the admittedly late evidence of a 1276 inquest which states that she granted the prebend of the church of Stretton, in the hundred of Alstoe North, to a chaplain

[68] Charles Pythian-Adams, 'Rutland Reconsidered', in *Mercian Studies*, ed. Ann Dornier (Leicester, 1977), 63–83.
[69] Tixover was granted to Robert, bishop of Lincoln, early in the reign at Henry's request See *RRAN* 2: 743. The other manors went, probably on the same occasion, to Michael of Hanslope, castellan of Rochester. *RRAN* 2: 887. See also Figure 1.
[70] See *Rutland Domesday*, ELc2; and Foster and Langley, edd., *Lincolnshire Domesday and the Lindsey Survey*, p. 11, entry 9, and xxxiii–v for a discussion of the status of the borough of Stamford.

named Albin.[71] The maps on pages 70 and 71 show the documentable continuity between the pre- and post-Conquest holdings in Rutland.

While no reliable estimate of the total revenues of any Anglo-Norman queen can be made, this survey of Matilda's revenues and holdings, tentative as it has been, suggests that her holdings both continued Anglo-Saxon traditions and set precedents for later reigns. And even though her wealth cannot be quantified, Queen Matilda obviously controlled considerable resources that would have ranked her among the wealthiest of England's magnates. These resources allowed her the latitude to exercise influence and play a public role in Henry's reign, and armed with some knowledge of the sources of her wealth, we now turn to a discussion of the use of those resources and the political activities of England's new queen.

[71] *VCH Rutland* 2: 150.

4

Godric and Godiva: Queen Matilda's Political Role

Almost from the day of her marriage, Matilda began to play a part in the public life of her new realm. Within a few weeks of the wedding, she and Henry celebrated the first Christmas of the reign with a formal crown-wearing at Westminster, where the new queen may have obtained her first glimpse of international intrigue.[1] Among the assembled guests was the future King Louis VI of France. According to Orderic Vitalis, Louis' stepmother, Bertrade of Montfort, sent a letter under the seal of the king of France commanding Henry to keep Louis imprisoned in England. After a 'long and animated discussion with his magnates', Henry decided to have no part in the plot.[2]

Matilda and Henry's court soon began to distinguish itself from that of the former king. William of Malmesbury reports that some of the Norman courtiers became disgruntled with the difference in tone between Henry's court and that of his brother and predecessor William Rufus. Some of the blame must have devolved upon Henry's bride, for William describes how a coalition of barons 'openly libeled their lord with sarcastic remarks', calling him 'Godric' and his lady 'Godiva' and secretly sent for Robert Curthose.[3] It seems probable that by deliberately choosing English names with which to deride the newlyweds these Norman courtiers were indicating their opinion of the English connection, perhaps trying to negate Matilda's role at court. If so, the tactic was singularly unsuccessful. Throughout the next eighteen years, Matilda was present at the councils where major policy decisions were made. Not only did she serve as a member of Henry's curia, but she was also the delegated head of the council during many of Henry's trips to Normandy. Working in conjunction with the king's barons and 'curiales', Matilda sat in judgement and issued charters dealing with a wide spectrum of cases. She had the means to patronize ecclesiastical institutions of her choice, and she also had a hand in determining the direction of Henry's patronage. Narrative sources confirm that Matilda played a part in the political crises of the first eighteen years of Henry's reign,

---

[1] *RRAN* 2: 524.
[2] *Orderic* 6: 50–2. The story is not corroborated in any other source and Chibnall dismissed it as reading like 'epic invention'. See also Simeon of Durham, 'Historia Regum', 2: 232 and the *Winchester Annals* 2: 41 for other accounts of Louis' visit.
[3] *Gesta regum*, 705.

from the investiture contest in the early years up to and including the question of papal legates in England and the Canterbury primacy in the last years of her life. At every turn, the sources reveal the queen intimately and actively involved in the public affairs of the kingdom, and none of the writers of these sources exhibit any surprise or dismay that this should be the case. By 1100, it had become a commonplace that the queen was, by right, entitled to the role specified in the coronation ritual: 'a participant in the affairs of the kingdom'.

Of course, the first duty of any medieval queen was to provide a male heir to the throne, and Matilda was no exception. She was 'in childbed' when Robert Curthose invaded England in the summer of 1101.[4] Her first pregnancy appears to have been a difficult one, and physicians from all over the realm were consulted. Faritius, abbot of Abingdon, along with his friend and lay colleague Grimbald, became her chief medical advisors. The *Abingdon Chronicle* reports that Faritius was called to the royal bedside in the summer of 1101. This summons, combined with Wace's romantic account of the chivalrous Curthose turning away from his proposed siege of Winchester on account of the queen's infirmity, makes it easy to see how historians have been misled into asserting that Matilda gave birth that summer to a child who died soon afterward. But, because it is known that Matilda's daughter and namesake was born in early February 1102 (most likely on the seventh), the biological realities do not allow the existence of a child born in July 1101. If Wace's account has any truth in it at all, we can only surmise that Matilda became pregnant in the early summer of 1101 and was threatening to miscarry by late July, when Curthose entered the city. If Matilda were confined to bed, this could have allowed Curthose the necessary excuse to withdraw from the city. Charter evidence backs up this interpretation as well, because Henry and Matilda continued to shower Faritius and Abingdon with gifts throughout the fall of 1101. The charters recording these gifts were issued from either the London area or near Abingdon, indicating that Faritius was probably in constant attendance on the queen that autumn and winter. Marjorie Chibnall's conclusion that the empress was born in a royal manor house at Sutton Courtenay, near Abingdon, is likely to be correct.[5] I would not be the first to accuse Master Wace of chivalric embellishment, but, whatever the case in July 1101, Matilda's good relations with her godfather served Henry quite well the following year. During Robert's court visit in 1102, Matilda evidently persuaded him to remand to her the three thousand marks (two thousand pounds) owed him yearly under the terms of the Treaty of Alton. He did so, William of Malmesbury tells us, because 'the queen desired it'.[6]

With Curthose temporarily out of the picture, Henry could turn his attention

---

[4] Wace, *Le Roman de Rou et de Ducs de Normandie*, ed. A. J. Holden (2 vols, Paris, 1970–4), 2: 440.
[5] See *RRAN* 2: no. 550, issued 3 September 1101, from Windsor by Henry, #553 issued sometime in 1101 from London, also by the king. Of Matilda's two charters (*RRAN* 2: 565, 567) from this period, one was issued at Sutton Courtenay, near Abingdon, and the second bears no place of issue. See also Chibnall, *The Empress Matilda*, 9, n. 10.
[6] *Gesta regum*, 719 ('quod illa peteret, condonavit'). See also Orderic 6: 15, and Wace, *Romans de Rou*, 2: 449–54. Robert of Torigni says that Robert collected the money from Henry and then turned it over to the queen. See *The Gesta normannorum ducum of William of Jumièges, Orderic Vitalis, and Robert of Torigni*, ed./trans. Elisabeth M. C. van Houts (2 vols, Oxford, 1992–5), 2: 221.

to other matters, chief among which was the problem of lay investiture. Anselm, in exile during the last years of Rufus' reign, had been summoned back to the kingdom shortly after Henry's coronation. With Henry's hold on the crown as tenuous as it was at the beginning of the reign, he desperately needed the archbishop's support and was prepared to be conciliatory. His coronation charter had promised to amend the evils that the English church had suffered under Rufus, and he apologized to Anselm for having been crowned in his absence. Henry could not have known that a troubling new issue was about to arise. The questions of episcopal fealty and lay investiture had not arisen during Rufus' reign, and Anselm personally seems not to have cared one way or another. But, having attended the Council of Rome in 1099, he now believed himself bound by papal decrees against practices that were standard in both England and Normandy. At first, both king and archbishop were willing to come to terms, and several delegations were sent between England and Rome to induce the Pope to defer to English custom. A temporary concession on Anselm's part allowed Henry to invest new bishops as long as he was not required to consecrate them, a truce that broke down in 1102 when Henry arranged for three appointees to receive consecration from the archbishop of York. One of the three, Matilda's chancellor Reinhelm, returned his ring and staff rather than accept uncanonical consecration, while William Giffard, the bishop-elect of Winchester, created a public scene by his refusal to allow the ceremony to proceed. The bishop-elect of Salisbury, Henry's chancellor Roger, was more circumspect, managing not to offend either party. When three separate delegations had returned from Rome with no definite word from the pope that would ameliorate the strained situation, Henry and his bishops convinced Anselm that he should go to Rome himself and seek advice from the pope.[7]

Although Matilda was careful to alienate neither the pope nor the archbishop, her own views about the Gregorian reform are difficult to ascertain from her surviving letters, which Sir Richard Southern has aptly termed 'full of wariness and political sophistication'.[8] However, her affection for the archbishop is beyond question, and her letters reveal that she served as an intermediary between the pope, king, and archbishop throughout Anselm's exile. Matilda declared her sympathies shortly before Anselm's departure (he left England on 21 April 1103) by witnessing a Rochester document as 'Matilldis reginae et filiae Anselmi archiepiscopi'.[9] During the two and a half years of Anselm's continental sojourn, he and the queen maintained a constant correspondence. Matilda worried about Anselm's diet and general health, while Anselm felt free to reprimand her for her mistreatment of churches in her demesne. Matilda turned this reprimand to her advantage, informing the archbishop that she required his presence as an advisor lest she fall into error. Anselm rejected that line of reasoning entirely, replying that he would return as soon as it became fitting. Meanwhile, he paid her the compliment of informing her that she had a fine

---

[7] See Kealey, *Roger of Salisbury*, 17, and Eadmer, *Historia novorum*, 141–6.
[8] Southern, *St Anselm and his Biographer*, 191.
[9] *Textus Roffiensis*, ed. Thomas Hearnes (Oxford, 1720), 227. The *Regesta* editors misread the attestation and rendered the signature 'Queen Matilda et filiae' *(RRAN* 2: 636).

mind of her own, clearly capable of discerning right and wrong behavior.[10] The investiture question remained unresolved throughout 1104 and 1105, becoming increasingly problematic as each party became more firmly wedded to his position. Henry saw the issue as one of traditional royal prerogatives being inexplicably diminished; Paschal was firmly committed to Gregorian reforms; and Anselm, first and foremost a monk, was committed to obey the papal decrees. Time worked against the royal position, particularly as Henry prepared to invade Normandy to 'liberate' the Norman churches from Robert's ineffective governance.

Matilda's letters to Anselm, which were at first restricted to pleas for personal guidance and the archbishop's return, became increasingly political in nature. She began to take on the role of intercessor between king and archbishop. When Henry seized the Canterbury revenues, Matilda persuaded him to mitigate the action, securing an allowance for Anselm's personal needs while on the continent. She also kept the archbishop apprised of Henry's actions, at times advising him on the proper way to approach the king or to demand concessions. Her letters informed Anselm of Henry's state of mind as well: '[The king] is more composed toward you than many men think, he who, with God approving and me suggesting what I am able, will become more fitting and agreeable to you. What he permits to be done in the present about your rents, he will permit the same and more fully in the future when according to time and circumstance you shall ask it.'[11] Anselm continued to serve as a spiritual advisor and heartily approved of her intercession, urging her to 'counsel these things, intimate these things, publicly and privately to our lord the king, and repeat them often. As much as it pertains to you, undertake this with zeal.'[12] In another epistle, he confided that he prayed that by her counsel God would turn the heart of the king away from his evil advisors.[13] He assured the queen that 'when you strive to mitigate the heart of the king toward me, you do what is fitting for you and what I judge to be useful to him [Henry]'.[14] However, Matilda's professions of intense devotion to Anselm were sometimes met with frostiness on the part of the prelate. Perhaps, as Southern suggested, he was suspicious that her enthusiasm was politically motivated.[15] When she saluted Anselm as the one who had consecrated her and raised her to the dignity of an earthly kingdom, Anselm denied any responsibility for her elevation. Although he was the agent of her queenship, he wrote, Christ was its author.[16] His response to her proud announcement that she had regained some of the confiscated Canterbury revenues for him was that he was entitled to all of them and would just as soon have nothing as a partial amount.[17] In 1106, Anselm refused to sanction

---

[10] See *Anselmi opera omnia* letter #242 (4: 150–2) for Matilda's concern about Anselm's overzealous fasting, #400 (5: 344) for her letter of consolation during a period of illness. For Anselm's reprimands see letter #346 (5: 284–5). Matilda's response to Anselm's letter of reprimand has not survived, but its contents can be inferred from Anselm's next letter in *Anselmi opera omnia* 5: 285–6, letter #347.
[11] *Anselmi opera omnia* 5: 248–9 (letter #320).
[12] *Anselmi opera omnia* 4: 216–17 (letter #296).
[13] *Anselmi opera omnia* 4: 156 (letter #246).
[14] *Anselmi opera omnia* 5: 250–1 (letter #321).
[15] Southern, *St Anselm and his Biographer*, 193.
[16] *Anselmi opera omnia* 4: 151–4 (letters #242 and 243).
[17] *Anselmi opera omnia* 5: 250 (letter #321).

Matilda's appointment of Ædulf, a monk and former sacristan of Winchester, to the abbacy of Malmesbury, even though Matilda had scrupulously refrained from investing him with the abbatial staff.[18] Finally, when the queen asked his assistance in interceding with Henry about someone who had been deprived of his property, Anselm replied that the matter had nothing to do with him.[19] In other cases, though, Anselm appeared appreciative of the queen's solicitations on his behalf. He also seemed to have been genuinely touched by some favor Matilda did for his nephew and namesake, whom Matilda had 'adopted' and promised to treat as her own kin.[20] When in Rome, Anselm must have informed the pope that Matilda's opinions had some influence with Henry. Sometime about December 1104, when Paschal II threatened to excommunicate the English king, he wrote first to the queen, urging that she 'beg, plead, and chide' the king to change his position. He also used this occasion to relay the message to the king that, if he would capitulate, Paschal would support him against all his enemies, which may have been an indication that he would favor Henry's attempts to displace his brother in Normandy.[21] The pope wrote to the queen on at least one other occasion. One of the archbishop's letters to the pope referred to Paschal's letters to the king and queen that Anselm had been carrying but which he destroyed after events rendered null the stern messages they evidently had contained.[22]

In the midst of the controversy, Matilda gave birth to her son William, who was probably born before the end of September 1103. The birth of the prince was celebrated throughout the kingdom as the fulfillment of a prophecy widely believed to have been revealed to Edward the Confessor on his deathbed. According to Edward's vision, England in 1066 was about to be delivered over to its enemies because of its sins, and 'devils' would range throughout the land. The ills would only be relieved when 'a green tree shall be cut through the middle and the part cut off, being carried the space of three acres, shall without any assistance, become united again to its stem, burst out with flowers, and stretch forth its fruit, as before, from the sap again uniting'.[23] In 1103, the green tree was interpreted as signifying the line of English kings, the three acres the reigns of Harold, the Conqueror, and Rufus, and the reunification of the tree the marriage of Henry and Matilda. Now that a son had been born, the tree was again flowering and bearing fruit. England could henceforth look forward to happier times.

Since Anselm was out of the country, it fell to his deputy, Gundulph of Rochester, to baptize the new prince. The *Vita Gundulphi* speaks, not implausibly, of a special fondness between the young queen and the elderly bishop. Matilda, because of her great respect for Gundulph's holiness and good works, especially desired that he should be the one to raise the child to the font and baptize him. With the birth of a son, Matilda had fulfilled her primary

---

[18] *Anselmi opera omnia* 5: 326–8 (letters #384 and 385).
[19] *Anselmi opera omnia* 5: 351 (letter #406).
[20] *Anselmi opera omnia* 5: 248–51 (letters #320 and 321).
[21] *Anselmi opera omnia* 4: 292 (letter #252).
[22] *Anselmi opera omnia* 5: 242–3 (letter #315).
[23] Barlow, ed., *Vita Aedwardi regis*, 75–6.

obligation as a twelfth-century queen. She apparently had no more children, although later chroniclers did posit the existence of others.[24] William of Malmesbury, who knew the queen well, reports that she 'ceased either to have offspring or desire them, satisfied, when the king was busy elsewhere, to bid the court goodbye herself, and spend many years at Westminster'.[25] The limited charter evidence available suggests that William was correct in perceiving Matilda's favorite palace to be Westminster. Of the twenty-two charters issued by the queen in which the place of issue can be identified, eight, or just over a third, were issued from Westminster. William was also correct in describing the living conditions at Westminster, where the queen 'forewent none of the state due to a queen' as visitors poured through her 'proud portals'.[26] Westminster Palace, rebuilt by Rufus in the final years of his reign, was fast becoming 'the ceremonial center of the Anglo-Norman kingdom'. The great hall, measuring 240 feet long by $67\frac{1}{2}$ feet wide, was by far the largest in England and probably in contemporary Europe.[27] But William's depiction of a passive queen far removed from the affairs of state is completely misleading. The queen's role was far more than ceremonial. As even a cursory reading of Matilda's charters and the chronicles shows, her activities and influence went far beyond merely enduring the absence of the court. Her participation in public affairs, far from diminishing after 1103, continued throughout her reign. The *Life of Gundulph* provides a typical illustration of the power of the queen to effect change at court. According to the hagiographer, Gundulph was as beloved of the English people as he was of the king and queen. He writes, 'when many at court were encumbered with some obligation they would beg the bishop to help, and he as a kind intercessor confidently approached the king or queen and often obtained from them some work of mercy or alleviation for those coming to him for help'.[28] Here the queen is mentioned alongside the king, equal in her ability to relieve the needs of Gundulph and his petitioners.

Much of the historical discussion on Matilda's political activities has focused on whether her role in Henry's government foreshadowed the Angevin office of chief justiciar. Most of the participants in the discussion have allowed that Matilda wielded a wide range of powers but admit that the vice-regal arrangements in Henry's reign were too fluid to allow Matilda the honor of being formally numbered among England's vice-regents. Francis West believed her powers to be real but too informal and ephemeral to be considered official.[29] The collaborators H. G. Richardson and G. O. Sayles disagreed, stating that 'in all probability the occasions when Matilda was left in charge of the kingdom . . .

---

[24] Gervase of Canterbury reports that Matilda had three children, a girl named after herself, a son named William, and a son named Richard, before she ceased having offspring. 'Richard' is probably Henry's bastard son by that name. See *Chronica Gervasi* (ed. William Stubbs, 2 vols, RS, London, 1870), 1: 91–2.

[25] *Gesta regum*, 755–7.

[26] *Gesta regum*, 757.

[27] See H. M. Colvin, ed., *The History of the King's Works* (6 vols, Oxford, 1963–73): 2: 491 and 1:45.

[28] See Rodney Thomson, ed., *Vita Gundulphi: The Life of Bishop Gundulph of Rochester* (Toronto, 1977), section #37, p. 61.

[29] Francis West, *The Justiciarship in England* (Cambridge, 1966), 14–15.

were not very frequent and never of any long duration'.[30] They concluded that Roger of Salisbury was the effective ruler of England during Henry's absences. Their position has largely been negated by recent scholarship that recognizes Matilda's role. Roger's biographer Edward J. Kealey championed Roger's claims but saw his rise to power as a gradual one. 'Although the respective strengths of queen regent and appointed viceroy cannot be measured', Kealey concluded, 'their responsibilities apparently never conflicted. Matilda was more than a figurehead, but Roger's power does not seem to have been diminished by her title.'[31] Warren Hollister saw Matilda within the context of 'a select and stable body of English-based vice-regal administrators' who contributed to the increasing centralization and professionalism of government that characterized Henry's reign.[32] Finally, in a provocative 1981 study of the origins of the justiciarship, David Bates rejected what he termed a 'narrowly administrative approach' and instead saw Matilda in the context of a widespread pattern among the European aristocracy, who delegated and shared power within kin groups. According to Bates, regents from the royal family exercised authority on the same terms as the king and in all probability possessed real power. He argued that Matilda's writs and other documents were issued in exactly the same form as those that the king issued, while Rannulf Flambard, Roger of Salisbury, and other non-related vice-regal figures possessed less authority in their own names. In Roger's case, Bates pointed out that the language of his writs almost invariably refers to the king's authority and/or that they are confirmed by a regal writ, and that even the most authoritative of Roger's writs puts off doing anything until the king's return from Normandy.[33] And, although Bates has possibly drawn too fine a distinction between the writs of the queen and those of Roger, his approach has much to recommend it. It may be tempting to look for the roots of a later office in the government of Henry and Matilda, but this approach tells us little about Matilda's activities or her own conception of her role as queen of England. When Matilda of Scotland sat in judgement, issued writs, offered advice, and performed countless other activities that later historians classify as regal or vice-regal, she was simply behaving as a member of a royal family, a consecrated queen, and therefore naturally a 'participant in the affairs of the kingdom'.

The thirty-three charters Matilda is known to have issued, as well as the numerous documents that she attested for Henry or confirmed for others, provide the primary evidence of the extent of her participation in public affairs. Very early in the reign, the king and queen jointly confirmed two charters issued by William, Count of Mortain, in favor of the monks of Cluny and of Tours.[34] As one of Henry's most consistent attestors, Matilda was normally

---

[30] Richardson and Sayles, *Governance of Mediaeval England*, 162.
[31] Kealey, *Roger of Salisbury*, 31.
[32] Judith Green takes essentially the same position in her study *The Government of England under Henry I* (Cambridge, 1986), 39–40. See C. Warren Hollister, 'The Rise of Administrative Kingship: Henry I', originally published in a co-authored article with John Baldwin (who covered Philip Augustus and France) *American Historical Review* 83 (1978): 867–905. Hollister's section is reprinted in *Monarchy, Magnates and Institutions in the Anglo-Norman World* (London, 1986), 223–46.
[33] Bates, 'Origins of the Justiciarship', 11.
[34] See *RRAN* 2: 645, 680.

present on the occasions when charters were drawn up. Matilda witnessed about sixty-five of the surviving charters of Henry's first eighteen years in office. The high status of Henry's queen-consort shows in the position of her name in charter witness lists. In all her attestations save one, her name occurs in the first or second position – after the king, but before the bishops and lay magnates. The sole exception occurs in a charter in favor of St Stephen's, Caen. Matilda's name appears third in this witness list, after those of Henry and her brother Edgar, the reigning king of the Scots.[35] Several times she served as a messenger between the royal court, where cases were heard and decisions were made, and the writing office, where writs recording those decisions were drawn up. This role, indicated by the 'per Queen Matilda' clause that appeared at the end of the charters, indicates that she was entrusted with the task of seeing that the contents of the final instrument were in conformance with what had actually been decided.[36]

Matilda's earliest datable attestations came in the spring of 1101, probably on 21 April.[37] On the same occasion, Henry formally deeded her 'Waltham with all the appurtenances'. This charter referred to a complex judicial system operating in the 'curia reginae' at Waltham, where 'canons shall answer according to their rule and the laymen according to secular law'.[38] Matilda then issued the earliest of her surviving charters, pardoning the canons of Waltham the money that they had formerly paid annually to the bishop of Durham for work on Durham Castle. This charter shows the queen acting in the manner of any feudal lord or lady on his or her demesne.[39] Most of Matilda's charters are of this nature. A smaller group clearly shows the queen acting with what amounts to vice-regal authority. With a few of the charters, it is difficult to tell whether the lands in question are under the queen's control because they belong to her demesne or because she is acting as Henry's agent in a judicial or governmental capacity. A case in point involves a series of charters issued in 1105–7 regarding the rival claims of the monks of Blyth and the canons of St Peter's, York, to the tithes of the church of Laughton-en-le-Moreton. This land and church had belonged to Roger de Builli at the time of the Domesday survey, when it had been worth £15 (£24 TRE).[40] Roger founded the monastery at Blyth in 1088, and the foundation charter cedes the monks 'two-thirds of the tithes of the halls in the lands and assarts, and all the small tithes in Laughton'.[41] According to Orderic Vitalis, when Roger died, his lands reverted to his kinsman, Robert de Bellême, who, after rebelling in favor of

---

[35] *RRAN* 2: 601.
[36] The 'per' clause occurs with respect to Matilda in *RRAN* 2: 568 and 569 and is discussed in *RRAN* 2, xxvii, and by Van Caenegem in *Royal Writs in England from the Conquest to Glanville* (London, 1959), 149–50. The editors of the *Regesta* note that the 'per' clause was rarely used after the first few years of the reign, because court procedure had evolved to the point that a clerk would normally be present in the curia where acts could be drawn up on the spot – another sign of the ever-increasing efficiency in Henry's reign.
[37] *RRAN* 2: 524.
[38] *RRAN* 2: 525. For the text of the charter see *Waltham Charters*, 4–5, entry 3.
[39] *RRAN* 2: 526. During Rufus' reign, Waltham belonged to the bishop of Durham, who used it as his London residence. See *Waltham Charters*, xxvi.
[40] *VCH Yorkshire* 2: 166.
[41] R. T. Timson, ed., *The Cartulary of Blyth Priory* (2 vols, London, 1973), 2: 207–9 (entry #325).

Curthose, surrendered his lands to Henry in 1102.[42] Shortly after Henry took possession of the castle, he issued a charter assuring the monks of Blyth that they could continue to hold the tithes of Laughton 'as on the day I received the castle of Blyth (Tickhill) for my own use'.[43] In 1105, probably in October, Henry again confirmed the monks in their possession of the tithes of the church.[44] But within two months of Henry's second confirmation, Matilda granted the church as a prebend to the canons of St Peter's, York.[45] Henry confirmed Matilda's gift on Christmas Day, 1105.[46] The transfer was contested, and in 1107 both Henry and Matilda issued writs ordering the monks of Blyth not to interfere with the tithes of the church, which were to go to St Peter's.[47] The key to ascertaining whether Matilda's 1105 donation and 1107 writ concern demesne lands or whether she was acting in a vice-regal nature lies in the terms of her 1105 gift. On the one hand, if Henry had given Matilda some of the lands taken from Robert of Bellême, then perhaps Matilda believed that she had the right to bestow the tithes of the church wherever she pleased. The 1107 writ was issued from France, when she and Henry were together, and would argue in favor of this interpretation, for the queen would most likely not be acting vice-regally if the king himself were present. On the other hand, if York had shown a better claim to the land than that of the monks of Blyth, the charters in question belong to Matilda's vice-regal activity. A charter from the reign of William Rufus that guaranteed the archbishop of York title to his lands 'at Launtona and elsewhere, with the rights that were enjoyed by Archbishop Aldred in the time of King Edward and King William I', may refer to the same church.[48] If it does, then perhaps Henry and Matilda had come to believe that Roger de Builli's title to Laughton had been doubtful and that the tithes ought to be restored to York. The surviving evidence does not allow for a firm conclusion as to the nature of the queen's grants, although perhaps this is a case where William of Malmesbury was correct in commenting that Matilda sometimes promised more than she could deliver.[49]

The distinction between the queen's regal power and her power as a feudal landholder has the merit of allowing the historian to separate governmental from private action, but it is also somewhat artificial. When Matilda the landholder endowed a leper hospital or gave a plot of land to the church, she

---

[42] Marjorie Chibnall's work casts doubt upon Orderic's claims concerning the disposition of the Honour of Blyth and point to the possibility that the lands remained in Builli hands while Henry received only the forfeit castle. Henry's charter claims possession of the castle only, which adds weight to Chibnall's case. See Chibnall, 'Robert of Bellême and the Castle of Tickhill', *Droits privés et institutions régionales: Etudes historiques offertes à Jean Yver* (Paris, 1976), 151–6.

[43] Timson, *Blyth Cartulary*, 2: 282, entry #437; calendared *RRAN* 2: 598.

[44] *RRAN* 2: 704.

[45] *RRAN* 2: 675; J. Raine, ed., *The Historians of the Church of York and its Archbishops* (3 vols, London, RS, 1879–94), 3: 31, entry #14, 2.

[46] *RRAN* 2: 720.

[47] *RRAN* 2: 808, text printed in Raine, ed., *Historians of York*, 3: 31, entry #14, 4. For Henry's writ, see *RRAN* 2: 807.

[48] *RRAN* 1: 375, issued c.1094–5. See also *VCH Yorkshire* 2: 166, n. 61.

[49] Hugh the Chanter, *History of the Church of York*, 24–5, believed the gift to have come from the king at the instigation of Archbishop Gerard. See also Charles Travis Clay, *York Minster Fasti* (2 vols, Yorkshire, 1958–9), 2: 49–50, who points out the value of the prebend in question. It was assessed at £63 6s 8d for the 1291 taxation.

was still the queen of England, and this is most likely the way that the recipients of her charitable acts would have viewed her. A striking illustration of this perception can be found within the pages of the *Abingdon Chronicle*. Both the king and the queen had heavily patronized Abingdon. In August 1104, Henry left the island for the first time since his coronation, remaining in Normandy until December. Matilda stayed behind in England, travelling throughout the kingdom. In mid-August, she was in Oxfordshire and stopped in to hear her old friend Faritius perform the Assumption Day services at his abbey at Abingdon. It was during that visit that she stayed at the house of a local landholder, 'Robert the son of Hervey', and persuaded him and his overlord, Robert Gernon, to deed his property to her. She promptly gave the land and house to Abingdon. Matilda may have considered that she was granting away her personal property to Abingdon, but the gift from the first Robert and the gracious consent of Robert Gernon can only have come because she was the queen.[50] In another instance, charters copied into the *Abingdon Chronicle* report that Matilda permitted Faritius to use the lead from the buildings at the royal hunting lodge at Andresey in order to repair the monastic buildings.[51] Another charter explicitly states that the gift of the houses was hers or at least that it had come because of her intervention. She had obtained the buildings from the king, who gave them to her and to the abbot. But whatever the legal technicalities, the Abingdon chronicler recorded that the gift had come from the queen. And even when the queen clearly acted in a non-royal role, concerning her own property, she could bestow protections and grant rights in a way that few private individuals could. For example, between 1108 and 1115 she granted a fair to the canons on her demesne at Waltham, promising them 'the king's peace and my own'.[52]

As can be ascertained from the language of her charters and letters, Matilda exploited her role as 'intercessor' and relished the power that her perceived persuasive abilities assured her. That she embraced the role is not surprising. The familiar image of the queen as intercessor gained new importance during the reform era for a variety of reasons. Chief among them was that the rise of administrative kingship coupled with changes in the structure of the noble family began to close down traditional means by which a female had sometimes directly exercised public power. As the possibility for direct exercise of power became more remote, writers began to stress the queen's duty to use the less direct, but no less potent, means of persuasion and intercession. The distinction between direct and indirect uses of power may not have meant as much to medieval queens as it sometimes does to modern theorists, and it is not clear that Matilda or her contemporaries ever saw intercession as a lesser means of accomplishing a goal than more direct action. In a world where Christ and the Virgin were worshipped as intercessory figures, and where churchmen derived their authority from their ability to intercede for humanity, medieval queens had a frame of reference largely lost to modern political theorists. The ability to intercede with the king and to influence his actions assured the medieval queen

[50] *Abingdon Chronicle* 2: 98–9.
[51] *Abingdon Chronicle* 2: 88–9.
[52] See also *RRAN* 2: 1090.

of her status within the court and kingdom, and medieval women cultivated and embraced this ability. Courtiers flattered or bribed the queen to intercede, churchmen wrote didactic treatises and epistles attempting to control the direction of her intercession, and it appears that some medieval queens were able to manipulate the language and ceremony of intercession themselves to their own advantage.[53] Matilda was among those women. Although she certainly wielded direct power on her own lands, and maintained considerable authority within the 'curia regis', the wording of Matilda's documents makes it clear that successful intercession with Henry was important to her as well. The example of the Old Testament queen, Esther, was used several times in writings for and about Queen Matilda. In one of her letters to Anselm, she herself 'borrowed' the voice of Esther to express her despair over the archbishop's protracted absence. Her threat to throw off her royal robes and tread them underfoot closely parallels the language of Queen Esther's contempt for her own royal robes.[54] When Matilda gave the buildings on Andresey to Faritius, she made it clear through whom the gift had come, and her letters to Anselm stress that it was she who had guided Henry in the right direction. The language of some of Henry's *acta* also indicates that Matilda had some influence over the direction of his patronage. A donation charter for Westminster includes notes that the gifts were made 'at the prayer of Queen Matilda', while one for Malling is even more explicit. It gives the nuns the right to hold a weekly market, and it includes the phrase 'I concede and confirm this for love of, and at the request of my wife, Queen Matilda.'[55] And, even though Henry's foundation for the Augustinian canons at Carlisle came after Matilda's death, some evidence survives to suggest that the original settlement may have been at the queen's instigation. A thirteenth-century manuscript at the British Library carries a marginal note to that effect, and a fourteenth-century manuscript bound with the *Anonimale Chronicle* again states that 'Rex Henricus primus per industriam et consilium Matildis regine constituit canonicas regulares in ecclesia Karleoli'.[56] This claim,

---

[53] The clerical and monastic encouragement of the intercessory role of aristocratic wives has been treated by Sharon A. Farmer in 'Persuasive Voices: Clerical Perspectives of Medieval Wives', *Speculum* 61 (1986): 517–43. See also John Carmi Parsons, 'The Queen's Intercession in Thirteenth-Century England', in Jennifer Carpenter and Sally-Beth MacLean, edd., *Power of the Weak: Studies on Medieval Woman* (Urbana, Il, 1995), 147–77. My essay in the same volume, 'Intercession and the High-Medieval Queen: The Esther Topos', 126–46, discusses both Queen Esther and Queen Matilda's manipulation of the language of the story of the biblical queen.

[54] *Anselmi opera omnia*, 5: 244–6, letter 317. Compare Matilda's phrasing, 'Si autem nec fletus mei nec publica vota sollicitant: postposita regia dignitate, relictis insignibus, deponam fasces, diadema contemnam, purpura byssumque calcabo et vadam ad te maeore confecta', with the passage where Esther pleads for God's help in saving her people. See the Vulgate Esther 14: 2, 15–16.

[55] Matilda may have cultivated ties to Westminster as the burial place of her kinsmen Edward the Confessor and his wife, Edith. She made several gifts of liturgical items and relics to the monastery and ultimately was buried there. See John Flete, *The History of Westminster Abbey*, ed. J. Armitage Robinson (Cambridge, 1909), 70, 72. Matilda also donated land along the abbot's wharf to Westminster *(RRAN* 2: 1180, discussed in Mason, ed., *Westminster Abbey Charters*, 59, #97). See also Mason, 'Westminster Abbey and the Monarchy between the Reigns of William I and John (1066–1216)', *Journal of Ecclesiastical History* 41 (1990): 199–216. For Henry's gift, 'precatu regine', see *RRAN* 2: 668. *RRAN* 2: 634 records a grant to the nuns of Malling. The phrase in question is 'hoc concedo et confirmo pro amore et deprecatione uxoris mee Mahaldis regine'. The text appears in the *Calendar of the Charter Rolls Preserved in the Public Record Office* (London, 6 vols, 1903–27), 5: 56–7.

[56] See V. H. Galbraith, ed., *The Anonimalle Chronicle* (Manchester, 1927), xlvi.

discussed more fully in the following chapter, is not difficult to believe in light of the queen's favor toward the Augustinians.

Another indication that successful intercession, or at least the appearance of such, was important to Matilda emerges from Eadmer's description of a royal procession in 1105. According to Eadmer, the procession was interrupted when Henry and Matilda were approached by a group of two hundred barefoot and poverty-stricken priests who had been ordered to relinquish their wives by Anselm's decrees and then had been impoverished by Henry's fines on offenders. When Henry ignored them, these priests surrounded the queen and begged for her intercession, but Matilda burst into tears and professed herself afraid to discuss the subject with the king.[57] The story is troubling. Matilda was not normally a shrinking violet, and this narrative demands integration with everything else known about her. There is some reason to suspect that Matilda's influence may have declined somewhat in 1105–6. Her letter to Anselm asking his aid in persuading Henry to return the seized property from an unknown courtier dates from about that period and indicates that she had been less than successful with her own petitions.[58] It is tempting to speculate about the reasons for her sudden failure and fears. Could she have overstepped the bounds of Henry's patience with regard to investiture? If Matilda took the advice of the churchmen, perhaps her constant nagging, pleading, begging, and chiding had begun to have the opposite effect to that which the archbishop and pope had envisioned. But this scenario is hardly likely, since Henry and Anselm had met on good terms while Henry was in Normandy in 1105, and every indicator pointed to a resolution of the crisis in the near future. Henry was also gearing up for his planned invasion of Normandy by 1105. Matilda, Duke Robert's goddaughter, may not have wholeheartedly approved. And, since much of Henry's need for funds grew out of the projected military expenses, the priests may simply have touched a raw nerve in asking her to intercede. However, nothing except Matilda's known friendship with Duke Robert supports that she did not favor the conquest of Normandy. A final possibility is that Matilda simply knew that, in this case at least, Henry would prove impervious to any plea she might make and was distressed by the call for her intercession. Having been turned down in a previous case, she could not risk a public rebuff. The position of any medieval queen rested on her degree of perceived influence at court rather than any formal institutional powers, and, from her own repeated references to the times when she had successfully intervened, it appears that Matilda realized that this was the case. By 1105, Henry's patience with monogamy may also have been waning. Although most of Henry's two dozen or so illegitimate children were born before his marriage, there were a few who had to have been born in the decade after 1105.[59] David Crouch has noted that much of Henry's extramarital

---

[57] Eadmer, *Historia novorum*, 173.
[58] *Anselmi opera omnia* 5: 351 (letter #406).
[59] A list of most of Henry's illegitimate children can be found in George E. Cokayne, ed., *Complete Peerage of England, Scotland, Ireland, Great Britain and the United Kingdom, extant, extinct or dormant* (new edition, London, 13 vols, 1901–59), 11: 112–20. See Hollister, *Henry I*, 41, n. 68, for corrections and emendations.

activity seems to have taken place in Oxfordshire, centered on his palace at Woodstock. Henry, in contrast to his grandson Henry II, seems to have preferred to keep his mistresses and wife separated. There is no evidence from attestations of charter issuances that Queen Matilda ever conducted any official business at Woodstock. In fact, we have no evidence that Matilda ever visited Woodstock at all, and this circumstance may have been in the back of William of Malmesbury's mind when he wrote of Matida being 'content to remain at Westminster' while Henry and the court were elsewhere occupied.[60] None the less, in the very public atmosphere of Anglo-Norman courtly society, Henry's taking of mistresses could not have been unknown to Matilda or others close to him, and this may have been a source of distress and personal embarrassment for her. But whatever her private fears, she retained Henry's trust to a degree sufficient for him to leave the kingdom in her hands when he sailed for Normandy in August 1106.

One of Matilda's official duties during this period of authority, that of greeting and escorting Anselm upon his long-awaited return to England, must have given her special pleasure. According to Eadmer's account, the queen met Anselm at the port. She arranged for the lavish processions that accompanied him on his way north, yet she never tarried to witness the scenes of welcome, because she would be riding ahead to the next stopping point to make further arrangements for the archbishop's comfort.[61]

Nor did Matilda suffer any long-lasting lessening of her informal influence over the king. A letter from the German Emperor Henry V, probably written in relation to his proposed marriage with Matilda's daughter, survives to illustrate that he considered the queen to be a good avenue for approaching the king. The letter addressed Matilda as the emperor's 'adiutrix', thanked her for previous favors, and expressed the hope that he could continue to rely on her good will. 'We have', he wrote, 'from experience come to know of your zeal in all those things that we ask from your lord.' In the last paragraph of his letter, the emperor mentioned that he was highly displeased about a certain count 'N'. The count in question may have been Robert of Normandy, which would mean the letter would have to have been written before the Battle of Tinchebrai in September 1106. The count in question had prohibited imperial messengers from crossing his territory. 'He has', writes the emperor, 'offended not only me, but also you and your lord; he dared to impede my messengers, whom I sent to both of you.' The implication is, of course, that the queen would cause something to be done to relieve the situation.[62]

In the long run, the queen's stress on her intercessory ability earned her the lasting gratitude of at least one group of subjects: the citizens of Exeter. According to a civic petition to King Henry VI in 1422, the mayor of Exeter

---

[60] Crouch, 'Robert of Gloucester's Mother and Sexual Politics in Norman Oxfordshire'. The William of Malmesbury passage cited is from *Gesta regum*, 757.
[61] Eadmer, *Historia novorum*, 183.
[62] From Udalrici Codex, in *MGH Monumenta Bambergensia* 5, *Bibliotheca rerum Germanicarum*, ed. Philip Jaffe (Berlin, 1869, repr. 1964) entry 142, 259. Discussed by Karl Leyser, 'England and the Empire in the Early Twelfth Century', originally appearing in *Transactions of the Royal Historical Society* 10 (1960): 61–83, reprinted in *Medieval Germany and its Neighbors: 900–1250* (London, 1982), 191–213.

had, during the reign of Henry I, murdered one of the king's servants, which caused Henry to repeal the traditional liberty of the town. Henry gave the city to 'Quene Maute, on whos saule God take mercy'. Matilda 'instantly labored the kynge's grace and gate the libertez of your citie to the maire, balifs and commualtie agayne: for that good dede your suppliants kepe a obbite yerely for the said quene'. The story does not appear elsewhere, but Matilda did hold the farm of the city of Exeter in 1107/8, when she gave two-thirds of it, amounting to £25 blanch, to her new foundation in London, Holy Trinity Aldgate.[63]

Henry's 'Norman Conquest' was effectively over with the Battle of Tinchebrai on 28 September 1106. Sometime after the battle, Matilda crossed the sea, probably for the only time in her life, and visited her husband's new domain. Her visit caused little comment from contemporary chroniclers and is only known through two charters, one issued by the queen from Lillebonne and a second that she attested from Rouen. It is also possible that Adelard of Bath played his cithara for the queen while she was in France.[64] She and Henry returned to England shortly before Easter, and Matilda turned her attention toward establishing a new foundation for Augustinian canons in London. It is also probable that much of her literary patronage dates from the period just after Tinchebrai. Matilda was present, along with Henry, at the Canterbury council of August 1107, that finally saw the consecration of England's bishops-elect, including her former chancellor, Reinhelm, to his bishopric at Hereford.[65] Henry returned to Normandy in July 1108, remaining on the continent until June of the following year. During this absence he committed care of the kingdom to Anselm rather than to either Matilda or Roger of Salisbury. Anselm had been too ill to see Henry off on his voyage, and Henry had sent messengers to the aged archbishop telling him not to exert himself but to 'indulge in plenty of rest'. At the same time, he committed his son and the care of the kingdom to Anselm, reassuring him that 'whatever you order shall be lawful, whatever you forbid will be a crime'.[66] Henry followed his verbal message with a letter to Anselm confirming that his word carried weight above that of his other justiciars. Kealey considered that Henry's choice of a viceroy during this continental sojourn 'was probably more a formal courtesy than anything else'. Given Anselm's age and the state of his health, he is probably correct, although the archbishop continued to exercise a great deal of authority until his death on 21 April 1109.[67]

---

[63] J. H. Wylie and James Wylie, edd., *Report on the Records of the City of Exeter* (Historical Manuscripts Commission 73, 1916), 391 (Miscellaneous Rolls XVII). For the gift to Holy Trinity, see *Cartulary HTA*, 224–5, entry #4.

[64] *RRAN* 2: 808, 809. The *Winchester Annals*, 40, s.a. 1107, report that Henry and Matilda returned to England ('hoc anno venuerunt rex et regina in Angliam'). Adelard, in a treatise difficult to date, speaks of having played before the queen and some French students. See Hans Wilner, ed., 'Des Adelard von Bath Traktat *De eodem et diversa* zum ersten Male hersausgegeben und historisch-kritisch untersucht', *Beiträge zur Geschichte der Philosophie des Mittelalters* 4 (1903): 25–6.

[65] *RRAN* 2: 826, also possibly #828, although the editors of the *Regesta* see that charter as suspicious in form.

[66] Eadmer, *Historia novorum*, 197. For the written confirmation, see *Anselmi opera omnia* 5: 410–11 (letter #461).

[67] Kealey, *Roger of Salisbury*, 33.

It was probably late in 1109 or early in 1110 that Matilda received a letter from Herbert Losinga, the bishop of Norwich, requesting confirmation of the exemption from geld that Thorpe, one of his manors, had previously enjoyed. Taking no chances, the bishop also approached Roger of Salisbury about the matter.[68] These letters, which are probably typical of the business that the queen and her advisors dealt with on a daily basis, provide some insight into the way in which petitioners approached royal government. It is clear that either Bishop Herbert was an outsider with no clear idea about the procedures to be followed or that royal administration had perhaps not developed to the point that there was a particular path for a petitioner to follow. From whom, Losinga asked, did he need his exemption? If the queen and Roger were not going to act, could they at least wait until he had had time to send a messenger to the king? Or, he suggested, perhaps the matter could simply be held off until Henry returned from Normandy. To Matilda, he offered an apology for adding to the burdens of administering the kingdom, which, he added, she was doing in a praise-worthy manner.[69] In his letter to Roger, Losinga informed him that he had already confided in Matilda about the problem and that 'you will not find the queen to be difficult in this matter, for out of her kindness, she has been a very mother to me'. This clause indicated that Bishop Herbert believed that any action taken would need the queen's approval. But, he added, 'it is well known that she takes your advice in everything'. Even if Losinga were only flattering Roger here, the phrase demonstrates that the queen and the bishop of Salisbury were working in tandem or at least that Losinga believed that they were. Losinga's letter to Matilda, in which he asked her to 'greet the bishop of Salisbury for me', strengthens the inference. Herbert eventually did approach the king and obtained a charter that freed Thorpe from any further exactions, although the manor was assessed the charge for the relief raised in 1109 for the marriage of the king's daughter.[70]

The years immediately following saw no large domestic crises or change in the queen's participation in political affairs. Her private life certainly changed when her eight-year-old daughter left for Germany at the beginning of the Lenten season of 1110 to be taught the German language and educated for her future role as Henry V's empress. We know next to nothing of the childhoods of either young Matilda or her brother William, but the queen must have participated somewhat in their education. It is clear that throughout Henry's reign Matilda continued to attend meetings of the 'curia regis' and to attest royal charters. She was visible enough during the dispute over whether Thomas II of York would profess obedience to Canterbury to have been included in Rannulf Flambard's attempt to influence royal justice when he offered the king a thousand marks of silver and the queen a hundred for a favorable verdict.[71] Only two of the many charters she witnessed during the period 1107–1111 allow for precise dating.

---

[68] Herbert Losinga, *Epistolae Herbert de Losinga, prima episcopi Norwiencis*, ed. Robert Anstruther (Caxton Society, 1846; repr. New York, 1969), 48–50, letter #25.
[69] *Epistolae Herbert de Losinga*, 49, letter #25.
[70] *Epistolae Herbert*, 49, letters #25 and #26. See also Alexander, 'Herbert of Norwich', 144–5 and *RRAN* 2: 946, issued 29 May 1110, from Windsor.
[71] Hugh the Chanter, *History of the Church of York*, 46–7.

She was present at the large council held in Nottingham on 17 October 1109, when the see of Ely was created, and from Bishop's Waltham on 8 August 1111 she attested a charter confirming the rights and privileges of the city of Bath and of its bishop.[72] Henry left soon after the Bath charter was issued for a trip to Normandy that would keep him out of England for nearly two years. Shortly after Henry's departure, Matilda traveled to Winchester, where, along with three bishops and five abbots, she witnessed the translation of the relics of St Æthelwold.[73]

By the end of the first decade of Henry's and Matilda's reign, it is clear that the administration was maturing to the extent that the personal authority of a member of the royal family was not necessary for day-to-day transactions. Increasingly after the Battle of Tinchebrai, when Henry must have finally considered his hold on the throne secure, bureaucratic functionaries were left to handle mundane matters. Matilda's responsibilities were weightier, and included presiding over the court of the Exchequer in Henry's absence. Francis West termed the Michaelmas meeting of 1111 'the first example of a designated regent treating the administration as his or her own'.[74] Whether or not Matilda's activity foreshadowed Angevin developments, she certainly displayed a firm command of administrative and judicial procedure on this occasion. Several charters survive to provide strong evidence of the confident control she had developed after eleven years of service within and at the head of Henry's 'curia regis'. One of the litigants to come before the court, Faritius of Abingdon, used the *Liber thesauro*, probably Domesday Book, to prove that his manor of Lewknor owed nothing to the hundred of Pryton. In the writ subsequently issued, Matilda had the names of all present listed and called the court 'my lord's and mine'.[75] A second case dealt with the manor of Ross, claimed by Bishop Rannulf Flambard for Durham. Rannulf's predecessor had already come to terms with Robert de Muschamps, who occupied the manor, but Robert had not kept his side of the agreement. The problem had come to Henry's attention in August, when from Portsmouth he commanded the sheriffs of Northumbria to see that the bishop regain full possession of the property, and if they did not, 'I shall order that Nigel d'Albini and my judiciary do it.'[76] Matilda carried out Henry's threat, ordering Nigel to 'see that Rannulf the bishop had full right from Robert'. The bishop, she informed the royal officer, 'will be able to show [you] that his predecessor remained in possession'.[77] Another charter, uncalendared in the *Regesta* but appearing in the cartulary of Worcester Cathedral Priory, was probably also issued during the Michaelmas accounting. In this charter, Matilda announced that Prior Thomas and 'his monks and all his men and lands are in the hands of the king and me, and they have the firm peace of the king and me'.[78] Only one of these charters, the one regarding Durham,

---

[72] *RRAN* 2: 919, 920.
[73] *Winchester Annals*, 44.
[74] West, *The Justiciarship in England*, 14.
[75] *RRAN* 2: 1000. Queen Edith had given the monks the manor in question.
[76] *RRAN* 2: 993.
[77] *RRAN* 2: 1001.
[78] R. R. Darlington, ed., *The Cartulary of Worcester Cathedral Priory, Register I* (London, 1968), p. 26, #40. The charter is definitely issued by Matilda as a deputy for the king. Darlington believed it to have

survives in the original. The queen's seal is attached, one of the earliest known seals of a European queen and a rare use of the seal of a queen-consort to seal an official document.[79] In another charter, issued from Westminster between August 1111 and May 1112, Matilda, again acting in precisely the manner that her absent husband would have, confirmed the gifts of Bishop Sampson to the church at Worcester.[80]

No documentation has survived to enable the historian to trace Matilda's itinerary with any precision from the end of 1111 until 1114, when it is known that she, along with her young son William, visited the newly-chosen site for Merton Priory.[81] Sometime in 1112 she was present at St Peter's, Gloucester, when Robert Gernon gave two churches from his estates to the monastic chapter.[82] A charter from the cartulary of Eye Priory, issued from Westminster most likely sometime between 1107 and July 1113, orders Hubert de Monchensy to return whatever he and his ministers have unjustly seized from the monks.[83] Henry was in England from July 1113 until the autumn of 1114, which helps to account for the lack of queenly charters issued during that period. There is also some indication that the queen may have suffered from an unidentified illness during this period. Hildebert of Lavardin, her friend and spiritual advisor, wrote a short letter, which Migne dated to 1113, inquiring about the queen's health, and a prayer, composed for the queen by Herbert Losinga, that asks for the aid of St John the Evangelist in securing her 'long-awaited recovery', may date from this period.[84] However, Matilda did continue to attest Henry's charters and to influence his decisions. When David, the queen's youngest brother, wished to marry one of the king's wards, the widow and heiress of the earl of Huntingdon, as well as a grand-niece of the Conqueror, Henry is said to have been 'persuaded by the arguments and petitions of the queen' to agree to the alliance.[85] In this case, as Judith Green has pointed out, Henry may not have needed much persuasion, since David was a favorite and much honored by Henry. The marriage took place sometime before Christmas 1113, when David began attesting royal charters as the earl of Huntington.[86]

been issued during Henry's absence, in either 1108–9 or 1111–13. The lack of even a courtesy referral to Anselm, the titular justiciar during the earlier absence, argues for the later date. The 'per' clause and the absence of witnesses are problematic.

[79] For the use of seals, see T. A. Heslop, 'English Seals from the Mid-Ninth Century to 1100', *Journal of the British Archaeological Association* 133 (1980): 1–16, and 'Seals', in George Zarnecki, Janet Holt, and Tristam Holland, edd., *English Romanesque Art, 1066–1200* (London, 1984), 305, and Figure 336, a photograph of Matilda's seal preserved in the Library of the Dean and Chapter of Durham Cathedral.

[80] For dating, see Darlington, ed., *Register of Worcester Cathedral Priory*, 139, entry #262. Text of charter in appendix, # VI.

[81] M. L. Colker, 'Latin Texts Concerning Gilbert, Founder of Merton Priory', *Studia monastica* 12 (1970): 241–72.

[82] Hart, cd., *Historia et cartularium monasterii Sancti Petri Gloucestriae*, 2: 166. See also *RRAN* 2: 1026 (Henry's confirmation of Robert's gift, dated 1113) and the *Abingdon Cartulary* 2: 77.

[83] Vivien Brown assumed that the charter was issued during the years the abbey was in royal custody, which is the most likely scenario. See Brown, ed., *The Cartulary and Charters of Eye Priory* (2 vols, Woodbridge, 1992–4), 1: 34, charter #26.

[84] *PL* 171, cols 289–90; *Epistolae Heribert de Losinga*, #18, pp. 33–7.

[85] See 'Vita et passio Waldevi comitis', in F. Michel, ed., *Chroniques anglo-normandes* 2: 126–7.

[86] See Green, 'Anglo-Scottish Relations', 59, and 'David I and Henry I', *Scottish Historical Review* 75 (1996): 1–19.

Henry also allowed the vacant archbishopric of Canterbury to be filled in 1114. The candidate of choice, both by Henry and by the Canterbury monks, was Faritius, the abbot of Abingdon. But two influential bishops, Roger of Salisbury and Robert Bloet of Lincoln, opposed the reform-minded abbot on the surprising grounds that he had been the queen's physician and that one who had formerly spent his time 'smelling women's urine' was unfit for episcopal office. The rejection of Faritius, who like Lanfranc and Anselm had come from Italy, has been explained as a sign of Norman 'nationalism' or possibly as indicative of a growing hostility and power-struggle between monks and members of the secular clergy. It is also possible that Roger and Robert were displaying fear of a formidable alliance between the queen and her reform-minded physician. The king did not press the issue, and a compromise candidate, bishop Ralph of Rochester, was chosen instead.[87]

When the king left in late September 1114 for a ten-month stay on the continent, he again left Matilda in charge of the kingdom of England. One of his last acts before sailing was to issue a charter in favor of Robert Bloet's cathedral of St Mary's, Lincoln, and to send word to the queen that he had done so.[88] There were again no major crises in England for the queen to handle in 1114–15, and Matilda's tenure as head of the 'curia regis' during that period has left no trace in the surviving diplomatic records. She reappears shortly after Henry's return in September 1115, when, wittingly or not, she served as a peacemaker between Ralph, the testy archbishop of Canterbury, and Robert of Meulan, one of the king's chief counselors. When the queen's chancellor, Bernard, was promoted to the bishopric of St David's, Robert of Meulan suggested that the king's chambers might be the appropriate place to perform the consecration. Ralph, ever vigilant when Canterbury privileges were concerned, retorted that he would consecrate no one save at Canterbury. After Henry quickly assured the archbishop that he could consecrate the chancellor wherever he chose, Ralph admitted that his church at Lambeth Palace would be suitable. But, because the queen wanted to attend the ceremony, the consecration was held at Westminster Abbey in the queen's presence.[89] A few months later, Henry and Matilda, along with many of England's lay and ecclesiastical magnates, traveled to St Albans to attend the dedication of the new church built on the site of the martyrdom of one of England's earliest saints.[90] Matilda's sister, Mary, who had married Count Eustace of Boulogne in 1102, died in the spring of 1115 (perhaps on 31 May). Sometime between her death and Henry's trip to Normandy the following year, Matilda issued a charter in favor of the monks of Durham, naming the

---

[87] See Eadmer, *Historia novorum*, 221–5. Also, William of Malmesbury, *Gesta pontificum anglorum*, 125–6, and *Abingdon Chronicle* 2: 287. Discussed in Denis Bethell, 'English Black Monks and Episcopal Elections in the 1120s', *English Historical Review* 84 (1969): 673–98. Mary Amanda Clark's doctoral dissertation, 'Ralph d'Escures: Anglo-Norman Abbot and Archbishop' (University of California, Santa Barbara, 1975), provides details of Ralph's political involvement before and after the election.

[88] *RRAN* 2: 1056.

[89] Eadmer, *Historia novorum*, 235–6.

[90] Thomas Walsingham, *Gesta Abbatum Monasterii Sancti Albani*, ed. Henry Thomas Riley (2 vols, RS, 1867), 1: 70–1. See also *RRAN* 2: 1102.

souls of her parents, brothers, and sister, as well as Henry and her children as spiritual beneficiaries of her action.[91]

In April 1116, Henry again went to Normandy, leaving Matilda to enjoy her last period of authority, which lasted until her death on 1 May 1118. During part of her tenure, their son William assisted her. From about 1115, Henry and Matilda had begun including him in government decisions. His first attestations for Matilda concerned her demesne property, but between 1116 and 1118 the queen and the prince issued three writs concerning the seized ship of the abbot of St Augustine's, Canterbury. It appears that the king had been involved in the case before his departure for Normandy as well, because, after several hearings, nothing was resolved, and it was finally decided to restore the property to the abbot 'as it had been on the day the king crossed the sea' and to hold any further litigation 'until he himself returns'.[92] The last of Matilda's surviving vice-regal writs concerns a group of hermit-monks who established their cell in the area of the royal forest near Luffield. From Oxford, Matilda ordered that Mauger and his servants be conveyed to the site, 'because the king has allowed that they may remain there'. These monks were also to be protected from all injury. Eventually, Robert of Leicester founded a house of Augustinian canons at Luffield, and the hermit Mauger became its first prior.[93]

A comparatively substantial amount of documentation for the queen's activity in administrative and judicial affairs survives from the year 1116. In the spring, the queen joined forces with the saints Benedict, Ætheldreda, and Sexburga to free a prisoner whom Henry's justiciar, Ralph Basset, had unjustly condemned on charges of usury and concealment of the king's treasure.[94] This prisoner, Bricstan of Chatteris, described by Orderic Vitalis as 'an honest man neither rich nor poor', had been wrongly accused and cast into a London prison. Bricstan, who evidently had been considering taking monastic vows even before he fell foul of the law, was not the type to suffer in silence. Instead, he 'never ceased to call upon St Benedict and St Ætheldreda with constant groans, sighs, sobs, and tears'.[95] The honest man's piety eventually paid off. According to the narrative, his wailing summoned both Benedict and Ætheldreda to Bricstan's cell. Although apparently uninvited, Sexburga came along as well. Benedict tore off the chains binding Bricstan and for good measure, hurled them against the wall and ceiling of the cell several times. The 'alarming clatter' from the chains woke the astonished guards. The guards notified Queen Matilda, who 'just happened' to be in London at the time. Matilda sent

[91] See RRAN 2: 1108. The charter survives with the original seal at the Library of the Dean and Chapter of Durham Cathedral (1.3. Ebor. 13).
[92] William, along with his uncle David, the earl of Huntingdon, attested a charter in favor of Durham concerning the disposition of Matilda's lands at Waltham Abbey. See RRAN 2: 1189, 1191 for William's writs.
[93] RRAN 2: 1198, Appendix I, # IV. See also G. R. Elvey, ed., Luffield Priory Charters, Part One (Welwyn Garden City, 1968), #4, pp. 16–17.
[94] There are three surviving medieval accounts of the miraculous release of Bricstan of Chatteris. The first appears in the Liber Eliensis, 266–9. Orderic Vitalis wrote a narrative account which appears in Orderic 3: 352–7. Finally, Gregory of Ely's poem on the life and miracles of St Ætheldreda also tells Bricstan's story. See Pauline A. Thompson and Elizabeth Stevens, edd., 'Gregory of Ely's Verse Life and Miracles of St Æthelthryth', Analecta Bollandiana 106 (1988): 333–90.
[95] Orderic 3: 352–3.

Ralph Basset to investigate the unusual occurrence. On speaking with Bricstan, Basset at first doubted his story, but was finally convinced that a miracle had indeed taken place.

The interpretation of a medieval miracle is often problematic for modern readers, and this tale may reveal more about the minds of the monks of Ely or the sleepy guards at the jailhouse in London than it does about the posthumous actions of Benedict and his virginal companions. But whatever went on in Bricstan's cell, the events surrounding the discovery and promulgation of the miracle demonstrate the queen's judicial powers. Ralph Basset led the former prisoner to the queen, who, 'being a good Christian', rejoiced in the event and ordered that special masses be held and that the bells in all of London's churches be rung in celebration. At Matilda's orders, Bricstan was paraded through the city as a 'living relic' ('vivas reliquias') before being allowed to retire to the monastery at Ely, and the queen is described as being present when the chains were delivered to Ely for safekeeping.[96] None of the narrative sources display any surprise that it was the queen to whom both the guards and the royal justiciar turned for disposition of the case. One of the accounts, Gregory of Ely's poem on the life and miracles of St Ætheldreda, does explain that the king was away from England at the time and that the queen was ruling the kingdom. The poet described her as 'Matilda, not dissimilar to the king in competence'.[97] The queen's participation in the royal justice system is confirmed by a letter from her episcopal correspondent, Hildebert of Le Mans, who once referred to her as having been given the power to judge crimes.[98]

About the time that Matilda, the good Christian, was dealing with Bricstan of Chatteris, Pope Paschal II turned his attention to the church in Britain as well. The Pope, who had long been irritated by the independence of the English bishops, had complained in 1115 because Ralph of Rochester had been translated to Canterbury without his permission. The letter also expressed papal displeasure because his legates were not being received in the island kingdom unless they obtained Henry's permission.[99] In the spring of 1116 the younger Anselm, now the abbot of St Saba in Rome, was sent to England with letters demanding the payment of Peter's Pence and also demanding that the British bishops and abbots receive him with full legatine authority. When Anselm caught up with Henry in Normandy, the king detained him while a message was sent to the bishops and abbots of England. Late in August, Matilda presided over the council of English prelates who met to discuss what action should be taken. A delegation consisting of Archbishop Ralph, Herbert Losinga of Norwich, Abbot Hugh of Chertsey, and William of Corbeil, then a canon at Chertsey, was chosen to go to the king in Normandy. In the words of Eadmer, they would 'inform the king of the ancient customs and liberties of the

---

[96] *Orderic* 3: 356–7.
[97] Thompson and Stevens, edd., 'Gregory of Ely', lines 194–5. According to the editors, the surviving manuscript of Gregory's poem dates from soon after 1116, certainly before 1131.
[98] *PL* 171: col. 290.
[99] Eadmer, *Historia novorum*, 231–3. See also P. Jaffe and S. Lowenfeld, edd., *Regesta pontificum romanorum ab condita ad annum post Christum natum MCXCVIII* (2 vols, Rome, 1885–9: 1, entry 6547.

kingdom', and, if Henry thought it necessary, they would go all the way to Rome to 'annihilate these innovations'.[100]

Matilda's last datable public actions took place during this council of 1116, although two of her charters could well have been issued subsequently. Both the charter dealing with the confiscated ship of the abbot of St Augustine's and the order to convey Mauger and his followers to Luffield date from Henry's last trip to Normandy before the queen died on 1 May 1118. After the queen died, her son William took her place as the head of the curia until his departure for Normandy in May 1119.[101] After William died, Roger of Salisbury finally emerged as the power second only to the king. But there was a difference between Roger's authority and that which had belonged to Matilda and William as members of the king's family. As Bates pointed out, nearly all of Roger's writs are either confirmed by the king, refer to the king's authority, or put off any action until the king's return.[102] Although the same could be said about some of Matilda's writs, there is another element to the wording of Matilda's charters that is wholly missing from those of Roger. Matilda clearly considered herself to be more than just a deputy or substitute for her absent husband. When Matilda referred to the exchequer as 'my court and the court of my husband' or offered to extend 'the king's and my peace' to the canons at Worcester or Waltham, she was using language that no mere vice-regent could have used. When she granted fairs or extensions of fairs and sealed exchequer documents with her own seal, that of 'Mathildis secunda regina Anglie', she was not acting solely as a substitute for the king but was exercising authority in her own right as queen. This queen was, as the monk of Ely described her, 'not dissimilar from the king in competence'. And, although Matilda recognized that her unofficial power as an intercessor was as important as the more visible authority she wielded in the curia, she did not consider herself to be just an adjunct to the king. When Matilda of Scotland was the queen of England, the queen was an integral part of the institution of monarchy.

Of course, to understand the queen as a political figure, more than just a narrative of her public activities is needed. Part of any analysis of the Anglo-Norman monarchy must involve the 'who' as well as the 'what' of history. In a very real sense, the political history of the early Anglo-Norman realm is the history of the great families who rose to prominence at the Conquest, and of the 'curiales' who rose to found new great families in the generations that followed. The shifting relationships among the king, the queen, their household officers, the 'curiales', and the great magnates of the realm (lay and ecclesiastical) provided the dynamic through which constitutional issues were raised and resolved. Those relationships were created and defined in the very public context of the court, and at court the queen was a major player in the contest for favor and patronage. Therefore, to unravel the political history of

---

[100] Eadmer, *Historia novorum*, 239. Roger of Hovedon has Ralph going over alone, by the counsel of the queen and certain of the nobles. See *Chronica Magistri Rogeri de Houedene*, 1: 171. Also, Simeon of Durham, 'Historia regum', 250.
[101] *Orderic* 6: 224.
[102] Bates, 'Origins of the Justiciarship', 11.

the Anglo-Norman state we need to know not only what the queen did and what her powers were but also who was present with the queen, whose advice she valued, and why and to whom she dispensed lands, offices, gifts, and all the other signs of royal favor.

Many fruitful studies of the Anglo-Norman elite have used the witness lists of royal and private charters as the focus of prosopographical studies of the court, but that approach alone will not serve here.[103] Too many of Matilda's charters have been lost, and there is no assurance that those that remain provide a representative sample of the whole. There are several chance references to Matilda's gifts surviving in sources other than her *acta*, indicating that many more charters must have been issued than now survive. With thirty-seven names from fewer than thirty charters as a basis, the lost charters become crucial, for one or two more attestations per person could considerably change the picture as it now stands. And, compounding the problem, in several of the charters that survive in cartulary copies, the scribe has indicated with phrases such as 'et aliis' that the witness list has been omitted or truncated. In one important charter, many more men are listed in the body of the instrument as present when the case was decided than actually appear as witnesses to the ensuing writ, raising questions about those charters that do not provide such convenient information.[104] The possibility has also been raised that witnesses to some *acta* may have been added after the instrument was actually issued. For instance, it may have been seen as good policy for the beneficiary to show the writ around in the locality it concerned and gain the assent of regional magnates to any transactions. But even with all these caveats, the witness lists to Matilda's charters can be used to provide clues about the makeup of Matilda's entourage. To the clues from the witness lists we can add information from the *arengae* and bodies of the charters and also narrative evidence that shows the queen at work with one or more members of the *curia regis*. When these scraps of information are pieced together, the outline, if not the detail, of the queen's activity becomes clearer. These charters show that Matilda and her advisors regularly met with and heard the pleas of what must have been a constant stream of visitors and petitioners to the court, both at Westminster and during her journeys. Although it is impossible to make claims about the relative importance of more than a few of her attestors, we can see that, throughout the reign, Matilda interacted with the groups of men who formed the 'select and stable body' of the *curia regis*, as well as with the local officials whom she consulted when the court traveled throughout England. Finally, like other members of the European royalty and aristocracy, Matilda relied on her family members as witnesses. Her brother

---

[103] For examples, see Everett Crosby, 'The Organization of the English Episcopate under Henry I', *Studies in Medieval and Renaissance History* 4 (1967): 1–89, and the work of C. Warren Hollister, especially 'The Rise of Administrative Kingship, Henry I and the Anglo-Norman Magnates', and 'Magnates and "curiales" in Early Norman England', originally published between 1973–1980 and reprinted in *Monarchy, Magnates and Institutions*. Also, 'The Viceregal Court of Henry I', in Bernard S. Bachrach and David Nicholas, edd., *Law, Custom, and the Social Fabric in Medieval Europe: Essays in Honor of Bryce Lyon* (Kalamazoo, 1990): 131–44. For scepticism about the value of the prosopographical approach, see Emma Mason's review of Hollister, *Monarchy, Magnates and Institutions*, in *Medieval Prosopography* 9 (1988): 105–13.

[104] *RRAN* 2: 1000.

David and her son William both served as witnesses to her deeds, William once and David three times. She also maintained her own staff, the *curia reginae*, who helped to administer and manage her demesne. The evidence tentatively suggests that the queen was expected to maintain these officials out of her own resources. The subsequent careers of many members of the queen's staff show that belonging to the queen's household carried prestige and the possibility of advancement to higher office and great wealth. The discussion below approaches the attestors to Matilda's charters in two groups. The first are those men who attested in a public capacity either as *curiales*, local officials, or landholders with an interest in the transactions being recorded. The second group of attestors consists of those men who were members of Matilda's own household.

In an article which first appeared in 1978, C. Warren Hollister analysed the vice-regal arrangements of Henry's reign and compiled lists of Henry's most consistent attestors from between c.1111 and c.1130, as well as of his household officers.[105] Most of Matilda's attestors appear on Hollister's lists, yet only a few of them witnessed the queen's charters with any consistency. This lack of consistency is attributable more to the paucity of the queen's charters than to any other cause. Of the vice-regal group, Roger of Salisbury was Matilda's most frequent witness by far, attesting eight times, including four of the six 'acta' definitely not connected with the queen's demesne lands. Roger's attestations are scattered throughout the eighteen years of Matilda's reign, confirming Kealey's conclusion that the bishop and the queen normally worked together during Matilda's lifetime.[106] Robert Bloet, the bishop of Lincoln, attested three times for the queen, twice in connection with the queen's gifts to churches and once on a vice-regal writ concerning land in his diocese.[107] Robert and his diocese were themselves objects of Matilda's patronage. Early in the reign, at Henry's request, Matilda ceded some of her demesne property to Robert and his cathedral church.[108] Walter, the castellan of Gloucester, is the only local magnate to appear on the queen's witness lists more than once, and it is possible that all three of his attestations took place within a short period surrounding the Michaelmas court of 1111.[109]

Two-time attestors include royal servants such as the stewards William de Curci and Adam de Port and Ranulf the Chancellor.[110] Other members of

---

[105] Hollister, 'Rise of Administrative Kingship', 226, 241.
[106] See *RRAN* 2: 567, 906, 909, 1000, 1090, and 1190, as well as both charters from the *Cartulary of Worcester Cathedral Priory*. For Matilda and Roger, see also Kealey, *Roger of Salisbury*, 31–2.
[107] *RRAN* 2: 906, 1180, 1198.
[108] *RRAN* 2: 526, 535.
[109] Walter of Gloucester appears as a witness to *RRAN* 2: 1001, and the writ extending the peace of the king and queen to the canons of Worcester (*Cartulary of Worcester Cathedral Priory*, entry #40, p. 26). He was also listed as being present when the case described in *RRAN* 2: 1000 was heard. He is the only witness listed in the Eye Priory Cartulary to the queen's charter in favor of the monks there (*Eye Cartulary* 1: 34).
[110] William's attestations are for *RRAN* 2: 971, 1000. William de Ponte and Geoffrey de Clinton attested *RRAN* 2: 906. For Adam de Port, see *Cartulary of Worcester Cathedral Priory*, 139, entry #262, and *RRAN* 2: 1000. Adam witnessed one of the Worcester charters (above) and *RRAN* 2: 1000. His first attestations seem to have been for Queen Matilda, and he attested with some regularity in England from 1111 to 1129. The editors of *Regesta* 2 imply that he died in 1131. He was a landholder in Herefordshire and a patron to the monastery of Holy Trinity at Tiron. Ranulf attested *RRAN* 2: 906 as chaplain, and #1090 as chancellor.

Henry's English vice-regency appear only once as attestors for the queen, although further study of the charters themselves sometimes adds to what can be gleaned from the witness lists. For instance, Richard de Belmeis, the bishop of London, only witnessed one charter, but analysis of other parts of the queen's *acta* show that she and the bishop worked together closely. Five of the queen's charters include the bishop among the addressees, and he is listed as present in 1111 at the Michaelmas accounting when Faritius of Abingdon made his plea. Since many of Matilda's patronage projects benefited the city of London and its surroundings, Bishop Richard must have advised and influenced the queen on many more occasions than is demonstrable by attestations alone.[111] The name of Nigel d'Oilli, castellan at Oxford, appears only once as an attestor in the surviving *acta*, although he may also have been present when Faritius appeared before the Exchequer.[112] One-time attestors also include the treasurers Geoffrey de Clinton and William de Ponte de l'Arche, Urse d'Abitot and the dapifers Hamo and Eudo.[113]

Although the witness lists cannot provide more than pointers toward those who influenced the queen, they do supplement what is known about the magnates and *curiales* of the early part of the twelfth century. Several men not among Hollister's list of vice-regal figures of 1111 attended Matilda's court and witnessed more than once for her. Robert Malet, England's first master chamberlain, died about five years too early to be included in Hollister's analysis, but he witnessed twice for the queen. His first attestation for Matilda was from London in 1104, and the next year he witnessed a charter issued in York, indicating that he was with the queen's itinerant court during the king's second trip to Normandy.[114] Robert's presence among the queen's advisors lends further support to Hollister's arguments against Orderic Vitalis' assertion that Robert was disseised and banished from court in 1102.[115] Another of Matilda's witnesses, Michael of Hanslope, held land of the queen and appears to have begun his rise to power in her service, possibly as one of her chamberlains.[116] Michael first appears as the castellan of Rockingham, in an area that

---

[111] Richard's sole attestion is *RRAN* 2: 971. He is among the addresses in *RRAN* 2: 902, 906, 909, 1090, 1180, all concerning grants to religious foundations in London or her lands at Waltham, which lay within the diocese of London, and is listed among those present when *RRAN* 2: 1000 was issued.

[112] *RRAN* 2: 1000 lists a William de Oilly among the witnesses to Faritius' case. Hollister notes that William was either an otherwise unknown relative of Nigel's or a scribal error for Nigel himself. See Hollister, 'Rise of Administrative Kingship', 227, n. 10 and 233, note to table two. Also, *RRAN* 2: xv.

[113] For William de le Pont de l'Arche and Geoffrey de Clinton, see *RRAN* 2: 906. Urse d'Abitot witnessed *RRAN* 2: 535 along with Hamo dapifer. Eudo was a well-rewarded royal servant and relative of the Mandeville clan who eventually held lands in England worth c.£500. See Hollister, 'The Misfortunes of the Mandevilles' (originally published in *History* 58 [1973]: 18–28), *Monarchy, Magnates and Institutions* 123–34, and 'Magnates and curiales', 109–10.

[114] *RRAN* 2: 674 (from London) and 765 (from York).

[115] See *Orderic* 6: 18, claiming that Malet was stripped of his possessions for supporting Curthose in 1101. That Robert continued to attest royal charters for several years after that date was noticed by Geoffrey H. White, 'The Fall of Robert Malet', *Notes and Queries* 12th series, 12 (1923): 390–1 and accounted for by Hollister, 'Henry I and Robert Malet', originally in *Viator* 8 (1977): 63–81, and reprinted in *Monarchy, Magnates and Institutions*, 129–36. Also, C. P. Lewis, 'The King and Eye: A Study in Anglo-Norman Politics', *English Historical Review* 104 (1989): 569–87.

[116] In 1141, Empress Matilda gave Barrowden, with its soke, to her chamberlain, William Mauduit, who paid a relief of 50 marks of silver for the property (*RRAN* 3: 581) William was Michael's son-in-law, and Michael had previously held the land. In between, Henry I had given the land at farm to William

formed a traditional part of the queen's holdings and which may also have belonged to Matilda. About 1106, Michael received large grants out of her lands in Rutland.[117] One of her charters in his favor was issued from Rockingham.[118] Michael witnessed a grant issued at Exeter in 1103, indicating that he might sometimes have traveled with the queen.[119] He became a major landholder in the shires of Huntingdon and Northampton, several times serving as a witness for Earl David.[120] Later in Henry's reign he became attached to the king's retinue and received many royal privileges that were passed on to his son-in-law and successor, William Mauduit, the founder of the influential Beauchamp family. Michael's gradual rise to power can be traced in the witness lists to the king's charters, where, over time, his name rises from among the last witnesses to a place of increasing prominence.[121]

Many of England's episcopal figures attended the queen's court or appeared before her from time to time when she traveled to their dioceses. Bishop William Warelwast of Exeter's sole attestation in the queen's 'acta' was to a grant issued in Devonshire.[122] Southern has argued that Rannulf Flambard, the bishop of Durham and former favorite of William Rufus, wisely avoided the court during Henry's reign. Certainly he never recovered anything like the prestige and influence that he had enjoyed under Rufus, but the charter evidence from Henry's reign indicates that he did not suffer unduly once he was restored to his see. A series of royal confirmations survives to show the process of his recovery of episcopal property that had been annexed by local landholders during the absences of both Flambard and his predecessor, William of St Carileph.[123] When Matilda traveled to the northern part of the kingdom, Flambard was in attendance. He witnessed the queen's charter in favor of Selby Abbey in either 1107 or 1108. He was also present at Winchester during the Canterbury/York debates in 1109, for at least part of the exchequer meeting of Michaelmas 1111, and he was with the court for the dedication of St Albans in

---

d'Albini. Empress Matilda's charter refers to giving land to 'William Mauduit, my chamberlain', land which her mother had given to his 'antecessor', Michael de Hansclape. The text does not specify whether Michael is his antecessor as holder of the land, or of the office, or both.

[117] Michael received the Rutland estates of Barrowden, Luffenham, Seaton and Thorpe. See *RRAN* 2: 1090 and 536. See also Gaimar, *L'estoire des Engleis*, lines 4132–40, for the Anglo-Saxon queen's relationship to Rockingham.

[118] *RRAN* 2: 743.

[119] *RRAN* 2: 632.

[120] See Lawrie, *Early Scottish Charters*, #LVII, p. 51, and no. LXXI, p. 58.

[121] See *RRAN* 2: 818a, for the queen's gifts. Michael may have had some connection with Bishop Maurice of London (See *RRAN* 2: 749, where Michael is the first witness to a concordat between the bishop and Eustace III of Boulogne). He held a fief created from the principal lands that had been held by Winemar the Fleming in 1086. The king and/or queen probably created the fief in return for services rendered and it may not have been heritable. Michael gradually garnered numerous royal privileges, including freedom from tolls and passage money throughout England *(RRAN* 2: 1674, 1846) and rights of pasturage in the royal forest *(RRAN 2*: 1847). After the queen's death, Michael traveled with the king's retinue in Normandy *(RRAN 2*: 1204). His lands were held in return for service and reverted to the crown upon Michael's death. The king later gave his daughter and heiress to William Manduit, along with many of Michael's former privileges. For brief discussions of Michael's origins and holdings, see Mason, 'Magnates, "Curiales", and the Wheel of Fortune', 133. See also Emma Mason, ed., *The Beauchamp Cartulary: Charters 1100–1268* (London, 1980), xxxvii.

[122] *RRAN* 2: 632.

[123] See *RRAN* 2: 540, 645, 560, 562, 575, 589, 590, 642, 925, 1181.

1115.[124] Everett Crosby's analysis of episcopal attestations placed him fifteenth in frequency of attestations among the forty-four men who headed English and Welsh dioceses during Henry's reign.[125] William Giffard, Rufus' chancellor, whom Henry elevated to the see of Winchester, also attested two of the queen's surviving charters.[126] Other bishops who served as witnesses to various of the queen's writs and donations include Hervey of Bangor and John of Bayeaux who each appear once in the surviving *acta*. John of Sees attested twice for the queen. The future bishops Thomas of York and Waldric of Laon each attested one of the queen's charters while still in the king's service.[127] Other infrequent attestors include members of the king's household, local officials, and regional magnates, such as William Peverel of Nottingham, who attested only when the royal household was visiting their areas.[128] Witness lists at best are only imprecise indicators of the interplay among those who attended court, but there can be little doubt that those who attested regularly, such as Roger of Salisbury and Robert of Lincoln, enjoyed some prominence within the royal circle. The negative side of the equation is more problematic, because, as the case of Ralph Basset makes clear, infrequent attestation does not necessarily indicate that an individual was not influential at court. Ralph Basset nowhere appears as an attestor for the queen, although his importance as a justiciar is apparent from many sources, including Orderic's narrative account of the case of Bricstan of Chatteris. Likewise, Thurstan, the king's chaplain and future archbishop of York, never witnessed for Matilda but was present for the exchequer session of 1111.[129]

[124] *RRAN* 2: 1001. Southern treats the career of Rannulf Flambard, including his decline and soft landing in Henry's reign, in 'Rannulf Flambard', in *Medieval Humanism and Other Studies*, 183–205. A more recent and sympathetic treatment is J. O. Prestwich, 'The Career of Ranulf Flambard', in Rollason *et al.*, ed., *Anglo-Norman Durham*, pp. 300–10.

[125] Crosby, 'Organization of English Episcopate', 6–7. Crosby's rankings are adjusted to allow for the length of time each man held the episcopate.

[126] *RRAN* 2: 526, 906.

[127] Hervey of Bangor, John of Sees, and John of Bayeaux attested *RRAN* 2: 675. Thomas the Chaplain appears as a witness to *RRAN* 2: 887 and is listed as present for the case described in *RRAN* 2:1000. John of Sees also signed *RRAN* 2: 808. Waldric served as Henry's chancellor from about Michaelmas 1102 until 1106. He captured Robert Curthose at the Battle of Tinchebrai (6 September 1106) and was promoted to (or bought) the bishopric of Laon the same year. See H. W. C. Davis, 'Waldric the Chancellor', *English Historical Review* 26 (1911): 84–9, and also the entry in the *Dictionary of National Biography* 7: 813 (listed under Galdric). This entry discusses gifts that Matilda sent to France that the bishop confiscated for his own use.

[128] William Peverel of Nottingham was probably a local justiciar under William II and during the early part of the reign of Henry I (see Hollister, 'Magnates and "Curiales" in Early Norman England', 226, Table 1). The one-time attestors not discussed above are Ralph of Tew (*RRAN 2*: 565), Grimbald the Physician (*RRAN* 2: 567), Roger de Courselles (*RRAN* 2: 674), Eudo Dapifer, 'T' fitz Count (*RRAN* 2: 887), and Giffard de Clare (*RRAN* 2: 906). Most of these men are identifiable in other records. Grimbald the Physician, an associate and countryman of Faritius of Abingdon, assisted the queen during her first pregnancy and appears later as a physician to the king, attesting Henry's charters from time to time. Roger Courselles was an occasional witness to royal 'acta' between 1104 and 1121. The editors of the *Regesta* believed 'T' fitz Count to be Ottuer, a son of earl Hugh of Chester, who died along with the king's son in the wreck of the White Ship. Giffard de Clare was probably a relative of bishop William of Winchester, part of the numerous and influential Clare family.

[129] For Thurstan, see *RRAN* 2: 1000 (appendix I, 1), and Nicholl, *Thurstan, Archbishop of York, 1114–1140* (New York, 1964). For Ralph Basset, see Doris M. Stenton, *English Justice between the Conquest and Magna Carta* (Philadelphia, 1964), 60–2, and W. T. Reedy, 'Were Ralph and Richard Basset Really Chief Justiciars in the Reign of Henry I?', in Bernard Levy and Sandro Sticca, edd., *The Twelfth Century* (Binghamton, NY, 1975): 74–103.

Turning to the second group of attestors, members of Matilda's household, we can infer from the charters that she employed a staff of (at minimum) about four men at any given time. Her staff included a chancellor ('cancellarius'), a chamberlain ('camerarius'), and one or more chaplains, whose duties included secular business as well as any religious duties they might perform. Matilda's first chancellor, Reinhelm, served the queen for only three years before being appointed to the see of Hereford. Only one of the queen's charters he attested survives. Reinhelm also attested two of Henry's charters in conjunction with the queen.[130] Bernard, who was already a clerk in the queen's service, replaced Reinhelm. Bernard witnessed seven of the surviving queenly 'acta', more than anyone other than Roger of Salisbury. He also witnessed three of Henry's charters, two in conjunction with the queen. His duties may have included serving as a liaison between the queen's officers and those of the king. The charter Bernard witnessed for Henry in the queen's absence is a confirmation of one of Matilda's charitable gifts.[131] Another of Henry's charters includes the clause 'per Bernard', indicating that his authority was accepted by the king's officials when he instructed the scribes to draw up the writ.[132] As the queen's chancellor, Bernard held property on the royal demesne in the city of Winchester for which he was released from the customary duties and fees.[133] Bernard served as the chancellor for twelve years before being promoted to the see of St David's, where, as the first Norman to head the diocese, he was both effective and controversial.[134] Matilda and Bernard must have worked well together, and it was certainly accepted that she would want to attend his consecration in September 1115. While he was bishop of St David's, Bernard was once called upon to testify about the terms of a donation he had witnessed while in the queen's service. Robert Gernon's gift of the church of Wraysbury to St Peter's, Gloucester, was contested by Gernon's successor, William de Montfichet. Bishop Alexander of Lincoln held an inquiry to determine the terms of the grant. Because he could not be present to testify orally, Bernard described the transaction in a letter to Lincoln's bishop. The letter details some of the ceremony that normally preceded the issuance of a donation charter. Bernard testified 'that I was present and saw and heard this: Robert Gernon gave to St Peter and to Peter, the abbot of Gloucester and his monks, the church of Wraysbury and the church at Laverkerstoke, and all things that pertain to those churches'. He informed Alexander that King Henry had issued a writ confirming those gifts and that he, Bernard, 'saw my lady, Queen Matilda, conduct Robert Gernon to the altar of St Peter's, Gloucester, when he,

---

[130] See *RRAN* 2: 571 (for the queen), and #544 and 613 (for the king). Reinhelm is always identified as the queen's chancellor in his attestations.
[131] For Bernard's attestations for Matilda, see *RRAN* 2: 565, 624, 675, 743, 808, 906, 971. He witnessed *RRAN* 2: 906, 1041, for Henry, in conjunction with the queen, and also appears as an attestor to Henry's confirmation of Matilda's grant to York (*RRAN* 2: 675 is Matilda's grant, #720 Henry's confirmation).
[132] *RRAN* 2: 698.
[133] Biddle, ed., *Winchester in the Early Middle Ages*, entry 83, p. 47. Bernard's holding was outside the west gate of the city on land held in part by the king and in part by the bishop of Winchester. By 1110, Bernard had encroached upon the king's street by a foot. He received 24s in rents on the property.
[134] See W. S. Davies, 'Materials for the Life of Bishop Bernard of St David's', *Archaeologia Cambrensis* n.s. 19 (1919): 299–322.

standing by the queen and several others, confirmed this gift by laying his knife on the altar'.[135]

Along with her chancellors, Matilda employed lesser staff functionaries: her chamberlains and chaplains. These men seldom or never attested for the king. Matilda's first known chamberlain, Aldwin, attested her charters as early as 1104 and remained in the household throughout Matilda's tenure as queen. He held large estates in Tottenham of her brother David and, after the queen's death, part of his rent was diverted to paying for an annual memorial service for the queen and her parents. Emma Mason conjectured that Aldwin also exercised local jurisdiction in Waltham because several of Matilda's charters concerning Waltham's property in Essex and nearby areas are addressed to him.[136] A charter granting the monks of Selby Abbey income from one of her manors just outside Rutland in Lincolnshire lists Aldwin among the addressees just before 'all her servants in Rockingham', indicating that he may also have held property of her in Rockingham.[137] The second Winchester survey lists property in the city formerly held by 'Alwin the Chamberlain', presumably the queen's servant, the only known royal chamberlain with that name in the period. Located not far from the royal palace on the south side of the High Street, the property was worth 110s 8d in 1148.[138] Aldwin's holdings at Waltham (and possibly in or near Rockingham) suggest that at least some of the queen's servants were maintained from the revenues of her demesne property. The queen also drew at least one chaplain, Geoffrey, from Waltham, for between 1108 and 1115 he attested a grant to Waltham as 'Geoffrey the queen's chaplain and canon of the said church'.[139] By 1115, Geoffrey had been named as dean of the chapter at Waltham. Other members of the queen's staff are known only by name. Odo Moricus, or Moire, attested several of the queen's charters. The *Regesta* editors deduced that he was probably attached to the queen's chapel, but nothing further is known of him.[140] Even more shadowy are the chaplains Albin, who received the prebend of the church of Stretton, part of the queen's demesne in Rutland, and John, who became the head of the leprosarium Matilda established at Holborn.[141] A document from the reign of Henry II describes John as one of Matilda's chaplains and the former head of the leprosarium, but his tenure cannot be dated securely. Concerning the church of Stretton, an inquest of 1276 revealed that 'queen Maud had the advowson and she gave it to a certain chaplain, Albin'.[142] It is just possible that this Albin may be the same person as Aldwin the chamberlain. There is no record that Aldwin the chamberlain was a priest, and he had at least one son who succeeded him on his lands in Tottenham. Of course, married priests, or at least priests with sons, were not

---

[135] *Gloucester Cartulary* 2: 166, entry #705.
[136] Aldwin witnessed *RRAN* 2: 675, 906, 971, 1090, 1108 and 1143. See also Emma Mason, 'Westminster Abbey and the Monarchy', Hollister, 'Vice-Regal Court of Henry I', 134–5, and especially G. W. S. Barrow, ed., *Regesta regum scottorum: The Acts of Malcolm IV, King of Scots 1153–65* (Edinburgh, 1960), 104–5, and #6, p. 134.
[137] *RRAN* 2: 887.
[138] Biddle, ed., *Winchester in the Early Middle Ages*, p. 81, entry 128.
[139] *RRAN* 2: 1090.
[140] *RRAN* 2: 674, 1090.
[141] *VCH Middlesex* 1: 206–10.
[142] *VCH Rutland* 2: 150.

uncommon at the Anglo-Norman court. It is also not impossible that Aldwin may have entered the priesthood late in life, as indeed did Bernard, who was consecrated as a priest only one day before receiving the bishopric of St David's. Alternatively, and more likely, this Albin could be an entirely different person, an otherwise unknown member of the royal household, whose income derived at least in part from Matilda's holdings in Rutland.

The queen's household also consisted of an unknown number of ladies-in-waiting. Three of these, Emma, Christina, and Gunnhilda, are known to history because they chose to enter the church after the queen's death. They seem to have attached themselves to a hermit near the present site of Kilburn Wells. In 1128 they were deeded land at Kilburn, where they established a house for Augustinian canonesses, or possibly Benedictine nuns. This house, founded in honor of St John the Baptist by Abbot Herbert of Westminster, remained a dependency of Westminster Abbey until the Dissolution. It used to be thought that the *Ancrene Riwle* was written for the nuns at Kilburn, but this view has been discredited by modern scholarship that shows the rule to date from the thirteenth century.[143]

The court of the Anglo-Norman kings and queens was exciting, lively, and turbulent. Under William Rufus, the court had been dominated by his military associates. Contemporaries complained about the decadence, perversion, and extravagance of the king and his servants. But after a series of royal reforms between 1105 and 1108 the court of Henry I and his wives became more and more a center of education, artistic and literary refinement, a virtual birthplace of the chivalric refinements of the later twelfth century. The court drew people from all classes, and under Henry I curial service brought with it the possibility of 'dazzling advancement'. But, as Emma Mason has made clear, the stakes were high, and the players must often have been desperate.[144] If a curial family could not succeed within a reasonable amount of time in making itself indispensable to the king or alternatively, too dangerous to be ignored, the family could and often did sink socially, politically, and economically until it finally fell out of the baronial class. But even though Henry and Matilda maintained a much more orderly establishment than had been the case in the wanton days of the Red King, their court still was not a place for everyone. Early in the reign, Matilda had employed a chaplain named Ernisius, but fed up with 'long conversations in court intrigues, and experienced in their manifold false subtleties, he at last by the mercy of God retired to the happy Sabbath of a hermit's life'.[145] Ernisius eventually teamed up with William, a refugee from the court of Rufus, and together they began to practice eremitical lives in an abandoned church in the

---

[143] Flete, *History of Westminster Abbey*, 87–8.
[144] Mason, 'Magnates, "Curiales", and the Wheel of Fortune', 118–40. For complaints about Rufus' court, see Eadmer, *Historia novorum*, 192, and *Anglo-Saxon Chronicle*, s.a. 1097 as well as Hollister, 'Courtly Style and Courtly Culture', 8–10.
[145] Translation of 'The History of Llanthony Prima' (BL Cotton Ms. Vespasian Dx), in Robert Atkyns, *The Ancient and Present State of Glocestershire* (second edition, London, 1768), 263. For Ernisius, see George Roberts, 'Llanthony Priory, Monmouthshire', *Archaeologia Cambrensis* 1 (1846): 201–45; E. W. Lovegrove, 'Llanthony Priory', *Archaeologia Cambrensis* 97 (1943): 213–29. Before leaving court, Ernisius witnessed *RRAN* 2: 675 for the queen.

old county of Monmouthshire in Wales. Within a few years, the two were persuaded to take on followers, and they founded what became the Augustinian house of Llanthony Prima, with Ernisius as the first prior. According to the history of the house, written in the late twelfth or early thirteenth century, Henry and Matilda wanted to enlarge the establishment, offering the canons extensive lands, but William and Ernisius, perhaps soured by their earlier experiences, politely refused, preferring to remain poor. This action, though, was not typical of officials of the Anglo-Norman church, many of whom maintained close and fruitful ties to the court. Deeply pious despite her refusal to become a nun herself, Matilda established several ecclesiastical foundations and, in addition, exercised a great deal of influence over the direction of Henry's patronage. The relationship between Matilda and the church is examined in Chapter 5.

5

Mater, Nutrix, Domina et Regina: Queen Matilda and the Church

If modern historians have found Matilda of Scotland worthy of mention at all, it is usually because they have found her interesting in one of the contexts of queenship discussed elsewhere in this book. They have cited her because her marriage symbolizes the blending of the English and Norman peoples after the Conquest, or because as a political figure she represents a final stage of the exercise of female power in the face of the rise of administrative kingship. Matilda was also a patron of art, music, and literature, and several modern authors have portrayed her as a harbinger of a new, courtly image of women created in the later twelfth century. But when chroniclers of her own day wrote of Queen Matilda, they were more likely to mention her religious dedication, benefactions, or good relationships with prominent churchmen than any other facet of her personality or her reign. Granted that most of these commentators were monks and so naturally inclined toward ecclesiastical concerns, it is still clear from the sources that Queen Matilda, both by inclination and because her royal position demanded it, was a major influence on the Anglo-Norman church.

Matilda's part in the political issues concerning the church, such as the Investiture Contest, the issue of papal legates in England, and the question of the Canterbury primacy, has been touched upon earlier. This chapter focuses on the less official side of the queen's relationship with the church, including what can be known about Matilda's religious sensibilities and personal piety. We will look at how that piety played out in her relationships with individual churchmen and in the ecclesiastical foundations that she patronized. As a landholder, the queen exercised jurisdiction over important monasteries, and out of her resources Matilda established several new foundations. As queen, she helped determine the direction of royal and aristocratic patronage. In particular, her sponsorship of the Augustinian canons was crucial to that order's success in England. Her influence extended well beyond the borders of the Anglo-Norman realm, for she corresponded with several continental bishops and sent gifts to their churches. In addition to the good works she accomplished because of her public position, her personal piety and obvious dedication to religion provided an example for both court and kingdom. Indeed, it is chiefly because of her many good works and gifts to churches that clerical and monastic chroniclers gave her the cognomen *Mathilda bona regina* which was often used to distinguish her from the numerous other Matildas of the Anglo-Norman period. The inscription on her tomb, which comes from earlier chronicler summaries, provides an oft-quoted example of the medieval assessment of her character: 'If we wished to speak of her goodness and probity of character, a day would not be sufficient.'[1] Fortunately, the engraver was exaggerating a little, for it is indeed our purpose here to reconstruct, as far as it is possible, 'her goodness' by examining the extent and direction of the queen's patronage. Only through exhaustive analysis of her gifts can we determine what the queen gave and to whom, and perhaps most importantly, why she chose to patronize a given foundation or order. Once again, her charters provide the bulk of the evidence, although in this instance, her letters and the chronicle notices are almost as revealing.

Several of the chroniclers who discussed the queen in a religious context included personal anecdotes describing some facet of Matilda's relationship with their particular houses. While some of these anecdotes seem too stereotypical to be authentic, they are still valuable for understanding both the contemporary reputation of Queen Matilda and the expectations about queenly piety that they reveal. One of these stories, narrating an event that apparently took place during the 1105 Easter court, appealed to the medieval imagination to the extent that some version of it was repeated by numerous chroniclers throughout the twelfth and thirteenth centuries. It eventually made its way into hagiographical legend when, in the fourteenth century, the hagiographer John of Tynemouth appended it to his abbreviated version of the *Life of St Margaret*. This story probably served as the basis for the seventeenth-century Bollandist investigations into Matilda's sanctity.[2] Because the story was so widespread and because it reveals so much of the queen's religious sensibilities, it is worth reading in full from the earliest of the medieval versions, that of Aelred of Rievaulx, who heard the story straight from Matilda's younger brother David. Aelred writes in David's voice:

> When I was a youth, serving at the royal court, one night I was in my quarters with my companions. I don't remember what we were doing, I went up to the queen's apartments when I was summoned by the queen herself. And, behold! The place was full of lepers, and there was the queen standing in the middle of them. And taking off a linen cloth she had wrapped around her waist, she put it into a water basin, and began to wash and dry their feet and to kiss them most devoutly while she was bathing and drying them with her hands. And I said to her, 'My lady! What are you doing? Surely if the king knew about this he would never deign to kiss you with his lips after you had been polluted by the putrefied feet of lepers!' Then she, under a smile, said, 'Who does not know that the feet of the eternal king are to be preferred over the lips of a king who is going to die? Surely for that reason I called you, dearest brother, so that you might learn such works from my

---

[1] See *Cartulary HTA*, 230.
[2] It forms the conclusion of John of Tynemouth's 'Life of St Margaret' in BL Cotton Tiberius Ei, printed in Horstmann, ed., *Nova legenda angliae*, 174–5. The Bollandists several times considered and rejected evidence for Matilda's sanctity. See *Acta Sanctorum*, 30 April, 1 May (Volume 1 for May, p. 4), 7 August (Volume 2 for August, p. 183), and 10 November (Volume 2 for November, p. 419).

example. Take some cloths and do in the same way what you see me doing'. At that behest I became greatly terrified, and I was unable to say anything in return to her. For I had not yet come to know the Lord, nor had his Spirit been revealed to me. And she began vehemently insisting, and I, to my shame, laughingly returned to my companions.[3]

Dramatic though it may be, this incident does not read like the invention of medieval churchmen. Queen Matilda, like her mother before her, took a special and personal interest in the most miserable of her subjects. Indeed, in this case, Matilda's action was probably taken in conscious imitation of the practices of her parents. As part of their Lenten devotions, Margaret and Malcolm fed and washed the feet of several hundred paupers daily, and their charitable activities are narrated in detail by the author of the *Vita Margaretae*.[4] If the *vita* were written shortly after the 1104 opening of the tomb of St Cuthbert, Matilda could have even been reacting directly to the stories she would have recently read.

It is difficult to appreciate the impact the queen's good works on behalf of the lepers had on the medieval imagination without recalling the fear and horror that the disease inspired during the Middle Ages. Leprosy, the 'unclean disease' of biblical times, had been rare in western Europe until the middle of the eleventh century, but it spread rapidly after that, particularly in urban areas. The symptoms of leprosy were imprecise, and the diagnosis covered many other conditions in addition to that which modern physicians diagnose as leprosy. Medieval people knew no cure for leprosy, and the only treatment was to segregate sufferers in order to confine the contagion. The spread of the disease reached its peak in England during the twelfth and thirteenth centuries, and during that time, those suspected of being carriers were gradually subjected to civil penalties which came to include the loss of common law rights. Sufferers were excluded from churches and other places where people assembled. Nor was the leper allowed to wash in springs or sunning water, touch women or children, or give any object to anyone. The afflicted were allowed to speak with others only in the open air and only when clothed in a distinctive costume that revealed their condition.[5]

When Matilda invited lepers into her chambers to set an example to others, it provided a graphic demonstration that the queen's faith and her concern for the victims of the disease were stronger than her fear of contagion. Judging by the number of times the story was repeated, the queen's gesture deeply impressed her contemporaries. And while the deed certainly had its intended effect, it was more than just a spontaneous and dramatic incident. In addition to the example she set by accepting the sufferers and actually touching their wounds, she showed her continuing concern for them through her patronage of institutions dedicated to their care. She founded a hospital dedicated to St Giles, which was still caring for up to fourteen lepers at the Dissolution in 1539. The leper population had declined by the sixteenth century, and Matilda's foundation would have housed many more than fourteen, although Kealey's figure of forty

---

[3] Aelred of Rievaulx, 'Genealogia regum anglorum', *PL* 195: 736.
[4] *Vita Margaretae*, paragraphs 18, 21–3.
[5] See Kealey, *Medieval Medicus*, 89–93 and 101–4; Honeybourne, 'Leper Hospitals', 4.

is perhaps high.[6] St Giles was located just outside the boundaries of the city of London, on the old Roman road which linked London to Oxford and the west of England. We have some idea of the size of the institution, both because of later land transactions and because Matthew Paris included a drawing of the complex, which he labeled a 'memorial for Queen Matilda', in the autograph manuscript of his *Chronica majora*.[7] It is impossible to determine if or how closely the foundation of the hospital was related to the incident in the queen's chambers, since the actual founding date of the hospital is not known. The best evidence points to a date late in the reign, perhaps as late as 1118. Matilda endowed the hospital with an annual income of sixty shillings from the revenues of Queenhithe, which was to be spent on food for the residents. The hospital also received the soke of the parish of St Giles. Later in the century, Matilda's grandson King Henry II added another ninety shillings and five pence per annum to provide candles and habits. Henry's charter refers to a former chaplain, John, who may have been the original chaplain appointed by Queen Matilda.[8]

In addition to founding and supporting St Giles, Queen Matilda was also a benefactor to the leprosarium at Chichester. It is even possible that she founded the hospital, dedicated to St James and Mary Magdalen. Kealey speculated that the queen also patronized a hospital of St James in Westminster that housed thirteen diseased women. While this is a possibility, the founding date of the Westminster hospital is not known. The earliest textual documentation of its existence is in a charter of Henry II, although archaeological evidence does support an earlier date.[9] The fact that the queen showed no repugnance for the disease and even braved the possibility of contagion so that she might demonstrate her Christian charity probably did have some effect in mitigating the mistreatment of lepers in the early part of the twelfth century.

Matilda, like her mother, was sometimes attracted to holy ascetics and both women were capable of the kind of humiliation of the body that medieval writers often seem to delight in describing. Margaret's fasting was so severe that she contracted a stomach infirmity that bothered her all her life. Matilda kissed the rotting feet of lepers and, according to William of Malmesbury, during the Lenten season walked barefoot between the palace and church in Westminster, clad in a haircloth tunic hidden under her royal robes.[10] Margaret's biographer describes how she approached the Scottish *culdees* (hermits) and tried to offer them material gifts. When these offerings were refused, Margaret requested that the holy men lay out some task for her, tasks that the biographer claims were never refused.[11] Matilda's best-known interaction with hermits is described by

[6] Kealey, *Medieval Medicus*, 90.
[7] 'Memoriale Matildis reginae scilicet hospitale Sancti Egidii quod est Londoniae'. Cambridge, Corpus Christi manuscript MS XVI–XXVI, f. 110v. The drawing is reproduced in Suzanne Lewis, *The Art of Matthew Paris in the Chronica majora* (Berkeley, 1987), Figure 47.
[8] *Monasticon* 6, part two, 635–6. See also *VCH Middlesex* 1: 206–10.
[9] Henry II's charter is printed in *Monasticon* 6,2: 635–6. See also *VCH Middlesex* 1: 206–10. The small hospital at Chichester is discussed in *VCH Sussex* 2: 99. For the London foundations, see *VCH London* (1909), 542–6, and Kealey, *Medieval Medicus*, 90. Honeybourne discusses the archaeological evidence for St James, Westminster, in 'Leper Hospitals', 54.
[10] *Gesta regum*, 757.
[11] *Life of Saint Margaret*, paragraph 19.

the late-twelfth- or early-thirteenth-century author of the history of the foundation of Llanthony Prima, the Welsh monastery founded on the site of the hermitage first inhabited by William and Ernisius, the queen's former chaplain. The author describes a meeting between the queen and the two holy men. William, a former knight who had once served William Rufus, continued to wear his mail shirt next to his skin under his outer clothing. Wearing the armor was to remind him that even though he had abandoned his former procession, he needed to remain armed against Satan, an even more formidable enemy. The queen, having heard of William's manner of dress, but 'not sufficiently acquainted with the sanctity of this gentle man', caused him great embarrassment when she asked him if she could put her hand inside his cloak and feel his undergarment. When the blushing hermit submitted to the Matilda's request, she used the occasion to slip a purse of gold into his shirt. According to the author of the monastic history, William desperately wanted to refuse the gift by was persuaded to keep it for his growing community so as not to offend the queen.[12]

There is simply no way of knowing whether this incident or anything like it, ever occurred. Matilda was in Gloucestershire on at least one occasion, but one should always suspect the details of an anecdote committed to writing ninety years or so after the event. It may have been based on oral tradition or even on written records that no longer survive. Llanthony's historian goes on to report that as William and Ernisius began to attract more followers, Henry and Matilda offered to enlarge their properties, but the monks of Llanthony preferred to remain free from court ties, and so managed to politely refuse their would-be royal patrons. But as the community continued to grow, and it became apparent that some form of organization was necessary, William and Ernisius began to examine the religious communities that they saw around them, seeking the most perfect rule. Eventually, on the advice of Archbishop Anselm, known to both men from their days in royal service, William and Ernisius decided to adopt the rule of the Augustinian canons.[13] The account does not say that Queen Matilda exerted any influence in this direction, but given her interest in both the house and the order, it would be surprising to find that she was not involved. The Augustinians were at the forefront of the English monastic revival of the twelfth century, a revival that culminated in the introduction and spread of the Cistercians later in the century. Introduced to England from the continent, the Augustinian rule stressed that the members of the clergy were obliged to follow the *vita apostolica*, which some were beginning to interpret meant interaction with the world rather than seclusion from it. In England, the Augustinian, or Austin, canons fed the hungry, nursed the sick, and generally took care of the physical needs of the urban communities in which they tended to live. This group appealed to the practical nature of England's queen, and Matilda became an early and fervent patron of the new order. The priory of St Botolph's at Colchester is generally reckoned to be the earliest Augustinian foundation in England, and Matilda witnessed both of

---

[12] British Library Cotton Julius Dx, 41v, translation adapted from Robert Atkyns, 'The History of Llanthony Prima', in *The Ancient and Present State of Gloucestershire*, 266.
[13] Atkyns, ed., 'History of Llanthony Prima', 265.

Henry's charters favoring the house. At the same time, Henry issued a charter confirming the gifts of Count Eustace of Boulogne to St Botolph's, so it is tempting to see a connection between the queen's interest and the interest of her brother-in-law, Eustace (Eustace was married to Matilda's sister Mary).[14] Matilda had definitely become a patron of the order by 1107 or 1108, when, on the advice of Archbishop Anselm, she founded the Augustinian priory of Holy Trinity at Aldgate in London. There is, however, some indication that she had begun to favor the order earlier, just possibly as early as 1102. The fourteenth-century *Anonimalle Chronicle*, produced at St Mary's York, is bound with some earlier prefatory material, including a few folios containing valuable information about the see of Carlisle. This material indicated that 'Henry I, because of the industry and counsel of Queen Matilda, placed regular canons in the church of Carlisle.'[15] This is nothing more than a possibility for historians remain uncertain about the foundation dates for the Augustinian abbey and later, the cathedral church and diocese of Carlisle. Antiquarian sources of the sixteenth and seventeenth century cite 1102 as the date for the foundation of the Augustinian house, about five years before the next appearance of Augustinian canons in England. Over a century ago, J. E. Prescott argued persuasively for 1122, corresponding with Henry's tour of the north during that year. A date four years after Matilda's death is too late to credit her with more than perhaps suggesting to Henry that Augustinian canons would be appropriate at that spot. But Prescott had not seen the marginal note in the Cotton manuscript, and he accused Leland of having invented the 1102 date.[16] V. H. Galbraith pointed out that the founding of a monastery is seldom a single, datable event, but rather a process that sometimes stretched over many years before being immortalized in a foundation document.[17] It is possible, as Prescott suggested, that an informal community had sprung up at Carlisle before any official foundation, and that Matilda had some interest in that community, perhaps urging Henry to persuade the recluses at that spot to adopt the Augustinian rule rather than affiliating with Benedictines or Cluniacs. The cases of Llanthony Prima and Luffield Priory, both of which enjoyed the queen's patronage, certainly fit this pattern. But however she first became interested in the Augustinians, she had certainly chosen them by 1107, when she began to work on the foundation of her own house, Holy Trinity Aldgate, in conjunction

---

[14] *RRAN* 2: 568, 569, 862, and 863. See also Dickinson, *Origin of the Austin Canons*, 98–103.

[15] 'Rex Henricus primus per industriam et consilium Matildis regine constituit canonicas regulares in ecclesia Karleoli'. See V. H. Galbraith, ed., *The Anonimalle Chronicle, 1333 to 1381*, xlvi. The chronicle is bound with a number of miscellaneous fragments including the one discussed here. The marginal notation also occurs on a British Library MS, Cotton Vitellius Dvii, f. 58r.

[16] For arguments in favor of 1102, see Leland, *De rebus Britannicis collectanea*, ed. Thomas Hearne (6 vols, London), 1: 120–1, as well as the discussion in *VCH Cumberland* 2:131. Prescott's arguments are in Prescott, ed., *The Register of the Priory of Wetheral* (London, 1897), 478–80. See also J. C. Dickinson, 'Walter the Priest and St Mary's, Carlisle', *Transactions of the Cumberland and Westmoreland Antiquarian and Archaeological Society*, n.s. 59 (1969): 102–14; H. S. Offler, 'A Note on the Early History of the Priory of Carlisle', *Transactions of the Cumberland and Westmoreland Antiquarian and Archaeological Society* 55 (1965), 176–81. The most recent and thorough treatment of the early diocesan history of Carlisle is by Henry Summerson, 'Old and New Bishoprics: Durham and Carlisle', in Rollason *et al.*, edd., *Anglo-Norman Durham*, 369–80.

[17] Galbraith, 'Monastic Foundation Charters', *Cambridge Historical Journal* 4 (1934), 214.

with Archbishop Anselm, who had been an early partisan of the Augustinians.[18] The chapter of Augustinian canons that she established in the heart of London became an enormously influential house that served to colonize many of England's later Augustinian foundations. In addition, Matilda was an early champion of Merton Priory, another important house begun in 1114 by the royal official Gilbert the Sheriff. Like Gilbert, other members of the royal curia followed the example of the queen and directed their religious patronage toward the order of Austin canons. Together, Holy Trinity and Merton colonized nearly a dozen daughter houses, all but a few of which were founded by members of the royal circle.[19]

The story of the foundation of the church of Holy Trinity, Aldgate, is preserved both in a full cartulary and through the *Historia fundationis*, a short chronicle account of the early days of the church that precedes the collection of charters in one manuscript. On the advice of Anselm, Matilda deeded property near London's 'Old Gate' to form the nucleus of a new foundation of Augustinian canons on the site of an unused church. The *Historia fundationis* supplies the foundation date of 5 April 1108, but it is unclear just what stage of the foundation that date signifies. It may have been the date of the rededication of the church, when the foundation charter was issued, when the canons moved into their dwellings, or perhaps when the prior took office.[20] The former church on that site had belonged to Waltham Abbey and had formerly paid the canons of Waltham a rent of thirty shillings a year. In return for the loss of the London church, the queen gave the clerks at Waltham the rights to at least one mill on her demesne land at Waltham.[21] She endowed Aldgate with the London gate and its soke and a cash income of two-thirds of the tolls from the city of Exeter, which amounted to £25 12s 6d annually.[22] Matilda chose Norman, a canon from St Botolph's in Colchester, to head the new community. Norman, who had probably once been a pupil of St Anselm, had been one of the first of the English churchmen to take serious notice of the Augustinian foundations springing up on the continent. He had gone to France with Anselm's aid to observe the canons there and had then returned to St Botolph's where the Augustinian rule was adopted. Holy Trinity was colonized with canons from Colchester but soon surpassed its mother house in size and importance. Norman used the queen's endowments to provide rich plates, books, copes, and other luxury items for the church. These purchases depleted his resources to the extent that the canons ran short of food and had to depend upon the generosity of local housewives who literally began to supply their daily bread.[23] Despite this less than auspicious beginning, Holy Trinity quickly flourished, becoming the first large-scale foundation of the Augustinian canons within England.

[18] J. C. Dickinson, 'Saint Anselm and the First Regular Canons in England', *Spicilegium Beccense* (Paris, 1959), 541–6.
[19] Dickinson, *Origin of the Austin Canons*, 129.
[20] *Cartulary HTA*, xiv, 224.
[21] See *RRAN* 2: 908. 909; also *Waltham Charters*, entry 6, pp. 5–6. The Holy Trinity Cartulary refers to one mill, but Ransford notes that there had been three mills at Waltham in 1086. See *Cartulary HTA*, xiii–iv, 1, 200, 224.
[22] *Cartulary HTA*, entry 4, pp. 224–5. See Parry, 'The Fee Farm of Exeter', and *VCH London*, 465.
[23] *Cartulary HTA*, 228.

A few years after Holy Trinity's foundation, Gilbert the Sheriff, who enjoyed a warm relationship with the queen, began to plan and build his own great house, which he located within easy range of London in the county of Surrey. The queen's hand can be seen in the early history of Merton, which is related in the foundation history, preserved in a single London manuscript.[24] According to the account, Matilda was quite fond of Gilbert, who is described in the *Historia* as an extremely successful courtier, and she often visited the site of the new foundation to see the progress of the building. On at least one occasion, Matilda took care to bring her son William, so that he could play on the grounds. Providing a rare glimpse of Queen Matilda as a mother, the author of the *Historia* notes that Matilda hoped that William's happy childhood memories associated with the site might induce him to remain a lifelong patron of the priory.[25] The Merton account also proudly reports that Matilda treated Gilbert as if he too were her own son. According to the chronicler, when Gilbert's mother died, he made no public announcement, fearing the sad news might affect the mood at court. Matilda noticed his sadness, and after making inquiries, summoned Gilbert to find out why she had not been notified. When Gilbert responded that he was afraid that excessive grief might disturb her royal dignity, Matilda took him by the hand and offered to adopt him as her own son and treat him with maternal affection as long as she lived.[26] Not surprisingly, Merton's historian reported that the premature deaths of the queen and the prince proved to be a great loss to the house.[27]

The impact of the queen's alliance with the Augustinian canons and their influence on the Anglo-Norman church was summed up a half-century ago by John C. Dickinson. Dickinson concluded that the enormous success of the Augustinians in England is probably attributable to the reputation quickly established by the canons at Holy Trinity and Merton, which captured the attention of both the aristocracy and the urban citizens who came into contact with the canons. Holy Trinity, he wrote, was 'founded at the hub of English life by two of the most venerable members of English society, under a prior full of primitive enthusiasm, at a time when the great flood of monastic revival had scarcely stirred the rather placid waters of English church life. Even without the testimony of [the *Historia*] we should be safe in surmising its enormous and instant popularity.'[28]

In discussing the queen's piety and religious benefactions, several authors have speculated that Matilda had a particular devotion to one or more of the saints. The queen gave relics to various foundations and was willing to accept that the saints had interceded on behalf of the imprisoned Bricstan of Chatteris, so it is clear that she shared in the medieval devotion to the cult of the saints. Denis Bethell surmised that she adhered to the cult of Mary Magdalen since she had donated relics of the repentant prostitute to Westminster Abbey. Mary Magdalen was also among those to whom Holy

---

[24] Colker, 'Latin Texts concerning Gilbert', 241–72.
[25] Colker, 'Latin Texts concerning Gilbert', 250.
[26] Colker, 'Latin Texts concerning Gilbert', 259.
[27] Colker, 'Latin Texts concerning Gilbert', 250.
[28] Dickinson, *Origin of the Austin Canons*, 129.

Trinity was dedicated.[29] Norman Cantor wrote of her particular devotion to the Virgin.[30] Others have suggested that she took an interest in the developing cult of Edward the Confessor.[31] The cult of John the Evangelist was becoming quite popular in England during the early twelfth century, particularly among the Augustinians. Alison Binns places John the Evangelist as the second most popular saint to whom Augustinian foundations were dedicated (the Virgin was first), 'in marked contrast to his relatively low position among the Benedictines'.[32] There is some evidence that Matilda may have shared in the new devotion. At some point during her reign Bishop Herbert Losinga of Norwich sent the queen a prayer to St John which he had composed for her. The prayer requests the saint's intercession in helping the queen recover from a long illness. Written in the first person a prayer to be read aloud by Matilda herself, the text promises the Evangelist that 'before all other saints I have chosen you alone; indeed, I have chosen as my patron the one whom I hear to have been beloved above all others'.[33] In a separate letter, Herbert associated the earthly queen with the Virgin Mary, the queen of heaven. Addressing Matilda directly, he added that, 'by the side of this queen, I say, you are standing, doing service with insatiable longing to her sons Christ and John'.[34] Matilda referred to the Evangelist in her correspondence, when chiding Anselm about his prolonged absence from the kingdom. 'Remember', she wrote to the exiled archbishop, 'that you hold the place of John, the apostle and beloved of the Lord, whom the Lord wished to survive him so that this virgin, cherished and chosen above others, might take care of the Virgin Mother. You have undertaken the care necessary of Mother Church.'[35] As further evidence of Matilda's devotion to the Evangelist, her donation to Westminster Abbey included relics of John's coffin.

Matilda's interest in the Evangelist did not rule out her interest in other heavenly intercessors. In her letters to Anselm, she made reference to St Martin of Tours, the saint on whose day she and Henry were married.[36] Finally, Matilda once asked the monks of Malmesbury about her relationship to their patron, Aldhelm, and appeared to know details of his life; she may have discussed this saint with Faritius and William of Malmesbury, both of whom wrote hagiographical accounts of Aldhelm. But, although the queen was associated with the cults of several saints, analysis of Matilda's benefactions, devotion, and of the literature written for the queen fails to prove a special and sustained interest in any save the Evangelist. Somewhat unexpectedly, there is no evidence that Matilda shared the devotion to the Holy Cross shown by both her mother and her brother David. Matilda's interest in Aldhelm and Edward the Confessor is likelier to have been more genealogical than devotional, and she made donations of all kinds of relics to various foundations. Her donations to

---

[29] Denis Bethell, 'The Making of a Twelfth-Century Relic Collection', in J. Cuming and Derek Baker, edd., *Popular Belief and Practice*, Studies in Church History 8 (Cambridge, 1972), 69–70.
[30] Cantor, *Church, Kingship, and Lay Investiture in England, 1089–1135* (Princeton, 1958), 297.
[31] For example Mason, 'Westminster Abbey and the Monarchy', 199–216.
[32] Alison Binns, *Dedications of Monastic Houses in England and Wales* (Woodbridge, 1989), 37.
[33] *Epistoli Heriberti*, letter #18, p. 35.
[34] *Epistoli Heriberti*, letter #25, p. 49.
[35] *Anselmi opera omnia*, 4: 151 (letter #242).
[36] *Anselmi opera omnia*, 4: 151 (letter #242).

Westminster included a liturgical garment and a bone from the fourth-century virgin and martyr Christina, as well as the relics of Mary Magdalen and John the Evangelist. The choice of Mary Magdalen as a dedicatee for Holy Trinity simply reflected the patron of the existing church on the site. Matilda expanded the dedicatees to include the Holy Trinity, and in her charters she always referred to the church as the church of the Holy Trinity. The Aldgate dedication may reflect the influence of Anselm and the Canterbury dedication, or that of her mother's foundation in Dunfermline. Matilda I's foundation in Caen is also dedicated to the Holy Trinity, so Matilda II may have seen dedicating her church to the Holy Trinity as a way of honoring both her mother and mother-in-law.

But if Queen Matilda had any particularly idiosyncratic direction to her piety, it was that she tended to ally herself with, and seek direction from, living churchmen. Like her mother, who discussed theological questions with the most learned men in the Scottish realm, Matilda turned often to spiritual prelates for her spiritual guidance. It is quite possible that some of Matilda's building projects were inspired by her conversations with the episcopal architect Gundulph of Rochester. The *Vita Gundulphi* records Matilda's devotion to the elderly bishop of Rochester and the fact that she turned to him for guidance during the early part of her reign.[37] Her letters to Anselm reveal that she considered him to be her spiritual father, just as in the preceding generation Matilda's mother had turned to Archbishop Lanfranc, Anselm's predecessor. After Norman was appointed to Holy Trinity, he became the queen's confessor. Other ecclesiastical figures also influenced the queen's spiritual development. Matilda received guidance and comfort from such well-known prelates as bishops Ivo of Chartres, Marbod of Rennes, and Hildebert of Lavardin. The letters and poems composed for the queen by her ecclesiastical advisors forms a body of evidence that shows these prelates at work guiding, admonishing, and exhorting the queen toward the image of an ideal queen. All the writers acknowledged that Matilda had a voice in determining public policy and the direction of royal patronage. Many of the letters reveal an attempt to mold the queen's religious thinking and inspire a sense of duty toward Rome, as was the case with the letters of direction written by Anselm and Pope Paschal during the Investiture Contest. The biography of Margaret, the letters of continental bishops, the poems of Hildebert and others all contain a similar message: the successful queen is one who supports the arts, effects commerce, influences legislation, and most of all, strives to bring England into closer conformance with the dictates of Rome. About a third of the text of the *Life of St Margaret* describes and praises the Scottish queen's attempts to bring about some of the very changes that were being called for during the Gregorian reform movement.[38] The text provides a not very subtle reminder to the queen that she has and should use the capacity to help bring about necessary changes within the realm.

There are some references to the Virgin Mary in the writings addressed to Queen Matilda. In an era when devotion to the Virgin, already well-established

---

[37] *Vita Gundulphi*, 61.
[38] *Vita Margaretae*, paragraphs 13–16.

in Anglo-Saxon England, was gaining popularity throughout western Europe, it was only natural that the image of the queen of heaven would be applied to her earthly counterparts. Some of Matilda's correspondents drew on Marian imagery in fleeting passages. Bishop Ivo of Chartres cited the special devotion of 'the queen of the Angles to the queen of the angels', and Hildebert of Le Mans saluted the queen by expressing the hope that one day she would stand 'at the right hand of God, clothed in a golden garment.' Hildebert was making direct reference to Psalm 44, which medieval churchmen interpreted as a reference to the Virgin.[39] Herbert Losinga drew on the same passage, standing Matilda 'next to that queen to whom none but queens do service; queens whose happiness increases according to how devoutly they pay her homage'.[40] Judith Abbott argued that the authors of the coronation *ordo* most likely adapted Marian hymns for the coronation of the Anglo-Norman queens to reinforce the queen's sacrosanctity and authority. Abbot believed that the *ordo* would also plant the idea that the earthly queen should be regarded as a representation of Mary in the same manner as the king was seen as the vicar of Christ.[41] Since there were many aspects to the medieval image of the Virgin, Marian language could easily be adapted to reinforce many roles played by the earthly queen. John Carmi Parsons has shown that, during the thirteenth century, both learned writers and ordinary petitioners were apt to stress the Virgin's capacity for merciful intercession and to draw on the language of Marian liturgy when requesting the earthly queen's intercession with her spouse.[42] Hildebert used the image of the rose, often associated with Mary, in a poem that may have been intended as a panegyric to Matilda.[43] But although Matilda was often asked to intercede with Henry, her petitioners did not draw on the Virgin's capacity for pity and mercy when they asked her for action. Rather, in the fleeting passages that do explicitly refer to the Virgin, the writers stress the regal aspects of the Queen of Heaven, reinforcing and legitimizing Matilda's authority as an earthly queen. The scarcity of direct Marian imagery does not imply that ecclesiastical writers did not see Matilda as both merciful and capable of pity. The so-called Hyde chronicler, writing in the middle of the twelfth century, lauded Matilda as the 'glory of monks, the honor of clerics, the refuge of paupers, the consoler of the wretched, and to all who fled to her, insofar as it was permitted, a refuge of safety'.[44] The Aldgate chronicler gave Matilda perhaps the highest encomium of all when he praised her as an 'assiduous visitor of the sick, a continual reliever of the poor, a co-sufferer with prisoners, a minister to the pregnant, and not only the consoler of the lepers but one who was a most humble washer of them; and who in everything showed herself to be a most humble servant of Christ'.[45] Nor

---

[39] For Ivo of Chartres' letter, see *PL* 162: columns 125–6, letter 107. For Hildebert, see *PL* 171, column 289.
[40] *Epistolae Heriberti de Losinga*, letter #25, p. 49.
[41] Abbott, 'Political Strategy in the Coronation of Queen Matilda', Abstract in *Anglo-Norman Anonymous* 9 (1991), 5.
[42] Parsons, 'The Queen's Intercession in Thirteenth-Century England', in Sally-Beth MacLean and Jennifer Carpenter, edd., *Power of the Weak: Studies on Medieval Women* (Urbana, IL, 1995), 147–77.
[43] *PL* 171: 1444.
[44] Edwards, ed., *Liber monasterii de Hyda*, 305.
[45] *Cartulary HTA*, 223.

was maternal imagery lacking in their praises. Matilda's correspondents as well as the chroniclers often portrayed the ideal queen in maternal terms. To her subjects, she should be 'a kind mother from whom no one goes away empty-handed'.[46] To her demesne tenants she is to be 'a mother, a nurse, a kind lady, and a queen'.[47] Anselm urged her, 'with as much feeling as I can, and as much as I dare to presume upon Your Highness, I beg, I entreat, I beseech and I faithfully counsel you to apply yourself to the peace and quiet of the church of England, and most of all to her feeble sons'. The queen was to become their mother. 'Succor these orphans of Christ', Anselm urged, 'console and nurture like an evangelical hen under the wings of her protection.'[48] The elderly bishop of Norwich, Herbert Losinga, claimed that the queen had always been a 'very mother to me' in times of financial distress.[49] Matilda accepted, adopted, and even manipulated this imagery. She showed her friendship and favor by creating ties of fictive kinship, as was the case with Gilbert the Sheriff and the younger Anselm. She was called, and in some sense was, 'the common mother of all England'.[50]

If Matilda's image of herself as mother stretched beyond her own offspring and friends to include the entire kingdom, then she may have been willing to admit that she had a favorite child in the city of London. While William of Malmesbury's claim that she was content to remain at Westminster after the births of her children is exaggerated, Matilda did spend much of her time in or near London.[51] Matilda drew a great deal of revenue from London's Queen-hithe, but in return she directed much of her energy and many of her resources toward improving London and bettering the lives of its inhabitants. Both of the queen's major foundations, St Giles and Holy Trinity, were located in or just outside of the city.

In addition to the leprosaria and religious houses, Matilda provided purely practical benefits for London. To the modern mind, discussion of these improvements in a chapter on the queen and church may seem misplaced. However, the queen and her subjects would have considered these projects to be 'good works' for the benefit of her soul as much as for the welfare of those whose lives they improved. On Queenhithe, Matilda paid for a large bath-house that included London's first public toilet facilities.[52] The queen also built several bridges linking London and the surrounding countryside. The nineteenth-century collaborators Owen Manning and William Bray repeated a seventeenth-century account claiming that Matilda built a bridge on the London–Portsmouth road, in the Surrey village of Cobham, after one of her ladies drowned while trying to ford the river during a flood. That the queen built the bridge is well attested in the place-names of the area. The drowning

[46] *Vita Margaretae*, paragraph 18.
[47] *Anselmi opera omnia*, 5: 284–5 (letter #346).
[48] *Anselmi opera omnia*, 4: 207–8 (letter #288).
[49] *Epistolae Heriberti de Losinga*, 50–2 (letter #26).
[50] *Epistolae Heriberti de Losinga*, letter #25.
[51] *Gesta regum*, 757.
[52] Torry, *The Book of Queenhithe*, 14–17, 35. Also, Ernest L. Sabine, 'Latrines and Cesspools of Mediaeval London', *Speculum* 9 (1934): 303–21.

story first appears in the thirteenth century.[53] Two of Matilda's other bridges linked London and Essex. One of these, an arched bridge over the Lea, was built from stone and was extremely well engineered for its day. Known as the 'Bow Bridge' for its arched shape, it provided the major crossing between London and Essex well into the nineteenth century. Antiquarian sources repeat the charming if unlikely story that the queen had decided to build the bridge after she herself had been 'well washed' while making the crossing. According to the plans drawn in the early nineteenth century just before the queen's bridge was replaced, Bow Bridge had a chapel dedicated to St Katherine of Alexandria at one end. Medieval patrons often did place a chapel dedicated to the saint who was charged with protecting the travellers on the river on or near a bridge, but there are no drawings precise enough to allow conjecture over whether this chapel was originally part of the bridge or a later addition. The earliest text reference to the chapel dates from 1455.[54] Matilda charged Barking Abbey with the upkeep of the bridges over the Lea, and to provide the funds to do so she bought a mill in West Ham and gave it to the nuns of Barking.[55]

Modern commentators have sometimes accused Henry I and Matilda of being less generous in their patronage than other royal figures. Edward Kealey, summing up Matilda's benefactions, posited that the queen seemed to have a short attention span. 'On the whole', he wrote, 'Matilda was more interested in establishing policies than executing them. She liked to begin things and normally moved directly, even brusquely, to her objective.'[56] He also accused her of having cleverly made the citizens of London responsible for the upkeep of the hospital of St Giles. Others have pointed out that there were economic motives for preferring the Augustinian canons to the Benedictines, because patronage of the former 'conferred far more prestige on its founder than was warranted by the financial outlay demanded'.[57] Augustinian houses tended to be small and to be located on the sites of existing houses that were simply refounded as colleges of regular canons. Holy Trinity does seem to have been under-endowed, at least in the early days when the canons were reduced to relying on the charity of local housewives for their food supply. But Matilda's foundations were given perpetual sources of income – St Giles had an annual income, and the three bridges Matilda built were all provided with grants of land or money for their upkeep. The author of the Aldgate foundation history uttered not one word of blame amidst the many words of praise he had for his foundress. Medieval chroniclers, including Eadmer of Canterbury, who had perhaps the deepest reservations about the queen, agreed with the acclaim of the Aldgate writer. Even

---

[53] See Manning and Bray, *The History and Antiquities of the County of Surrey* (3 vols, London, 1909), 2: 732. The story was recorded in an *inspeximus* of 23 Henry III, the original of which was reported lost in 1780. See also *VCH Surrey* 3: 442.

[54] Alfred Burges, 'Account of the Old Bridge at Stratford-le-Bow, Essex', *Archaeologia* 27 (1893), 77–95, quoting Morant's history of Essex and the antiquarian John Stow.

[55] *VCH Essex*, 6: 44–5, 59–60, 90.

[56] Kealey, *Medieval Medicus*, 19.

[57] Jane Herbert, 'The Transformation of Hermitages into Augustinian Priories in Twelfth-Century England', in W. J. Sheils ed. *Monks, Hermits, and the Ascetic Tradition*, Studies in Church History 22 (Oxford: 1985): 144–5. See also Southern, *Western Society and the Church*, 245–8.

those who had some quarrel with Matilda agreed that, overall, she was deserving of praise for her piety, her generosity, and her ecclesiastical policies. But, however much contemporaries liked to stress the queen's piety and devotion to her subjects, there is a strain of tension in the accounts that cannot be ignored. At least at the beginning of her reign, the relationship between the queen and her tenants was not entirely harmonious. Her need for income led her to tax her churches harshly, giving rise to William of Malmesbury's often-quoted lament:

> The news of her liberality consequently spread throughout the world, and hither flocked in troops any scholars who had a name for singing or turning verses; happy he thought himself, the man who could please his lady's ear with a new song. Nor were they the only recipients of her bounty; it went to all sorts of men, especially to foreigners, who might accept her presents and then advertise her fame in other countries. So deeply is the love of glory set by nature in the minds of men that scarce anyone is content with the precious fruits of a good conscience, and does not count it sweet, if he does something well, to have it spread abroad. Hence it was, they say – and indeed it was true, that our lady was beguiled into sweetening with presents all the foreigners she could, and kept the others dangling with promises that were sometimes honoured, and sometimes – indeed, more often – empty. Thus it came about that she did not escape the vice of prodigality, laid all kinds of claims upon her tenantry, used them despitefully and took their livelihood, winning the name of a generous giver but ignoring the wrongs of her own people.[58]

William's complaints cannot be dismissed as an aberration. Letters between Matilda and her continental correspondents bear witness to the truth of these allegations. These letters show a pattern wherein the queen would be approached by a churchman who paid tribute to her reputation for piety and generosity, then requested some benefit for himself or his church. As an example, early in the reign Bishop Ivo of Chartres wrote praising her prudence and holiness and suggesting they had interests in common that would make it fitting that they 'learn to esteem each other with a mutual love'. He had two of the canons from his church deliver the letter and added that 'they will acquaint you with the needs of our church and will accept as a blessing the gift that God will inspire you to give'.[59] That Matilda took the hint is evident from a later letter thanking her for sending church bells and for promising to provide a new roof for the church. The cathedral did eventually receive its new roof, as evidenced from an entry in the Chartres necrology. The scribe noted that among the queen's many gifts were 'a leaden covering for the church, a chasuble worked in gold, and forty pounds of money for the use of the brothers'.[60] An early letter from Anselm to Matilda corroborates William's complaint that Matilda mistreated the churches in her demesne. Sometime in late 1103, he wrote to chasten her. 'Scarcely had I left England', he reprimanded, 'than I

---

[58] *Gesta regum*, 757.
[59] *PL* 162, Epistola 107, columns 125–6.
[60] *PL* 162, Epistola 142, columns 148 and 149. The gifts are enumerated in Eugene de Lépinois and Lucien Merlet, edd., *Cartulaire de Notre Dames Chartres* (3 vols, Chartres, 1862–5), 3: 204.

began to hear, concerning the churches that are in your care, that you were behaving other than is right for them and for your soul.' He went on to admonish her to behave in such a way that, 'not only in those churches of which I speak, but also among the entire English church', she might be known as 'a mother, a nurse, a kind mistress, and a queen'.[61]

Matilda's reaction to Anselm's reprimand was both prompt and crafty, for she used the occasion not only to express her regret for her behavior, but also to point out that if Anselm had not left the kingdom, her errors would never have arisen. If her later actions are any indicator, her repentance was sincere. From that point onward, her relationship to the English church was harmonious, earning her the cognomen 'Matilda the Good Queen', from the priests and monastic chroniclers who commented on her life and reign. Hildebert went so far as to call her a defender of the church. When he wrote to her, evidently as she was recovering from a period of ill health, he praised her as one whose protection and respect for the law preserved the status and well-being of the church.[62] Even William of Malmesbury tempered his complaint, using the well-worn device of placing the blame for the queen's excesses on her greedy and grasping servants rather than on the queen herself. William may truly have believed royal servants to be the problem, but it is more likely that he was employing a convenient literary ruse. Even if he did believe the queen to be guilty of rack-renting, he ended his comments by pointing out that, in every other respect, Henry's queen was 'admirable and godly'.[63] It is difficult to know how much credence to give William's complaints, which were written soon after the queen's death. If Matilda did have tenurial rights at Malmesbury, then William's complaints that she continually misused her tenants might be treated with some caution, for it may indeed be the case that this was a simple instance of sour landlord–tenant relations. It may, of course, also be true that the queen did slip back into the practice of overtaxing her demesne properties, particularly after 1109, when Archbishop Anselm was no longer alive to restrain her.

Certainly Matilda of Scotland never showed a sustained and generous interest in any one foundation the way her predecessor Matilda of Flanders had done toward her foundation at Caen. But here is no need to see Matilda II as less than generous toward those foundations she did favor. Several modern writers have noted that the second quarter of the twelfth century saw a trend in aristocratic patronage toward smaller gifts and more conservative gifting.[64] Although Matilda died in 1118, perhaps her preference for smaller gifts to numerous establishments is best seen in light of this European trend. However, those who have accused Queen Matilda of 'sharing King Henry's gift for generosity on the cheap', are not entirely on the wrong track.[65] Analysis of Matilda's gifts to some Benedictine foundations points to the conclusion that she often did benefit

---

[61] *Anselmi opera omnia*, 5: 284–5 (letter #346).
[62] *PL* 171, column 290.
[63] *Gesta regum*, 757.
[64] See Stephen White, *Custom, Kinship, and Gifts to Saints: The Laudatio parentum in Western France 1050–1150* (Chapel Hill, 1988), especially pp. 22–3, and also Sharon A. Farmer, *Communities of St Martin: Legend and Ritual in Medieval Tours* (New York, 1991), 96.
[65] Brooke and Keir, *London, 800–1200*, 323.

from a reputation for generosity that cost her very little in actual lands or money. For instance, Abingdon, where her physician Faritius was abbot, was the recipient of several gifts soon after each of her children was born. None of these gifts came from lands directly controlled by the queen, nor did she lose anything because of her generosity to Faritius and his monks. A series of charters concerned the lead roofs and building materials from the isle of Andresey. These buildings where part of an elaborate complex that had formerly fallen under the abbey's jurisdiction but had been taken over as a royal hunting preserve shortly after the Conquest. By 1100, the buildings were uninhabited and beginning to fall into ruin when Matilda and Henry deeded them to the Abingdon monks.[66] Matilda received credit for a gift that technically was probably not even hers to give. Clauses in the donation charters indicate that her role had been to 'persuade' the king to cede the buildings to Faritius.[67] Two other gifts to Abingdon, which the queen confirmed, came to the abbey from the property of Robert Gernon, who, we may infer, found it difficult to say no to the queen. Charter evidence affirms that he and his heirs later repented of the grants that he made at the urging of Queen Matilda.[68]

Despite the fact that most of the actual benefits that accrued to Abingdon came from the king or members of the landed aristocracy, the abbey's historian shrewdly recognized the queen's role in directing patronage toward his abbey, and she received high praise in the pages of Abingdon's chronicle. The queen's patronage of other large Benedictine houses appears to have been less systematic than her relationship to Abingdon, leading to the conclusion that Abingdon benefited because of the personal relationship between the royal couple and Abbot Faritius rather than because of any special tie between the court and the house itself. Faritius had been Henry's choice to succeed Anselm as the archbishop of Canterbury, and the Abingdon chronicle tells us that Henry relied on the abbot's skill as a physician to the extent that he followed Faritius' prescriptions even when he disregarded the advice of others.[69] Robert of Meulan, Henry's chief lay advisor, had at least one of his twin sons educated at the abbey. Certainly Faritius was skilled at extracting tangible signs of the royal favor he so clearly enjoyed. During his tenure as abbot, Abingdon grew in size from twenty-eight to eighty monks, with its endowment and buildings growing at a commensurate rate.[70] And, as further evidence for the reason Abingdon was so favored, Edward Kealey has noted that royal patronage to Abingdon dried up almost immediately upon Faritius' death.[71]

We may detect personal motives behind much of the attention Matilda lavished upon the religious houses of England and France. Many of the gifts that enhanced the beauty of the churches of England and France of which the chroniclers spoke were exchanged between Matilda and her ecclesiastical

[66] Colvin, *History of the King's Works* 2: 895–6; *Abingdon Chronicle* 2: 49–52.
[67] *RRAN* 2: 565, 567.
[68] *Abingdon Chronicle* 2: 97–100, 106–7, 109–11. See also *RRAN* 2: 742.
[69] *Abingdon Chronicle* 2: 55.
[70] *Abingdon Chronicle* 2: 287–9; see also G. Lambrick, 'Abingdon Abbey Administration', *Journal of Ecclesiastical History* 17 (1966): 159–83.
[71] Kealey, *Medieval Medicus*, 68.

correspondents. Several letters of gratitude or solicitation are preserved in the letter collections of the leading churchmen of France. Hildebert of Lavardin wrote the queen a fulsome letter of thanks for the metal candlesticks she had recently had sent to him.[72] Another opulent candlestick went to the abbey of Cluny.[73] Matilda also gave gifts of liturgical garments embroidered in gold, the famous *opus anglicana* that was highly prized in medieval Europe. A gift to Westminster Abbey appears in a fifteenth-century inventory, and Ivo of Chartres once wrote asking for a high-quality cope. Ivo's letter makes the interesting but unsubstantiated claim that the queens of England had traditionally held the Virgin in high veneration, an excuse that he, as a servant of the queen of the angels, used as a premise through which to approach the queen of the Angles. In addition to the gifts we know of through surviving documentation, there were probably numerous other relics and precious liturgical objects commissioned by the queen for the men and houses she wished to favor. Waldric, the ill-fated bishop of Laon and one-time royal chancellor, is said to have confiscated for himself a gift that the queen had sent through Laon, evidently intended for a church in his diocese.[74]

Many of the donations that Matilda made to houses within England can also be linked to a personal connection. The queen extended the privilege to collect wood in the royal forest to Wilton, the abbey where she had been educated. The Pipe Roll of 1130 lists revenues in the amount of 41s for the customs of wood that Matilda gave to the church of St Edith at Wilton, as well as 35s 7d in respect to the fair that the king and queen conceded to the same church.[75] Matilda also made several gifts to Salisbury Cathedral, probably as signs of favor to Bishop Roger. Among these gifts were her rights in the markets of Salisbury and also the 'logs and beams and other wooden materials from the king's forest for restoring and conserving the church of Salisbury'.[76] The latter gift is another sign of the queen's interest in building projects of all types. Two gifts of manors from Matilda's demesne to Lincoln Cathedral were directed to its bishop, Robert Bloet, another member of the royal *curia*.[77] The gift of the land of Archil Morel to Tynemouth Priory must have given Matilda particular pleasure. Several chroniclers report that Archil had murdered the queen's father, King Malcolm, and while this tradition is uncertain, the fact that Matilda gave this gift for the benefit of her father's soul does tend to argue that Matilda believed her father had been murdered. Matilda often gave gifts for the benefit of the souls of her ancestors, but only in this single instance does Malcolm appear as the specific beneficiary of the queen's gift. In addition, Tynemouth Priory was dependent upon its mother church, that of St Albans, located just outside of London. It

---

[72] Hildebert, *PL* 171, columns 16–62.
[73] Joan Evans, *Monastic Life at Cluny 910–1157* (Oxford, 1931, repr. 1968), 94. See also Frank Barlow, *The English Church, 1066–1154* (London, 1979), 185, n. 35.
[74] Kate Norgate made this claim in her entry on Waldric in the *Dictionary of National Biography* (7: 813). I have been unable to locate her source.
[75] Hunter, ed., *Magnum rotulum scaccarii*, 12–13.
[76] *RRAN* 2: 1199 details the market privileges granted to the cathedral chapter; for the privileges of the royal forests see Jones and Macray, edd., *Charters and Documents Illustrating the History of the Cathedral, City, and Diocese of Salisbury*, 12.
[77] *RRAN* 2: 535, 743.

commemorated an early British martyr, and the cathedral was being rebuilt in the Norman style during the first two decades of the twelfth century. All of these factors together made St Albans an appealing target for the queen's generosity. St Albans' historians record that the queen and king were present for the rededication of the church on 28 December 1115, one of the few secure dates for the latter part of Matilda's reign.[78]

Matilda was a sporadic patron of Westminster Abbey, the resting place of her kinsman Edward the Confessor and his queen, for whom she had originally been named. Her most substantial gift, in material terms, was land along the abbot's wharf in London that had previously been held of her by the sheriff Hugh de Buckland. The ceding of the land to the abbey probably corresponded to Hugh's death in either 1116 or 1117.[79] According to one cartulary copy, some of Henry's gifts to Westminster were given 'at the prayer of his queen'.[80] Matilda was also a benefactor to St Mary's, York, to which she gave £6 worth of land in Belton-in-Axelholme. A large gift that she gave to the canons of St Mary's Huntingdon was probably prompted by family loyalty after her brother David became earl of Huntingdon. The land which she gave, in the Buckingham hundred of Stoke, had belonged to Robert Gernon in 1086. Perhaps her gifts to St Mary's, like the donations to Abingdon and Gloucester, were more royal confirmations than donations in their own right.[81]

In some instances, the circumstances surrounding Matilda's gifts are unknown, so her motives are impossible to discern. This is certainly the case with her gifts to St Mary's, York, and with land she ceded to Selby Abbey in 1107–8. The only known personal connection between Selby and the royal family is the uncertain tradition that Henry I had been born there.[82] The language of the register of Norwich Cathedral priory implies that Matilda played some part in the decision to turn the royal manor of Thorpe over to Bishop Herbert Losinga. The bishop approached 'the king and Queen Matilda, who is called "Matilda the Good", and by divine will procured the manor with all appurtenances and woods, for himself and his monks'.[83]

A few of Matilda's gifts bear the mark of impulsive generosity. She donated lands, revenues, and prebendary churches to houses in both York and Tavistock during royal visits to the counties of the recipients.[84] In some of these instances William of Malmesbury's report of the queen's tendency to promise more than she could deliver is borne out. As we saw in the previous chapter, it is not clear whether Matilda made the gift to York out of her own resources or whether this

---

[78] *Gesta abbatum S. Albani*, 1: 70–1.
[79] RRAN 2: 1180; John Armitage Robinson, *Gilbert Crispin, Abbot of Westminster: A Study of the Abbey under Norman Rule* (Cambridge, 1911), 155, entry #38. See also Emma Mason, 'Westminster Abbey and the Monarchy', 210.
[80] Armitage Robinson, *Gilbert Crispin*, 143–4.
[81] *Monasticon* 6, 1: 79–80. The queen's gift is known only through a confirmation charter King Henry issued c.1130. See *RRAN* 2: 1659.
[82] *RRAN* 2: 887. See J. T. Fowler, ed., *The Coucher Book of Selby Abbey* (2 vols, Yorkshire, 1891–3), 1: 25, entry 23; and Hollister, *Henry I*, 32.
[83] Saunders, ed., *The First Register of Norwich Cathedral Priory*, 28–9.
[84] For the York donation, see *RRAN* 2: 675, 808. For the donation to St Mary's, Tavistock, see *RRAN* 2: 632, and H. P. R. Finberg, 'Some Early Tavistock Charters', *English Historical Review* 62 (1947), 352–77.

charter was issued when she was acting in a vice-regal capacity during Henry's absence. Whatever the case, it does seem that the queen's gift was not fully thought out, or if it were, that the king and queen had not come to any agreement about the disposition of the prebend before Matilda made her bequest.

Perhaps the best example of Matilda's reputation for generosity outweighing the tangible benefits she conferred can be detected, throughout her reign, in the relationship she established with the monks of Durham. Sometime between 1107 and 1116, Matilda bestowed the Northumbrian church of Carham-on-the-Tweed on the monks of Durham.[85] But after the queen's death, the great northern baron Walter Espec gave the same church to his priory at Kirkham, a gift that Henry confirmed. Matilda's charter clearly claims jurisdiction over the church, and since the church did carry a dedication to St Cuthbert, the monks of Durham must have possessed it at some point. It may be that Matilda's gift was intended for her lifetime only. After her death, however, the monks of St Cuthbert continued to claim the property. The legal wrangling between the monks of Durham and the canons at Kirkham continued until March 1253 when an accord was finally reached and the monks renounced their claims.[86] The queen's relationship to the bishop of Durham and his monastic foundation was further complicated by the fact that the abbey of Waltham Holy Cross, which Henry gave to Matilda in demesne, had previously belonged to Durham and had owed rents and services to the northern bishop. When Matilda relieved the Holy Cross canons of these burdens, it cost the queen nothing but ultimately subtracted from the patrimony of St Cuthbert. For example, one of Matilda's earliest acts was to pardon the canons at Waltham from the annual duty to provide for the works and upkeep of the episcopal castle at Durham.[87] No compensation is recorded for the revenues lost to the northern bishop, who in any case was then in disgrace in Normandy. In another instance, Matilda ordered that land 'unjustly seized' by the bishop be returned to the canons of Waltham.[88] Later in the reign, however, Matilda did direct some of Waltham's revenues toward Durham, perhaps partly to compensate for earlier losses. When Brunig, a canon of Waltham, died, Matilda allowed his son Adam to inherit some property that Brunig had held of her, with the proviso that 14s annually of his rents should go to the monks of Durham. The strong minatory language in Henry's confirmation of Matilda's gift to Durham indicates that the diversion was understandably not welcomed by the canons of Holy Cross.[89] Durham was still the eventual loser, for it appears that the canons enjoyed the advantage of proximity and gradually regained control over the revenues of Adam's property.[90] Finally, Matilda's gift of the lands of Bewick and Lilleburn to the monks at Tynemouth Priory, a dependency of St Albans, was of lands previously

---

[85] *RRAN* 2: 1143.
[86] John Hodgson, *A History of Northumberland in Three Parts* (3 parts in 7 vols, Newcastle upon Tyne, 1858), Part 3, vol. 2: 150, and Kenneth Vickers, *A History of Northumberland* (15 vols, 1894–1940), 11: 12–13.
[87] *RRAN* 2: 526.
[88] *Waltham Charters*, entry 10, p. 7; calendared in *RRAN* 2: 902.
[89] *Waltham Charters*, 8. See also *RRAN* 2: 1109, printed in full on p. 332.
[90] *Waltham Charters* 7–10; see especially the dating note to entry #14, p. 9.

claimed by the monks of Durham. Those lands continued to be a source of contention throughout the Middle Ages. Our only medieval drawing of the queen comes from the margins of a fourteenth-century St Albans manuscript, a propaganda piece depicting the queen holding out a charter upon which it was confidently and emphatically asserted that 'Queen Matilda gave Lilleburn and Bewick to us.'[91]

There is another factor in the queen's connections to Durham and that concerns the royal relationship to Durham's bishop, the controversial Rannulf Flambard. Although Flambard had been restored to his see after supporting Curthose in the early years of Henry's reign and continued to participate in some court occasions, he never came close to regaining the trust and prestige he had enjoyed during the reign of William Rufus. As we have seen throughout the analysis of Queen Matilda's relationship to, and influence on, the Anglo-Norman church, the queen was always likely to lavish her gifts and attention on the churches pastored by men whom she liked and admired. There is no indication that Flambard ever belonged to that charmed inner circle of the queen's advisors. With no tie to Durham's bishop to encourage her benefactions, the question is why Matilda even tried to patronize St Cuthbert and his church. The answer lies in Matilda's close identification with her natal family. During the reign of Malcolm Canmore in Scotland, the monks of Durham had been highly favored by members of the Scottish royal house. Malcolm had been present when the foundations of Durham Cathedral had been laid, and Margaret held St Cuthbert in special veneration. Reginald of Durham's description of Margaret's gifts in the Durham treasury indicates that the Scottish monarchs had been generous to the monastery. An entry in Durham's *Liber vitae* records a confraternity agreement in which the monks received money to provide for the poor in return for masses for the souls of Matilda's parents as well as Matilda and her siblings.[92] The author of the *Life of St Margaret* had been a monk at Durham, and Margaret's confessor also joined the community after the Scottish queen died. In Matilda's generation, Durham continued to benefit from the patronage of the children of the royal house. Edgar, first of Margaret's sons to rule Scotland, gave the monks several villages and churches as well as rights of fishing and shipwreck along the Northumbrian coast.[93] Alexander, who succeeded Edgar I in 1109, was the only layman present at the opening of St Cuthbert's tomb in 1104.[94] As kings, both Alexander and David also favored the Durham community. One of Matilda's extant Durham charters includes a long list of family members whom the queen wished to commemorate through her gift: 'For the welfare of my lord King Henry and my son William and the welfare of my own soul and those of my brothers, and for the souls of my father and mother and brothers and sister[s]'.[95] The witnesses to the donation included Matilda's brother David, and in one of his earliest appearances in the record sources, her son William. Given Matilda's strong

---

[91] BL MS Cotton Nero Dvii.
[92] Stevenson, ed., *Liber vitae Ecclesie Dunelmensis*, 54.
[93] Lawrie, *Early Scottish Charters*, 16–18, entries 18–22.
[94] Simeon of Durham, *Historia regum*, 236.
[95] Durham, Library of the Dean and Chapter of Durham Cathedral, 1.3. Ebor.13.

interest in her ancestry and her close relationship with her siblings, it is not surprising that she, along with other members of her natal family, wished to show her devotion to St Cuthbert and his monks.

In light of the less-than-profitable relationship between Queen Matilda and the see and monastic chapter of Durham, it is remarkable that Durham's chroniclers showed no open hostility toward the queen. Rather, Simeon and Reginald of Durham, both writing in the twelfth century, maintained a circumspect silence about the queen and her affairs. Simeon commented briefly on the king's marriage and the queen's death but never expressed an opinion about Matilda. His reluctance to comment on Matilda stands in sharp contrast with the praise he lavished upon Margaret.[96] The failure to praise Margaret's daughter seems to be deliberate and is especially striking in light of the close relationship between Durham and members of Matilda's natal family. However, as we have seen, the brothers at Durham had very little reason to be grateful to the queen herself. In the case of Durham, that Matilda was mentioned at all probably had to do with any monastery's desire to credit members of the royal family with some sort of fondness for their houses. Like the monks of Abingdon, the brothers of Durham were quite aware that royal patronage of an abbey or order often brought benefits far beyond the value of the lands bestowed by the monarchs, because barons and members of the local aristocracy were often apt to direct their gifts toward foundations known to be favored by the king and queen.

In the final analysis, the key to understanding Matilda's impact on the people and the institutions of the Anglo-Norman church lies in personalities, not policies. There is no evidence to support the contention that she was a fervent backer of the papal reform, nor that she had a special devotion to any particular saint other than John the Evangelist. Although she did not share in her mother's devotion to the cross, she did share in Margaret's personal piety, and to some extent, her ascetic practices. Matilda's devotion to the church is evident. She used her visibility to teach others by example, both in the Lenten austerities she practiced and as a benefactor to various religious houses and orders. There are some constant features that emerge from an analysis of her patronage. Her concern for the needs of the citizens of London led to a lifelong interest in good works of a useful nature such as improving hygiene and caring for lepers. She seemed fascinated by building projects of all kinds. Her bridges and the lavatory complex at Queenhithe were among the most structurally advanced of their day. Several of the monastic foundations she favored were undergoing extensive rebuilding during the years of her reign. Most of all, the Augustinian canons benefited from her patronage. It is here that the queen's influence is perhaps most dramatically seen and most easily quantified, for the introduction of the Augustinian canons into England and the tremendous success of that order changed the spirit of the English church. But overall, in the relationship between

---

[96] Simeon of Durham, 'Historia regum', 192, 222. Simeon's passages on Margaret bear a close resemblance to passages in her *vita*. The earliest extant catalog of the Durham library, dating from about the middle of the twelfth century, reveals that the monks possessed a copy of the *vita*. See Thomas Rud, ed., *Codicum manuscriptorum ecclesiae cathedralis Dunelmensis* (Durham, 1825), 212.

Matilda of Scotland and the Anglo-Norman church, personal factors reigned supreme. Places associated with Queen Matilda's childhood or her ancestry were likely to be favored, as were those institutions headed by her friends and counselors. Anselm, whom she considered to be her spiritual father, backed her continual support of the Augustinian canons. Later in the reign, Prior Norman, who became her confessor, may have filled Anselm's place. The alliance between Queen Matilda and the prominent churchmen of the early twelfth century benefited the church in tangible ways. She used her own funds and demesne land for the benefit of the church, and she influenced the king and the Anglo-Norman magnates to do the same. She often interceded with the king in matters of policy toward the church or individual churchmen, although she was never the innocent dupe of her ecclesiastical allies. As we have begun to see in this chapter, and will continue to see in the following chapter, the queen's interest in the church also helped to further the arts. Some of her patronage involved funding works of great beauty, and she helped to finance some of the great achievements of Norman Romanesque architecture. Matilda was also a great lover of music, poetry, and literature, and in the final chapter devoted to the biography of the queen, I will explore Matilda's role in furthering the arts and making the Anglo-Norman church a center of artistic production and patronage.

6

Queen Matilda and the Arts

The period of Matilda of Scotland's life and reign was one in which a European 'high culture' flourished as never before. Architecturally, the Normans led the way in the creation and perfection of the techniques of stone vaulting and sculpture characteristic of the Romanesque style. At the same time, Anglo-Saxon craftsmen continued to practice the minor arts, at which they excelled, in post-Conquest England. The Conquest itself provided an impetus for both the production and the consumption of literature. The first extant verses in the Anglo-Norman dialect of French date from the turn of the twelfth century, and, at the same time, Latin poetry gained an audience in England largely through the works of continental poets such as Hildebert of Lavardin, Marbod of Rennes, and Baudri of Bourgeuil. As literacy became more widespread, so did the demand for books, and it again became a status symbol for members of Europe's aristocratic classes to own and use deluxe and expensive books, such as the Gospel Book owned by Matilda's mother, Margaret. Queen Matilda displayed a lively interest in many forms of the arts, and, under her influence, the Anglo-Norman court became a center of literary and artistic patronage. This chapter is devoted to an analysis of that patronage. The first aim of this analysis is to discern which artists and media the queen favored and why, and also to discover how far the queen's influence spread. Another goal of this chapter is to look at the messages that Matilda received in the literature directed to her. That literature, which took the form of history, saints' lives, the biography of her mother, courtly correspondence, and poetry, often contained didactic messages, and by examining its content, we can learn a great deal about contemporary ideals concerning queenship and a woman's place in feudal society. We will see Matilda reacting to those ideals by changing her behavior to reflect the texts she read. A secondary aim will be to discover, as far as possible, the degree of 'courtliness' that existed in the court of Henry I and Matilda, and how far activities at their court contributed to or were a part of the movement known as the Twelfth-Century Renaissance. Finally, I will look at the literary portraits of Queen Matilda and how writers of the mid-twelfth century and beyond exploited her good reputation to create an image of ideal queenship that soon existed independently of any historical reality.

In any survey of artistic production in post-Conquest England, commentators invariably and rightly stress the building programs of the Normans. Impressive achievements of both secular and ecclesiastical architecture are extant throughout England, and it is easy to imagine the effect these fortresses and fortress-like structures must have had on the native population, which had done very little in the way of large-scale construction. William of Malmesbury, who himself carried the blood of both Normans and Anglo-Saxons, commented on the difference in taste between the conquerors and their subjects, remarking that the English lived extravagantly in small and humble buildings, while the Normans and French lived moderately in large and proud structures.[1] The greatest skill of the Anglo-Saxon artisan lay in the production of portable and highly-perishable items such as jewelry, liturgical objects, and textiles woven or embroidered with precious metals and incrusted with jewels. These textiles, often made into liturgical garments, were sometimes designed and made by women, particularly women in convents. While the Normans appreciated the small-scale work of English artisans, their own skill and taste tended to be expressed in large and technically daring buildings epitomized by the cathedral at Durham. It is worth bearing this difference in mind when exploring the artistic taste and patronage of Queen Matilda, who after all has been held up as a representative of the blending of the Anglo-Saxon and Norman peoples.

At first glance, Matilda's taste seems to be completely Norman, with a special interest in building projects that showed the Normans at their ingenious best. Neither the leprosarium near London nor the priory of Holy Trinity in London, the two buildings with which she was most intimately associated, are extant, but surviving descriptions indicate that they were of the fashionable style and formidable scale introduced at the Conquest. The same scale is evident in other buildings associated with the queen. Matilda's demesne abbey at Waltham, although founded by the unquestionably Anglo-Saxon King Harold, had been ceded to the bishop of Durham and had undergone extensive rebuilding by Durham-influenced artisans. Other churches patronized by Queen Matilda, including Abingdon Abbey, Merton Priory, Selby Abbey, and the church of St Albans, had been either founded by Normans or rebuilt in the Norman style following the Conquest. The queen's bridge-building, especially the fact that at least one of them was built with stone arches, also indicates an interest in Norman-style building works. It is unquestionably true that Matilda shared in the Norman passion for erecting large buildings. However, the chroniclers who recorded the queen's involvement with building projects were in most cases themselves Norman, and probably more apt to notice the activities that conformed to their own aesthetic interests. Upon a closer reading of the sources, it becomes clear that Matilda also patronized the types of activity associated with her Anglo-Saxon ancestors. Indeed, in giving gifts of Anglo-Saxon metalwork and needlework to her French correspondents, Matilda helped to foster a continental taste for insular art. Furthermore, in return for the rich gifts the queen sent, she received panegyric poetry that spread the fame of her ancestors and so helped raise the prestige of the Anglo-Norman monarchy within the European community.

[1] *Gesta regum*, 459.

With its emphasis on deep colors and shining surfaces, the Anglo-Saxon standard of beauty informs contemporary descriptions both of the Scottish royal palace at which Matilda was born and the convent at Wilton where she was educated. According to Margaret's biographer, who as a former sacristan had an eye for such things, the Scottish queen filled her home with precious objects. The public areas of the palace as well as the living quarters of the royal family seemed to shine with the reflected gleam of gold and silver.[2] Margaret and Malcolm also donated many liturgical objects made of precious metals and jewels for use in various religious institutions. Like many of her countrywomen, Margaret was a skilled needleworker. She and her ladies made liturgical garments in the women's quarters of the palace. Owing to the fragile nature of their art, none of these garments survives, but Margaret's encomiast tells something of their quality when he assures us that, in looking at some of the articles displayed in the palace, 'you would have thought they came out of some heavenly workshop'.[3] Another indication of the wealth of the Scottish monarchs comes from the description of the luxurious furs and other gifts presented to Edgar Ætheling and his party when they left Scotland in 1074 to meet with King William on the continent: 'King Malcolm and his sister Margaret gave him and his men great gifts, many treasures in skins faced with purple cloth, marten-skin robes, miniver and ermine-skins, costly robes, vessels of gold and silver.' After the seemingly luckless Edgar and his followers were shipwrecked and most of the treasure lost, the party was outfitted a second time with gifts of the same type and quality.[4]

When the young princesses Edith and Mary went south for their convent education, they were exposed to more of the same style of art that they were accustomed to seeing in the Scottish palace. Little remains of the buildings at either Romsey or Wilton where eleventh-century women and girls lived and worshipped, but the anonymous encomiast of Edward the Confessor and the hagiographer Goscelin of St Bertin have left us some description of Wilton in that era. The Confessor's queen had rebuilt the monastery in stone, although the complex was described as 'modestly planned' and not of the scale which would have impressed contemporary Normans.[5] Some of Goscelin's descriptions, such as that of the shrine of Edith, or of a richly-embroidered alb, also associated with that saint, are among the most specific of existing accounts of the lost treasures of the Anglo-Saxons.[6] Edith's shrine, constructed out of gold donated by King Cnut, portrayed the stories of the Massacre of the Innocents and scenes from the life, passion, and resurrection of Christ.[7] The alb, made in the tenth century and said to have been designed by St Edith herself, was extant and

---

[2] *Life of St Margaret*, paragraph eleven.
[3] *Life of St Margaret*, paragraph seven. St Edith, as well as the Confessor's queen, were described as expert needleworkers, and after the Conquest, Matilda of Flanders patronized Anglo-Saxon embroideresses. For St Edith, see Wilmart, ed., 'La legende de St Edith', 79; for Queen Edith see Osbert of Clare as printed in Barlow, ed., *Vita Aedwardi regis*, 14, and William of Malmesbury, *Gesta regum*, 353.
[4] *Anglo-Saxon Chronicle*, s.a. 1074.
[5] Barlow, ed., *Vita Aedwardi regis*, 46–8. The complex is described as being 'moderatius ceptum'
[6] Wilmart, ed., 'La légende de Ste Edith', 89–90. See also C. R. Dodwell, *Anglo-Saxon Art: A New Perspective* (Manchester, 1982), 33.
[7] Wilmart, ed., 'La légende de Ste Edith', 280–1.

displayed when the Scottish Edith was a girl. Goscelin marveled at the quantity of golden thread, pearls, and colored stones used in its making, and described the figures of Christ and the apostles that were embroidered around the hem. St Edith portrayed herself (or had herself portrayed) as Mary Magdalen, prostrate and kissing the feet of Christ.[8] This garment may not have been very different from those produced in the workshop in Margaret's quarters in the palace at Edinburgh or those made in England for Matilda of Flanders.[9] The sources indicate that Matilda II continued to patronize Anglo-Saxon needleworkers. Ivo, bishop of Chartres, wrote to Henry's queen, requesting that she send him a robe or other ecclesiastical vestment as a reminder of their friendship. When making his request, Ivo specified that the garment was to be 'of such a kind as is fitting for a queen to give, and for a bishop to wear while celebrating the divine offices'.[10] It has been suggested that requests for gifts of clothing are a medieval topos, meant to recall or reinforce a patron/client relationship rather than to be taken literally. However, in this case, the Chartres necrology confirms that Ivo was requesting a garment of the famed *opus Anglicana*.[11] A fifteenth-century inventory from Westminster Abbey, if accurate, also attests that Matilda sometimes gave liturgical garments to favored institutions. It records a black woven girdle with the words of the hymn 'Nesciens mater' and the prayer 'Deus qui salutis' embroidered in gold letters upon it among the gifts given by 'Matildis bona regina'.[12] Matilda patronized metalworkers as well as needleworkers. She gave the monks of Cluny a candlestick so lavish that it drew venom from Bernard of Clairvaux in his famous tirade against the Cluniac lifestyle. Bernard complained that the Cluniacs substituted 'great trees of brass, fashioned with wondrous skill, glittering with jewels as much as with candlelight' for the utilitarian objects he preferred.[13] A pair of candlesticks that Matilda sent to Hildebert of Lavardin, the bishop of Le Mans, were most likely similar to that given to Cluny.[14] The cathedral at Chartres was a recipient of a set of church bells that served to 'proclaim her dignity abroad', as William of Malmesbury would have it. Ivo's thank-you letter assured the queen that her gift would not go unnoticed. 'I will', he wrote, 'cause them to be set up in a much-frequented location, for crowds of people to hear, and daily, as often as they are rung to mark the canonical hours your memory will be renewed in the hearts of the hearers.'[15]

When Matilda provided luxury items for churches, was it simply because of

---

[8] Wilmart, ed., 'La légende de Ste Edith', 79.
[9] For Matilda of Flanders' patronage of Anglo-Saxon embroidery, see Musset, ed., 'Les actes de Guillaume le Conquérant et de la Reine Mathilde', entry 16, pp. 112–13. Domesday Book mentions an Anglo-Saxon woman, Leofgeat, who 'made and makes embroideries in gold for the king and queen'. See *Domesday Wiltshire*, 67: 86.
[10] Ivo of Chartres, *PL* 162: columns 125–6, letter 107.
[11] Therese Latzke, 'Der Topos Mantelgedicht', *Mittellateinisches Jahrbuch* 6 (1970): 109–31. The Chartres necrology commemorates Queen Matilda for her many gifts to the church, including a chasuble worked in gold. See de Lépinois and Merlet, edd., *Cartulaire de Notre Dame Chartres*, 3: 204.
[12] Flete, *History of Westminster*, 72.
[13] Bernard of Clairvaux, 'Apologia ad Guillelmum, Sancti Theodorici Abbatem', *PL* 182, column 915. See Evans, *Monastic Life at Cluny 910–1157*, 94, and Barlow, *The English Church, 1066–1154*, 185, n. 35.
[14] The gift to Hildebert is mentioned in *PL* 171, columns 160–2.
[15] *PL* 162, epistola 142, columns 148–9.

a desire, conscious or not, to continue the insular traditions with which she was familiar? It is true that this type of gift had a long history, but in reading the letters that responded to these gifts, it is clear that other factors were also at work. Women in the medieval world were primary producers of food and clothing, and in one sense, Matilda was fulfilling an age-old role when she provided liturgical garments and objects for the altar, which after all, was a table upon which a meal was prepared. But assisting in the preparation of this particular meal gave a woman a special sacral significance. Both Ivo and Hildebert stressed that, in giving gifts used in God's service, Matilda became an active participant in the liturgy. Ivo compared Matilda to the Hebrew women of old, who supplied gold, silver, gems, and rich dyes that were used for making vestments. According to Ivo, Matilda ought especially to value being recalled to memory when the bells were rung to commemorate the exact moment when 'that unique sacrificial lamb' was consecrated on the Lord's table, a time when God was especially inclined toward mercy. Ivo asserted that the benefit of mercy would, without doubt, 'extend to the ministers of God who are rich in goods, which for His honor and love, they use to supply those who are lacking'.[16] Going further along the same lines, Hildebert asserted that, because the queen provided the objects for the table where the eucharist was prepared, she took part in the eucharistic service. Her role, although different from that of a priest, was of no less value. And, like Ivo, Hildebert offered a biblical analogy. In presenting Christ with the candlesticks, he said, Matilda acted in the manner of the women who offered Christ their tears at the crucifixion and who brought spices to the tomb. 'You also', he wrote, 'are present when Christ is sacrificed'. In the reform era, when members of both the laity and the clergy were struggling to redefine their roles in religious life, sentiments of this kind may have gone a long way toward defining an active and meaningful role for women of the upper classes.[17] We know little of how royal and aristocratic women perceived their situations in the opening and middle years of the twelfth century. Often, we do not even have direct evidence that most noblewomen enjoyed wielding the kinds of power that they often did in situations such as Matilda's. It is, however, quite likely that some noblewomen particularly relished these affirmations of their importance as their opportunities for direct action in the political sphere were diminishing.

Patronage of and interest in secular literature also provided a voice for women in the courts. Relationships between aristocratic women and the written word and indeed, questions of medieval lay literacy itself have been subjects of recent scrutiny that has tended to show that the ability to read Latin was more widespread than is sometimes thought. A distinction has been made between practical literacy, or the ability to manipulate the formulae of legal documents and records, and the sort of literacy, involving the ability to read and appreciate

---

[16] *PL* 162, epistola 142, columns 148–9.
[17] *PL* 171, columns 160–1. I owe Deborah McBride thanks for sharing her insights into Hildebert's letters with me on several occasions.

Latin literary sources, that required a clerical education.[18] The usefulness of this distinction becomes clear when looking at the career of someone like Roger of Salisbury, who was responsible for many of the administrative innovations in the reign of Henry I, but who more educated contemporaries could also describe as 'almost illiterate'.[19] Practical literacy of the kind possessed by Bishop Roger appears to have been fairly widespread among the members of the Anglo-Norman aristocracy, but, because of her superb education, Matilda can be counted among the 'truly literate' of her age. Her practical abilities are evident in her day-to-day dealings in political affairs that called for an understanding of the language of charters and other governmental records. As one example among many, the charters of Henry I that include the clause 'per Queen Matilda' demonstrate that, early in the reign, she carried information between the 'curia regis', where decisions were made, and the places where scribes recorded those decisions and issued charters.[20] Within a few months of her coronation, Matilda was issuing charters in her own name. Perhaps the queen simply announced her decisions or even dictated her charters in French or English to a scribe who prepared their Latin texts, but this would not negate her understanding of the value of the written word nor her ability to manipulate the information she found in record sources. Whoever prepared the texts of the queen's charters, their content demonstrates that Matilda was sophisticated in the use of documents. She understood the value of a written record, and could evaluate evidence contained in the records she examined. In 1111, she allowed written evidence, possibly from Domesday Book, to be used to prove a claim concerning payments owed by the monks of Abingdon. In another case, Matilda ordered a petitioner to accept written proof of another's ownership of land that he claimed.[21] Although her charter does not specifically state that she herself had examined the documents, it may be presumed that she had. In a similar instance, when she issued a charter augmenting a fair, she referred to the privileges that had previously existed and were enumerated 'per breve regis'. Here, the language of the queen's charter so closely parallels that of the king's that it must be assumed that the scribe had a copy of Henry's charter before him as he wrote.[22]

There is no question that Matilda was at the forefront of the systematization of written records that characterized the administration of Henry I, but she was far more than just practically literate. Though no single surviving book or manuscript can definitely be attributed to her patronage, evidence that Queen Matilda was intimately involved with the written word survives even from her earliest childhood. Although her father, Malcolm, was described as 'illiteratus',

---

[18] See, for example, Ralph V. Turner, 'The *miles literatus* in Twelfth- and Thirteeth-Century England: How Rare a Phenomenon?', *American Historical Review* 83 (1978): 929–45; Michael Camille, 'Seeing and Reading: Some Visual Implications of Medieval Literacy and Illiteracy', *Art History* 8 (1985): 26–50.

[19] William of Newburgh referred to Roger as 'fere illiteratus'. See William of Newburgh, *Historia rerum anglicarum*, ed. Hans Claude Hamilton (London, 1856, repr. Vaduz, 1964, two volumes in one), 1: 26.

[20] *RRAN* 2: 568 and 569. See also Van Caenegem, *Royal Writs in England from the Conquest to Glanville*, 149–50.

[21] For the Abingdon case, see *RRAN* 2: 1000; for the case ordering examination of the documents, see *RRAN* 2: 1001.

[22] *RRAN* 2: 971.

he had respect for learning and evident pride in his wife's devotion to the written word. Margaret's education, eloquence, and love for books greatly impressed her biographer, who commented that, although she was terribly busy with worldly affairs, she nevertheless kept scholars at court, and that she was often to be found in the midst of them, easily discussing difficult subjects with obvious enjoyment. Margaret, like other women of her social status, owned a number of books, but her love for them seems to have gone beyond the purchase of a few prestigious and expensive volumes. Her biographer complained that she exhausted him in her search for interesting volumes to purchase.[23] Our knowledge of mother–child interaction in the Middle Ages is woefully incomplete, yet there are several tantalizing accounts of royal and aristocratic mothers teaching their offspring their letters by holding them on their laps and looking at Psalters or Gospel Books together.[24] This may have been the way in which the young Edith was first introduced to the written word since Margaret's biographer points out that she taught her children the rudiments of the Christian faith. Matilda may even have seen the Gospel Book, now preserved at the Bodleian Library at Oxford, that legend states was miraculously preserved after being dropped into a stream. The book has numerous golden initials throughout the text as well as full-page illustrations with the bright colors typically seen in late Anglo-Saxon painting.

After leaving Scotland to be educated at Romsey and Wilton, the Scottish princesses received the best education available for eleventh-century girls in the British Isles. There is no question but that Matilda was literate in Latin, and she probably read French as well. In her writings, she displayed familiarity with the Bible, the liturgy, and the major patristic authors. She was also able to use classical writers to some extent. For example, in one of her letters to Anselm, she cited Cicero's *De senectute*, the Gospels of Matthew, Luke, and John, and the liturgical offices for the feast of St Martin.[25] The inclusion of the liturgy of St Martin's Day may have been intended to reinforce the archbishop's memory of the king's and queen's wedding, which he performed on the day of the feast of St Martin in 1100. In another of her letters to the exiled archbishop she cited the Psalms, Paul's letters to Timothy and to the Thessalonians, and the rather obscure Old Testament story of the over-zealous royal servant Giezi.[26] A third epistle contains references to Cicero, St Paul, and the church fathers Jerome, Augustine, and Gregory.[27] Of course, it could be argued that, since these letters were undoubtedly prepared by scribes, they reflect the erudition of the queen's staff rather than the queen herself. The question of the authorship of the queen's letters only highlights how little we know of how documents were generated in the medieval world. All of the surviving letters to and from the queen are in

---

[23] *Life of St Margaret*, paragraphs 10 and 11.
[24] On this point see Susan Groag Bell, 'Medieval Women Book Owners: Arbiters of Lay Piety and Ambassadors of Culture', in Erler and Kowaleski, edd., *Women and Power in the Middle Ages*, 162–6. For another point of view, consult Richard Gameson, 'The Gospels of Margaret of Scotland and the Literacy of an Eleventh-Century Queen', in Jane H. M. Taylor and Lesley Smith, edd., *Women and the Book: Assessing the Visual Evidence* (London, 1997), 149–71.
[25] *Anselmi opera omnia*, 4: 150–1 (letter #242).
[26] From 4 Kings (Vulgate) 4:27. See *Anselmi opera omnia* 5: 244–5 (letter #317).
[27] *Anselmi opera omnia* 5: 326–7 (letter #384), and Schmitt's notes to lines 29–30, 37, and 45–6.

Latin, a language that Matilda understood, but how conversant was she with the learned Latin of her ecclesiastical correspondents? Did she read their letters herself, or did an intermediary read them aloud to her? Did that intermediary supply commentary and explanation, perhaps even a translation into one of the vernacular languages? When the queen needed to send a letter, did she dictate in Latin, or did she ask a scribe to write a draft which she then approved? Would the draft have been in French or even English, only to be put into Latin in the final version? There is, unfortunately, no real way of finding answers to these questions. At the very least, even if her scribes supplied the entire content of the letters, Matilda was sufficiently educated that she desired to project an image of herself as a participant in literate culture. But there are clues that point to the fact that the queen read texts herself. In one of her letters to Anselm, she thanked him for a recent letter, 'I hug the little letter sent from you. . . . I cherish it in my heart; I *reread with my lips* (emphasis mine) the words flowing from the sweet fountain of your goodness.'[28] The author of the *Life of St Margaret* congratulated Matilda for wanting not only to hear of her mother's saintly deeds, but also to have those deeds presented to her in writing so that she could consult the 'written-down letters' as often as she wanted. The Latin phrase 'impressam litteris' is difficult to render in colloquial English, but the passage strongly implies that the queen would see the words as well as hear them.[29] In another instance, William of Malmesbury wrote to Matilda's daughter, telling of the circumstances that led to the commissioning of his monumental work, the *Gesta regum anglorum*. William related that the queen asked about her relationship to Malmesbury's patron saint, Aldhelm. When told that it was through her West Saxon royal ancestors, Matilda inquired about the exact relationship, and after it was explained to her orally, she replied that she wished to have a more permanent account, and requested that the details be supplied to her in written form. When this work was completed, the queen began to believe that her ancestral history required an even 'more dignified treatment' and thus commissioned William to write a fuller history.[30] These clues combine to demonstrate that the queen participated in the literate mentality of the twelfth century, appreciating the permanence of the written word and valuing written texts above oral accounts. In another letter, this time to Matilda's brother David, William flattered him by pointing out that, 'for certainly your family is known to love the study of letters . . . our lady your sister, among her other virtues, never ceased to support literature and to advance those who were devoted to it'.[31] William's narrative also implies that Matilda had some prior knowledge of the seventh-century abbot and bishop Saint Aldhelm. Matilda's physician and favorite, Faritius, had written a *Life* of Aldhelm, and it is conceivable that Matilda's knowledge stemmed from discussions with Faritius

---

[28] *Anselmi opera omnia* 5: 248–9 (letter #320). The italics are mine.
[29] *Life of St Margaret*, paragraph one. See also James Westfall Thompson, *The Literacy of the Laity in the Middle Ages* (repr NY, 1963), 170–1.
[30] *Gesta regum* 4–5. See also Thomson, 'Willliam of Malmesbury as Historian', 391, 410, and Könsgen, 'Zwei unbekannte Briefe', 213–14.
[31] Faritius' *Life of St Aldhelm* is printed in *PL* 89, columns 63–84; see William of Malmesbury, *Gesta pontificum*, 330–443.

or a reading of his *Life*. Another possibility is that Aldhelm's work, which included saints' lives and a treatise on virginity directed toward women, was read and discussed as part of Matilda's convent education. William's account of his first encounter with Queen Matilda makes clear that the queen's main interest in Aldhelm was his relationship to her, and it was this interest in her ancestry and heritage that stimulated her to commission both the biography of her mother and, ultimately, William's great work of history. Although a generation of scholarship on the medieval nobility shows that paternal bloodlines became increasingly important during the period of Matilda's life, medieval women, particularly the 'matron' of royal and aristocratic houses, often commissioned works of history that commemorated the deeds of their own blood relatives. Matilda's literary commissions demonstrate that she saw herself as a member of an ancient lineage whose deeds were worth recording. These commissions, along with the benefactions recorded in her charters, suggest that, although the queen valued all members of her natal family and relished the status that came with being the daughter of a crowned king, she largely identified with her maternal, Anglo-Saxon heritage over that of her Scottish father. This identification with her mother's ancestry is not surprising. After all, Malcolm and Margaret named five of their seven sons and one of their two daughters after Margaret's royal relatives, suggesting that the children must have been nurtured on stories of their Anglo-Saxon ancestors. In the case of the daughters, their early training was no doubt reinforced throughout their years under Christina at Romsey and then at Wilton, where their Anglo-Saxon forebears were commemorated daily. For example, in addition to the hagiographic accounts of Edith and Wulfhilde, the queen and her sister may have read William of Malmesbury's lost verse account of the miracles of their maternal kinswoman Ælgifu, mother of King Edgar and possibly abbess of Wilton.[32] The value of Matilda's tie to the Anglo-Saxon kings was of course stressed repeatedly at her marriage and when her children were born.

Matilda's identification with her mother and her Anglo-Saxon ancestors must have been known to many of those who wrote for her. The author of the *Vita Margaretae* congratulated her for wanting to learn more about the habits of the mother she had scarcely known and also included an elaborate genealogical section emphasizing her blood-ties to the Confessor. Elisabeth van Houts has collected nine surviving poems written for Matilda, and noted that eight of them make some mention of her mother.[33] One, by Hildebert of Lavardin, Bishop of Le Mans, refers to the mother's virtue being reborn in her offspring, so that, even while enclosed in the tomb, the mother lives again through her daughter.[34] Matilda maintained close ties to her natal family after her marriage. The charters recording her many gifts to monastic houses reveal that gifts were

---

[32] For the lost account of Aelgifu's miracles, see *Gesta pontificum* 186–7.
[33] Elisabeth M. C. van Houts, 'Latin Poetry and the Anglo-Norman Court 1066–1135: The Carmen de Hastingae Proelio', *The Journal of Medieval History* 15 (1989): 39–62.
[34] Marjorie Chibnall believed the poem to refer to the Empress (Chibnall, *The Empress Matilda*, 47), but I believe that the weight of the admittedly scanty evidence suggests that the elder Matilda was the original patron. See Therese Latzke, 'Der Fürstinnenpreis', *Mittellateinisches Jahrbuch* 14 (1979): 22–65. A. Brian Scott, the most recent editor of Hildebert's poems and Elisabeth van Houts argue for the elder Matilda. See Scott, ed., *Hildeberti Cenomannensis Episcopi carmina minora* (Leipzig, 1969).

made almost as often for her parents and siblings as they were for her own soul and those of her husband and children.[35] Her continental correspondents knew that she was close to her brothers. In a letter of consolation written to the queen after Edgar died in 1107, Ivo promised her that he would pray for the soul of the king but also assured her that Edgar would ascend quickly to heaven 'if he lived his life as it is said'.[36] Edgar, along with his successors and brothers Alexander and David, visited the Anglo-Norman court during the reigns of both Rufus and Henry. In fact, David spent so much time with Henry and Matilda that William of Malmesbury admitted that he had 'rubbed off all the barbarian gaucherie of Scottish manners' among the civilized southerners.[37] As kings of Scotland, Matilda's three brothers carried Anglo-Norman governmental practices, religious institutions, and artistic ideas north with them. Matilda's role in furthering David's career has been noted, and we may assume that she also played no small part in the 1102 marriage of her sister Mary to Eustace, count of Boulogne. When Mary died in 1116, she was buried in Bermondsey Abbey in a splendid marble tomb that depicted her crowned ancestors and celebrated her bloodline in a verse engraved in golden letters.[38] Mary, like her elder sister, was evidently keenly aware of her royal origins. Some indication of the depth of Matilda's pride in her ancestry can be gauged by reading one of her letters to Pope Paschal in which she asserted her need for Anselm to guide her: 'Of what use are our life and lineage', she asked, 'while we are descending into errors?'[39] The passage is a direct quotation of Psalm 29:10. Matilda, who had recently given birth to the child who was seen as restoring to 'green tree' of England, chose to identify with King David and his reference to the illustrious bloodline that was to produce the Christ child.

Largely because of the interests of his queens, the court of Henry I developed into a center for the patronage of literary activities, for it has become a commonplace that it was his wives, rather than Henry himself, who were primarily responsible for the cultured tone of the court. The predominance of Matilda and Adeliza should not be surprising. Women in the European courts have been recognized as leading patrons of the burst of literary activity at the beginning of the twelfth century, the burst that had developed into the creation of a full-blown 'courtly ethos' by the end of the century. The courtly movement had broad consequences for European society, and the terms associated with the court carry many connotations. It is worth considering the meanings of these terms before discussing to what degree the household of Henry I, which has

---

[35] Only eight of Matilda's charters contain clauses naming those who are to benefit from her gifts. Of these eight, one mentions her father only, three are for the welfare of Henry, herself, and their children, and two are for the souls of Henry, Matilda, and their parents. The two surviving originals have the most elaborate beneficiary clauses, naming Matilda's brothers and sister, as well as her ancestors, husband, and offspring. The longer lists in the originals suggest that some clauses may have been abbreviated or deleted in cartularies by copyists who did not share Matilda's familial devotion.
[36] See *PL* 162: column 177, letter #174.
[37] *Gesta regum*, 727.
[38] John of Fordun, *Chronica gentis scotorum*, as quoted in Otto Lehmann-Brockhaus, *Lateinische Schriftquellen zur Kunst in England, Wales, und Schottland vom Jahre 901 bis zum Jahre 1307* (5 vols, Munich, 1956), 1: entry 304, p. 304.
[39] *Anselmi opera omnia* 5: 254, (letter #323).

been called 'the first patronizing court' in English history, merits the appellation 'courtly'.[40]

Although in modern usage the term 'court' refers to a specific place, historians have tended to see the medieval court in terms of its administrative function. Because of the itinerant nature of Anglo-Norman kingship and the need for personal rule, the 'court' of the Anglo-Norman monarchs was never a specific site. Rather, the court was peripatetic, consisting of the king, his closest advisors who formed the inner circle, and lesser household functionaries who were charged with the myriad mundane tasks associated with the logistics of providing for a large group of people who were constantly on the move. The *Constitutio domus regis* enumerates the king's servants and divides them into those who lived at court and those who did not, providing some sense of the complexity of the king's household and the fluid nature of his retinue.[41] Thus, when historians speak of the 'court' of Henry I, they are more likely to be referring to the king and his followers, wherever they were, than to any specific physical place.

The use of the term 'court' to describe the king and his retinue has worked very well for strictly political discussions. Social scientists and literary critics, however, employ a much broader definition of the terms 'court' and 'courtly' and import insights and terminology from these disciplines into discussions of medieval culture. For example, Norbert Elias and C. Stephen Jaeger have discussed the court from an anthropological perspective, seeing it in terms of a 'civilizing institution' that draws society's warriors and artists into line with the ruling parties and provides a sense of stability for the state.[42] According to Jaeger, chivalric ideals, which were the means of stabilizing European feudal society, were first articulated by 'the educated members of courts, the curiales who served kings, bishops, and secular princes, and the entire class of men who aspired to that position'.[43] Joachim Bumke used the German word 'höfische' to refer to 'the social setting of literary activity'. Thus, any piece of literature, of whatever genre, can be (and has been) described as 'courtly' as long as it was produced at court or for or by a member of the court circle. Using this definition, the reign of Henry I was certainly 'courtly' in that secular biography, hagiography, a bestiary, law codes, numerous poems, histories, and letters were all associated with court patronage.[44] However, this use of the word tells us only of the site, and not the tone of a literary work, and in the following discussion I will only use the word 'courtly' to refer to the medieval aristocratic social ideals

---

[40] So described by Karl Julius Holzknecht, *Literary Patronage in the Middle Ages* (Menasha, WI, 1923), 218. See Van Houts, 'Latin Poetry', 50–2. Other relevant discussions include M. D. Legge, 'L'influence littéraire de la cour d'Henri Beauclerc', in *Melanges offerts à Rita Lejeune, Professeur à l'Universite de Liège I* (Gembloux, 1969), 679–87, Thompson, 'Literacy of the Laity', 170, and Bezzola, *Origines et la formation de la littérature courtoise*.

[41] See *Constitutio domus regis*, xlix–lii, 128–35.

[42] C. Stephen Jaeger, *The Origins of Courtliness* (Philadelphia, 1985), and Norbert Elias, *Über den Prozess der Zivilisation. Sociogenetische und psychogenetische Untersuchungen* (2 vols, Frankfurt, 1979 [originally published 1939]), in translation as *The Civilizing Process* (trans. Edmund Jephcott, New York, 1978). References herein are to the English translation.

[43] Jaeger, *The Origins of Courtliness*, 4.

[44] Joachim Bumke, *Courtly Culture: Literature and Society in the High Middle Ages* (Berkeley, 1991), 59–60.

characterized by an emphasis on ritual, dress, manners, and sentiment. Thus, in its totality, 'courtly' implies not only a literary style but also a social and administrative setting and a way of life that embraces and makes use of refined ideals in etiquette, dress, leisure activities and all other forms of meaningful social interaction. I will employ the word here in its fullest sense. At what point does a king's retinue become 'courtly'? Certainly the Carolingian and Ottonian societies of the early Middle Ages were centrally organized around a court society, but of course not all European societies were equally 'courtly' at any given time. The reign of Malcolm Canmore in Scotland marks a transitional period between a king surrounded by an informal group of military and administrative officials and a king who was the focus of a true courtly society. Here we see the hand of Queen Margaret in the transition as she 'made the magnificence of royal honor much more magnificent for the king and she conferred more glory and graces to all the nobles of the kingdom and to their servants'. Among other things, the queen 'ordered that merchants coming to her from land and sea would bring different kinds of costly things to sell, things that until then were unknown in Scotland'. Under her influence, the Scots began to wear more varied and refined clothing that undoubtedly marked those who belonged to the court circle. According to her biographer, Margaret even 'made submissions to the king more sublime, and when he went out, on foot or riding, he was accompanied by a great throng of retainers showing him much honor'.[45]

Can we truly speak of 'courtliness' in the reign of Henry I, and if so, to what degree was Queen Matilda a participant in the creation and maintenance of courtly society? Certainly some of the necessary elements of a court culture were present in Henry's reign. There was a more-or-less stable core of administrative personnel, a great throng of hangers-on, the presence of educated clerics who participated in the learned culture of the era, and even a rudimentary court school where sons of the nobility were educated and trained for future service.[46] But to what extent did this society participate in the chivalric lifestyle depicted in courtly literature? Geoffrey Gaimar, who wrote a vernacular verse history shortly after the death of Henry I, ended his account with Henry's accession, claiming that the reign had been covered in detail by David, who had written at the request of Henry's widow, Adeliza. Although David's work has been lost, we know what it did not contain because in the last few lines of Gaimar's history, he could tell 'a thousand things' about King Henry that David never wrote. Among these omitted details, the poet disclosed, were 'verses about the fairest deeds; that is, about love and gallantry; and of woodland sports and jokes; and of feasts and splendor; of largesses and riches; of the barons whom he led; of the great gifts he gave'.[47] But can Gaimar's boast be trusted? Modern critics have not always been willing to do so. For Richard Southern, the salient point was that Gaimar did not even attempt to provide the description or praise of the king he called 'the best that ever was'. Pointing to the disjunction between what he

---

[45] *Vita Margaretae*, paragraph 11.
[46] See C. Warren Hollister, 'Courtly Culture and Courtly Style in the Anglo-Norman World', *Albion* 20 (1988): 1–17, especially p. 16.
[47] Gaimar, *L'estoire des Engleis*, lines 6483–518.

considered to be the historical facts of Henry's reign and Gaimar's poetic fancies, Southern concluded 'it is hard to see what there was to joke about. It was an unlovable reign.'[48] Others have agreed that Gaimar presented an ideal rather than a realistic picture of court life during Henry's reign. But some scholars have taken Gaimar at his word, seeing him as a reliable witness to events, attitudes, and practices of his day. Certainly there are reasons to believe that Henry's reign was not so grim as Southern would have us believe. Particularly during the years of Prince William's adolescence, there were plenty of high-spirited sons of the nobility present at court. Henry himself had fathered a number of out-of-wedlock children who were just older than William and who associated with him. Henry was famous for his love of the hunt. Is it indeed the case, as Hollister argued, that 'the age of chivalry dawned in the Anglo-Norman world' sometime between the reign of William the Conqueror and the death of Henry I?[49] The monastic chroniclers do make clear that court life under the Anglo-Norman kings became more and more sophisticated and stylized. During the last years of the reign of William Rufus and the first years of Henry's reign, members of the king's retinue had begun to adopt fashions and hairstyles that marked them as members of the court circle. The long hair, flowing beards, fancy garments, mincing gait, and curly-toed shoes of the courtiers drew derision from the clerical commentators, but they also served to distinguish members of the courtly society from those who were outside it.[50] Some members of the court also adopted a lifestyle of privilege and excess. Eadmer was disgusted by the lewd and wasteful practices of William Rufus and his retinue, and the author of the 1097 entry into the *Anglo-Saxon Chronicle* vividly described the suffering in the countryside that followed a visit from the king. Since the complaint was echoed in the entry for 1104, we can assume that the practices of the first years of Henry's reign did not differ much from those of his brother. But the years between 1105 and about 1110 saw a gradual reform of the court, brought about because of the systematization and order imposed by the king. According to William of Malmesbury, Henry set down rules governing how much his followers could take from the residents of the areas through which they passed, and established just prices for other needs. Transgressors were subject to heavy punishment.[51] Even the hairstyles of the king and his followers were reformed. Orderic Vitalis tells how, during the 1105 Easter ceremonies in Rouen, Henry and his followers were stirred by the sermon of Serlo, bishop of Bayeaux, who disapproved of the 'effete' long locks worn by members of his audience. When the king promised to mend his ways, Serlo immediately produced scissors and snipped the king's flowing locks.[52]

The improvement in the moral tone of Henry's court may reflect the influence of Queen Matilda. Some of the literature suggests that she was too

---

[48] Southern, 'King Henry I', in *Medieval Humanism and other Studies* (Oxford, 1970), 230; Gaimar, *L'estoire des Engleis*, lines 6504–5.
[49] Hollister, 'Courtly Style and Courtly Culture', 17.
[50] For descriptions of the dress and manners prevalent at Henry's court, see *Orderic* 4: 186–8. See also Bumke, *Courtly Culture*, 128–55, regarding the need for distinctive dress and manners among insiders in a court setting.
[51] Eadmer, *Historia novorum*, 192–3. See also *Gesta regum*, 725.
[52] *Orderic* 6: 64–6.

old-fashioned for the stylish Normans who formed part of the king's retinue during the early years of his reign. According to William of Malmesbury, these courtiers began to blame Henry's married state for the less rollicking style preferred in the years after 1100. A few of them were so disgusted with the staid life of Henry and his queen, whom they mocked as 'Godric and Godiva', that they were willing to send for Robert Curthose just to liven things up. The poetry addressed to Queen Matilda also reflects the sober portrait drawn by William and does not project an image of the 'courtly lady' who became the standard female role later in the century. While Hildebert several times referred to Matilda's beauty and noble lineage, and Marbod of Rennes praised her excellent manners and 'fluent, honeyed speech' these are standard tropes, and Marbod's poem indicates that Matilda had little interest in the latest frills and fashions for courtly ladies. Marbod contrasted Matilda's lack of artifice with the practices of women who painted their faces with false colors and bound up their prominent breasts to appear more slender. Matilda, according to Marbod, was so beautiful she needed no artificial means to enhance what nature had given her.[53] The seal that Matilda used on official documents confirms that she had little interest in the latest clothing, for the outfit she is depicted wearing had been out of style for a generation before she ascended the throne. Her seal is similar to that used by Henry's sister Cecilia, abbess of Caen, and both probably derived from the seal of Matilda of Flanders. T. A. Heslop suggested that Matilda II simply copied the matrix of Matilda of Flanders' seal without worrying about projecting a fashionable image.[54]

Altogether, the panegyric poetry written for and about Queen Matilda shows her to have been proud of her bloodline, praiseworthy, moral, and possibly somewhat uninspired in matters of style. Of course, the tone of the poems may reflect the values of their clerical authors as much as it does the actual personality of their subject. But whether or not the poems tell us anything about Queen Matilda herself, they do, combined with letters of advice and other didactic literature, provide glimpses into the ideals contemporary writers had about the queen, and more rarely, the institution of queenship. The clerical commentators approved of anything that would improve the moral tone of the court, and if we look at the literature directed at the queen, we see that contemporaries perceived her to be in a position to effect that moral reform. According to the churchmen who wrote to and for Matilda, the king's wife had a clear role in shaping the law and could be praised as one who sought peace and justice for the kingdom. One anonymous poet likened Matilda to a heavenly body complementing the seven principal stars and went on to praise her for persuading Henry to abolish unjust laws in the kingdom.[55] In a letter, Hildebert praised her as the queen 'whose safety preserves reverence for the laws and the undamaged state of the church . . . through whom the

---

[53] *PL* 171: 1660.
[54] Heslop, 'Seals', 3. See also Heslop, 'English Seals from the Mid-Ninth Century to 1100', and C. H. Hunter Blair, 'Armorials in English Seals from the Twelfth to the Sixteenth Century', *Archaeologia* 89 (1943): 1–26.
[55] Discussed by van Houts, 'Latin Poetry', and printed in André Boutemy, 'Notice sur le recueil poétique du manuscrit Cotton Vitellius Axii du British Museum', *Latomus* 1 (1937, repr. 1964): 278–313, at 304–5.

integrity of the law and the state of the church continue uninjured' and as 'the queen to whom the power of judging crimes has been conferred, whose character is an example of honesty'. In one of his poems, he commended her for preserving a peace that allowed England's natural prosperity to flourish.[56] The author of the Anglo-Norman version of the *Voyage of St Brendan* praised her for seeking and encouraging peace, claiming that her wisdom and counsel strengthened both human and divine law.[57] The theme is echoed in the biography of Margaret, when the author praised Margaret as the queen whose counsel caused the laws of the kingdom to be 'put in order'.[58] The biographer also provided Matilda with the example of a queen who raised the moral tone of the court. Not only did Margaret introduce refinements in dress, manners, and royal pomp, but her innovations were accomplished so effectively that wherever the court traveled, no one 'was permitted to seize anything for himself, nor would any one of them dare to oppress or injure the country people or the paupers in any way'.[59] This description of the changes in the Scottish court echo the clerical descriptions of the changes that were then being effected in England, possibly influenced by the queen. It is likely that the biographer was expressing praise of his patron as well as of his subject in these passages describing the lifestyle of the king, the queen, and the nobles who attended their court. Clerical writers recognized the need for ostentation in dress and manners among royal and aristocratic families, but also warned lest the splendor become an end in itself. Margaret's biographer carefully reminded his reader that, although Margaret loved finery, she knew that underneath, she was but dust and ashes.[60] Hildebert likewise warned the queen not to become dependent on her earthly riches, because death put an end to earthly privilege, and as he put it, 'makes the scepter equal to the hoe'.[61] In one of his letters, Anselm begged Matilda to take care lest fondness for the glories of this world hinder her journey to the next one.[62] The clerical writers whom Matilda favored cautiously accepted the chivalric lifestyle, and from what we know of the queen's behavior, her attitude seems to have been much the same.

In addition to the works that can specifically be linked to the queen's patronage, several other texts and authors have been associated with Queen Matilda. The Anglo-Norman version of the *Voyage of St Brendan* was written for a queen at the court of Henry I, but it is not clear whether Matilda or Adeliza commissioned the piece. Three of the four extant manuscripts of the dedicatory preface have some version of the name Adeliza but the oldest and most reliable among them names Matilda. Dominica Legge, pointing out that some elements of the poem derive from neither French, Latin, nor Anglo-Saxon sources, believed that the fabulous stories of the seafaring sixth-century Irish abbot must

---

[56] *PL* 171: columns 289–90. For the poem, see *Carmina minora*, 24.
[57] *The Anglo-Norman St Brendan*, ed. Edwin G. R. Waters (Oxford, 1928), lines 2–6.
[58] *Vita Margaretae*, paragraph 6.
[59] *Vita Margaretae*, paragraph 11.
[60] *Vita Margaretae*, paragraph 12.
[61] Hildebert, *Carmina minora*, 2.
[62] *Anselmi opera omnia* 5: 284–5.

have been known to Matilda from her Scottish childhood.[63] Legge's analysis of the content of the poem accords well with the other evidence that has been adduced in favor of Matilda as the poem's patron, and this attribution has been hesitantly accepted by most literary scholars.[64]

But even if scholars have come to a basic consensus about the date and patronage of the poem, other problems remain unresolved. Among these areas of uncertainty is the genre to which the poem belongs. Nearly all critics agree that, despite its title, the work is not a piece of hagiography, and should not be classified as such.[65] Some have gone so far as to suggest that *St Brendan* represents the first romance of the type later associated with Chrétien de Troyes.[66] In addition to the problem of genre, other controversial areas include the identity of the author, the logic of the narrative structure, and the audience for which the mysterious 'li apostoiles danz Benedeiz' wrote.[67] The hero of the poem, Brendan, lived from c.486 to c.575. Very few details of his life can be verified, but like other early-medieval Celtic saints, he traveled widely, and may have helped found monasteries in Scotland and Brittany. His legend grew over time, culminating in the tale that he and fourteen companions embarked on a quest to find heaven and hell. During the medieval period, the Brendan legend enjoyed great popularity, and the tale survives today in well over one hundred medieval manuscripts.[68] Benedeiz did not merely translate the *Navigatio* from Latin into the vernacular. He completely recast the journey into a livelier framework stressing the dangers and fantastic nature of the adventures Brendan and his companions underwent during their seven-year quest. Robin F. Jones

---

[63] Legge, 'La précocité de la litterature anglo-normande', *Cahiers de civilisation médiévale* 8 (1965): 329–30. The Anglo-Norman *St Brendan* owes much to the Irish *immrana*. See Jill Tattersall, 'Expedition, Exploration and Odyssey: Extended Voyage Themes and their Treatment in some Early French texts', in Sally Burch North, ed., *Studies in Medieval French Language and Literature Presented to Brian Woledge in Honour of his 80th Birthday* (Geneva, 1988), 192–214. See also John Fox, *A Literary History of France: The Middle Ages* (London, 1974), 34–9.

[64] Citations to the *Anglo-Norman Voyage of St Brendan* are to the Waters edition (see note 58 above). Waters, after some hesitation in which he admitted Matilda's possible patronage, opted in favor of Henry's second wife, Adeliza of Louvain (See xxii–vi). Subsequent arguments in favor of Matilda's patronage include Robert L. Ritchie, 'The Date of the "Voyage of St Brendan"', *Medium Aevum* 14 (1960): 64–6 and Legge, *Anglo-Norman Literature and its Background*, 9. The editors of the most recent publication of the text, Ian Short and Brian Merrilees (*The Anglo-Norman Voyage of St Brendan* [Manchester, 1979]) used a single manuscript and did not attempt to resolve dating and patronage questions. See also Fox, *A Literary History of France*, 34–42. Fox (p. 36) accepts Matilda as the poem's patron as well as Ritchie's dating to c.1106.

[65] See, for example, Legge, *Anglo-Norman Literature*, 10, and Robin F. Jones, 'The Precocity of Anglo-Norman and the Voyage of St Brendan', in *The Nature of Medieval Narrative*, ed. Minnette Grunmann-Gaudet and Robin F. Jones (Lexington, 1980): 145–58, esp. 155–6. For a more conservative view, see Fox', *Literary History of France*, p. 34.

[66] See Legge, *Anglo-Norman Literature*, 17–18; Ruth J. Dean, 'What is Anglo-Norman?', *Annuale Mediavale* 6 (1965), 38–46, esp. p. 41; Jones, 'The Precocity of Anglo-Norman', 156–7.

[67] The identity of the author remains a mystery. He identifies himself as 'li apostoiles danz Benedeiz' in the preface *(St Brendan,* line 8), but aside from this reference, nothing is known of him. Legge believed that his use of language suggested that he was a Norman monk who had also lived in England for some time. See *Anglo-Norman Literature and its Background*, 9. For speculation concerning the author's identity, see Emmanuel Walberg, 'Sur le nom de l'auteur du Voyage de S. Brendan', *Studia Neophilologia* 12 (1939): 46–55, and Legge, 'Les origines de l'anglo-normand littéraire', *Revue de linguistique romaine* 31 (1967), 47–8. Merrilees and Short provide a summary of the speculation in their edition, 5–6.

[68] Fox, *Literary History of France*, 34–43.

has suggested that the poem was written for a carefully-cultivated audience, asserting that it 'may well be the first story in the vernacular composed in the privacy and freedom of an author's imagination and set down in writing to be read rather than sung to an audience'.[69] Arguing that the poem was to be 'read to a select company of gentlefolk gathered together in the bower or solar, Jones contrasts the work to the *chansons de geste* that were 'performed for frequently boisterous, mixed audiences, in church, market place, and great hall'.[70] Pointing out that the poem is divided into three parts of approximately six hundred lines each, R. N. Illingworth speculated that 'it is likely that the tripartite structure imposed by the repetition of large- and small-scale themes arises from the contingencies of performance . . . a segment of some 600 lines ending on a suitable climax would provide the material for one evening's recitation, the whole being performed in three separate sessions'.[71]

The subject-matter of the poem, its uncertain genre, and the difficulties involved in understanding its audience provide clues about when it was likely to have been performed. The poem is about a saint and his adventures, yet it does not resemble other hagiographic pieces of the era. It is clearly written to be read aloud, yet not to be performed in the same raucous manner expected of the *chansons de geste*. I believe that Matilda asked Benedeiz to provide a poem as entertainment for one of the occasions when the court gathered for some seasonal festival. Because of the subject matter and the length of the poem, it is likely to have been first sung over the course of one of the festive Easter courts attended by both the king and the queen. The Easter festival is a prominent theme in the poem, in which passage of time is marked only by the annual feast, always eaten on the back of a giant fish. The poem, which provides a lively story with an edifying theme, would provide perfect entertainment for the three nights of entertainment during the final days of Lent, days that culminated with the Easter Sunday crown-wearing and the singing of the *laudes regiae*. Ritchie believed that *St Brendan* was written after the conquest of Normandy in September 1106, chiefly because the prologue emphasizes the queen's role in bringing peace and order to the kingdom.[72] Since Henry celebrated Easter in Normandy in 1109, and then discontinued regular, formal crown-wearings shortly after that time, the poem may have been first performed during the Easter festivities in either 1107 or 1108. However, the passages referring to the improvements the queen will bring about are in the future tense, and an earlier date in the reign, even a date soon after Matilda's marriage, is not impossible. The number of surviving manuscripts as well as the fact that it was ultimately re-dedicated to Matilda's successor Adeliza show its popularity among twelfth-century audiences.

St Brendan is not likely to have been the only work composed for

---

[69] Jones, 'Precocity of Anglo-Norman', 146. Legge believed that the poem was written to be sung to music. See *Anglo-Norman Literature*, 15.

[70] Jones, 'Precocity of Anglo-Norman', 6.

[71] R. N. Illingworth, 'The Structure of the Anglo-Norman Voyage of St Brendan', *Medium Ævum* 55 (1986): 217–29, at p. 227. See also Robin F. Jones, 'The Mechanics of Meaning in the Anglo-Norman Voyage of St Brendan', *Romanic Review* 71 (1980): 105–13, and her 'Precocity of Anglo-Norman', 151 as well as M. Burrell, 'Narrative Structures in Le Voyage de St Brendan', *Parergon* 17 (1977): 3–9.

[72] *St Brendan*, lines 2–6. See also Ritchie, 'Date of St Brendan', 64–6.

performance at the court of Henry I and Matilda. We know from William of Malmesbury that music was one of Matilda's chief interests, and he makes it clear that musicians from far and wide made a point of visiting the English queen in hope of gathering fame and riches. Little is known about the specific musicians or even the type of music that flourished at the Anglo-Norman court. Tentative evidence suggests that Adelard of Bath may have played his cithara for the English queen when she was in Normandy in 1106. Adelard wrote of having played before the queen and some French students in the year before he wrote *De eodem et diversa*. Precise dating of the treatise has proven impossible, but internal evidence places it in the period between 1105 and 1116. But even though Adelard's treatise definitely dates to the reign of Queen Matilda, Adelard may have been referring to the French queen, Bertrada of Montfort, who was queen consort until 1108. There was no queen-consort in France between 1108 and 1115, but even if the treatise were written after the death of Philip I, Adelard could have been referring to Queen Bertrada in her role as the queen-mother. However, because of Matilda's known love for exotic music and because of Adelard's later documented ties to the Anglo-Norman court, it is quite possible that Adelard could have been referring to playing for Queen Matilda.[73]

Only two other court musicians from the period are known by name, and neither can be specifically associated with Queen Matilda. The first, William LeHarpur, benefited from court patronage in that he received favorable taxation rates on four and a half bovates of land granted him by Henry I.[74] The second, Rahere, was a Norman tenant of Bishop Richard Belmeis of London. Rahere had been a minstrel for William Rufus, but appears in the records as a prebendary canon of St Paul's shortly after 1115, and he is known to have made a pilgrimage to Jerusalem in 1120. Other than his ties to the bishop of London and Rufus, there is nothing to link him to Henry's court, and no evidence that the queen favored him. The earliest manuscript of the *Song of Roland* dates from the turn of the twelfth century and seems to be the work of a single, gifted poet, and John Southworth suggested Matilda as the poem's patron. There is no evidence whatsoever for his position other than the queen's known love of music, and the subject-matter of the poem differs greatly from what is known of Matilda's tastes. Stronger arguments have been made for other candidates as patrons of the poem, but it is probably the case that the *Song of Roland* was at least performed at Henry's and Matilda's court. It is also likely that Matilda had some interest in the later works of the famed poet and hagiographer Goscelin of Canterbury, whose ties to the monastery of Wilton stretched back many years, and who wrote many accounts of the saints of the house of Wessex. Unfortunately, these few names are all that can be known of the musical entertainment that Queen Matilda favored and that undoubtedly provided a

---

[73] Hans Willner, ed., 'Des Adelard von Bath Traktat *De eodem et diversa*', 25–6. The bishop to whom the treatise is dedicated, William of Syracuse, is not mentioned in surviving documents as bishop until 1112, but that reference implies that he had been in office for some time. His predecessor had died in 1104. For a general treatment of courtly music, see Laurence Wright, 'The Role of Musicians at Court in Twelfth-Century Britain', *Art and Patronage in the English Romanesque* (London, 1986), 97–106.

[74] Southworth, *The English Medieval Minstrel* (Woodbridge, 1989), 39.

background for the courtly activity in the royal palace in the early years of the twelfth century.

Disappointing as it is to be able to locate so few pieces that can be definitely associated with Queen Matilda's patronage, there is no doubt that her court was a focal point for both literary and musical activity in the opening years of the twelfth century. The panegyric literature especially allows us to glimpse the ideals of queenly behavior to which she aspired, and judging by her posthumous reputation, usually attained.

Conclusion:
Matilda of Blessed Memory
The Legacy of 'Matilda Bona Regina'

On the first day of May, in the year 1118, Queen Matilda died in her favorite palace of Westminster. There is little indication that she had been suffering from any lingering illness, and nothing that hints at the cause of her death. William of Malmesbury simply explained that she 'shared in the lot of her relations, who almost all departed this life in the flower of their age'.[1] The nearby monks of Westminster Abbey took possession of the queen's body, despite the outrage of the canons at Holy Trinity Aldgate, who claimed that she had expressed a desire to be buried in their church. At the time Matilda died, the canons of St Paul's were doing their best to establish themselves as the leading church of London, and Holy Trinity was legally subject to the cathedral church of St Paul's. The canons may have especially desired Matilda's tomb in order to counter the growing cults of Edith and Edward at Westminster. When Henry returned from Normandy, they lodged a protest against the monks of Westminster for taking possession of the Queen's body. Ultimately, they were forced to settle for a royal confirmation of all Matilda's donations to Holy Trinity, accompanied by a gift of relics that had been sent from the Byzantine emperor to the king and queen of England.[2] Nothing survives to document the queen's own desire, but it is indeed possible that she may have wished to be interred in the church she had founded. There was ample precedent for such a choice. Matilda's mother Margaret of Scotland had been buried at Holy Trinity, Dumfermline, which she had founded; Matilda of Flanders had chosen to be buried in her foundation, Holy Trinity, Caen; and Matilda of Scotland may have been echoing their choices with her foundation at Holy Trinity Aldgate.[3] It is also possible that Matilda, who had always identified with her Anglo-Saxon heritage, would have chosen to be entombed at Westminster Abbey near her kinsman King Edward the Confessor and his wife Edith.

The 'Hyde Chronicler' provided a full description of the queen's funeral service, which was attended by most of the secular and ecclesiastical dignitaries of the kingdom. Bishop Roger of Salisbury preached her funeral sermon, and the most noble clerks of the kingdom, 'whom she had greatly loved while living', spent thirty days mourning at her tomb. Spurred on by Roger, the kingdom's

---

[1] *Gesta regum*, 759.
[2] *Cartulary HTA*, 230.
[3] For discussion, see John Carmi Parsons, '"Never was a Body Buried in England with such Solemnity and Honour": The Burials and Posthumous Commemorations of English Queens to 1500', in Duggan, ed., *Queens and Queenship in Medieval Europe*, 317–37.

lay and ecclesiastical lords paid for masses and prayers for the queen, as well as for charitable acts to be performed in her memory. The 'Hyde Chronicler' is typical in his fulsome praise of the queen. He explained that Henry chose Matilda as his bride because 'no woman in her time could withstand comparison to her', describing her as a 'truly incomparable woman'. During her lifetime, England flourished to the point that 'from the time England first became subject to kings, out of all the queens none was found to be comparable to her, and none will be found in the time to come, whose memory will be praised and whose name will be blessed through the ages'.[4] The number of gifts that poured into the churches of England upon the death of the queen was 'unable to be comprehended by any man', but he provides a summary of eight days' worth of the donations: 47,000 masses, 9,000 psalms, 80 'tricennaria' (a cycles of masses said for thirty days after a death), and daily sustenance for 67,820 paupers.[5]

Details of other memorials for the queen can be gleaned from later records. Henry set up a fund to maintain a perpetual tomb-light at his wife's gravesite.[6] Matilda's brother David repaid his sister's devotion by establishing an annual memorial service to be performed by the monks of Westminster. The money to pay for these services was to come from the rents from lands held of David by Matilda's chancellor, Aldwin.[7] The cathedral chapter at Exeter also celebrated an anniversary mass for the queen, purportedly out of gratitude for her part in persuading Henry to restore the liberties of their city.[8] The Norman chronicler Robert of Torigni spoke of a 'Life of Queen Matilda', and while it is possible that he was mistakenly referring to the *Life of Margaret*, there may also have been a lost *Life of Matilda* written for her descendants. Robert of Torigni was well-acquainted with the Empress Matilda, and it is certainly possible that she might have commissioned a biography of the mother she scarcely knew in the same way that the elder Matilda had done for Margaret.[9]

Within a short time after Matilda's death, 'signs and miracles' were taking place at her tomb, indicating to contemporaries that 'her soul certainly now dwelt in heaven' and hinting that a cult of sanctity was beginning to arise around 'Good Queen Maud'.[10] Sanctity was still a fluid status in the twelfth century, perhaps more often first recognized by the community of believers than by the church hierarchy. But even in the twelfth century, official recognition of Matilda's cult would have required a testimonial from the bishop of London or his deputies, the canons of St Paul's. In light of the rivalry between the canons of St Paul's and the monks of Westminster, it is difficult to see this testimonial forthcoming without some pressure from the king, who was away in Normandy and seems to have made no official notice of Matilda's death there. If Matilda and Henry's

---

[4] *Liber monasterii de Hyda*, 312–13.
[5] *Liber monasterii de Hyda*, 312.
[6] Mason, ed., *Westminster Abbey Charters*, #79.
[7] For David's charter, see Barrow, ed., *Regesta regum scottorum* 1: 6 (p. 134).
[8] J. H. Wylie and JamesWylie, edd., *Report on the Records of the City of Exeter* (London, 1916), 391.
[9] Van Houts, ed., *Gesta normannorum ducum* 1: lxxxvii–viii, and 2: 242–3.
[10] *Gesta regum* 2: 495.

only son, William, had not died in the wreck of the White Ship in 1120, Henry might have taken an interest in promoting the cult of his dead wife for the sake of his heirs. But during the early 1120s, Henry must have thought it unlikely that any of Matilda's descendants would ever ascend the English throne. Her son William was dead, and her daughter, married to the German Emperor Henry V, remained childless. Henry, meanwhile, remarried after William's death, presumably with the hope of producing more sons. The Westminster monks chose to use their energy to promote the cult of Edward the Confessor.

Yet the popular memory of Queen Matilda persisted. In the mid-1120s, papal indulgences in memory of King Edward and Queen Matilda were granted to those visiting the abbey during the major feasts of St Peter, 'inasmuch as the holy King Edward and Queen Matilda are buried there'.[11] When a delegation from Savigny visited Westminster in 1122 or 1123 to announce the death of their abbot, the Westminster monks inscribed his funeral roll with a request for prayers for their royal patrons: Kings Edward, Edgar, Offa, and Queen Matilda.[12] For a short time, it appeared that Matilda might join her mother and other illustrious ancestors in the ranks of England's royal saints. But after this auspicious beginning to the creation of the legend of 'Good Queen Maud', Stephen of Blois seized the throne in 1135. His partisans argued that Matilda's daughter and namesake should be barred from the throne because of bastardy. According to their lights, the marriage of Henry and Matilda II should never have been allowed to take place because of the time that Matilda had spent in the convent. Although this line of reasoning failed at the papal court in Rome, rumors of impropriety were rife throughout the rest of the century.[13] The scandal probably stanched any incipient cult growing up around Matilda of Scotland. Even with the prestige of St Anselm to safeguard the queen's reputation, later commentators were ambiguous and varied in their treatment of the royal marriage. Eadmer's defense of the archbishop was not widely disseminated, so writers in the reign of Henry II and beyond often confused the details of Matilda's early years. For instance, Walter Map claimed that Matilda had been a nun at Winchester, and when she wished to marry, 'Rome said neither yes nor no, but allowed it.'[14] By the time of Matthew Paris, who wrote toward the middle of the thirteenth century, Matilda had truly become 'another Esther in our own times': a reluctant bride who left the convent unwillingly, sacrificing herself to the Norman king only to save her suffering race from further oppression under the cruel conquerors. Matthew even accounted for the tragic fates of Matilda's children by having her curse the descendants of the marriage that called her from her true vocation as a nun.[15]

---

[11] Quoted in Mason, 'Westminster Abbey Charters', #187, #189.

[12] Leopold Delisle, ed., *Rouleau mortuaire du B. Vital, Abbé de Savigni, comtenant 207 titres, écretis en 1122–23 dans différentes églises de France et d'Angleterre* (Paris, 1909).

[13] John of Salisbury (*Historia pontificalis*, ed./trans. Marjorie Chibnall (Oxford, 1986), 83–6) and Gilbert Foliot (*The Letters and Charters of Gilbert Foliot*, letter #26, pp. 60–6) wrote independent accounts of the papal hearing of 1139 in which Stephen's partisans claimed the Empress to be illegitimate of impropriety. See also Adrian Morey and C. N. L. Brooke, ed., *Gilbert Foliot and his Letters* (Cambridge, 1965), 112–21.

[14] Walter Map, *De nugis curialium*, 474.

[15] Matthew Paris, *Historia Anglorum*, ed. Frederic Madden (RS, London, 1866), 188–9.

Although Matilda's reputation was tainted by the rumors that developed during Stephen's reign, chroniclers of the next reign, that of her grandson Henry II, tended to treat her memory very well. Aelred of Rievaulx wrote a genealogical account of the English royal line at Henry II's request wherein he compared Matilda to the biblical queen Esther.[16] The records from Henry III's renovation of Westminster Abbey in the thirteenth century show that she was at that time still commemorated as a member of the royal *stirpes*. King Henry ordered four silver dishes to be made for holding tomb lamps. Two of these lamps were hung over the grave of the Confessor, the third over his wife Edith, and the fourth was placed over the unmarked tomb of Matilda, queen-consort of Henry I.[17] Matilda's tomb was probably renovated at that time, and the following legend inscribed upon it:

> Here lies Matilda II, the good queen of the English, formerly the wife of King Henry I, mother of the Empress Matilda, and daughter of Lord Malcolm the former king of the Scots and his consort, Saint Margaret. She died on the first day of May in the year of grace 1118, and if we wished to speak of her goodness and probity of character, a day would not be sufficient. May her spirit be greatly soothed. Amen.[18]

The later thirteenth and fourteenth century witnessed only occasional references to the queen, and nothing in the way of original scholarship devoted to Matilda. If chroniclers chose to comment upon her, it was usually in reference to her pious foundations or to repeat the stories of her interaction with lepers. In 1522, the city fathers of Exeter claimed still to be celebrating the anniversary of Queen Matilda in gratitude for her role in restoring their liberties. But within a few years, the memory of 'Mathilda bona regina' had certainly faded. Perhaps most symbolic of her disappearance into history is the notice entered into the Exeter city archives on 4 September 1528: 'the recever schall pay no more money for the obytt of Queen Molde to the parsons and curates of the citie for as moche as they have nott keptte the same obytt in tymes past as they schulde have done'.[19] By the dawn of the modern era, Good Queen Maud was passing from legend into oblivion.

What, then, should modern readers conclude about the life and legacy of Matilda of Scotland? I have tried to argue throughout this work that she stands at the apogee of opportunity for medieval women to exercise public authority. England had a precedent of strong, competent, and active queen consorts from at least the time of Queen Aelfthryth in the later tenth century. The circumstances of the Conquest and the cross-channel *regnum* required a sharing of regal authority, and until the middle part of Henry's reign, it was most practical that it be a member of the king's family who shared in that authority. Even after Henry's administration had gained the sophistication to operate independently

---

[16] *PL* 195: column 736.
[17] Jocelyn Perkins, *Westminster Abbey: Its Worship and Ornaments* (Alcuin Club 34, 3 vols, 1936–52), 2: 42.
[18] *Cartulary HTA*, 230. The quotation from earlier chronicles, the reference to the first King Henry and to Margaret as a saint make it impossible that the inscription on the tomb was the original one.
[19] Wylie and Wylie, ed., *Report on the Records of the City of Exeter*, 404–5.

of personal authority for most matters, we see the queen presiding at solemn occasions such as the treasury accounting of 1111 or in unusual circumstances such as the freeing of Bricstan of Chatteris in 1116. Clearly the queen carried public authority second only to the king during the lifetime of Matilda II. But we must stop short of speaking of the development of 'institutions' of queenship, as the life and reign of Matilda's immediate successor demonstrates. Adeliza of Louvain, Henry's second wife, played little part in the public life of the kingdom while married to Henry. Adeliza's successor, Matilda of Boulogne, was called upon to play other strong, visible, and unusual roles during the English civil war. The next queen consort, Eleanor of Aquitaine, was personally flamboyant, but left little mark on the institutional development of queenship. Indeed, it was probably because of her 1173 disgrace that the queen's household became financially subsumed under that of the king.

I argued at the beginning of this study that personal factors should not be ignored in trying to reconstruct the history of any medieval court. I hope it has become clear that one key to understanding Matilda's success is to look at her relationships with other powerful people of her era. The fact that she was able to maintain a generally harmonious relationship with Henry in spite of what must have been a challenging marital situation provided her the opportunity and responsibility to play a public role. Her friendships with men such as Anselm of Canterbury, Gundulph of Rochester, and Faritius of Abingdon allowed her to share in their goals and projects, and also allowed her to draw upon their experience and resources as she developed her own interests and patronage patterns. She left indelible marks on the city of London in the form of physical monuments, and her interest in the Augustinian canons helped that group flourish on English soil.

I have also shown that Matilda was prepared, as few other women could have been, to exercise her public authority. Her bloodline, her excellent education, her lifelong interest in the works of her predecessors, and her personal abilities combined to place Matilda in a position to succeed. She was ideally suited, by her birth, bloodline, and education, to serve as England's queen at a time when parts of England were still adjusting to the finality of the Norman Conquest. The marriage itself represents an acceptance of that finality. As Hollister put it, '[Matilda] was clearly proud of being, through her mother, a member of the west Saxon royal line, and she must have realized, as most people of her time did, that there was little chance of her line reascending the English throne except through a marriage.'[20] The fact that she only had one son initially proved problematic and probably cost her the distinction of sanctity, but with the accession of her grandson Henry II in 1154 the descendants of Alfred of Wessex regained England's throne.

Matilda's life after her marriage also puts another nail in the coffin of the strictly agnatic noble family as imagined by modern theorists. Clearly even after her marriage and coronation Matilda continued to identify with her natal family and to see herself as a Scottish and Anglo-Saxon princess. She was invaluable in promoting the interests of her younger brother David and her

---

[20] Hollister, *Henry I*, 127–8.

sister Mary. The ties she had to them influenced the course of English and Scottish history for several generations, for David became Matilda's daughter's most loyal adherent during the English civil war. At the same time, Matilda of Boulogne carried on traditions of queenship she had learned from the direct example of her aunt, Matilda of Scotland.

Finally, Matilda of Scotland shows us, perhaps more clearly than any other English queen, what the medieval world desired and admired in a royal consort. She, like her mother before her, became a model, or mirror, of good queenship. Over and over, through her own relationships with churchmen and the letters and poems addressed to her, we see the ideal of queenly behavior held up to us in the person of Matilda of Scotland. Her personal probity and moral qualities seemed almost beyond reproach. She was praised as a suitable helpmeet to the king, admonished to act as an intercessor in case of his harsh behavior, counseled to be a wise lawgiver, urged to be an effector of commerce, all of which she did to the best of her considerable ability. She was known as a patron of the arts, a friend of the church, and mother to the heirs and to the nation at large. If we are willing to listen to the voice of medieval commentators, modern thinkers have no choice but to conclude with them that Matilda of Scotland was an unparalleled success in her role as England's queen.

Appendix I

A Handlist of Matilda of Scotland's Acta

This handlist provides a reference to all of Matilda's known acta. Most have been printed in readily available sources, but one is printed here for the first time. I have divided Matilda's thirty-two known acts into two groups. Group I charters all show the queen acting in a regal capacity. Group II acta are more complicated. The majority show the queen exercising dominion over her own lands. When there is any doubt as to whether an act reflects a demesne act or a vice-regal one, I have chosen the more conservative option and listed as the former, although, as we have seen, the line is sometimes difficult to draw.

Most of the listed actions are based on extant charters or good cartulary copies. Other acta of the queen are known to us only through later confirmation charters, and several are inferred because of mentions of the queen's gifts in other sources. The notes to each act document the source and context. I have normally gone with the dating of acta based on the information in *RRAN* 2, but in some cases I have been able to narrow down a possible range of dates or to suggest an alternative date. Again, the notes to each act document any dating controversies or uncertainties.

Group I: The Vice-Regal Acta

I. (*RRAN* 2: 1000)
PLACE OF ISSUE AND DATING INFORMATION: Winchester, 30 September 1111.
PRINTED: Stevens, ed., *Abingdon Chronicle* 2: 116–17.
ACTION: Queen Matilda notifies Robert Bishop of Lincoln, Thomas of St John and all the Oxfordshire barons, French and English, that Abbot Faritius of Abingdon has appeared at the treasury, her court and that of her husband, and has proved by the 'Liber thesauro' that the manor of Lewknor owed nothing to the hundred of Pryton. Listed as present at the hearing: Roger Bishop of Salisbury, Robert Bishop of Lincoln, Richard Bishop of London, William de Curci, Adam de Port, Turstin the chaplain, Walter of Gloucester, Herbert the chamberlain, William d'Oilli, Geoffrey fitz Herbert, William de Anesy, Ralph Basset, Geoffrey de Mandeville, Geoffrey Ridel, Walter Archdeacon of Oxford.
WITNESSES: Roger Bishop of Salisbury, William de Curci, and Adam de Port.

II. (*RRAN* 2: 1001)
PLACE OF ISSUE AND DATING INFORMATION: Winchester, 30 September 1111.
PRINTED: Van Caenegem, *Royal Writs*, #143.
ACTION: Queen Matilda orders Nigel de Albini to do full right to Ranulf Bishop of Durham concerning lands that Robert de Muschamps seized after an agreement between Bishop William and Robert Earl of Northumberland.
WITNESSES: Walter of Gloucester.

III. (*RRAN* 2: 1190)
PLACE OF ISSUE AND DATING INFORMATION: Westminster, 1116 × 1118.
PRINTED: Hardwick, ed., *Historia Monasterii S. Augustini Cantuariensis*, 354; also Van Caenegem, *Royal Writs*, #59.
ACTION: Queen Matilda orders Ansfrid the Dapifer to ensure that the ship belonging to the Abbot of St Augustine's, Canterbury, is returned to him, along with all its goods. Further, the queen orders that the men who seized the ship are to find sureties so that they might stand before the king when he so wills.
WITNESSES: Roger Bishop of Salisbury.

IV. (*RRAN* 2: 1198)
PLACE OF ISSUE AND DATING INFORMATION: Oxford, 1116 × 1118.
PRINTED: Elvey, ed., *Luffield Priory Charters*, 1.
ACTION: Queen Matilda orders Vitalis Engaigne and William de Lisors, keepers of the forest in Northamptonshire, to convey Malger the monk and his servants to Luffield, and to protect them there, because the king has allowed them to stay there.
WITNESSES: The Bishop of Lincoln.

V. (Uncalendared in *RRAN*)
PLACE OF ISSUE AND DATING INFORMATION: Winchester, January–June 1109 or August 1111–July 1113.
PRINTED: *Register of Worcester Cathedral Priory*, p. 26, entry #40.
ACTION: Queen Matilda informs Walter of Gloucester, Sheriff Roger of Worcester, Hugh of Leicester and all the barons and ministers of the king and queen that Thomas Prior of Worcester and all his monks and lands are in royal hands and should have the peace of the king and the queen.
WITNESSES: Roger Bishop of Salisbury, Walter of Gloucester. 'Per' Osbert the chaplain.[1]

VI. (Uncalendared in *RRAN*)
PLACE OF ISSUE AND DATING INFORMATION: Westminster, before May 1112.
PRINTED: *Register of Worcester Cathedral Priory*, p. 139, entry #262.
ACTION: Queen Matilda notifies the French and English barons and all of England that she has, on the part of herself and her lord the king, confirmed the gifts that Bishop Sampson gave to the monks and the church at Worcester. She

---

[1] For the use and meaning of the 'per' clause, see Chapter 4, page 80.

orders that they be allowed to hold these gifts as honorably and freely as did Sampson and his predecessors.
WITNESSES: Roger Bishop of Salisbury, Adam de Port, etc.

VII. (Not calendared in *RRAN*)
PLACE OF ISSUE AND DATING INFORMATION: Westminster, probably 1111 × 1113.
PRINTED: Brown, ed., *The Cartulary and Charters of Eye Priory* 1: 34, charter #26.
ACTION: Queen Matilda informs Hubert de Montchesny that the possessions of the monks of St Peter at Eye are to be left in peace and she orders that everything that Hugh and his officials have unjustly seized be returned to the church, Hubert the prior, and Robert the chamberlain.
WITNESSES: Walter of Gloucester

Group II: The Demesne Acta

VIII. (*RRAN* 2: 565)
PLACE OF ISSUE AND DATING INFORMATION: Sutton Courtenay, probably between September 1101 and February 1102.
PRINTED: *Abingdon Chronicle* 2: 51.
ACTION: Queen Matilda orders Hugh of Bocland to allow Abbot Faritius of Abingdon to have the lead from the houses of Andresey for use in the church at Abingdon.
WITNESSES: Ralph of Tew and Bernard the clerk.

IX. (*RRAN* 2: 567)
PLACE OF ISSUE AND DATING INFORMATION: Probably between September 1101 and February 1102.
PRINTED: *Abingdon Chronicle* 2: 51–2.
ACTION: Queen Matilda notifies Hugh de Bocland and all the faithful subjects in Berkshire that she has given Abbot Faritius of Abingdon the houses on the island of St Mary to use in repairing the church at Abingdon, and that the king has confirmed her gift.
WITNESSES: Roger the chancellor and Grimbald the physician.

X. (*RRAN* 2: 526)
PLACE OF ISSUE AND DATING INFORMATION: 1100 × 1101.
PRINTED: Ransford, ed., *Waltham Charters*, 5.
ACTION: Queen Matilda announces that she has pardoned the canons of Waltham from the money which they used to have to give yearly to William Bishop of Durham for the building of Durham Castle.
WITNESSES: William Giffard the chancellor and others.

XI. (*RRAN* 2: 535)
PLACE OF ISSUE AND DATING INFORMATION: Winchester, 1101 × 1108
PRINTED: Foster, ed., *Registrum Antiquissimum* 1, entry 62, p. 42.

ACTION: Queen Matilda notifies Osbert the sheriff, Ranulf Meschin, the barons, and all the faithful subjects in Lincolnshire that, at her request, King Henry has given to Robert, Bishop of Lincoln the manor of Nettleham and everything pertaining to it, which was in her fee.
WITNESSES: Hamo Dapifer and Urso d'Abitot.

XII. (*RRAN* 2: 571)
PLACE OF ISSUE AND DATING INFORMATION: Whitsuntide, probably 25 May 1102.
PRINTED: *Calendar of Patent Rolls: Richard II, vol. 6, AD 1396–99*, entry 9, p. 75.
ACTION: Queen Matilda notifies Osbert, Sheriff of Lincoln, and all the king's barons that she has given six pounds worth of land in Belton, which she used to have, to the church of St Mary's, York, to hold freely.
WITNESSES: Reinhelm the queen's chancellor.

XIII. (*RRAN* 2: 624)
PLACE OF ISSUE AND DATING INFORMATION: London, 1102 x 31 July 1106.
PRINTED: Gibson, *History of the Monastery at Tynemouth*, 2, Appendix #xix.
ACTION: Queen Matilda notifies Roger Picot, the barons, and all her faithful subjects in Northumberland, both French and English, that she has given the land of Archil Morel to God and to St Alban, St Oswin, and Abbot Richard for the soul of her father. She wishes that they hold the land peacefully and honorably with all customary rights.
WITNESSES: Bernard the chancellor.

XIV. (*RRAN* 2: 632)
PLACE OF ISSUE AND DATING INFORMATION: Exeter, 1103, probably in January.
PRINTED: Finberg, 'Early Tavistock Charters', 354–5.
ACTION: Queen Matilda notifies her ministers in Lifton that she has given to the church of St Mary in Tavistock all the rights that she had in 'Oddetriwe' (Guthery?) namely 22d. and one awm of rye.
WITNESSES: William de Warelwast and Michael de Hanslope.

XV. (*RRAN* 2: 674)
PLACE OF ISSUE AND DATING INFORMATION: London, 1104, after 15 August.
PRINTED: *Abingdon Chronicle* 2: 98–9.
ACTION: Matilda, queen of the English, advises Robert Bishop of Lincoln, Hugh de Bocland, and all the French and English barons of Buckinghamshire that she has given Robert, son of Hervey, with all of his land, to God and the church of St Mary at Abingdon, because Robert Gernon gave them to her. She wishes that the abbot be allowed to hold this land, with all its customs, as well and as peacefully as he holds his other lands, and they are to see that she hears no more about the matter.
WITNESSES: Roger de Curci, Robert Malet and Odo Moire.

XVI. (*RRAN* 2: 675)
PLACE OF ISSUE AND DATING INFORMATION: York or Evreux, 1101–3. Henry's confirmation charter (*RRAN* 2: 720) is dated Christmas Day, and the witness list of his charter is generally compatible with either 1101–3 or 1105. The *RRAN* 2 editors prefer 1105, and read 'Ern' capellano' in the witness list as 'Everard' rather than Ernisius. Everard, one of Henry's chaplains, does not appear in any of the queen's other charters. Ernisius the queen's chaplain appears elsewhere in conjunction with Aldwin, another of the queen's household chaplains, but he had left the queen's service by 1103.
PRINTED: Raine, *Historians of the Church of York*, 3: 30, entry #14, 2.
ACTION: Queen Matilda informs Richard, son of Gotze, Roger de Lovetot and all the barons on the Honour of Blyth that she has given the church of Laughton-en-le-Moreton to St Peter's, York, for a prebend. She wishes and orders that this prebend be held quietly and free from all customs as are the other prebends of this church.
WITNESSES: Bishop Hervey, Bernard the Chaplain, John of Bayeaux, John of Sées, Ernisius the chaplain, Robert Malet and Aldwin the chaplain.

XVII. (*RRAN* 2: 743)
PLACE OF ISSUE AND DATING INFORMATION: Rockingham, 1106.
PRINTED: Foster, ed., *Registrum Antiquissimum*, 1, entry #16, p. 18.
ACTION: Queen Matilda notifies the Abbot of Peterborough, Earl Simon, Sheriff Robert de Pavilli, and Michael de Hanslope, and all the faithful barons, French and English, of Northamptonshire, that she has, with the king's permission, given Tixover and everything pertaining to it to Robert Bishop of Lincoln. She wishes and orders that they be allowed to hold it as well and as honorably as she herself held it.
WITNESSES: Waldric the chancellor, Bernard the chaplain, Eudo Dapifer, William Peverel of Nottingham and Michael de Hanslope.

XVIII. (*RRAN* 2: 808)
PLACE OF ISSUE AND DATING INFORMATION: Lillebonne, Easter 1107.
PRINTED: Raine, *Historians of York*, 3: 31, entry 14, p. 4.
ACTION: Queen Matilda orders William Peverel of Nottingham, Richard son of Gotze, and Roger of Lovetot to see that the church of Laughton-en-le-Moreton, which she gave in prebend to St Peter's of York, be allowed to have its tithes fully and without molestation. Neither the monks of Blyth nor anyone else may interfere. The addressees are to see that her alms are not diminished, and no one is to interfere with them except the canons of York themselves.
WITNESSES: John of Sées and Bernard the chaplain.

XIX. (*RRAN* 2: 818a)
PLACE OF ISSUE AND DATING INFORMATION: Unknown place of issue, 22 June 1103 or 1105 × 1107.
PRINTED: Mason, ed., *Beauchamp Cartulary*, entry #165, p. 18.
ACTION: Queen Matilda notifies all her French men that she has given Michael

de Hanslope the land which she used to hold in Barrowden, Luffenham, Seaton, and Thorpe-by-the-Water.
WITNESSES: David the queen's brother.

XX. (*RRAN* 2: 887)
PLACE OF ISSUE AND DATING INFORMATION: Winchester, 1107 × 8.
PRINTED: Fowler, ed., *Coucher Book of Selby Abbey*, 1: 25, entry #23.
ACTION: Queen Matilda notifies Archbishop Gerard of York, Robert Bishop of Lincoln, Hugh Sheriff of Northamptonshire, and all the barons of Northamptonshire and Aldwin the chamberlain and all her ministers at Rockingham that she has given, at the wish of the king, all that she possessed concerning the manor of Stamford, namely £4 and the service of two knights, to God and the church of St German of Selby. The gift is for the welfare of her lord and herself and for the souls of her ancestors, to be held with all the privileges which it had when it was in her custody. She orders her ministers to defend and maintain the manor appropriately.
WITNESSES: Rannulf bishop of Durham, 'T' son of the Count, and Thomas the chaplain.

XXI. (*RRAN* 2: 902)
PLACE OF ISSUE AND DATING INFORMATION: 26 July 1108 × 1118. (After the consecration of Richard de Belmeis to the bishopric of London.)
PRINTED: Ransford, Waltham Charters, #10, p. 7.
ACTION: Queen Matilda notifies Richard Bishop of London and others ('etc' in cartulary copy) that she has given to God and to the canons of the Holy Cross at Waltham two and a half hides of northland that Bishop Walcher of Durham had unjustly seized from the church. And she orders that they hold it quietly, as they used to do before it was taken away. She does this for the welfare of the body and the soul of her lord King Henry and for her children.
WITNESSES: List omitted, although the presence of witnesses noted ('Hiis testibus' in cartulary copy).

XXII. (*RRAN* 2: 906)
PLACE OF ISSUE AND DATING INFORMATION: Westminster, May 1108 × April 1109.
PRINTED: *Cartulary HTA*, entry #4, pp. 224–5.
ACTION: Matilda, Queen of England by the Grace of God, notifies Bishop Richard of London and all the faithful sons of the Holy Church, that she has, with the advice of Archbishop Anselm and with the permission and confirmation of her lord, King Henry, given and confirmed Christ Church within the walls of London to Prior Norman and the canons there serving God. They are to hold the church free from subjection to either Waltham or any other church except St Paul's of London and the bishop. She does this in perpetuity for the redemption of their souls and the souls of their parents. Likewise, she gives them the gate of Aldgate, with the 'soc' and 'sac' that pertained to it when it was in her demesne, and also she gives two-thirds of the rents from the city of Exeter. She orders that the canons hold the land and the church and everything

pertaining to them freely and honorably, as King Henry has confirmed by his charter.
WITNESSES: William Bishop of Winchester, Roger Bishop of Salisbury, Robert Bishop of Lincoln, Rannulf and Bernard the chancellors, Walter Giffard of Clare, Geoffrey de Clinton, William de Pont and Aldwin.

XXIII. (The act is calendared in *RRAN* 2: 909 as a more general notification)
PLACE OF ISSUE AND DATING INFORMATION: After Bishop Richard was consecrated, 26 July 1108, at the foundation of Holy Trinity, Aldgate.
PRINTED: There were evidently two separate charters announcing this act, one possibly issued at the foundation of Holy Trinity, 1107 × 1108, and this one, issued a little later. They are identical except for the addressees. The first, calendared in *RRAN* 2, and printed in Ransford, *Early Charters*, #6, pp. 5–6, was addressed to 'all her faithful men, etc'. The cartulary also contains a second act, addressed more specifically, which Ransford did not print in full. The text below is from BL MS Additional 37665, f. 10r.[2]
ACTION: Queen Matilda notifies Richard Bishop of London, all the faithful sons of the church of God and her ministers in Waltham that she has given the Church of the Holy Cross at Waltham her mills and everything pertaining to them in exchange for the church of Holy Trinity in London. And just as the canons of Holy Trinity may possess and freely alter their church, the canons of Waltham are free to enlarge and use their mills.
WITNESSES: Roger Bishop of Salisbury and others.
TEXT: Titulus: Carta Mathildis regine de molendinus. Matilda regina Anglorum Ricardo episcopo London' omnibus filiis sanctis Dei ecclesie et ministris suis de Waltham, salutem. Sciatis me concessisse et dedisse ecclesie Sancte Crucis de Waltham molendina eiusdem Waltham tam in aqua quam in silva et in multura et in omnibus libertatibus quas ego ipsa ea habui pro escambio ecclesie Sancte Trinitatis de Londonia. Et sicut licet canonicis Sancte Trinitatis in omnibus que possunt ecclesiam suam emendare ital liceat canonicis de Waltham molendina sua in omnibus que possunt crescere et moliare. Teste Rogero episcipo Salesberiensis, etc.

XXIV. (Uncalendared in *RRAN*)
PLACE OF ISSUE AND DATING INFORMATION: Early in the reign, before #XXV, below.
PRINTED: Notification of the act in Brewer and Martin, edd., *Registrium Malmesburiense* 2: 333.
ACTION: Queen Matilda confirms the order of King Henry I *(RRAN* 2: 494, 29 September 1100) that the abbot of Malmesbury may hold a five-day fair, which had been conceded to him earlier by William I for three days and extended to five days by William II. If Malmesbury was part of the queen's dower, as I have

---

[2] If the two charters were issued at separate times, it would imply that someone in the royal writing office was keeping copies of outgoing documents that could be retrieved for later use. This practice seems intuitive to modern minds, but may not have been so in the twelfth century. See Michael T. Clanchy, *From Memory to Written Record: England 1066–1307* (Oxford, 2nd ed., 1993), for more on the development of medieval record keeping.

suggested, then Matilda issued her confirmation charter after her marriage to Henry on 11 November 1100, but before her second charter (1108 × 1115) granting a further augmentation of the fair to a total of eight days.
SOURCE OF TEXT: Brewer and Martin, edd., *Registrium Malmesburiense* 2: 333, from a manuscript in the Public Record Office. Checked against BL Landsdowne 417, f. 31v, another copy of the register.
TEXT: Titulus: Item de feria: Matildis anglie regine. Require ut supra.

XXV. (*RRAN* 2: 971)
PLACE OF ISSUE AND DATING INFORMATION: Westminster, after 1108 and before Bernard became bishop in September 1115.
PRINTED: Brewer, ed., *Registrium Malmesburiense* 1: 329.
ACTION: Matilda notifies Roger Bishop of Salisbury and Walter son of Edward, and all the barons and Humphrey de Bohun and all the king's ministers in Wiltshire and at Malmesbury that she has given to St Aldhelm a three-day augmentation of the fair beyond the five days that the monks used to have. Specifically, they are to have three days before the festival, the festival day itself, and four days after the fair, freely and quietly with all the customs and privileges inside and outside the town which they had before by the king's writ.
WITNESSES: Richard Bishop of London, Bernard the chancellor, William de Curci and Aldwin the chamberlain.

XXVI. (*RRAN* 2: 1090)
PLACE OF ISSUE AND DATING INFORMATION: Westminster, 13 September 1108 × 1117, probably before 1115, which is the date Brooke and Keir give for the death of Hugh de Bucland.[3]
PRINTED: Ransford, *Waltham Charters*, #15, p. 10.
ACTION: Queen Matilda informs Richard Bishop of London and Hugh de Bucland and Aldwin the chamberlain and all the ministers of the king and queen, and all the men, both French and English, of Essex, that she has given to the Church of the Holy Cross at Waltham and to the canons serving God there a fair to be held on the festival of the Holy Cross with all the customs pertaining to the fair. And she does this for the welfare of her lord the king and for their children. She orders that they hold the fair as quietly and honorably as was done when she herself had the fair. And all coming to the church are to have the firm peace of the king and the queen.
WITNESSES: Roger Bishop of Salisbury, Nigel d'Oilli, Ranulf the chaplain, and Geoffrey the queen's chaplain, canon of the aforementioned church, and Aldwin the chamberlain and Odo Moire.

XXVII. (*RRAN* 2: 1108)
PLACE OF ISSUE AND DATING INFORMATION: Westminster, April 1115 × April 1116, after the death of Mary Countess of Boulogne in April 1115 and before Henry left for the continent in April 1116.
PRINTED: Ransford, *Waltham Charters*, #11, pp. 7–8. This charter, with its seal,

---

[3] Brooke and Keir, *London 800–1216*, 204.

is extant in the Library of the Dean and Chapter of Durham Cathedral, 1.3. Ebor. 13.
ACTION: Queen Matilda notifies Geoffrey the deacon and Aldwin the chamberlain and all the canons of Holy Cross and all her faithful men and ministers at Waltham that she has given, to God and St Cuthbert, for the work of the monks of Durham, one and a half hides of land that Bruning the canon held in Epping and a half hide in Nazeing, which the aforesaid Bruning held on the day of his death. This land will be held with all customary rights and freedom from service as it was when it was in her demesne. St Cuthbert and his monks are to hold this land as well and as quietly as they do any of their other land in England, which they have and hold. She gives this to the saint and the monks for the welfare of her lord King Henry and her son William and her brother and for the welfare of the souls of her mother and father and brother and sister. And all this land is to be held from St Cuthbert and his monks by the canon Adam for his lifetime, in return for 14s. rent annually. She wishes her grants to be held by St Cuthbert and his monks in perpetuity without any disturbance.
WITNESSES: William the queen's son, Count David, and Aldwin the chamberlain.

XXVIII. (*RRAN* 2: 1143)
PLACE OF ISSUE AND DATING INFORMATION: Windsor, April 1107 × 1116.
PRINTED: Hodgson, *History of Northumberland*, 3: 2, p. 150. This charter and its seal are extant in the Library of the Dean and Chapter of Durham Cathedral, Durham 1.2.Spec.23*.
ACTION: Queen Matilda notifies Rannulf Bishop of Durham and the sheriffs Alaric and Liulf and all the barons of Northumberland, French, and English, that she has given the church of Carham and everything pertaining to it, as far as it pertains to her to do so, to God and to St Cuthbert and to the monks serving him. She does this for the welfare of herself, her lord the king and for their children and for the souls of her parents and the king's parents. And the addressees are to see that no one disturbs the work of the monks. WITNESS: Aldwin the chamberlain.

XXIX. (*RRAN* 2: 1180)
PLACE OF ISSUE AND DATING INFORMATION: Westminster, c. December 1113–c.1115.
PRINTED: Robinson, *Gilbert Crispin*, entry #38, p. 155.
ACTION: Queen Matilda informs Bishop Richard and the sheriff and barons of London, both French and English, that she has given to St Peter and Abbot Gilbert of Westminster all that Hugh de Bucland had held of her on the wharves of London. She does this for the welfare and salvation of King Henry, herself and their children.
WITNESSES: Robert Bishop of Lincoln and Count David.

XXX. (*RRAN* 2: 1199)
PLACE OF ISSUE AND DATING INFORMATION: Northampton, 1101 × 1118.
PRINTED: *Reg S. Osmundi episcopi*, 1: 202–3.

ACTION: Queen Matilda announces that she has given the church of St Mary at Salisbury her rights in the market of Salisbury. There is a scribal error in the manuscript at this point, and after a short break, the scribe appends part of a text of a charter of Henry I, dated 8 September 1131, to the opening of Queen Matilda's act.
WITNESSES: None listed

XXXI. (Notice of Henry's general confirmation of gifts made to the canons of St Mary at Huntingdon, *RRAN* 2: 1659).
PLACE OF ISSUE AND DATING INFORMATION: The queen's charter has been lost; it was most likely issued after 1113, when her brother David became earl of Huntingdon. We know of the queen's gift only because it is listed in a charter of Henry I in favor of the monks of Huntingdon, which confirms a number of earlier gifts, by other people.
PRINTED: (Henry's charter) *Monasticon* 6, 1: 79–80.
ACTION: Henry confirms the gift of 60s. of land in Stoke, with all of its privileges which Queen Matilda gave to them and confirmed by her charter.
WITNESSES: None; charter has been lost.

XXXII. (Not calendared in *RRAN*, no surviving text).
PLACE OF ISSUE AND DATING INFORMATION: None; the charter does not survive and its existence is only inferred because it is mentioned in the concession in the Pipe Roll of 1130.
ACTION: Payment rendered in the amounts of 41s for the customs of wood which Matilda gave to the church of St Edith at Wilton and 35s. 7d. collected in respect of the fair which the king and queen had conceded to the same church (indicating at least one charter issued in favor of Wilton).
WITNESSES: Not applicable; charter not extant.

XXXIII. (Gift of the land in Langley Marish, confirmed by Henry I in *RRAN* 2: 1402)
PLACE OF ISSUE AND DATING INFORMATION: Henry's charter orders William de Montfichet to return whatever he has taken from the land of Langley Marish, land which Queen Matilda gave to the monks of Abingdon. The land had previously been held by Robert Gernon, and may have been contested like the gift described in #XIV, above, and discussed in Chapter 3, pp. 00. Robert Gernon gave the church of Langley Marish to the monks of Gloucester in 1112 and Queen Matilda was the sole witness of Henry's confirmation charter *(RRAN* 2: 1026); another possibility is that her charter giving the church to Abingdon was issued at that time as well.

Appendix II

A Translation of
The Life of St Margaret of Scotland

There are two extant medieval manuscripts containing the long version of the *Vita Sanctae Margaretae*. The first, British Library Cotton Tiberius Diii, is a collection of British saint's lives in a deluxe edition with red, blue, and green colored initials. The manuscript seems to date from about the middle of the thirteenth century. The *vita* was edited for the Surtees Society by Hodgson Hinde and printed in 1868. Several printed translations have appeared since. The second manuscript, Madrid, Biblioteca del Palacio Real, II. 2097 (text on fols. 26–41v) was recently discovered in Madrid along with a copy of the *Miracles of St Margaret*, which had been presumed lost. I have not yet been able to see the original manuscript. Professor Robert Bartlett of the University of St Andrews has edited and translated the miracles, which will appear in a future volume of the Oxford Medieval Texts series. I have not yet been able to see the original manuscript, but I have seen reproductions.[1] I have not been able fully to compare the two manuscripts from the copies, but it does appear that there are few significant variants between the two texts. The Madrid manuscript is longer and later than the British Library text. Among other changes, the Madrid manuscript contains less emphasis on Matilda's relationship to Edward the Confessor, and it explains the coming of the Normans to England. It supplies the author's name as Turgot. While further study is needed, it does appear that the original version of this manuscript was prepared in the middle of the thirteenth century for Margaret's canonization procedures.

A third manuscript, now lost, was used for the version of the *Life* appearing in the *Acta sanctorum* and in Pinkerton's 1789 *Vita antique sanctorum*. Daniel Papebroch, who edited the *Life* for the Bollandists, described his exemplar only as '*ex membraneo Codice Valcellensis in Hannonia monasterii, nunc nostro*'.[2] I have collated the manuscript with *the Acta sanctorum* edition here for the first time. Although parts of the Cottonian manuscript were burned beyond legibility, in the passages that remain there are surprisingly few variants between the Cottonian and Bollandist texts, and only one or two changes of any significance. Differences in meaning between the two texts have

---

[1] Professor Bartlett, just before this manuscript went to press, kindly allowed me to consult his photostatic reproductions of a microfilm copy of the manuscript.
[2] *Acta sanctorum*, 10 June.

been noted in the translation. Minor orthographic variations, such as "tanquam" for "tamquam" or "antedictum" for "ante dictum'," have not been noted at all. The paragraph numbers are inserted for clarity in citing the text. The British Library MS indicates paragraph divisions with the use of coloured initials.

There is a shorter version of the *Life* in the British Library, with the shelf mark Cotton Tiberius Ei. This codex is John of Tynemouth's collection of condensed versions of British saints' lives, entitled *Nova legenda angliae*. The shortened *Life of St Margaret* consists of four folio pages, with a table of Margaret's descendants through the mid-fourteenth century drawn at the foot of the final page. The final paragraph is not from the *vita* itself, but is an extract from Aelred of Rievaulx, describing Matilda's washing the lepers' feet during the 1105 Easter court. The shorter version is clearly a condensation of the longer.

THE LIFE OF ST MARGARET OF SCOTLAND

PROLOGUE: To Matilda, queen of the English, excellent in honor and honorable in excellence, from Theodore, servant of the servants of St Cuthbert. I hope that in the present you will have the benefit of peace and health, and in the future, the benefit of every good.

(1) In requesting you have commanded and in commanding you have requested, that I should offer to you in writing an account of the way of life of your mother of blessed memory, whose manner of living you have often heard lauded with the suitable praise of many people. You said that you entrusted this task to me on account of my great familiarity with her, and because you had heard that I had access to many of her private thoughts. I freely embrace these commands and these wishes, embracing I much revere, and revering I congratulate you that, having been made Queen of the Angles by the King of the Angels, you have desired not only to hear, but also to be able continuously to inspect the written down words about the life of your mother, the queen, who always used to aspire eagerly to reach the realm of the angels. Now, even though you only knew your mother's outward appearance slightly, you may have a full account of her virtues. And indeed, I want to carry out those things that you have commanded of me, but I confess my ability falls short, for to be sure, the things to be carried out are greater than my skill, either in writing or in speaking.

(2) Therefore, there are two things from which I suffer and I am pulled from one side to the other. On account of the magnitude of the matter I am terrified to obey and on account of the authority of the one commanding and the memory of the woman who is to be written about, I dare not contradict your order. But even though I am not worthy to tell such a thing, nevertheless I ought to tell just as much as I am able, assuming it to be proper, because these things are required out of love for her and by your command. For the grace of the Holy Spirit, who gave her the ability to be virtuous, will I hope, help me by supplying aid in narrating those virtues. For, as the Holy Scriptures say, 'The Lord will give

words to the Evangelists',[3] and again, 'Open your mouth and I shall fill it.'[4] And neither can he fail with words who believes in the Word: 'In the beginning was the Word and God was the Word.'[5] But from the very beginning I want you to know, and for you to tell others so they will also know, that if I should attempt to tell all things which ought to be told about her, I would be thought in praising her to be flattering you on account of the loftiness of your royal dignity. But, far be it from my old grey head either to be accused of lying or meddling with the virtues of so great a woman. In setting these things forth, as God is my witness and my judge, I swear that I have added nothing to the facts, but have kept back many things in silence, so that these matters will not seem incredible, or lest, like the saying of the orator, I shall be said to adorn the crow with the colors of the swan.[6]

CHAPTER ONE: The nobility of the queen's family and her motherly virtues.

(3) Many people, as we read, have drawn the origins of their name from some quality of their mind, so that their name shows and corresponds with the qualities they have received through grace. It was for this reason that Christ took the name 'rock' and gave it to Peter on account of the firmness of Peter's faith; and the sons of Zebedee were called 'sons of thunder' because of their thunderous preaching of the gospel.[7] And in this woman of excellence, this same thing is found, although the beauty which showed in her name was overshadowed by the greater beauty of her soul. For she was called Margaret, which is Latin for 'the pearl' and she was a precious pearl in the sight of God because of her faith and good works. And for that reason she was a pearl to you and me, but indeed, she was also the pearl of Christ, and because she belonged to Christ more than to us, she has left us behind, having been assumed by God. I contend that the pearl has been taken up from the dungheap of this world and now glows golden in eternity, having been placed there as an ornament of the king. I imagine that no one will doubt this after reading about her life and about the manner of her death. When I recall her conversations with me, seasoned with the salt of wisdom, when I consider the tears which she explained as coming from her stinging heart, when I remember her sober demeanor and the orderliness of her habits, I rejoice, and while rejoicing, I weep. I rejoice because she has gone on to God, which she longed to do; I weep because I do not rejoice with her in the heavens. I say I rejoice for her, because she now sees there in the land of eternal life the blessings of God in which she believed;[8] moreover, I weep for myself because while I am mortal I suffer the miseries of this life. Daily I am forced to cry out: 'I, unlucky man, who shall free me from this body of death.'[9]

(4) And now, although my task is to speak about the nobility of her mind, which she had in Christ, yet it also seems something should be said about her

---

[3] Psalms 67:12 (all Biblical references are to the Vulgate).
[4] Psalms 80:11
[5] John 1:1.
[6] In medieval writings, "the Orator" usually refers to Cicero. I have not located this aphorism in any of the extant works of Cicero nor in any other classical writer.
[7] Matthew 16:18; Mark 3:17.
[8] Psalms 27:13
[9] Romans 7:24.

worldly qualities. Her grandfather, King Edmund, stood out on account of his strength in combat, because he was invincible against his enemies, and from the excellence of his virtues he had been given the honor of a nickname in the English language, 'Edmund Ironside'. Edmund's half-brother (they had the same father but not the same mother) was that pious and gentle king, Edward, who showed himself to be a 'father of the fatherland' and in some way another Solomon, because he protected his kingdom more by peace than by arms. He bore his spirit victorious over anger, contemptuous of greed, straightforward and wholly free from haughtiness. Nor was this an astonishing thing; for just as his ancestors had bequeathed him the glory of rank, he had, almost as if from some hereditary right, also acquired from his grandfathers, King Edgar of the English and Count Richard of the Normans, not only his high nobility but also his extreme religious piety. About Edward's grandfather Edgar, let it be known only briefly how great he was in the world and what sort of Christian he was. Edgar was predestined to be a king as well as to become a lover of justice and peace. For, at Edgar's birth, the blessed Dunstan heard the holy angels in the sky rejoicing, saying 'Let there be peace, let there be joy in the church of the English, for however long the newborn boy shall hold the kingdom and Dunstan shall run the road of mortal life.'

(5) Richard too, the father of Edward's mother Emma, stood forth as deserving so great a grandson. Richard was a man of every strength and deserving to be praised by everyone. For no one of his ancestors was either more fortunate in the honor of his warband nor more fervent in love of religion. Having been placed at the summit of riches, he was very poor in spirit, like a second David. Having been made a lord of men, he was a humble servant of the servants of Christ.[10] Among other things that he did as a monument to his religious devotion, that pious Christian constructed a monastery at Fécamp, in which he himself, although dressed in secular clothes, acted as a monk and was often to be found in conversation with the monks, and he was accustomed to serve meat and drink during meals, so that, following scripture, by as much as he was exalted, by that much would he humiliate himself in everything.[11] He who desires to know more of his magnificence and works of virtue, let him read the *Deeds of the Normans*, which contains the acts of this man.[12] From such renowned and illustrious ancestors, the grandson Edward degenerated in nothing. As I said before, Edward was the half-brother (through the father) of King Edmund, whose son was Margaret's father, and the fame of Margaret's merits greatly adorns the illustrious line of her ancestors.

(6) Therefore, when she was still flourishing in her youthful state, she began to lead a sober life, and also to love God above all things, and to occupy herself in the study of divine readings, and to cultivate her mind in these things with delight. She had a keen acuteness of intellect for judging whatever matter there was to be understood, a tenacity of memory for retaining many things, and a favored facility for expressing things in words. Thus, although she used to

---

[10] Luke 22:26.
[11] Ecclesiasticus 3:20.
[12] The author is probably referring to the work of Dudo of St Quentin; see Dudo, *History of the Normans: Translaiton with Introduction and Notes*, ed. Eric christiansen (Woodbridge, 1998).

meditate on the law of God by day and night,[13] and like another Mary sitting at the feet of the Lord delighted to hear his word,[14] none the less, by the wish of her people – or rather, by God's ordination – more than by her own will, she was joined together in marriage with the most powerful Malcolm, king of the Scots, son of King Duncan. But although she was compelled to attend to things which are of this world, nevertheless she disdained to fix her desire in the things which are of this world; for she delighted more in good works than in the possession of riches. From temporal things she made herself eternal rewards, because she placed her heart in heaven, where her treasure was.[15] And especially because she used to seek the kingdom of God and His justice, the great grace of the All-Powerful kept abundantly adding honors and riches to her. All things which were fitting were carried out by order of the prudent queen: by her counsel the laws of the kingdom were put in order, divine religion was augmented by her industry, and the people rejoiced in the prosperity of affairs. Nothing was firmer than her faith, more constant than her countenance, more tolerant than her patience, more pleasant than her conversation.

(7) And so, as soon as she had ascended to the summit of honor, she erected a church as an eternal monument of her name and religious devotion in the place where her wedding had been celebrated. In building this church she had intended three things which lead to salvation: namely, to do a good deed on behalf of the soul of the king, then to attain her own redemption, and finally to obtain prosperity in this life and in the future for her children. She decorated this church with various kinds of ornaments, among which (as is well known) more than a few were of solid gold and pure silver. I can speak of this with certainty since, at the queen's command, I myself was put in charge of the care of these ornaments for a long while. The queen also placed a cross of incomparable worth there. The cross held an image of the Saviour which she commissioned to be covered with gemstones that shone among the purest gold and silver, and even today this cross plainly demonstrates her devotion to those who gaze upon it. Similarly, she bequeathed signs of her faith and sacred devotion to other churches, of which the Church of St Andrew is an example. She had erected there a very old crucifix, signs of which can be discerned even today because a copy remains.

Her chamber was never empty of articles pertaining to the cultivation of the divine service, things which, as I shall tell, seemed to be from the workshop of a heavenly craftsman. You could see there caps for singers, chasubles, stoles, altar cloths, and other sacred vestments and decorations for the church. Some were still being prepared by the hand of the artisan, and others already completed and deemed worthy of admiration were kept back for display.

(8) Women of noble birth, judged worthy to be present in the service of the queen because of their sufficiently sober-minded manners, were entrusted with these works. No man had ever entered among these women unless accompanied by the queen, since sometimes she permitted them to go in with her. None of her women was ever morally degraded by familiarity with men and none ever by

[13] Psalms 1:2.
[14] Luke 10:49
[15] Matthew 4:20–1, see also II Corinthians 4:18..

the wantonnness of levity. For the queen carried so much severity mixed with pleasantness and so much pleasantness in her severity, that all who were in her service, men and women, both esteemed her with fear and feared her with esteem. Because of this esteem and fear, not only would no one dare to do an execrable deed in her presence, no one even dared to offer a disgraceful word. For she, repressing all crimes in herself, was joyful in dignity but could grow righteously angry. She never had too much hilarity in loud laughter, and growing angry, never did she pour forth her anger in great wrath. From time to time she grew angry with the sins of another person, but always with her own. Her anger ought to be praised, because it was always inclined toward justice, the kind of anger which the Psalmist commanded: 'You shall be angered', he said, 'and not sin.'[16] Since her whole life had been conducted with the highest management of discretion, she was a very image of virtues. Her manner of speaking was seasoned with the salt of wisdom, her silence was filled with the good thoughts she was always thinking. Thus, her character agreed with the sobriety of her manners, so that it was possible to believe that she had been born solely to show the virtues of life. So that I might sum it all up briefly, in everything she said, in everything that she did, she showed herself to be thinking of heavenly matters.

(9) She poured out care to her children not less than to herself, seeing that they were nurtured with all diligence and that they were introduced to honest matters as much as possible. And because she knew the Scripture, 'who spares the rod hates the child',[17] she had ordered her household steward that, whenever the children committed some childish mischief, as young children will, that they should be punished by him with threats and beatings. And because of the religious zeal of their mother, the children's manners were far better than those of other children older than they. And they never fought among themselves, and the younger children always displayed respect to the elder ones. For this reason, during solemn mass, when they followed their parents up to the altar, the younger never tried to outdo the elder but went up by age, oldest first. Margaret had her children brought to her very often, and she taught them about Christ and faith in Christ, using words suitable to their age and understanding. She admonished them diligently: 'Fear the Lord', she said, 'O my children, because those that fear him will not be in need,[18] and if you delight in him, O my flesh, he returns goodness to you through prosperity in the present life and by giving you a happy afterlife with all the saints.' This was the desire of the mother, these were the admonishments, this was the prayer that she prayed day and night, with tears on behalf of her offspring, so that they might come to know their Creator in faith which works through love,[19] and knowing, that they might worship, worshipping, that they might love him in everything and above all things, loving, that they might arrive at the glory of the heavenly kingdom.

---

[16] Psalms 4:5; see also Ephesians 4:26.
[17] Proverbs 13: 24
[18] Psalms 33:10
[19] Galatians 5:6

CHAPTER TWO: Her concern for the honor of the kingdom and the church disciplines imposed by Margaret, and the abuses that were corrected.

(10) It is no wonder that the queen regulated herself wisely and her people with guidance, because she was always guided by the wisest teaching of Holy Scripture. I admire the fact that among the tumult of lawsuits, among the manifold cares of the kingdom, she worked hard at divine reading with wonderful zeal, about which she used to engage in discussions with the most learned men of the kingdom sitting beside her, asking subtle and wise questions. And just as no one among them was more profound in mental ability, so no one was more profound in eloquence. It more often came about that the wisest men themselves went away from her wiser than when they had come. Certainly she was more than a little full of holy passion for sacred books, and my intimate affection for her along with affectionate intimacy with her caused me to tire myself out trying to procure many books for her. Nor in this manner did she seek only her own salvation, but also the salvation of others, and above everyone else, she, with God helping her, made the king himself more obedient to justice, compassion, charity, and good works of merit. He learned from her to continue frequently in the vigil of the night, he learned, from her urging and example, to pray to God with a groaning heart accompanied by a profusion of tears. I confess I used to marvel at the great miracle of God's compassion, when sometimes I used to see such exertion in the King, such compunction in the breast of a secular man saying his prayers.

(11) Since the king had perceived Christ truly to live in her heart, he dreaded to displease that queen of such venerable life in any manner but rather he used to rush to comply with her wishes and prudent plans in all things. Anything she rejected, he also rejected, and anything she loved, he loved because of his desire for her love. And for this reason, even though he was illiterate, he would hold the books that she used for reading or to assist in her prayers in his hands and look at them. When he learned from her that a book was especially dear to her, he himself would hold that one dear, kissing it and handling it more often than the others. And occasionally, calling in a goldsmith, he commanded a book to be richly adorned with gold and gems. Then the king himself would personally present it to the queen as a token of his devotion. There are other things too: Margaret, that most noble jewel of the royal race, made the magnificence of royal honor much more magnificent for the king and she conferred more glory and graces upon all the nobles of the kingdom and to their servants. For she had ordered merchants coming to her from land and sea to bring different kinds of costly things to sell, things which until then were unknown in Scotland. And among these riches, the people of Scotland, compelled by the queen, bought garments of diverse colors and with various decorations on the clothes, and at her insistence they followed one another in a fitting manner with various refinements of their dress. She even made ceremonies of submission to the king more elaborate, and when he went or rode out, he was accompanied by a great throng of retainers showing him much honor. All this was accomplished with so much discretion that wherever they went, none of them was permitted to seize anything for himself, nor would any one of them dare to oppress or injure the country people or the paupers in any way. And she even multiplied the

ornaments of the royal hall, so that not only did it shine with the diverse beauty of its coverings, but also the whole house glittered with the reflections off gold and silver. And the table utensils with which the stewards offered food and drink to the king and the queen and the nobles of the kingdom were either pure gold and silver or gold and silver plated.

(12) And she had done these things, not because she delighted in the honor of the world, but because she was compelled to carry out those things which royal dignity demanded from her. For, while she went about with costly, refined clothing as befitted a queen, in her mind, like a second Esther, she trampled upon all her ornaments, and underneath the gems and gold she considered herself nothing but dust and ashes.[20] In short, in so much loftiness of rank she always held onto a great concern for the preservation of humility. For, because the fragile, transitory nature of human life never fled from her mind, she was more easily able to repress the swelling of pride derived from every worldly honor. For she always used to remember that maxim: 'Man, born from woman, living for a short time, is full of miseries, which, just as the flower blooms and is destroyed and flies away like a shadow, never remains in the same state.'[21] And she always used to ponder in her mind that saying of the Blessed Apostle James, 'Our life', he said, 'What is it? It is a vapor appearing for a limited time, and soon it is exterminated.'[22] And, because as the Scripture says, 'Blessed is the one who is always fearful',[23] she used to present the appointed Day of Judgment unceasingly to herself in her mind's eye, in much trembling and fear. Because of her fear, she used to ask me repeatedly that if I were to perceive anything in her, either word or deed, which ought to be reprimanded, that I should not hesitate to point it out to her, reproving her in secret. Because I used to do this more rarely and tepidly than she might wish, she used to press her assertions on me, and she used to accuse me of sleeping or neglecting her. 'Let the just man rebuke me in compassion', she said, 'and chide me. Moreover, let not the oil that is the flattery of sinners pour forth on my head.[24] Wounds from people who love you are better than the flattering kisses of enemies!'[25] Saying these things, for the sake of advancing her virtues she sought a rebuke for herself that anyone else might count as an insult.

(13) The queen, holy and worthy of God, with mind, word, and deed directed her course toward the heavenly fatherland and she even used to induce others to go with her on the immaculate road, on which they were able to arrive at true blessedness with her. When she saw an evil man, she admonished him so that he might become a good man; when she saw a good man, she exhorted him so that he might be better; the better, that he might strive to be the best. Since zeal, glowing with apostolic faith, for the house of God which is the church consumed her,[26] for this reason she worked to eradicate thoroughly everything

---

[20] Esther 14:16
[21] Job 14: 1–2
[22] James 4:15
[23] Proverbs 28:14
[24] Psalms 140:5
[25] Proverbs 27:6.
[26] Compare Psalms 68:10 and John 2:17.

illicit which had sprung up in it. For when she saw that many things in Scotland were done contrary to the rule of faith and the holy custom of the universal church, she set up many councils, so that by whatever means she prevailed, she might lead the erring ones toward the way of truth given by Christ. Of all these councils, the one that stands out above all the others is well-known to be that one in which she alone, for the space of three days, with a very few of her own people, fought with the sword of the spirit (that is, with the word of God),[27] struggling against those who defended false customs. You would have thought another Helena to be there, because just as Helena, using the dictates of Scripture, proved the Jews to be mistaken, now similarly did this queen prove wrong the erring. And in this conflict the king himself remained as her distinguished helper, most ready to say and do whatever thing she ordered in this matter. He, because he knew perfectly the language of the Angles as well as his own, was a vigilant interpreter for both sides at this council.

(14) And so the Queen, after an introductory statement had been made, right away stated that those belonging to the Catholic church, who served God in one faith, ought not to differ from the universal church by insisting on new or foreign customs. So, first she told them that they did not observe the Lenten fast legitimately, because it was not their custom to begin the fast with the holy church everywhere else, on the fourth holy day at the beginning of Lent. They used to begin the fast on the second day of the following week. Against her objections they said, 'The fast which we carry out, by Evangelical authority, we observe for exactly six weeks.' After a pause, she said, 'You are in disagreement with the Gospel in this matter, for we read that the Lord fasted for forty days, and this is not what you are doing. Because, when the six days of the Lord (Sundays) are subtracted from the fast, it is clear that only thirty-six days remain for fasting. Therefore, it is an established fact that you do not fast for forty days, but for thirty-six days. Moreover, it is also true that you should begin to fast with the rest of the church during the four days from the beginning of Lent, if you wish to observe the abstinence for forty days, following the example of the Lord. Otherwise, against the authority of the Lord himself and of the entire holy church, you alone will be opposed to the instruction.' They, having been convinced by the clear reason of truth, one after another began the religious rites of the holy fast just as the holy church everywhere is accustomed to do.

(15) Another thing, too, the queen proposed and ordered: that they show by what reason on the holy Easter day, they neglected to consume the sacraments of the body and blood of Christ following the custom of the holy and apostolic church. They, responding, said, 'The Apostle, talking about these things, said, "whoever eats and drinks unworthily, eats and drinks judgment to himself".[28] And so, because we recognize ourselves to be sinners, we hold back from approaching that mystery, lest we eat and drink judgment to ourselves.' To this opinion the queen responded, 'What! According to you, all who are sinners shall not eat the sacred mystery? No one therefore ought to eat it, because no

---

[27] Ephesians 6:17.
[28] I Corinthians 11:29.

one is without sin, not even an infant who has only lived one day on earth! If, therefore, no one ought to take it, why does the Gospel show the Lord saying "Unless you shall eat the body of the son of man and you shall drink his blood, you will not have life within you?"[29] But clearly it is necessary that the opinion that is put forth by the Apostle ought to be understood in another manner, following the Fathers, for not all sinners will consume the sacrament of salvation in an unworthy manner. For, when it was said, "he eats and drinks judgment to himself", it was added "not discerning the body of the Lord",[30] meaning not using faith to separate the sacrament from food for the body. It is that one who eats and drinks judgment to himself. But we, who for many days before have prepared ourselves by confessing our sins, we who have been chastened by penances, weakened from fasting, and have been cleansed from the filth of sin through tears and charity, in the day of the resurrection of the Lord, when we approach his altar, in Catholic faith we approach the Body and Blood of the Immaculate Lamb Jesus Christ, and we obtain not judgment, but the remission of sins for the purpose of wholesome preparation for perceiving the blessedness of eternity.'

When they considered her arguments, they were not able to offer a response, and from then on they observed all the commands of the church about receiving the sacred mystery.

(16) Further, there were some in certain places in Scotland who were accustomed to celebrating the Mass against the customs of the entire church. I do not know what barbarous rite they followed, but the queen, burning with the zeal of God, desired to destroy and annihilate those customs totally, so that afterward, no one in the whole race of the Scots would dare do such things. The Scots were also accustomed to neglect the Lord's day. Thus on Sundays, they would persist in their earthly labors, just as if it were any other day. This labor on earthly works is not permitted, which she showed to them equally by reason and by authority. 'Let us hold the Lord's day in veneration', she said, 'on account of the Lord who on this day was resurrected, and on it, let us not do servile labors, for it is on this day that we knew ourselves to have been redeemed from the service of Satan.' And this the blessed Pope Gregory affirms, saying 'Cease from earthly labors on the Lord's day, and persist in every manner of prayers, so that if anyone has neglected something during the six days of the week, this negligence can be expiated through prayer on the day of the Lord's resurrection.' And this same Pope Gregory, delivering a strict rebuke to a man on account of earthly work which he did do on the Lord's day, excommunicated for two months those who had advised him to carry out his labor.[31] Those at the council did not have strong arguments to counter the reasoning of the wise queen, and thus, afterward, they observed the reverence of the Lord's day by her order, so that no one was permitted either to carry out his own burdens on this day nor would he dare to compel another person to do any work.

Also, the illicit marriage of surviving sons with their widowed stepmothers,

---

[29] John 6:54
[30] 1 Corinthians 11:29
[31] No reference to this case is found in Gregory's surviving works.

and likewise the marrying of the widow of a dead brother by a younger brother, which used to be the custom in former times, she showed to be exceedingly execrable, and to be avoided by the faithful even as death itself. And she condemned in that council many other things which had sprung up against the faith and the rules of ecclesiastical observance that had been instituted and she took pains to see that these bad customs were driven out from the borders of her kingdom. For all those things which she had proposed she corroborated by the testimony of the Holy Scripture or by the opinions of the Fathers, so that to all these things, no one was able to offer any resistance or response at all. On the contrary, having renounced their obstinate behavior, they freely undertook everything that had to be fulfilled.

CHAPTER THREE: Margaret's customary charity toward paupers, especially through the time of 'Double Lent', and her zeal for praying.

(17) Since the venerable queen, with the help of God himself, had been eager to purge the house of God from sordid conduct and errors, she herself, with her heart radiated by the Holy Spirit, daily merited to be made his temple, which I know that she was in the highest manner, because I saw both her outer self and because I came to know her inner conscience when she opened herself plainly for me. That is, she spoke most familiarly to me and deigned to reveal her secrets, not because there was anything good in me, but because she used to think there was. For when she spoke to me concerning the welfare of the soul and the sweetness of eternal life, she brought forth every word full of grace, which words the Holy Spirit, who inhabited her heart, used to sound forth through her mouth. Truly, she was moved so much in speaking that she was cleansed, when everything would be loosened in tears, and because she was so moved, I too was moved to tears. Truly, more than any mortal whom I now know, she was given to zeal for praying and fasting, and works of compassion and charity.

Therefore, I shall speak first concerning prayer. In church, nothing was quieter than her silence, but in praying, no one who prayed was more intent. For it was her custom in the house of God never to speak of secular things or engage in anything worldly, but only to pray. In praying she would pour out tears. Indeed, she was on earth only in her body, because in mind she was near to God, for in her simple prayer she sought nothing except God and things which were of God. Moreover, what shall I say about her fasting? Only that through excessive abstinence she incurred the trial of a very great infirmity.

(18) To these two things, that is, prayer and abstinence, she added the benefits of compassion. For what was more clement than her breast? Who could be more benign toward those in need? Indeed, if she had been permitted, she would have given not only her things, but also her very being to the poor. For she was poorer than all the paupers, for they, who did not have anything, desired to have things, but she, who had goods, truly desired to dispose of them. Whenever she was walking or riding in public, crowds of widows and wretched orphans would flock toward the pious mother, and no one of them ever went away from her without receiving something in the way of consolation. And after she had distributed everything she carried around with her for the use of the needy, she

had the habit of requesting clothing or some such thing from whatever the rich men or officials who were with her had near at hand, which she would then give away to the poor, so that none of them would go away sorrowing. And these requests were not taken badly by her retainers; rather they used to struggle among themselves to offer things to her, because they knew for sure she would return everything back to them twice over.

Now and then she would even take something or another belonging to the king which she would then give away to some needy man, and the king always gracefully accepted her pious thievery. He had commanded that some gold coins be set aside for him to give out to paupers whenever he went out to partake of the eucharist or to hear mass, and the queen quite often used to pilfer this treasury so that she could give abundantly to the paupers who cried out to her. And indeed, even though the king knew full well that she did this, he would often pretend not to know. He greatly loved this sort of jest. Sometimes he would seize her hand full of the coins and lead her to me for justice, joking that he wanted to accuse her in court.

Not only to the native poor, but to members of almost every nation who had rushed to her after hearing reports of her compassion, she showed the munificence of her generosity with a cheerful heart. Truly, we are permitted to say of her: 'She has dispersed, she gave to the poor, and on that account her justice remains throughout the ages.'[32]

(19) Who, moreover, would be able to calculate the numbers of those captives from the Anglo-Saxon nation for whom she paid ransom? How often and how freely would she restore to liberty those who had been reduced to slavery by the violence of the enemy! For she had sent out her secret explorers throughout the provinces of Scotland so that she could find out which captives were enduring the harshest conditions or who were treated more inhumanely than others, and these spies would secretly report back to her where the captives were and by whom they were being maltreated, and she, who empathized with them from the very bottom of her heart, hastened to restore liberty to the ones she had redeemed.

At that time there were in the kingdom of Scotland many people who enclosed themselves in little cells in diverse places, and although they lived in human bodies they did not follow after the needs of the flesh, so that they led angelic lives on earth. And the queen delighted to venerate Christ through them, and she very often would go to to visit and converse with them, and it pleased her to commend herself to their prayers. And when she was not able to get them to accept any gift from her, she would firmly beg them to tell her what charitable or compassionate deed she could carry out at their order. And she never delayed in devotedly carrying out whatever they had commanded her to do, whether it be bringing paupers back from poverty or helping the afflicted so that they might be relieved from the miseries that oppressed them.

(20) And because the church of St Andrew draws crowds of religious people coming from everywhere, on each shore of the sea which still divides Scotland from Lothian she constructed small dwelling places, so that after the labor of the

---

[32] Psalms 51:9 and 2 Corinthians 9:9.

journey, pilgrims and paupers could be directed there, and when they arrived they would find prepared for them all the necessary things which they might require in order to refresh their bodies. She placed servants there for this very reason alone, that they might, with great solicitude, minister to those who had come and provide them with whatever things might be necessary. For this reason she even assigned ships to carry across people either going or returning, and never at any time did she demand payment from those who were carried across.

(21) I have spoken about the daily conversation of the venerable queen, also told something about her daily works of compassion, so now I shall attempt briefly to tell how she was accustomed to spend the time forty days before Christmas and all of Lent.

After she had rested a little in the beginning of night, she entered the church, and also, she complete the first of the matins of the Holy Trinity, next of the Holy Cross, and after that, St Mary. When she had finished, she began the offices of the dead, after which she began the Psalter, and she did not cease until she had gone through to the end. At the hour that the priests convened for the morning Lauds to be sung, she was either finishing her Psalter, or having been through one time, she would start all over again. Then, after the Lauds were over, she returned to her chamber with the king himself to wash the feet of six paupers, and she would always ask the king for a little something so that the paupers' troubles could be relieved. In this, the chamberlain took the greatest pains, because each night before the queen entered, he had to bring in the paupers so that when she went in to serve them she would find them there ready.

When these things had been carried out, she rested her body, and slept.

(22) And truly, when she had arisen early from her bed, for a long time she continued in prayers and Psalms, and among the Psalms, she would carry out a work of compassion. For she had nine little baby orphans, destitute of all aid, brought to her to be fed at the first hour of the day. For them she had ordered soft foods, which infants of that age need, to be prepared for them each day. When these babies had been brought in, she placed them on her lap and made little drinks for them, and with the spoons that she herself used, she deigned to put food in their mouths. Thus the queen, who was honored by all the people, filled on behalf of Christ the role of servant and most pious mother. She was ably to say fully, in the words of the Blessed Job, 'Pity came into existence with me from infancy, and went out with me from my mother's womb.'[33]

During these works, three hundred paupers were usually led into the queen's hall, and they would be seated in a line, and when the king and queen entered, the doors were shut by the servants, for excepting certain religious chaplains and other servants, no one was permitted to be with them while they carried out their works of charity. And with the king on one side and the queen on another, they would serve Christ in these paupers, and with great devotion they would bring in food and drink that had been specially prepared for this purpose. And when these things had been completed, the queen customarily went into the

---

[33] Job 3:18.

church, where with long prayers and sighing tears she would offer herself up as a sacrifice for God. For, during these Holy Days, besides the hours of the Holy Trinity, the Holy Cross, and St Mary, she completed within the span of a day and a night two or three Psalters, and before the public mass was celebrated, she had five or six private masses sung for her.

(23) When these things had been completed, and the time for refreshment drew near, she fed twenty-four paupers before her own meal, humbly serving them herself. And in addition to all those charities which I related above, for as long as she lived she continued to support paupers of that number (that is, twenty-four) through the course of a whole year. She arranged for these paupers to remain with her wherever she went, and wherever she proceeded, they would follow after her. And after she had devotedly served Christ in these paupers, she would then refresh her own little body also. In her meals, since in eager desiring (following the apostle) she did not take care of the flesh, she held strength for the necessities of life.[34] With a slight and frugal refreshment, she stirred up a greater hunger than she satisfied. She seemed only to taste her meal rather than to consume it. Hence, I ask, from these examples, might it be considered how great and of what sort would be her continence in fasting, when she showed such great temperance in feasting? And, although she led her whole life in great restraint, nevertheless in the forty days before Easter and Christ's birth she would weaken herself with incredible abstinence. And because of this excessive rigor in fasting, up until the end of her life she suffered from very harsh pains in her stomach, yet this bodily infirmity did not diminish the excellence of her good works. Zealous in sacred reading, persistent in prayer, unflagging in charity, she carefully kept herself totally occupied in all things which were of God. And because she knew the Scripture, 'Whom God esteems he rebukes, moreover, he scourges every son whom he receives',[35] she freely accepted her sorrows of body with patience and thanksgiving, like a beating from a most clement father.

(24) Therefore, because she was devoted to these works and to other works of this kind, she suffered constant infirmities, so that, since according to the Apostle, 'virtue is perfected in infirmity',[36] she was restored better from day to day, passing from virtue to virtue. Abandoning in her mind all earthly things, she used to burn with total desire, thirsting after heavenly things, saying with the Psalmist with her heart and her mouth, 'My soul thirsts for the living spring. When shall I come and appear before the face of God?'[37] Let others admire in others tokens of miracles, in Margaret I admire to a much greater extent works of compassion. For signs are common to both good and evil people, but works of true piety and charity are exclusive to the good. The former sometimes reveal sanctity, certainly the latter create sanctity. Let us, I say, more worthily admire in Margaret the deeds which effected her sanctity rather than portents (if she had caused any) which showed her very great sanctity to people. Let us, I say, more worthily admire in her, through whose zeal for justice, piety, compassion

---

[34] Compare Romans 13:14 and 1 Thessalonians 4:5.
[35] Proverbs 3: 11–12 and Hebrews 12:6.
[36] 2 Corinthians 12:9.
[37] Psalms 41:3.

and charity we contemplate the deeds rather than the wonders of the ancient fathers. Nevertheless, I am going to tell about a certain thing which relates to evidence of her religious life, and I hope that I am not speaking unsuitably.

(25) She had a Gospel Book, throughly covered over with gems and gold, in which images of the four evangelists were embellished with paint mixed with gold, and indeed, throughout, each capital letter glowed reddish with gold. This book she had always loved more dearly than the others in which she studied and read. Once, while this book was being transported, it happened that she crossed over through a ford in a river, and the book, having been incautiously wrapped in cloths, fell into the river. The person carrying the book continued to ride along, unconcerned because he had no idea that the book had been dropped. Indeed, it was a long time later, when he wished to bring out the book, that he realized for the first time that it was not there. For a long time the book was sought, but it was not found.

At length, the book was found, lying open at the bottom of a deep river, and its pages were being swept back and forth continuously by the rapid motion of the water. There had been some little silk protective cloths that covered the golden letters to prevent them from being worn away by continuous contact with the facing pages, but the cloths had been swept away by the force of the river. Who would think that the book would be worth anything any longer? Who would believe even one letter would still appear in it? But without a doubt, it was drawn up from the middle of the river intact, uncorrupt, and undamaged, so much so that it scarcely seemed to have been touched by the water! The pages remained as white as before, and everything was intact, and the forms of the letters remained just as they had been. The only damage was to the final leaves, where some signs of moisture could just barely be seen. At once, the book was brought back to the queen, and the miracle was related to her, and she returned thanks to Christ, and from then on the queen loved the book even more than she had before.

Now, other people should consider what they think about this event; I myself have fancied it to be a sign from God of his esteem for the venerable queen.

CHAPTER FOUR: The death of the queen; her foreknowledge of its approach and of the manner of her pious death.

(26) Meanwhile, while the omnipotent God was preparing to give back eternal rewards for her pious works, she was preparing herself for her entrance into the other life even more eagerly than she had been accustomed. For, as I will shortly make clear, she seemed to have anticipated her departure from this life as well as certain other things. So, speaking to me more privately, she began to tell me about all the events of her life, one by one, and to pour out rivers of tears with each word. In the end, she had poured out so many tears while she was speaking, that it seemed to me without a doubt that there was nothing which, at that moment, she could not have obtained from Christ. She was weeping, and I wept, weeping, we were for a long time silent because, breaking out in tears, we did not know how to offer words. Indeed, the flame of remorse, which her heart had burnt down, had also lit my mind from her spiritual words. And while I was hearing the words of the Holy Spirit through her tongue, and I

was discerning her conscience through his words, I judged myself unworthy of the favor of so much intimacy.

(27) When she had finished this conversation about necessary things, she turned back and began to speak to me. 'Farewell', she said, 'I shall not remain in life for much longer after this. You, however, will live after me for not a little time. Therefore, there are two things which I ask of you: One, that you will remember me in your prayers and in masses for my soul; secondly, that you will be the caretaker of my sons and daughters, and particularly that you give them love. You shall teach them to fear and to love God, and you shall never cease teaching them, and whenever you shall see one of them exalted to the summit of earthly dignity, you shall approach that one especially as a father and a teacher. Warn that one, and when the occasion shall demand it, accuse him or her, lest he or she swell in pride on account of the fleeting honor, or offend God on account of avarice, lest on account of the prosperity of this world, he or she neglects the happiness of eternal life. These are things', she said, 'that I ask you to do, and now, in the presence of God, who stands among us as a third party, I ask that you promise to me.' And bursting into tears at these words, I promised to do diligently these things which she had asked, for I shall not go against the order of one whom without a doubt I heard to predict the future. Those things which she had predicted are now in being – it has come about in that I live after her death and I also see her offspring at the loftiest rank of honor. With this conversation ended, about to return home, I said my last farewell to the queen, for I never saw her face ever after.

(28) A little later, she was attacked by a harsher infirmity than she had been suffering earlier, and before the day of her homecoming she was being wasted away by the fire of a long illness. Thus I shall narrate the story of her death just as I learned it from her priest, whom she had loved more than the other ministers on account of his simplicity, innocence, and chastity; and who after the death of the queen; handed himself over to the service of Christ. For the sake of her everlasting soul, he took the habit of the monks at the tomb with the uncorrupt body of the most holy father, Cuthbert and offered himself up as a sacrifice for her. He had been inseparable from the queen at the end of her life, and he had himself commended her soul to Christ when it went out of her body. He had witnessed the events of her departure in sequence, and since I used to ask him over and over about them, he was in the habit of telling me the story through his tears.

(29) For a little over six months, he said, she had not once been strong enough to sit on a horse, and rarely had she been able to get out of bed. On the fourth day before her death, when the king was on a military expedition, and separated from her by a large stretch of land, so that she could not have heard from any messenger, however swift, what the king was doing on that day, suddenly she grew very sad. She said to those of us who were sitting next to her, 'It so happens that a great evil has today weakened the kingdom of the Scots, an evil so great that its equal has not occurred for many ages back.' And truly, when we heard those things from her we paid little attention, but after some days, when a messenger had arrived, we discovered that the king had died on the very day that the queen had spoken. And earlier, she, as if knowing what the future

held, had forbidden the king to go out with the army to any place at all. I don't know what reason he had for not obeying her warning.

(30) And so, on the fourth day after the king was murdered, she felt a little better, and went into her oratory to hear Mass. She knew that her death was imminent and so she took care to secure her future with the most holy viaticum, the Body and Blood of the Lord. When she had been refreshed by such a wholesome taste, her pain began to worsen and she was being violently pushed toward death with an increasing affliction. Now, what should I do? Why should I delay? As if I could make her live longer by putting off telling about the death of my Lady! But nevertheless, I fear to come to her end! But, since all flesh is like straw and all the glory of the flesh like a flower of straw, the straw dries out and the flower is cut down.[38]

Her face had already become deathly pale when she commanded me and the others with me, ministers of the sacred altar, to stand by and assist her, by singing Psalms, to commend her soul to Christ. And she ordered that the cross which she used to call the 'Black Cross', which she had always held in the greatest veneration, to be brought to her. When it took a long time to open up the container where it was locked in, the Queen sighed heavily, saying 'O we miserable ones! We blameworthy people! We shall not merit a last sighting of the Black Cross!' Nevertheless, when it had been withdrawn from its place and brought to her, she took it with reverence, to embrace and to kiss, and she strove to seal her face with it. And now, with her whole body growing frigid, the warmth of vitality nevertheless beat in her breast and she kept praying and singing the fiftieth Psalm in proper order, at the same time placing the cross before her eyes by holding it in front of herself with both hands.

(31) Meanwhile her son, who now at present governs the kingdom after his father, returning from the army, entered the bedroom of the queen. What distress awaited him there! What agony for his soul! He stood there with adversity on both sides, and he knew not where to turn! For he had come to tell his mother that his father, along with his older brother, had been killed, and now he found his mother, whom he especially loved, about to die! He knew not whom he should mourn first! But above all, the departure of his sweet mother pierced him with bitter pain, when he saw her lying almost dead before his very eyes. And more than this, concern for the state of the kingdom was disturbing him, because he knew for certain that it was about to be thrown into confusion by the death of his father. He was united in that on every side he found grief, on every side he found pain. The queen, who was lying there in such agony that those present thought her to have been seized away, suddenly collected her strength and spoke to her son. She asked him about his father and his brother, but he was afraid to tell her the truth because he feared that if she heard about their death, she herself might suddenly die. He replied that they were well. But she sighed heavily, saying 'I know, my son, I know. By this Holy Cross, and the closeness of our blood relationship, I order that you declare the truth so that it might be known.' Because he was compelled by her command, he told her everything just as it had happened.

---

[38] 1 Peter 1: 24.

And what do you think she did? Who would believe, that in such adversities, she would not start murmuring against God? For all at the same time, her husband had been murdered, her son had perished, and she herself was suffering from a fatal illness! But through all these events, she did not sin with her lips, and said nothing foolish against God, but rather, raising her hands to heaven she burst out in praise and thanksgiving, saying, 'I give back praise and thanksgiving to you, Omnipotent God, who has willed that I should endure such anguish at my death, and through these burdens, cleanse myself, I hope, from some of the stain of sin.'

(32) Feeling the presence of Death, she began saying the prayer that the priest usually says after giving thanks for the Body and Blood of the Lord: 'O Jesus Christ, who, out of the willingness of the Father and the cooperation of the Holy Spirit, have given life to the world through your death, deliver me!' And while she was saying 'Deliver me!', her soul was delivered from the chains of the body toward true liberty, and she migrated to Christ, the maker of true liberty, whom she had always loved. She became a participant with those whose examples of true virtue she had always followed. Her departure was accomplished with so much tranquility, so much quietness, that it is not to be doubted that her spirit migrated to that region of eternal rest and peace. Also, (and this is a wonder!) her face, which in the manner of the dying had paled totally in death, after her death was infused by red mixed with white, so that it was possible to believe that she was not dead, but sleeping. Thus, her body was honorably shrouded as befitted a queen, and we carried her to Holy Trinity, which she had herself constructed, and there, just as she had ordered, right by the altar and the venerable sign of the Holy Cross which she had erected, we surrendered her to the grave. And thus her body now rests in that place where in former times she had often kneeled, pouring out tears while offering up vigils and prayers.

Bibliography

Manuscripts

Durham, Library of the Dean and Chapter of Durham Cathedral:
  Charters 1.3. Ebor. 13 and Durham 1.2.Spec. 23*.
London, British Library:
  Additional 37665. Records of Waltham Abbey.
  Cotton Claudius Div. Miracles of St Cuthbert and Durham cartulary.
  Cotton Claudius Dx. Records of Llanthony Priory, Monmouthshire.
  Cotton Tiberius Diii. Collection of saints lives, including the Vita Margaretae.
  Cotton Tiberius Ei. John of Tynemouth. Nova Legenda Angliae.
  Landsdowne 417. Register of Malmesbury Abbey.
  Stowe 944. Hyde Abbey Register.
Madrid, The Escorial:
  Madrid, Biblioteca del Palacio Real, II. 2097, fols. 26–41v.
Oxford, Bodleian Library:
  Latin liturgical f5. Gospel Book of St Margaret.

Primary Sources

Adelard of Bath. 'Des Adelard von Bath Traktat *De eodem et diversa* zum ersten Male hersausgegeben und historisch-kritisch untersucht'. Edited by Hans Wilner. *Beiträge zur Geschichte der Philosophie des Mittelalters* 4 (1903): 1–112.
Aelred of Rievaulx. 'Genealogia regum anglorum'. *Patrologia latina* 195: columns 711–58.
Aldhelm. *Aldhelm: The Prose Works*. Translated by Michael Herren and Michael Lapidge. Totowa New Jersey: Rowman and Littlefield, 1979.
Anderson, Alan Orr, ed. *Early Sources of Scottish History AD 500–1286*. Two volumes. Edinburgh: Oliver and Boyd, 1922.
Anselm of Canterbury. *S. Anselmi Cantuariensis archiepiscopi opera omnia*. Edited by Francis S. Schmitt. Six volumes. Stuttgart: Friedrich Fromann Verlag, 1946–61, reprint 1968.
Arnold, Thomas, ed. *Memorials of St Edmund's Abbey*. Three volumes. Rolls Series, London, 1890–6.
Asser. *Asser's Life of Alfred and other Contemporary Sources*. Edited and translated by Simon Keynes and Michael Lapidge. Harmondsworth: Penguin Books, 1983.
Assman, Bruno, ed. *Angelsächsische Homilien und Heiligenleben*. Three volumes. Kassel, 1889; repr. Darmstadt: Wissenschaftliche Buchgesellschaft, 1964.
Barlow, Frank, ed. *Vita Ædwardi regis: The Life of King Edward Who Rests at Westminster*. London: Thomas Nelson and Sons, Ltd., 1962.
Barrow, G. W. S., ed. *The Acts of Malcolm IV, King of Scots 1153–65*. Volume One, *Regesta regum Scottorum*. Edinburgh: University of Edinburgh Press, 1960.

BIBLIOGRAPHY: PRIMARY SOURCES

Bates, David, H. W. C. Davis, Charles Johnson, H. A. Cronne and R. H. C. Davis, edd. *Regesta regum Anglo-Normannorum*. Four volumes. Oxford: The Clarendon Press, 1913–98.

Bateson, Mary, ed. 'A London Municipal Collection of the Reign of King John, Part One'. *English Historical Review* 17 (1902): 480–511.

Bede. *Opera historica*. Translated by J. E. King. Two volumes. Cambridge, Mass: Harvard University Press, 1929.

Benedeit. *The Anglo-Norman Voyage of St Brendan*. Edited by Ian Short and Brian Merrilees. Manchester: Manchester University Press, 1979.

—— *The Anglo-Norman Voyage of St Brendan by Benedeit*. Edited by Edwin G. R. Waters. Oxford: The Clarendon Press, 1928.

Beowulf. Translated by Michael Alexander. Harmondsworth: Penguin Books, 1973.

Bernard of Clairvaux. 'Apologia ad Guillelmum, Sancti Theodorici abbatem'. *Patrologia latina*, 182, columns 895–919.

Birch, Walter de Gray. *Cartularium Saxonicum: A Collection of Charters Relating to Anglo-Saxon History*. Three volumes. London: Whiting and Company, 1885–93; repr. New York: Johnson Reprint House, 1964.

Blake, E. O., ed. *Liber Eliensis*. Camden Society, third series, Volume 92. London: Royal Historical Society, 1962.

Boethius, Hector. *Scotorum historiae a prima gentis origine*. Edinburgh, 1540; repr. Norwood, New Jersey: Walter J. Johnson, Inc., 1977.

Bolland, Jean, et al. *Acta sanctorum quotquot toto orbe coluntur vel a catholicis scriptoribus celebrantur*. . . . .. 66 volumes, Paris:, Antwerp and Brussels, 1643– .

Bouquet, Martin, et al., ed. *Recueil des historiens des Gaules et de la France*. 24 volumes. Paris: Aux dépens des Libraire Associés, 1738–1904.

Boutemy, André, ed. 'Notice sur le recueil poétique du Manuscrit Cotton Vitellius A: xii, du British Museum'. *Latomus* 2 (1937, repr. 1964): 296–313.

Bradley, S. A. J., ed. *Anglo-Saxon Poetry: An Anthology of Old English Poems in Prose Translation with Introduction and Headnotes*. Everyman's Library, Volume 1794. London: Dent Publishing, 1982.

Brewer, J. S., and Charles T. Martin, edd. *Regestrium Malmesburiense*. Two volumes. Rolls Series, London, 1879–80.

Brooke, Z. N., Adrian Morey and C. N. L. Brooke, edd. *The Letters and Charters of Gilbert Foliot*. Cambridge: Cambridge University Press, 1967.

Brown, Vivien, ed. *The Cartulary and Charters of Eye Priory*. Two volumes. Woodbridge: The Boydell Press, 1992–4.

Calendar of Charter Rolls Preserved in the Public Record Office. Six volumes. Public Record Office Texts and Calendars. London: His Majesty's Stationery Office, 1903–27.

Campbell, Alistair, ed. *Encomium Emmae reginae*. Camden Society, third series, Volume 72. London: Offices of the Royal Historical Society, 1949.

Chaplais, Pierre, ed. *Treaty Rolls Preserved in the Public Record Office*. Two volumes. London: Her Majesty's Stationery Office, 1955.

Clay, Charles Travis. *York Minister fasti: being notes on the dignitaries, archdeacons and prebendaries in the church of York prior to the year 1307*. Two volumes. Wakefield: Yorkshire Archaeological Society, 1958–9.

Colker, M. L., ed. 'Latin Texts concerning Gilbert, Founder of Merton Priory'. *Studia monastica* 12 (1970): 241–72.

Cotton, Bartholomew. *Historia anglicana*. Edited by Henry Richards Luard. Rolls Series, London, 1859.

Darlington, R. R., ed. *The Cartulary of Worcester Cathedral Priory, Register I*. London: Pipe Roll Society, 1968.

—— 'Winchcombe Annals, 1049–1181'. In *A Medieval Miscellany for Doris Mary Stenton*. Edited by Patricia M. Barnes and C. F. Slade. London: Pipe Roll Society, 1960, 111–37.

Davies, James Conway, ed. *Episcopal Acta and Cognate Documents Relating to Welsh Dioceses 1066–1272*. No place of publication cited. Volume 1, Historical Society of the Church in Wales, 1946.

Davies, W. S. 'Materials for the Life of Bishop Bernard of St David's'. *Archaeologia Cambrensis* n.s. 19 (1919): 299–322.

Delisle, Leopold, ed. *Rouleau mortuaire du B. Vital, Abbé de Savigni, comtenant 207 titres, écretis en 1122–23 dans différents églises de France et d'Angleterre*. Paris: Libraire Honoré Champion, 1909.

Dodwell, Barbara, ed. *The Charters of Norwich Cathedral Priory, Part One*. London: Pipe Roll Society, 1974.

Douglas, David C., and George Greenaway, ed. *English Historical Documents, 1042–1189*. Second edition. London: Eyre Methuen, 1981.

Dugdale, William. *Monasticon Anglicanum: A History of the Abbies and other Monasteries, Hospitals, Friaries, and Cathedral and Collegiate Churches . . .* Revised edition edited by John Caley, Henry Ellis, and Bulkeley Bandinel. Six volumes in eight. London: Longman, Hurst, Rees, Orme and Brown; Lackington, Hughes, Harding, Mavor and Jones; Joseph Harding, 1817–30.

Eadmer of Canterbury. *Historia novorum in Anglia*. Edited by Martin Rule. Rolls Series, London, 1866, repr. 1964.

—— *Eadmer's History of Recent Events in England*. Translated by Geoffrey Bosanquet. London, The Cresset Press, 1964.

Edwards, Edward, ed. *Liber monasterii de Hyda*. Rolls Series, London, 1866, repr. 1964.

Elvey, G. R., ed. *Luffield Priory Charters, Part One*. Welwyn Garden City: Broadwater Press, Ltd., 1968.

Faritius of Abingdon. 'Vita Aldhelmi'. *Patrologia latina* 89: columns 63–84.

Finberg, H. P. R. 'Some Early Tavistock Charters'. *English Historical Review* 62 (1947): 352–77.

FitzNigel, Richard. *Dialogus de Scaccario: The Course of the Exchequer*. Edited and translated by Charles Johnson, F. E. L. Carter, and D. E. Greenway. Oxford: The Clarendon Press, 1983.

Flete, John. *The History of Westminster Abbey*. Edited by J. Armitage Robinson. Cambridge: Cambridge University Press, 1909.

Florence of Worcester. *The Chronicle of Florence of Worcester, with Two Continuations*. Edited and translated by Thomas Forester. London: Henry G. Bohn, 1854.

—— *Chronicon ex chronicis*. Edited by Benjamin Thorpe. Two volumes. London: Sumptibus Societas, 1848; reprint Vaduz: Kraus Reprint, Ltd., 1964.

Forbes-Leith, W. *The Gospel Book of St Margaret: Being a Facsimile Reproduction of St Margaret's Copy of the Gospels Preserved in the Bodleian Library, Oxford*. Edinburgh: David Douglas, 1896.

Foster, C. W., ed. *The Registrum antiquissimum of the Cathedral Church of Lincoln*. Hereford: The Hereford Times Ltd. for the Lincoln Record Society, 1931.

—— and Thomas Langley, edd. *The Lincolnshire Domesday and the Lindsey Survey*. Lincoln Record Society, 1924, repr. Gainsborough: G. W. Belton Ltd., 1976.

Fowler, J. T., ed. *The Coucher Book of Selby*. Two volumes. Yorkshire: Yorkshire Archaeological Society and Topographical Association 10 (1891) and 13 (1893).

Fulbert of Chartres. *The Letters and Poems of Fulbert of Chartres*. Edited by F. Behrends, Oxford: Oxford University Press, 1976.

Gaimar, Geoffrey. *L'estoire des Engleis*. Edited by Alexander Bell. Oxford: Basil Blackwell

for the Anglo-Norman Text Society, 1960. Repr. NY: Johnson Reprint Corporation, 1971.
Galbraith, Vivian H., ed. *The Anonimalle Chronicle.* Manchester: Manchester University Press, 1927.
Gervase of Canterbury. *Chronica Gervasi.* Edited by William Stubbs. Two volumes. Rolls Series, London, 1870.
Goscelin of Canterbury. 'La vie de Sainte Vulfhilde'. Edited by Mario Esposito. *Analecta Bollandiana* 32 (1913): 10–26.
Guy of Amiens. *The Carmen de Hastingae Proelio of Bishop Guy of Amiens.* Edited and translated by Catherine Morton and Hope Muntz. Oxford: The Clarendon Press, 1972.
Hariulf. *Chronique de l'abbaye de Saint-Riquier.* Edited by Ferdinand Lot. Paris: Alphonse Picard et fils, 1894.
Harmer, F., ed. *Anglo-Saxon Writs.* Manchester: University of Manchester Press, 1952.
Hart, William Henry, ed. *Historia et cartularium monasterii Sancti Petri Gloucestriae.* Three volumes. Rolls Series, London, 1863–7.
Hearnes, Thomas, ed. *Textus Roffiensis.* Oxford: Sheldonian, 1720.
Hermann of Tournai. 'Liber de restauratione S. Martini Tornacensis'. *MGH Scriptores* 14 (1956): 274–317.
—— *The Restoration of the Monastery of Saint Martin of Tournai.* Translated with an introduction and notes by Lynn H. Nelson. Washington DC: The Catholic University of America Press, 1996.
Hildebert of Lavardin. *Opera omnia. Patrologia latina* 171.
—— *Hildeberti Cenomannensis episcopi carmina minora.* Edited by A. Brian Scott. Leipzig: BSB B.G. Verlagsgesellschaft, 1969.
Hincmar of Reims. 'De ordine palatii'. Edited by A. Boetius. *MGH Capitularies* 2. Hanover, 1883.
—— 'Coronation Iudithae Karoli II filiae'. Edited by A. Boetius. *MGH Capitularies* 2 Hanover, 1883 (repr. 1960): 425–7.
Hodgett, Gerald, ed. *The Cartulary of Holy Trinity Aldgate.* London: London Record Society, 1971.
Horstmann, Carl, ed. *S. Editha, sive Chronicon vilodunense im Wiltshire dialekt, aus Ms. Cotton. Faustina B III.* Heilbron: Gebr. Henninger, 1883.
—— *Nova legenda Anglie as collected by John of Tynemouth, John Capgrave, and others, and first printed, with new lives, by Wynkyn de Worde, A. D mdxui; now re-edited with fresh material from ms. and printed sources by Carl Horstman.* Two volumes. Oxford: The Clarendon Press, 1901.
Howlett, Richard, ed. *Chronicles of the Reigns of Stephen, Henry II, and Richard I.* Four volumes. Rolls Series, London, 1882–9.
Hugh Candidus. *The Chronicle of Hugh Candidus, a monk of Peterborough.* Edited by W. T. Mellows. Oxford: Oxford University Press, 1949.
Hugh the Chanter. *The History of the Church of York, 1066–1127.* Edited and translated by Charles Johnson; revised with corrections by M. Brett, C. N. L. Brooke, and M. Winterbottom. Oxford: The Clarendon Press, 1990.
Hunter, Joseph, ed. *Magnum rotulum scaccarii, vel magnum rotum pipae, de anno trecesimo-primi regni Henrici primi (ut videtur) quem plurimi hactenus laudarunt pro rotolo quinti anni Stephani regis.* London: Record Commission, 1833; repr. 1929.
Ingulph. *Ingulph's Chronicle of Croyland Abbey.* Translated by Henry T. Riley. London: Henry G. Bohn, 1854.
Ivo of Chartres. 'Epistolae'. *Patrologia latina* 162: 11–290.

Jaffe, Philipp, ed. 'Codex Udalrici'. *Monumenta Bamburgensia, Bibliotheca rerum germanicarum* 5 (MGH). Berlin, 1869, repr. 1964.

——, and S. Loewenfeld, edd. *Regesta pontificum romanorum ab condita ad annum post Christum natum MCXCVIII*. Two volumes. Rome: Vatican printing Office, second edition 1885–8.

John of Salisbury. *Historia pontificalis*. Edited and translated by Marjorie Chibnall. Oxford: Oxford University Press, second edition, 1968.

Jones, W. H. Rich, and W. Dunn Macray, edd. *Charters and Documents Illustrating the History of the Cathedral, City, and Diocese of Salisbury in the Twelfth and Thirteenth Centuries*. Rolls Series, London, 1891.

Kemble, John M., ed. *Codex diplomaticus ævi Saxonici*. Six volumes. London: Publications of the Royal Historical Society 1839–48; repr. Vaduz: Kraus Reprint, Ltd., 1964.

Kemp, B. R., ed. *Reading Abbey Cartularies*. Camden Fourth Series, volumes 31 and 33. London: Offices of the Royal Historical Society, 1986–7.

Könsgen, Ewald. 'Zwei unbekannte Briefe zu den Gesta regum anglorum de Wilhelm von Malmesbury'. *Deutsches Archiv für Erforschung des Mittelalters* 31 (1975): 204–14.

Lanfranc of Bec. *The Letters of Lanfranc, Archbishop of Canterbury*. Edited and translated by Helen Clover and Margaret Gibson. Oxford: The Clarendon Press, 1979.

Lawrie, Archibald C, ed. *Early Scottish Charters (prior to A.D. 1153)*. Glasgow: James MacLehose and Sons, 1905.

de Lépinois, Eugène, and Lucien Merlet, edd. *Cartulaire de Notre Dame Chartres*. Three volumes. Chartres: Garnier, 1862–5.

Losinga, Herbert. *Epistolae Herbert de Losinga*. Edited by Robert Anstruther. Caxton Society, 1846; repr. NY: Burt Franklin, 1969. (Burt Franklin Research and Source Works, 154).

Luard, Henry Richards, ed. *Annales Monastici*. Five volumes. Rolls Series, London, 1864.

Macray, W. D., ed. *Chronicon Abbatiae de Evesam*. Rolls Series, London, 1863.

—— *Chronicon Abbatiae Rameseiensis*. Rolls Series, London, 1886.

Map, Walter. *De nugis curialium (Courtier's Trifles)*. Edited and translated by M. James. New York: Oxford University Press, 1983.

Mason, Emma, ed. *The Beauchamp Cartulary: Charters 1100–1268*. London: The Pipe Roll Society, 1980.

——, ed. *Westminster Abbey Charters 1066–1214*. London: London Record Society, 1988.

Michel, Francisque, ed. *Chroniques Anglo-normandes*. Three volumes in one. Rouen: Edouard Frère, Libraire de la bibliothèque de la ville, 1836.

Migne, J. P., ed. *Patrologiae cursus completus, seu, Bibliotheca universalis omnium SS. patrum, doctorum scriptorumque ecclesiasticorum, series latina, in qua prodeunt patres, doctores scriptoresque ecclesiae Latinae a Tertulliano ad Innocentium III*. 221 volumes. Paris: Garnier, 1878–90.

Morris, John, ed. *Domesday Book: A Survey of the Counties of England*. Chichester: Phillimore Books, 1975– .

Musset, Lucien, ed. 'Les actes de Guillaume le Conquérant et de la reine Mathilde pour les abbayes caennaises'. *Mémoires de la société des antiquaries de Normandie* 37 (1967).

Nelson, Janet L., ed and trans. *The Annals of St Bertin*. Ninth-Century Histories, Volume One. Manchester: University of Manchester Press, 1991.

Orderic Vitalis. *The Ecclesiastical History of Orderic Vitalis*. Edited and translated by Marjorie Chibnall. Six volumes. Oxford: Oxford University Press, 1969–80.

Paris, Matthew. *Historia Anglorum*. Edited by F. Madden. Rolls Series, London, 1866.

—— *Chronica majora*. Edited by H. R. Luard. Seven volumes. Rolls Series, London, 1866–9.

Pinkerton, John. *Vitae antiquae sanctorum qui habitaverunt in ea parte Britannia nunc vocata Scotia vel in ejus insulis*. London: Typis Johanis Nichols, 1789.

Prescott, John E. *The Register of the Priory of Wetherhal*. London: Cumberland and Westmorland Antiquarian and Archaeological Society, 1897.

Prynne, William. *Aurum reginae: Or a compendious Tractate and Chronological Collectum of Records in the Tower and Court of Exchequer Concerning Queen's Gold . . .* London: Thomas Ratcliffe, 1668.

Raine, James B., ed. *The Historians of the Church of York and its Archbishops*. Three volumes. Rolls Series, London, 1879–94.

Ransford, Rosalind, ed. *The Early Charters of the Augustinian Canons of Waltham Abbey, Essex 1062–1230*. Woodbridge: The Boydell Press, 1989.

Reginald of Durham. *Libellus de admirandis beati Cuthberti quae novelis patratae sunt temporibus*. Edited by James Raine. Surtees Society 1, 1835.

Riley, Henry Thomas, ed. *Munimenta Gildhallae Londoniensis: Liber albus, Liber custumarum, et Liber Horn*. Rolls Series, London, 1860.

Robert of Gloucester. *The Metrical Chronicle of Robert of Gloucester*. Edited by William Aldis Wright. Rolls Series, London, 1887.

Robert of Torigi et al. *The Gesta normannorum ducum of William of Jumieges, Orderic Vitalis, and Robert of Torigni*. Edited and translated by Elisabeth van Houts. Two volumes, Oxford: The Clarendon Press, 1992–5.

Robertson, A. J., ed. *Anglo-Saxon Charters*. Cambridge: Cambridge University Press, 1939.

Roger of Hovedon. *Chronica Magistri Rogeri de Hovedene*. Edited by William Stubbs. Four volumes. Rolls Series, London, 1868–71.

Roger of Wendover. *Flores historiarum*. Edited by Henry J. Hewlett. Three volumes. Rolls Series, London, 1886–9.

Saunders, H. W. *The First Register of Norwich Cathedral Priory*. No place of publication cited: Norfolk Record Society, 1939.

Sedulius Scottus. *Liber de rectoribus Christianis*. Edited by S. Hellmann. Munich: Quellen und Untersuchungen zur lateinischen Philologie des Mittelalters, 1906.

—— *On Christian Rulers and the Poems*. Translated by Edward Gerard Doyle. Binghampton, New York: State University of New York Medieval and Renaissance Texts and Studies, 1983.

Simeon of Durham. *Symeonis Dunelmensis opera et collectanea*. Edited by Hogdson Hinde. Surtees Society 51, 1868.

—— *Symeonis Dunelmensis opera omnia*. Edited by Thomas Arnold. Two volumes. Rolls Series, London, 1882–5, repr. 1965.

Smith, Sidney, ed. *The Great Roll of the Pipe for the Seventh Year of King John, Michaelmas, 1205*. London: Pipe Roll Society, 1941 (New series, Volume 19).

Stenton, Frank M. *Transcripts of Charters Relating to the Gilbertine Houses of Sixle, Ormsby, Catley, Bullington and Alvington*. Horncastle: Lincoln Record Society 18, 1920.

Stevenson, Joseph, trans. *The chronicles of John and Richard of Hexham. The chronicle of Holyrood. The chronicle of Melrose. Jordan Fantosme's chronicle. Documents respecting Canterbury and Winchester. Translated from the original texts, with preface and notes.* London: Seeleys, 1856, repr. Dyfed, 1988.

——, ed. *Chronicon monasterii de Abingdon*. Two volumes. Rolls Series, London, 1858.

——, ed. *Liber vitae ecclesie Dunelmensis*. Surtees Society, 1841.

Symons, Thomas, ed. *Regularis concordia angliae nationis monachorum sanctimonialiumque*. London: Thomas Nelson and Sons, 1953.
Tacitus. *The Agricola, Germania, and Dialogus*. Translated by M. Hutton. Revised by M. Ogilvie, H. Warmington, W. Peterson, and M. Winterbottom. Cambridge, Massachusetts: Harvard University Press, 1930.
Theobald of Étampes. 'Epistolae'. *Patrologia latina* 163: columns 759–60.
Thomson, Rodney, ed. *Vita Gundulphi: The Life of Gundulph of Rochester*. Toronto: Pontifical Institute of Medieval Studies, 1977.
Timson, R. T., ed. *The Cartulary of Blyth Priory*. Two volumes. London: Her Majesty's Stationery Office, 1973.
Thompson, Pauline A., and Elizabeth Stevens, edd. 'Gregory of Ely's Verse Life and Miracles of St Æthelthryth'. *Analecta Bollandiana* 106 (1988): 333–90.
Turgot (?). 'Life of St Margaret'. In *Acta sanctorum quotquot toto orbe coluntur vel a catholicis scriptoribus celebrantur*. Edited by Jean Bolland, Godfrey Henschenius, Daniel Papenbroch, *et al*. Brussels and Antwerp, 1643– , Volume 1 for June, 10 June. Antwerp 1658, repr. Brussels 1966.
Wace. *Le Roman de Rou et de Ducs de Normandie*. Edited by A. J. Holden. Two volumes. Paris: A & J Picard, 1970–4.
Walsingham, Thomas. *Gesta abbatum Monasterii Sancta Albani*. Edited by Henry Thomas Riley. Two volumes. Rolls Series, London, 1867.
Whitelock, Dorothy, ed. and trans. *Anglo-Saxon Wills*. Cambridge: Cambridge University Press, 1930.
——, David C. Douglas and Susie I. Tucker, edd./trans. *The Anglo-Saxon Chronicle*. New Brunswick, New Jersey: Rutgers University Press, 1961.
William of Jumieges. *Gesta normannorum ducum*. Edited by J. Marx. Rouen: Sociéte de l'histoire de Normandie, 1914.
William of Malmesbury. *Gesta regum anglorum: The History of the English Kings*. Edited and translated by R. A. B. Mynors, R. M. Thomson, and M. Winterbottom. Volume 1. Oxford: The Clarendon Press, 1998.
—— *Gesta pontificum anglorum*. Edited by N. E. S. A. Hamilton. Rolls Series, London, 1870.
—— *Vita Wulfstani*. Edited by R. R. Darlington. Camden Society, third series, 1928.
William of Newburgh. *Historia rerum anglicarum*. Edited by Hans Claude Hamilton. Two volumes in one. English Historical Society: London, 1856; repr. Vaduz, 1964.
William of Poitiers. *Histoire de la Guillaume le Conquerant*. Edited and translated into French by Raymonde Foreville. Paris: Société d'édition les belles-lettres, 1952.
Wilmart, Andre, ed. 'Une lettre inedite de S. Anselme à une moniale inconstante'. *Revue Bénédictine* 40 (1928): 319–32.
Wright, Thomas, ed. *The Anglo-Latin Satirical Poets of the Twelfth Century*. Two volumes. Rolls Series, London, 1872, repr. 1964.

Secondary Studies

Abbott, Judith Elaine. 'Political Strategies at the Coronation of Queen Matilda I, 1068'. Unpublished paper delivered at the Annual Meeting of the Charles Homer Haskins Society, Houston, Texas, November 1990.
—— 'Queens and Queenship in Anglo-Saxon England, 954–1066: Holy and Unholy Alliances'. Ph.D. dissertation, University of Connecticut, 1989.

Alexander, James W. 'Herbert of Norwich, 1091–1119: Studies in the History of Norman England'. *Studies in Medieval and Renaissance History* 6 (1969): 115–232.
Atkyns, Robert. *The Ancient and Present State of Glocestershire*. Second edition. London: F. Spilsbury for W. Herbert, 1768.
Baker, Derek. 'A Nursery of Saints: St Margaret of Scotland Revisited'. In Baker, ed., *Medieval Women*, 119–42.
——, ed. *Medieval Women*. Oxford: Basil Blackwell for the Ecclesiastical History Society, 1978.
Barlow, Frank. *Edward the Confessor*. Berkeley: University of California Press, 1970.
—— *The English Church, 1066–1154*. London: Longman, 1979.
—— *William Rufus*. Berkeley: University of California Press, 1983.
Barnett, T. Radcliffe. *Margaret of Scotland, Queen and Saint: Her Influence on the Early Church of Scotland*. Edinburgh: Oliver and Boyd, 1926.
Barrow, G. W. S. *The Anglo-Norman Era in Scottish History*. Oxford: The Clarendon Press, 1980.
—— *David I of Scotland (1124–1153): The Balance of New and Old* (The Stenton Lecture, 1984). Reading: University of Reading, 1985.
—— *The Kingdom of the Scots: Government, Church and Society from the Eleventh to the Fourteenth Century*. London: Edward Arnold, 1973.
—— *Kingship and Unity, Scotland 1000–1306*. Edinburgh: Edinburgh University Press, 1981.
—— 'Scottish Rulers and the Religious Orders 1070–1153'. *Transactions of the Royal Historical Society*, Fifth series, 3 (1953): 77–100.
Bates, David. 'The Origins of the Justiciarship'. *Anglo-Norman Studies* 4 (1981): 1–12.
—— 'Review of C. Warren Hollister, '"Monarchy, Magnates and Institutions in the Anglo-Norman World"'. *Albion* 19 (1987): 591–3.
Bedos-Rezak, Brigitte. 'Women, Seals and Power in Medieval France, 1150–1350'. In Erler and Kowaleski, edd., *Women and Power in the Middle Ages*, 61–82.
Bäuml, F. 'Varieties and Consequences of Medieval Literacy and Illiteracy'. *Speculum* 55 (1980): 237–64.
Bell, Susan Groag. 'Medieval Women Book Owners: Arbiters of Lay Piety and Ambassadors of Culture'. In Erler and Kowaleski, ed., *Women and Power in the Middle Ages*, 149–88.
Bennett, Matthew. 'Poetry as History: The Roman de Rou of Wace as a Source for the Norman Conquest'. *Anglo-Norman Studies* 5 (1982): 21–39.
Bethell, Denis. 'English Black Monks and Episcopal Elections in the 1120s'. *English Historical Review* 84 (1969): 673–98.
—— 'The Making of a Twelfth-Century Relic Collection'. In *Popular Belief and Practice* (Studies in Church History, 8). Edited by J. Cuming and Derek Baker. Cambridge: Cambridge University Press, 1972, 61–72.
Bezzola, R. R. *Les origines et la formation de la littérature courtoise en occident, 500–1200*. Paris: Bibliothéque de l'ecole des hautes etudes 226, 1978.
Biddle, Martin. 'Seasonal Festivals and Residence: Winchester, Westminster and Gloucester in the Tenth to Twelfth Centuries'. *Anglo-Norman Studies* 8 (1985): 51–72.
——, ed. *Winchester in the Early Middle Ages*. Oxford: The Clarendon Press, 1976.
Biles, Martha. 'The Indomitable Belle: Eleanor of Provence, Queen of England'. In *Seven Studies in Medieval English History and Other Historical Essays*. Edited by Richard H. Bowers. Jackson, Mississippi: University Press of Mississippi, 1983, 113–31.
Binns, Alison. *Dedications of Monastic Houses in England and Wales*. Woodbridge: The Boydell Press, 1989.

Blair, C. H. Hunter. 'Armorials in English Seals from the Twelfth to the Sixteenth Century'. *Archaeologia* 89 (1943): 1–26.

Blake, D. W. 'Bishop William Warelwast'. *The Devonshire Association for the Advancement of Science, Literature, and Art* 104 (1972): 15–33.

Brett, Martin. *The English Church under Henry I*. Oxford: Oxford University Press, 1975.

—— 'Forgery at Rochester'. In *Fälschungen im Mittelalter: Internationaler Kongreß der Monumenta Germaniae Historica, Teil IV, Diplomatische Fälschungen (II)*, 397–412, (MGH Schriften 33: 4). Hanover: Hahnsche Buchhandlung, 1988.

Brooke, Christopher N. L. 'Married Men among the English Higher Clergy, 1066–1200'. *Cambridge Historical Journal* 12 (1956): 187–8.

—— 'Princes as Patrons of Monasteries in Normandy and England, 1049–1122'. In *Il monachesimo e la riforma ecclesiastica, 1049–1122*. Miscellanea de Centro di Studi Medievali 6. Milan: La Mendola, 1971, 125–52.

——, and Gillian Keir. *London, 800–1216: The Shaping of a City*. Berkeley: University of California Press, 1975.

Broun, Dauvit. *The Irish Identity of the Kingdom of the Scots in the Twelfth and Thirteenth Centuries*. Woodbridge: The Boydell Press, 1999.

Bruce, W. Moir. 'Saint Margaret and her Chapel in the Castle of Edinburgh'. *The Book of the Old Edinburgh Club* 5 (1913): 1–66.

Brückmann, J. 'The *ordines* of the Third Recension of the Medieval English Coronation Order.' In *Essays in Medieval History Presented to Bertie Wilkinson*. Edited by T. A. Sandquist and M. R. Powicke. Toronto: University of Toronto Press, 1969, 99–115.

Buchtal, Hugo. *Miniature Painting in the Latin Kingdom of Jerusalem*. Oxford: The Clarendon Press, 1957.

Bumke, Joachim. *Courtly Culture: Literature and Society in the High Middle Ages*. Translated from the German by Thomas Dunlap. Berkeley: University of California Press, 1991.

Burges, Alfred. 'An Account of the Old Bridge at Stratford-le-Bow, Essex'. *Archaelogica* 27 (1893): 77–95.

Burrell, M. 'Narrative Structures in *Le Voyage de St Brendan*'. *Parergon* 17 (1977): 3–9.

Burton, Janet E. 'Monasteries and Parish Churches in Eleventh- and Twelfth-Century Yorkshire'. *Northern History* 23 (1987): 39–50.

Camille, Michael. 'Seeing and Reading: Some Visual Implications of Medieval Literacy and Illiteracy'. *Art History* 8 (1985): 26–50.

Campbell, Miles W. 'Emma, reine d'Angleterre, mère dénaturée ou femme vindicative?' *Annales de Normandie* 23 (1973): 97–114.

—— 'The Encomium Emmae reginae: Personal Panegyric or Political Propaganda?' *Annuale Mediaevale* 19 (1979): 27–45.

—— 'Queen Emma and Ælgifu of Northampton: Canute the Great's Women'. *Mediaeval Scandinavia* 4 (1971): 66–114.

Cantor, Norman F. *Church, Kingship and Lay Investiture in England, 1089–1135*. Princeton: Princeton University Press, 1958.

Carpenter, Jennifer, and Sally-Beth MacLean, edd. *Power of the Weak: Studies on Medieval Women*. Urbana, Illinois: University of Illinois Press, 1995.

Chaplais, Pierre. 'The Authenticity of the Royal Anglo-Saxon Diplomas of Exeter'. *Bulletin of the Institute of Historical Research* 39 (1966): 1–34.

Chibnall, Marjorie M. *The Empress Matilda: Queen Consort, Queen Mother, and Lady of the English*. Oxford: Basil Blackwell, 1991.

—— 'Robert of Bellême and the Castle of Tickhill'. In *Droit privé et institutions regionales: Etudes historiques offert à Jean Yver*. Paris: Presses Universitaires de France, 1976, 151–76.

Christie, A. G. I. *English Medieval Embroidery*. Oxford: Oxford University Press, 1938.

Clanchy, Michael T. *From Memory to Written Record: England 1066–1307*. Second Edition. Oxford: Blackwell, 1993.

Clark, Mary Amanda. 'Ralph d'Escures: Anglo-Norman Abbot and Archbishop'. Ph.D. dissertation, University of California, Santa Barbara, 1975.

Clay, Rotha Mary. *The Medieval Hospitals of England*. London: Methuen and Company, 1909.

Cokayne, George Edward. *Complete Peerage of England, Scotland, Ireland, Great Britain and the United Kingson, extant, extinct, or dormant*. New edition, revised and enlarged by Vicary Gibbs, H. A. Doubleday, Duncan Warrand, Lord Howard de Walden, and Geoffrey H. White. London, Office of the Master of Arms, 12 volumes in 13 parts, 1901–38.

Colvin, H. M., ed. *The History of the King's Works*. Six volumes. Oxford: Oxford University Press, 1963–73.

Corbett, William John. 'The Development of the Duchy of Normandy and the Norman Conquest of England'. *Cambridge Medieval History* 5 (1926, repr. 1968): 505–13.

Cowdrey, H. W. C. 'The Anglo-Norman *Laudes regiae*.' *Viator* 12 (1981): 38–78.

Craster, H. H. E. 'A Contemporary Record of the Pontificate of Ranulf Flambard'. *Archaeologia Aeliana*, fourth series, 7 (1930): 33–56.

Crépin, André. 'Waltheow's Offering of the Cup to Beowulf: A Study in Literary Structure'. In King and Stevens, edd., *Saints, Scholars and Heroes*, 45–58.

Crooke, B. M. 'General History of Lewes Priory in the Twelfth and Thirteenth Centuries'. *Sussex Archaeological Collections* 81 (1940): 68–96.

Crosby, Everett. *Bishop and Chapter in Twelfth-Century England: A Study of the Mensa Episcopalis*. Cambridge: University of Cambridge Press, 1995.

—— 'The Organization of the English Episcopate under Henry I'. *Studies in Medieval and Renaissance History* 4 (1967): 1–89.

Crouch, David. *The Beaumont Twins: The Roots and Branches of Power in the Twelfth Century*. Cambridge: Cambridge University Press, 1986.

—— 'Robert of Gloucester's Mother and Sexual Politics in Norman Oxfordshire'. *Historical Research* 72 (1999) 323–32.

Cutler, Kenneth E. 'Edith, Queen of England 1045–66'. *Mediaeval Studies* 35 (1973): 222–31.

David, Charles Wendell. *Robert Curthose, Duke of Normandy*. Cambridge, Massachusetts: Harvard University Press, 1920.

Davies, R. H. 'The Land and Rights of Harold, son of Godwine, and their Distribution by William I'. M.A. Thesis, University College, Cardiff, 1967.

Davis, H. W. C. 'Waldric the Chancellor'. *English Historical Review* 26 (1911): 84–9.

Dean, Ruth J. 'What is Anglo-Norman?' *Annuale Medievale* 6 (1965): 38–46.

DeBirch, Walter de Gray. 'On the Succession of the Abbots of Malmesbury'. *Journal of the British Archaeological Association* 27 (1871): 314–43.

DeMause, Lloyd, ed. *The History of Childhood*. New York: Psycho-History Press, 1974.

Deshman, Robert. 'Christus rex et magi reges: Kingship and Christology in Ottonian and Anglo-Saxon Art'. *Frühmittelalterliche Studien* 10 (1976): 367–405.

Dickinson, John Compton. 'Saint Anselm and the First Regular Canons in England'. *Spicilegium Beccense*. Paris, 1959.

—— *The Origins of the Austin Canons and their Introduction into England*. London: SPCK, 1950.

—— 'Walter the Priest and St Mary's, Carlisle'. *Journal of the Cumberland and Westmoreland Antiquarian and Archaeological Society* 59 (1969): 102–14.

Dodwell, C. R. *Anglo-Saxon Art: A New Perspective*. Manchester: Manchester University Press, 1982.

Douglas, David C. 'Companions of the Conqueror'. *History*, n.s., 28 (1943): 129–47.

—— 'The Song of Roland and the Norman Conquest of England'. *French Studies* 14 (1960): 99–116.

—— *William the Conqueror: The Norman Impact upon England*. Berkeley: University of California Press, 1964.

Duby, Georges. *The Chivalrous Society*. Translated by Cynthia Postan. Berkeley: University of California Press, 1977.

Duggan, Anne, ed. *Queens and Queenship in Medieval Europe*. Woodbridge: The Boydell Press, 1997.

Duncan, Archibald A. M. *Scotland: The Making of the Kingdom*. Edinburgh: Oliver and Boyd, 1975.

Dyson, Anthony G. Review of *The Ecclesiastical History of Orderic Vitalis*, Vol. III, Edited and translated by Marjorie Chibnall, *The Journal of the Society of Archivists* 4 (1970–3): 667–78.

Elias, Norbert. *The Civilizing Process: A History of Manners*. Translated by Edmund Jephcott. Two volumes. New York: Urizen Books, 1978–9.

Elkins, Sharon. *Holy Women of Twelfth-Century England*. Chapel Hill: University of North Carolina Press, 1988.

Enright, Michael J. 'Lady with a Mead-Cup: Ritual, Group Cohesion and Hierarchy in the Germanic Warband'. *Frühmittelalterliche Studien* 22 (1988): 170–203.

Erler, Mary, and Maryanne Kowaleski. *Women and Power in the Middle Ages*. Athens, Georgia: University of Georgia Press, 1988.

Evans, Joan. *Monastic Life at Cluny 910–1157*. Oxford: Oxford University Press, 1931. Repr., Archon Books, 1968.

Farmer, Sharon. *Communities of Saint Martin: Legend and Ritual in Medieval Tours*. Ithaca, New York: Cornell University Press, 1991.

—— 'Persuasive Voices: Clerical Perspectives of Medieval Wives'. *Speculum* 61 (1986): 517–43.

Fleming, Robin. 'Domesday Estates of the King and the Godwines: A Study in Late Saxon Politics'. *Speculum* 58 (1983): 987–1007.

Foreville, Raymonde. 'L'école de Caen au XIe siècle et les origines normandes de l'Université d'Oxford', *Etudes medievales offerts à M. doyen Augustin Fliche*. Montpelier, 1952, 81–100.

—— 'Le sacre des rois anglo-normandes et angevins et le serment du sacre (XIe–XXIIe siècles)'. *Anglo-Norman Studies* 1 (1978): 49–62.

Fox, John. *A Literary History of France, Volume One: The Middle Ages*. London: Bowes Ltd., 1974.

Freeman, Edward A. *The History of the Norman Conquest of England: Its Causes and Results*. Third edition. Oxford: The Clarendon Press, 1877–9.

—— *The Reign of William Rufus and the Accession of Henry the First*. Two volumes. Oxford, 1882. Reprint AMS Press: New York, 1970.

Frohlich, Walter. 'Die bischoflichen Kollegen des hl. Erzbischofs Anselm von Canterbury, Zweiter Teil: 1100–1109'. *Analecta Anselmiana* 2 (1970): 117–68.

—— 'The Letters Omitted from Anselm's Collection of Letters'. *Anglo-Norman Studies* 6 (1983): 58–71.

Galbraith, Vivian H. 'Monastic Foundation Charters'. *Cambridge Historical Journal* 4 (1934): 205–22.

Gameson, Richard. 'The Gospels of Margaret of Scotland and the Literacy of an Eleventh-Century Queen'. In *Women and the Book: Assessing the Visual Evidence*.

Edited by Jane H. M. Taylor and Lesley Smith. Toronto: University of Toronto Press, 1997, 149–71.
Garnett, George. 'Franci et Angli: The Legal Distinctions between Peoples after the Conquest'. *Anglo-Norman Studies* 8 (1986): 109–37.
Gathagan, Laura L. 'Embodying Power: Gender and Authority in the Queenship of Mathilda of Flanders'. Ph.D. dissertation, The City University of New York, 2002.
—— 'The Trappings of Power: The Coronation of Mathilda of Flanders'. Forthcoming in *The Haskins Society Journal: Studies in Medieval History*.
Georgi, Annette. *Das lateinische und deutsche Preisgedicht des Mittelalters in der Nachfolge der genus demonstrativum*. Berlin: Erich Schmidt Verlag, 1969.
Gem, Richard. 'A Recession in English Architecture in the Early Eleventh Century and its Effect on the Development of the Romanesque Style'. *Journal of the British Archaeological Association*, third series, 38 (1975): 28–49.
Gomme, Laurence, and Philip Norman, edd. *London County Council Survey of London. Volume 5: 'The Parish of St Giles in the Fields'*. London: London Record Commission, 1914.
Gransden, Antonia. *Historical Writing in England c.500–c.1307*. London: Routledge and Kegan Paul, 1974.
Green, Judith. 'Anglo-Scottish Relations, 1066–1174'. In *England and Her Neighbors: Essays in Honour of Pierre Chaplais*. Edited by Michael Jones and Malcolm Vale. London: The Hambledon Press, 1989, 53–73.
—— 'Aristocratic Loyalties on the Northern Frontier of England, c.1110–1174'. *England in the Twelfth Century: Proceedings of the 1988 Harlaxton Symposium*. Woodbridge: The Boydell Press, 1990, 83–100.
—— 'David I and Henry I'. *Scottish Historical Review* 75 (1996): 1–19.
—— *The Government of England under Henry I*. Cambridge: Cambridge University Press, 1986.
—— 'The Sheriffs of William the Conqueror'. *Anglo-Norman Studies* 5 (1982): 129–45.
Grinnell-Milne, Duncan. *The Killing of William Rufus*. Newton Abbott: David and Charles Ltd., 1968.
Harper-Bill, Christopher, Christopher Holdsworth, and Janet Nelson, edd. *Studies in Medieval History Presented to R. Allen Brown*. Woodbridge: The Boydell Press, 1989.
Harvey, John H. 'The Origins of Gothic Architecture: Some Further Thoughts'. *The Antiquaries Journal* 48 (1968): 87–99.
Haskins, Charles Homer. *Studies in the History of Mediaeval Science*. Harvard Historical Studies 27. Cambridge, Massachusetts: Harvard University Press, 1927.
Heales, Alfred C. *Records of Merton Priory in the County of Surrey*. London: Henry Froude, 1898.
Herbert, Jane. 'The Transformation of Hermitages into Augustinian Priories in Twelfth-Century England'. In *Monks, Hermits, and the Ascetic Tradition*. Studies in Church History 22. Oxford: Basil Blackwell for the Ecclesiastical History Society, 1985, 109–29.
Heslop, T. A. 'English Seals from the Mid-Ninth Century to 1100'. *Journal of the British Archaeological Association* 133 (1980): 1–16.
—— 'The Production of Deluxe Manuscripts and the Patronage of King Cnut and Queen Emma'. *Anglo-Saxon England* 19 (1990): 151–95.
—— 'Seals'. In *English Romanesque Art, 1066–1200*. Edited by George Zarnecki, Janet Holt, and Tristam Holland. London: Arts Council of Great Britain, 1984.
Hill, Rosalind. 'Marriage in Seventh-Century England'. In King and Stevens, edd., *Saints, Scholars and Heroes: Studies in Medieval Culture in Honour of Charles W. Jones*, 1: 67–75.

Hodgson, John. *A History of Northumberland in Three Parts*. Three parts in seven volumes. Newcastle-upon-Tyne: Thomas and James Pigg, 1820–58.
Holland, T. E. 'The Origin of the University of Oxford'. *English Historical Review* 6 (1891): 238–49.
Hollister, C. Warren. 'Courtly Culture and Courtly Style in the Anglo-Norman World'. *Albion* 20 (1988): 1–17.
—— 'The Greater Domesday Tenants-in-Chief'. In *Domesday Studies*. Edited by J. C. Holt. Woodbridge: The Boydell Press, 1987, 219–14.
—— *Henry I*. Edited and completed by Amanda Clark Frost. New Haven: Yale University Press, 2001.
—— *Monarchy, Magnates and Institutions in the Anglo-Norman World*. London: The Hambledon Press, 1986.
—— 'St Anselm on Lay Investiture'. *Anglo-Norman Studies* 10 (1988): 145–58.
—— 'The Viceregal Court of Henry I'. In *Law, Custom, and the Social Fabric in Medieval Europe: Essays on Honor of Bryce Lyon*. Edited by Bernard S. Bachrach and David Nicholas. Kalamazoo: Medieval Institute Publications, 1990, 131–44.
Holzknecht, Karl Julius. *Literary Patronage in the Middle Ages*. Menasha, Wisconsin: The Collegiate Press, 1923.
Honeybourne, M. B. 'The Leper Hospitals of the London Area'. *Proceedings of the Middlesex Archaeological Society* (1962): 4–61.
Hooper, Nicholas. 'Edgar Ætheling: Anglo-Saxon Prince, Rebel and Crusader'. *Anglo-Saxon England* 14 (1985): 197–214.
Howell, Margaret. *Eleanor of Provence: Queenship in Thirteenth-Century England*. Oxford, Blackwell, 1998.
—— 'The Resources of Eleanor of Provence as Queen Consort'. *English Historical Review* 102 (1987): 373–93.
Huneycutt, Lois L. 'The Audience and Patronage of the Anglo-Norman Voyage of St Brendan'. Unpublished paper presented at the annual meeting of the Charles Homer Haskins Society, Houston, Texas, November 1992.
—— 'The Idea of the Perfect Princess: The *Life of St Margaret* in the Reign of Matilda II (1100–1118)'. *Anglo-Norman Studies* 12 (1990): 81–98.
—— 'Intercession and the High-Medieval Queen: The Esther Topos'. In *Power of the Weak: Studies on Medieval Women*. Edited by Jennifer Carpenter and Sally-Beth MacLean. 126–46.
—— '"To Proclaim her Dignity Abroad": The Literary and Artistic Network of Matilda of Scotland, Queen of England 1100–1118'. In *The Cultural Patronage of Medieval Women*. Edited by June Hall McCash. Athens, Georgia: University of Georgia Press, 1996, 155–75.
—— 'Public Lives, Private Ties: Royal Mothers in England and Scotland, 1070–1204'. In *Medieval Mothering*. Edited by John Carmi Parsons and Bonnie Wheeler. New York: Garland Publishing, 1996, 295–313.
Illingworth, R. N. 'The Structure of the Anglo-Norman Voyage of St Brendan'. *Medium Aevum* 55 (1986): 217–29.
Jaeger, C. Stephen. *The Origins of Courtliness: Civilization and the Formation of Courtly Ideals 939–1210*. Philadelphia: University of Pennsylvania Press, 1985.
Jamison, Catherine. *The History of the Royal Hospital of St Catherine by the Tower of London*. London: Oxford University Press, 1952.
John, Eric. 'The *Encomium Emmae Reginae*: A Riddle and a Solution'. *Bulletin of the John Rylands Library* 63 (1980): 58–94.
Jones, Adrienne. 'The Significance of the Regal Coronation of Edgar in 973'. *Journal of Ecclesiastical History* 33 (1982): 375–390.

Jones, Robin F. 'The Mechanics of Meaning in the Anglo-Norman Voyage of St Brendan'. *Romanic Review* 71 (1980): 105–13.

—— 'The Precocity of Anglo-Norman and the Voyage of St Brendan'. In *The Nature of Medieval Narrative*. Edited by Minnette Grunmann-Gaudet and Robin F. Jones. Lexington: French Forum Publishers, 1980, 145–58.

Kapelle, William E. *The Norman Conquest of the North: The Region and its Transformation 1100–1135*. Chapel Hill: University of North Carolina Press, 1979.

Kealey, Edward J. *Medieval Medicus: A Social History of Anglo-Norman Medicine*. Baltimore: The Johns Hopkins Press, 1981.

—— *Roger of Salisbury: Viceroy of England*. Berkeley: University of California Press, 1972.

Keefe, Thomas K. 'Counting Those who Count: A Computer-Assisted Analysis of Charter Witness Lists and the Itinerant Court in the First Year of the Reign of Richard I'. *The Haskins Society Journal: Studies in Medieval History* 1 (1989): 135–45.

Kemp, B. E. 'Monastic Possession of Parish Churches in England in the Twelfth Century'. *Journal of Ecclesiastical History* 31 (1980): 133–60.

King, Margot H., and Wesley J. Stevens. *Saints, Scholars and Heroes: Studies in Medieval Culture in Honour of Charles W. Jones*. Two volumes. Ann Arbor, Michigan: University Microforms, 1979.

Kirshner, Julius, and Suzanne Wemple, edd. *Women of the Medieval World: Essays in Honor of John Hine Mundy*. Oxford: Basil Blackwell, 1985.

Knowles, David. *The monastic order in England: A history of its Development from the Times of St Dunstan to the Fourth Lateran Council, 940–1216*. Second edition. Cambridge: Cambridge University Press, 1963.

——, Christopher N. L. Brooke and Vera London, edd. *The Heads of Religious Houses, England and Wales 942–1216*. Cambridge: Cambridge University Press, 1972.

——, and R. Neville Hadcock. *Medieval Religious Houses: England and Wales*. London: Longman, Green and Company, 1953.

Lambrick, G. 'Abingdon Abbey Administration'. *Journal of Ecclesiastical History* 17 (1966): 159–83.

Larson, Laurence Marcellus. *The King's Household in England before the Norman Conquest*. Madison, Wisconsin: University of Wisconsin Press, 1904; reprint New York: Greenwood Press, 1969.

Latzke, Therese. 'Der Fürstinnenpreis'. *Mittellateinisches Jahrbuch* 14 (1979): 22–65.

—— 'Der Topos Mantelgedicht'. *Mittellateinisches Jahrbuch* 6 (1970): 109–31.

Legg, J. Wickham, ed. *Three Coronation Orders*. London: Harrison and Sons, 1900.

Legge, Mary Dominica. *Anglo-Norman Literature and its Background*. Oxford: The Clarendon Press, 1963.

—— 'L'influence littéraire de la cour d'Henri Beauclerc'. In *Mélanges offerts à Rita Lejeune I*. Gembloux, 1969, 679–87.

—— 'Les origines de l'anglo-normand litteraire'. *Revue de linguistique romane* 31 (1967): 44–54.

—— 'La précocité de la littéraire anglo-normande'. *Cahiers de civilisation médiévale* 8 (1965): 327–51.

Lehmann-Brockhaus, Otto. *Lateinische Schriftquellen zur Kunst in England, Wales und Schottland vom Jahre 901 bis zum Jahre 1307*. Five volumes. Munich: Prestal Verlag, 1956.

Leland, John. *De rebus Britannicis collectanea*. Edited by Thomas Hearne. Second edition. Six volumes. London: B. White, 1774.

LePatourel, John. *The Norman Empire*. Oxford: The Clarendon Press, 1976.

Lethaby, W. R. 'The Palace of Westminster in the Eleventh and Twelfth Centuries'. *Archaeologia* 60 (1906): 131–48.
—— 'The Priory of Holy Trinity, or Christ Church, Aldgate'. *The Home Counties Magazine* 2 (January, 1900): 45–53.
Lewis, C. P. 'The Earldom of Surrey and the Date of Domesday Book'. *Historical Research* 63 (1990): 329–336.
—— 'The King and Eye: A Study in Anglo-Norman Politics'. *English Historical Review* 104 (1989): 569–87.
Lewis, Suzanne. *The Art of Matthew Paris in the Chronica majora.* Berkeley and Los Angeles: The University of California Press, 1987.
Leyser, Karl. *Medieval Germany and its Neighbors 900–1250.* London: The Hambledon Press, 1986.
Lifshitz, Felice. 'The *Encomium Emmae reginae:* A Political Pamphlet of the Eleventh Century?' *The Haskins Society Journal: Studies in Medieval History* 1 (1989): 39–50.
LoPrete, Kimberly. 'The Anglo-Norman Card of Adela of Blois'. *Albion* 22 (1990): 569–89.
Lovegrove, E. W. 'Llanthony Priory'. *Archaeologia Cambrensis* 97 (1943): 213–29.
Madan, Falconer. 'The Evangelistarium of St Margaret, Queen of Scotland'. *The Academy: A Weekly Review of Literature, Science, and Art* 32, 796 (6 August 1887): 88–9.
Manning, Owen, and William Bray. *The History and Antiquities of the County of Surrey.* Three volumes. London: John White and Company, 1809.
Mason, Emma. 'Magnates, Curiales and the Wheel of Fortune'. *Anglo-Norman Studies* 2 (1979): 118–40.
—— 'Review of C. Warren Hollister, *Monarchy, Magnates and Institutions in the Anglo-Norman World'. Medieval Prosopography* 9 (1988): 105–13.
—— 'The Site of King-making and Consecration: Westminster Abbey and the Crown in the Eleventh and Twelfth Centuries'. In *The Church and Sovereignty c.590–1918.* Edited by Diana Wood. Basil Blackwell for the Ecclesiastical History Society, 1991, 57–96.
—— 'Westminster Abbey and the Monarchy between the Reigns of William I and John (1066–1216)'. *Journal of Ecclesiastical History* 41 (1990): 199–216.
—— 'William Rufus: Myth and Reality'. *Journal of Medieval History* 3 (1977): 1–20.
Mason, J. F. A. 'The Honour of Richmond in 1086'. *English Historical Review* 78 (1963): 703–4.
McBride, Deborah. 'The Bishop and the Court: A Look at the Exchanges between Hildebert of Lavardin and the Courtly Personages with whom he Corresponded'. Unpublished seminar paper, University of California, Santa Barbara, March 1991.
—— 'Feasts, Families, and Fashion at the Court of Henry I'. Unpublished paper delivered at the annual meeting of the North American Conference on British Studies, New Orleans, Louisiana, November 1990.
McLaughlin, Mary Martin. 'Survivors and Surrogates: Children and Parents from the Ninth to the Thirteenth Centuries'. In *The History of Childhood,* ed. DeMause, 101–82.
McNamara, JoAnn, and Suzanne Wemple. 'The Power of Women through the Family in Medieval Europe, 500–1100'. In *Women and Power in the Middle Ages,* edd. Erler and Kowaleski, 83–102.
Meyer, Marc Anthony, ed. *The Culture of Christendom: Essays in Medieval History in Commemoration of Denis L. T. Bethell.* London: The Hambledon Press, 1993.
—— 'Patronage of West-Saxon Royal Nunneries in Late Anglo-Saxon England'. *Revue Bénédictine* 91 (1981): 332–58.

—— 'The Politics of Possession: Women's Estates in Later Anglo-Saxon England.' *The Haskins Society Journal: Studies in Medieval History* 3 (1992): 111–129.

—— 'The "Queen's Demesne" in Later Anglo-Saxon England'. Iin Meyer, ed., *The Culture of Christendom: Essays in Memory of Denis L. T. Bethel.* London: The Hambledon Press, 1993, 75–113.

—— 'Women and the Tenth-Century Monastic Reform'. *Revue Bénédictine* 87 (1977): 34–61.

Mitchell, Linda E., ed. *Women in Medieval Western European Culture.* New York and London: Garland Press, 1999.

Moore, R. I. *The Formation of a Persecuting Society: Power and Deviance in Western Europe, 950–1250.* Oxford: Basil Blackwell, 1987.

Morey, Adrian, and C. N. L. Brooke. *Gilbert Foliot and his Letters.* Cambridge: Cambridge University Press, 1965.

Mussett, Lucien. 'La reine Mathilde et la fondation de la Trinité de Caen (abbaye aux dames)'. *Mémoires academie sciences et belles-lettres et arts Caen,* n.s. 21 1984): 191–210.

Nagy, Kazmer. *St Margaret of Scotland and Hungary.* Glasgow: John S. Burns and Sons, 1973.

Nelson, Janet L. 'Medieval Queenship'. In *Women in Medieval Western European Culture,* ed. Linda Mitchell. New York and London, 1999, 179–207.

—— 'Perceptions du pouvoir chez les historiennes du haut moyen age'. In *La femme au moyen âge.* Edited by Michel Rouche and Jean Heuclin. Maubeuge: Jean Touzot, 1990.

—— *Politics and Ritual in Early Medieval Europe.* London: The Hambledon Press, 1986.

—— and Margaret Gibson, edd. *Charles the Bald: Court and Kingdom. Papers based on a colloquium held in London, April 1979.* Oxford: British Archaeological Reports, 1980.

Newman, Charlotte. *The Anglo-Norman Nobility in the Reign of Henry I: The Second Generation.* Philadelphia: University of Pennsylvania Press, 1988.

Nicholl, Donald. *Thurstan, Archbishop of York (1114–1140).* New York: The Stonegate Press, 1964.

Norgate, Kate. 'Waldric of Laon'. In Leslie Stephen and Sidney Lee, edd. *Dictionary of National Biography.* Old series. 63 volumes. London, 1885–1900. Volume 7: 813.

Offler, H. S. 'A Note on the Early History of the Priory of Carlisle'. *Transactions of the Cumberland and Westmoreland Antiquarian and Archaeological Society* 55 (1965): 176–81.

Orme, Nicholas. *From Childhood to Chivalry: The Education of English Kings and Aristocracy, 1066–1530.* London: Metheun Press, 1984.

Parkes, M. B. 'The Literacy of the Laity'. In David Daiches and Anthony Thorlby, edd. *The Medieval World.* London: Aldus Books, 1973, 555–77.

Parry, H. Lloyd. 'The Fee Farm of Exeter'. *Reports and Transactions of the Devonshire Association* 81 (1949): 197–9.

Parsons, John Carmi. *Eleanor of Castile: Queenship and Society in Thirteenth-Century England.* New York: St Martin's Press, 1995.

——, ed. *Medieval Queenship.* New York: St Martin's Press, 1993.

—— 'Mothers, Daughters, Marriage, Power: Some Plantagenet Evidence, 1150–1500', In Parsons, ed., *Medieval Queenship,* 63–79.

—— '"Never was a Body Buried in England with such Solemnity and Honour": The Burials and Posthumous Commemorations of English Queens to 1500,' In Duggan, ed., *Queens and Queenship in Medieval Europe,* 317–37.

—— 'The Queen's Intercession in Thirteenth-Century England.' In Carpenter and MacLean, edd., *Power of the Weak: Studies on Medieval Women,* 147–77.

—— and Bonnie Wheeler, edd. *Medieval Mothering*. New York: Garland Publishing, 1996.

Perkins, Jocelyn. *Westminster Abbey: Its Worship and Ornaments*. Alcuin Club 34. Three volumes. London: Oxford University Press, 1936–52.

Poole, Austin Lane. *From Domesday Book to Magna Carta, 1087–1216*. Second edition. Oxford: Clarendon Press, 1955.

Poole, Reginald Lane. *The Exchequer in the Twelfth Century*. Oxford: Clarendon Press, 1912.

—— *Studies in Chronology and History*. Oxford: Oxford University Press, 1934.

Pope-Hennesy, Una. *Agnes Strickland: Biographer of the Queens of England*. London: Chatto and Windus, 1940.

Prah-Perochon, Anne. 'La role officiel du Mathilde, femme du Guilliaume le Conquérant'. Ph.D. dissertation, College de France, Université d'Aix-Marseille, 1973.

Press, Alan R. 'The Precocious Courtesy of Geoffrey Gaimar'. In *Court and Poet: Selected Proceedings of the Third Congress of the International Courtly Literature Society*. Edited by Glyn S. Burgess. Liverpool: Francis Cairns, 1981, 267–76.

Prestwich, J. O. 'The Career of Ranulf Flambard'. In Rollason *et al.*, edd. *Anglo-Norman Durham*, 300–310.

Pythian-Adams, Charles. 'Rutland Reconsidered'. In *Mercian Studies*. Edited by Ann Dornier. Leicester: University of Leicester Press, 1977, 63–83.

Reedy, W. T. 'Were Ralph and Richard Basset Really Chief Justiciars in the Reign of Henry I?' In *The Twelfth Century*. Edited by Bernard S. Levy and Sandro Sticca. Binghamton, New York: The Center for Medieval and Early Renaissance Studies, 1975, 74–103.

Rézbányay, J. 'St Margaret of Hungary: The Queen of Scotland'. *Katholikus Szemle* 10 (1896): 68–97.

Rice, D. Talbot. *English Art 871–1100*. Oxford: Oxford University Press, 1952.

Richardson, H. G. 'The Coronation in Medieval England: The Evolution of the Office and the Oath'. *Traditio* 16 (1960): 111–202.

—— 'The Letters and Charters of Eleanor of Aquitaine'. *English Historical Review* 74 (1959): 193–213.

——, and G. O. Sayles. *The Governance of Mediaeval England from the Conquest to Magna Carta*. Edinburgh: University of Edinburgh Press, 1963.

Ridyard, Susan. *The Royal Saints of Anglo-Saxon England*. Cambridge: Cambridge University Press, 1988.

Ritchie, Robert L. 'The Date of the Voyage of St Brendan'. *Medium Aevum* 14 (1960): 64–6.

—— *The Normans in Scotland*. Edinburgh: University of Edinburgh Press, 1954.

Roberts, George. 'Llanthony Priory, Monmouthshire'. *Archaeologia Cambrensis* 1 (1846): 201–45.

Robinson, Joseph Armitage. *Gilbert Crispin, Abbot of Westminster: A Study of the Abbey under Norman Rule*. Cambridge: Cambridge University Press, 1911.

Rollason, David, Margaret Harvey, and Michael Prestwich, edd. *Anglo-Norman Durham, 1093–1193*. Woodbridge: The Boydell Press, 1994.

Ronay, Gabriel. *The Lost King of England: The European Adventures of Edward the Exile*. Woodbridge: The Boydell Press, 1989.

Ross, Margaret Clunies. 'Concubinage in Anglo-Saxon England'. *Past and Present* 108 (1985): 3–34.

Rud, Thomas. *Codicum manuscriptorum ecclesiae cathedralis Dunelmensis*. Durham: F. Humble, 1825.

Ruud, Marylou. 'Monks in the World: The Case of Gundulph of Rochester'. *Anglo-Norman Studies* 11 (1989): 245–60.
Sabine Ernest L. 'Latrines and Cesspools of Mediaeval London'. *Speculum* 9 (1934): 303–21.
Salter, Elizabeth. *English and International: Studies in the Literature, Art, and Patronage of Medieval England.* Edited by Derek Pearsall and Nicolette Zeeman. Cambridge: Cambridge University Press, 1988.
Sawyer, Peter H. *Anglo-Saxon Charters: An Annotated Handlist and Bibliography.* London: Offices of the Royal Historical Society, 1968.
Schramm, Percy Ernst. *A History of the English Coronation.* Oxford: The Clarendon Press, 1937.
Searle, Eleanor. 'Emma the Conqueror'. In *Studies in Medieval History Presented to R. Allen Brown.* Edited by Christopher Harper-Bill, Christopher J. Holdsworth, Janet L. Nelson. Woodbridge: The Boydell Press, 1989, 281–8.
—— 'Possible History'. *Speculum* 61 (1986): 799–86.
—— 'Women and the Legitimization of Succession at the Norman Conquest'. *Anglo-Norman Studies* 3 (1980): 159–70.
Smith, R. A. L. 'The Place of Gundulph in the Anglo-Norman Church'. *English Historical Review* 58 (1943): 257–72.
Southern, Richard William. *Medieval Humanism and other Studies.* Oxford: Basil Blackwell, 1970.
—— *St Anselm and his Biographer: A Study of Monastic Life and Thought.* Cambridge: Cambridge University Press, 1963.
—— *Saint Anselm: A Portrait in a Landscape.* Cambridge: Cambridge University Press, 1990.
—— *Western Society and the Church in the Middle Ages.* London: The Penguin Group, 1970.
Southworth, John. *The English Medieval Minstrel.* Woodbridge: The Boydell Press, 1989.
Spear, David. 'The Norman Empire and Secular Clergy, 1066–1204'. *Journal of British Studies* 21 (1982): 1–10.
—— 'The School of Caen Revisited'. Unpublished paper presented at the Twenty-sixth International Congress on Medieval Studies, Western Michigan University, Kalamazoo, Michigan, May 1991.
Stafford, Pauline. 'Charles the Bald, Judith, and England'. In *Charles the Bald: Court and Kingdom (Papers based on a Colloquium held in London in April 1979).* Edited by Janet Nelson and Margaret Gibson. London: British Archaeological Reports, 1981.
—— 'Cherchez la femme: Queens, Queens' Lands, and Nunneries: Missing Links in the Foundation of Reading Abbey'. *History: The Journal of the Historical Association* 85 (January 2000): 4–27.
—— 'The King's Wife in Wessex, 800–1066'. *Past and Present* 91 (1981): 3–27.
—— 'The Portrayal of Royal Women in England, Mid-Tenth to Mid-Twelfth Centuries'. In Parsons, ed., *Medieval Queenship,* 143–67.
—— *Queen Emma and Queen Edith: Queenship and Women's Power in Eleventh-Century England.* Oxford: Blackwell, 1997.
—— *Queens, Concubines and Dowagers: The King's Wife in the Early Middle Ages.* Athens, Georgia: University of Georgia Press, 1983.
—— 'Sons and Mothers: Family Politics in the Early Middle Ages'. In Baker, ed., *Medieval Women,* 79–100.
—— 'Women and the Norman Conquest', *Transactions of the Royal Historical Society,* Series 6, Volume 4 (1994): 221–49.
—— 'Women in Domesday'. In *Medieval Women in Southern England.* Edited by

Malcolm Barber *et al.* Reading: Graduate Centre for Medieval Studies, University of Reading, 1989.

Stenton, Doris Mary. *English Justice between the Conquest and Magna Carta*. Philadelphia: American Philosophical Society, 1964.

Stenton, Frank M. 'Introduction to Rutland Domesday'. *VCH Rutland* 1: 121–36.

Stephen, Leslie, and Sidney Lee. *Dictionary of National Biography*. 22 volumes. Oxford: Oxford University Press, 1968.

Stow, John. *A survey of London, by John Stow; reprinted from the text of 1603, with introduction and notes by Charles Lethbridge Kingsford*. Two volumes. Oxford, The Clarendon Press, 1908.

Strickland, Agnes. *Lives of the Queens of England from the Norman Conquest from the Official Records and other Private and Public Documents*. Philadelphia: G. Barrie, 1902.

Sturman, Winifred Maud. 'Barking Abbey: A Study of its External and Internal Administration from the Conquest to the Dissolution'. Ph.D. thesis, University of London, 1961.

Summerson, Henry. 'Old and New Bishoprics: Durham and Carlisle'. In Rollason *et al.*, edd, *Anglo-Norman Durham, 1093–1193*, 368–80.

Tatlock, J. S. P. 'Muriel: The Earliest English Poetess'. *Publications of the Modern Language Association of America* 48 (1933): 317–21.

Tattersall, Jill. 'Expedition, Exploration, and Odyssey. Extended Voyage Themes and their Treatment in Some Early French Texts'. In *Studies in Medieval French Language and Literature Presented to Brian Woledge in Honour of his 80th Birthday*. Edited by Sally Burch North. Geneva: Librarie Droz S.A., 1988, 191–214.

Thiébaux, Marcelle. *The Writings of Medieval Women*. New York: Garland Press, 1987.

Thomson, Rodney. 'William of Malmesbury as Historian and Man of Letters'. *Journal of Ecclesiastical History* 29 (1978): 387–413.

Thompson, James Westfall. *The Literacy of the Laity in the Middle Ages*. Berkeley, 1939; repr. New York: Burt Franklin, 1963.

Thorndike, Lynn. *A History of Magic and Experimental Science*. Eight volumes. New York: Columbia University Press, 1923–58.

Torry, Gilbert. *The Book of Queenhithe: The History of a Harbour and City Ward*. Buckingham: Barracuda Books, 1979.

Tout, T. F. *Chapters in the Administrative History of Medieval England*. Six volumes. Third edition. Manchester: University of Manchester Press, 1967.

Trindade, Ann. *Berengaria: In Search of Richard the Lionheart's Queen*. Dublin: Four Courts Press, 1999.

Turner, Ralph V. 'The Children of Anglo-Norman Royalty and their Upbringing'. *Medieval Prosopography* 11 (1990): 17–44.

—— 'Eleanor of Aquitaine and her Children: An Inquiry into Medieval Family Attachment'. *Journal of Medieval History* 14 (1988): 321–36.

—— 'The *miles litteratus* in Twelfth and Thirteenth Century England: How Rare a Phenomenon?' *American Historical Review* 83 (1978): 928–45.

Van Caenegem, R. C. *Royal Writs in England from the Conquest to Glanville*. London: Selden Society, 1959.

Van Houts, Elisabeth. 'Latin Poetry as a Source for Anglo-Norman History: The Carmen de Hastingae Proelio'. *The Journal of Medieval History* 15 (1989): 39–62.

—— 'Medieval Historiography and Oral Tradition: The Norman Conquest of England in 1066'. Paper presented to the Medieval Group, University of Cambridge, October 1990.

—— *Memory and Gender in Medieval Europe, 900–1200*. Toronto: University of Toronto Press, 1999.

—— 'The Ship List of William the Conqueror'. *Anglo-Norman Studies* 10 (1987): 159–83.

Vaughn, Sally N. 'Anselm and the English Investiture Controversy'. *Journal of Medieval History* 6 (1980): 61–86.

—— *Anselm of Bec and Robert of Meulan: The Innocence of the Dove and the Wisdom of the Serpent.* Berkeley: University of California Press, 1987.

—— 'St Anselm and Women'. *The Haskins Society Journal: Studies in Medieval History* 2 (1990): 83–93.

Vickers, Kenneth *et al.*, edd. *A History of Northumberland issued under the direction of the Northumberland County History Committee.* Newcastle-upon-Tyne: A. Reid Sons and Company; London, Simpkin, Marshall, Hamilton, Kent,and Company, Ltd., 1893–1940.

Victoria Histories of the Counties of England:

Buckingham. Five volumes, ed. William Page. London: Archibald Constable and Company, 1905–27; reprint 1969.

Cumberland. Two volumes, ed. James Wilson. Vol I, London: Archibald Constable and Company, n.d. Vol. II, London: James Street, 1905.

Essex. Six volumes, ed. W. R. Powell, William Page *et al.* Seven volumes. London: Archibald Constable and Company and St Catherine's Press; Oxford: Oxford University Press, 1903–78.

Herefordshire. Four volumes. Edited by William Page. Westminster: Archibald Constable and Company, Ltd., 1902–14.

Middlesex. Nine volumes. Vol. I. Edited by J. S. Cockburn, H. P. F. King and K. G. T. McDonnell. Oxford: Oxford University Press, 1969.

Rutland. Two volumes. Vol I, London: Archibald Constable and Company, Ltd, 1908. Vol. II, London: St Catherine's Press, n.d.

Somerset. Seven volumes, 1906–99. Volume I, edited by William Page. London: Archibald Constable and Company, 1906.

Surrey. Four volumes, 1902–12. Volumes II and III, edited by H. E. Malden. London: Archibald Constable and Company., 1905–11.

Sussex. Nine volumes, 1902–99. Volume II, edited by William Page. London: Archibald Constable and Company, 1907.

Yorkshire. Three volumes. Edited by William Page. London, 1907–13; repr. London: University of London Institute of Historical Research, 1974.

Victoria History of London. Edited by William Page. London: Archibald Constable and Company, 1909.

Vogelsang, Theo. *Die Frau als Herrscherin im höhen Mittelalters: Studien zur 'consors regni' Formel.* Frankfurt: Musterschmidt Wissenschaftlicher Verlag, 1954.

Wainwright, Francis. 'Æthelflæd, Lady of the Mercians'. In Clemoes, ed., *The Anglo-Saxons*, 53–69.

Walberg, Emmanuel. 'Sur le nom de l'auteur du "Voyage de Saint Brendan"'. *Studia Neophilologica* 12 (1939): 345–61.

Wall, Valerie. 'Malcolm III and the Foundation of Durham Cathedral'. In *Anglo-Norman Durham, 1093–1193.* Edited by David Rollason *et al.*, 325–37.

Ward, P. L. 'An Early Version of the Anglo-Saxon Coronation Ceremony'. *English Historical Review* 57 (1942): 345–61.

Warren, F. E. 'The Evangelistarium of St Margaret, Queen of Scotland'. *The Academy: A Weekly Review of Literature, Science, and Art* 32, 800 (3 September 1887): 151.

Warren, Wilfrid Lewis. 'The Myth of Norman Administrative Efficiency (The Prothero Lecture)'. *Transactions of the Royal Historical Society* 34 (5th series, 1984): 113–32.

Watson, George. 'The Black Rood of Scotland'. *Transactions of the Scottish Ecclesiological Society* 2 (1906–9): 27–46.
Wemple, Suzanne. *Women in Frankish Society: Marriage and the Cloister 500–900*. Philadelphia: University of Pennsylvania Press, 1985.
West, Francis. *The Justiciarship in England*. Cambridge: Cambridge University Press, 1966.
Westwood, I. O. 'The Evangelistarium of St Margaret, Queen of Scotland'. *The Academy: A Weekly Review of Literature, Science, and Art* 32, 798 (20 August 1887): 120.
White, Geoffrey H. 'The Fall of Robert Malet'. *Notes and Queries*. 12th series, 12 (1923): 390–91.
White, Stephen D. *Custom, Kinship, and Gifts to Saints: The Laudatio parentum in Western France, 1050–1150*. Chapel Hill: University of North Carolina Press, 1988.
Wilmart, André. 'Alain le Roux et Alain le Noir, Comptes de Bretagne'. *Annales de Bretagne* 38 (1929): 578–602.
—— 'La destinaire de la letter de Saint Anselm sur l'etat et le voeux de religion'. *Revue Bénédictine* 38 (1926): 331–4.
—— 'Eve et Goscelin'. *Revue Bénédictine* 46 (1934): 414–38.
—— 'La légende de Saint Edith en prose et vers par le moine Goscelin'. *Analecta Bollandiana* 56 (1938): 5–101, 265–305.
Wilson, R. M. *The Lost Literature of Medieval England*, 1952; repr. New York: Cooper Square Publishers, Inc., 1969.
Wolffe, B. P. *The Royal Demesne in English Constitutional History: The Crown Estate of the Realm from the Conquest to 1509*. Athens, Ohio: Ohio University Press, 1971.
Wormald, Patrick. 'Bede, Beowulf, and the Conversion of the Anglo-Saxon Aristocracy'. In *Bede and Anglo-Saxon England*. Edited by Robert Farrell. London: British Archaeological Reports, 1978, 32–95.
Wright, Laurence. 'The Role of Musicians in the Court of Twelfth-Century Britain'. *Art and Patronage in the English Romanesque*. Edited by Sarah Macready and F. H. Thompson. London: The Society of Antiquaries of London, 1986, 97–106.
Wylie, J. H. and James Wylie, edd. *Report on the Records of the City of Exeter*. London: Historical Manuscripts Commission 73, 1916.
Zarnecki, George, Janet Holt, and Tristam Holland, edd., *English Romanesque Art, 1066–1200*. London: Hacker Art Books, 1984.

Index

Abbott, Judith, 37, 38, 52, 113
Abingdon Abbey, 42, 47, 48, 59, 62, 74, 82, 118, 120, 126, 130, 154, 160
  Abingdon Chronicle, 47, 48, 59, 74, 82
d'Abitot, Urse, 96, 154
Adam, son of Brunig, canon of Waltham, 121, 159
Adelard of Bath, 86, 142
Adeliza of Louvain, Queen of England, 61, 64, 66, 134, 136, 139, 141, 149
Ædulf, abbot of Malmesbury, 65, 77
Ælfflæd, Queen of England, 38
Ælfric, 39
Ælfgifu, mother of Edgar, King of England, 133
Ælfgifu of Northampton, 41, 43
Ælfsige, Abbot of Peterborough, 42
Ælfthryth, Queen of England, 35–39, 42, 44, 48, 49, 52, 57, 69, 70, 148
Ælred of Rievaulx, 3, 6, 104, 148, 162
Æthreldreda, St, 91, 92
Æthelflæd, Lady of the Mercians, 31
Æthelnoth, Archbishop of Canterbury, 43
Æthelred II, King of England, 38, 39–41, 44
Æthelred, Prince of Scotland, 10
Æthelwold, Bishop of Winchester, 36, 37
Æthelwulf, King of Wessex, 35
Alan the Black, Count of Richmond, 21–24
Alan the Red, Count of Richmond, 21–25
Alaric the Sheriff, 159
Albin, chaplain, 72, 100
d'Albini, Nigel, 88, 152
Aldhelm, St, 111, 132–133, 158
Aldwin, Queen's Chamberlain, 62, 100, 101, 146, 155, 156, 157, 158, 159
Alexander I, King of Scotland, 17, 122, 134
Alexander, Bishop of Lincoln, 99
Alexius Comnenus, Byzantine Emperor, 145
Alfred 'the Great', King of England, 45, 149
Alfred, Prince of England, 41, 45
Alstoe North, Rutland, 6, 71
Alstoe South, Rutland, 69
Ancrene Riwle, 101
Andresey, Isle of (Oxfordshire), 62, 153
d'Anesy, William, 151
Anglo-Norman architecture, 124, 125–129
Anglo-Saxon Chronicle, 21, 27, 31, 40, 137

Annals of St Bertin, 35
Anonimalle Chronicle, 83, 108
Anselm of Bec, Archbishop of Canterbury, 4, 19, 25, 26, 65, 84, 90, 117, 118, 123, 124, 147, 149, 156
  Correspondence with Queen Matilda, 111, 112, 114, 116–117, 131, 132, 139
  Opposes marriage of Henry I and Matilda, 28–29, 30
  Performs wedding and crowns Matilda queen, 29–30
  Returns to England, 85
  Role in Investiture Controversy, 75–78
  Sponsor of Augustinian canons in England, 106–108
  Vice-regal authority, 86
Anselm, Abbot of Bury St Edmunds, 92, 114
Ansfrid dapifer, 152
Archil Morel, 22, 25, 59, 119, 154
Asser, 34–35
Augustine of Canterbury, St, 20
Augustine of Hippo, St, 131
Augustinian canons, 1, 84, 101, 106–107, 115, 123, 149

Baker, Derek, 11–12
Barking Abbey, 37, 62, 63–64, 115
Barlow, Frank, 48
Barrow, G. W. S., 11
Barrowden (Rutland), 62, 70, 71
Bartlett, Robert, 161
Basset, Ralph, 91–92, 98, 151
Bates, David, 51, 79, 93
Bath, 88
Baudri of Bourgeuil, 125
Bede, 19, 31, 33–34
deBellême, Robert, 80–81
deBelmeis, Richard, Bishop of London, 96, 142, 151, 156, 157, 158, 159
Belton-in-Axelholme, 62, 120, 154
Benedeiz, 140, 141
Benedict, St, 91, 92
Beowulf, 32–33
Berengaria of Navarre, Queen of England, 69
Bermondsey Abbey, 134
Bernard, Abbot of Clairvaux, 128

INDEX

Bernard, Bishop of St David's, 90, 99, 101, 153, 154, 155, 157
Bertha, Queen of Kent, 31, 34
Bertrada of Montfort, Queen of France, 73, 142
Bethel, Denis, 110
Bewick (Northumberland), 62, 121, 122
Bible, 131, 134
Binns, Alison, 111
Bishop's Waltham (Hampshire), 88
Bloet, Robert, Bishop of Lincoln, 15, 62, 90, 95, 98, 119, 151, 152, 154, 155, 156, 157, 159
Blyth Abbey, 80–81, 155
Bow Bridge, Essex, 115
Bray, William, 114
Brendan, St, 140
Bricstan of Chatteris, 91–92, 98, 110, 149
Brooke, C. N. L., 66
Brunig, canon of Waltham, 121, 159
deBuckland, Hugh, Sheriff of London, 120, 153, 154, 158, 159
deBuilli, Roger, 80
Bumke, Joachim, 135
Bury St Edmund's Abbey, 42, 60

Caen, 50
  Holy Trinity Abbey, 50, 52, 112, 117, 145
  St Stephen's Abbey, 50, 80
Campbell, Miles, 43
Canterbury,
  Christchurch Cathedral, 41, 42, 112
  St Augustine's Abbey, 42, 91, 93, 152
Cantor, Norman, 111
Capitulaire de villis, 33
Carham (Northumberland), 59, 62, 121, 159
Carlisle, Augustinian foundation, 83, 108
Carmen de Hastingae proelio, 49
Cecilia, Abbess of Holy Trinity, Caen, 138
Charlemagne, Emperor of the Romans, 33
Charles the Bald, King of the West Franks, 35
Charters as historical sources, 4, 55–56, 94–101, Appendix I
Chartres Cathedral, 116, 128
Chibnall, Marjorie, 74
Chichester, 106
Christina, St, 112
Christina, nun of Romsey and possible abbess of Wilton, 17, 28, 133
Christina, member of Matilda of Scotland's household, 101
Cicero, Marcus Tullius, 131
deClinton, Geoffrey, 96, 157
Cluny, Abbey of St Peter, 79, 119, 128
Cnut, King of England, 40–43, 44
Cobham (Surrey), 114
Colnbrook (Buckinghamshire), 59, 62
Constitutio domus regis, 135

Coronation rituals, 30, 34–35, 39, 51
Crosby, Everett, 98
Crouch, David, 84
deCurci, William, 95, 151, 154, 158
Cuthbert, St, 15, 122, 123, 159, 176
Cutler, Kenneth, 43, 45

David (Biblical king), 134
David I, King of Scotland, 3, 6, 17, 89, 95, 97, 100, 104, 111, 120, 122, 132, 134, 146, 149, 150, 156, 159, 160
David the Poet, 134
Devonshire, 41
Dialogus de scaccario, 4, 60
Dickinson, John C., 110
Domesday Book, 4, 47, 49, 71, 88, 130
Duncan, King of the Scots, 165
Dunstan, Archbishop of Canterbury, 35, 38, 164
Durham,
  castle, 80, 153
  cathedral church of, 14, 21, 59, 62, 88–89, 90, 91, 121, 126
  Liber vitae, 15, 26

Eadburgh of Mercia, 34
Eadmer of Canterbury, 3, 28–29, 30, 84, 92, 115, 137
Eadgyth Swan-Neck, 21, 24
Ealdgyth, Queen of England, 49
Eanflæd, Queen of Northumbria, 34
Ebba of Coldingham, St, 4, 14
Edgar Æthling, Prince of England, 17, 22, 66, 127
Edgar 'the Peaceable', King of England, 26, 35, 38, 39, 42, 147, 164
Edgar, King of Scotland, 10, 19, 22, 58, 59, 80, 122, 134
Edith of Wilton, St, 10, 18, 19, 26, 127–128, 134
  Her shrine at Wilton, 127–128
Edith, Queen of England, 10, 19, 44–49, 52, 57, 68, 69, 70, 71, 120, 145, 148
Edith of Scotland, see Matilda of Scotland
Edith Weston (Rutland), 70
Edmund Ironside, 9, 41, 164
Edmund, Prince of Scotland, 10
Edward 'the Confessor', King of England, 9, 14, 27, 28, 40, 41, 43, 44, 52, 57, 70, 77, 111, 120, 145, 147, 148, 161, 162
  Life of King Edward, 19, 45, 46, 127
Edward the Elder, King of England, 38
Edward 'the Martyr', King of England, 36
Edward, Prince of Scotland, 10, 22, 24
Eleanor of Aquitaine, Queen of England, 60, 61, 63, 64, 69, 149
Eleanor of Castile, Queen of England, 63

INDEX

Eleanor of Provence, Queen of England, 63, 64, 68
Elias, Norbert, 135
Ely, 88
Ely Abbey, 42, 92
Emma, Queen of England, 39, 40–44, 45, 48, 49, 69, 164
Emma, member of Matilda of Scotland's household, 101
Encomium Emmae Reginae, 40, 42, 43, 46
Engaigne, Vitalis, 152
Epping (Essex), 62, 159
Ernisius, prior of Llanthony, 101–102, 155
Espec, Walter, 121
d'Escures, Ralph, Archbishop of Canterbury, 90, 92
Esther, Biblical queen of Persia, 6, 35, 39, 83, 147, 148, 168
Eudo dapifer, 96, 155
Eustace III, Count of Boulogne, 58, 69, 90, 108, 134
Eve of Wilton, 19
Everard the Chaplain, 155
Evesham Abbey, 42
Evreux, 155
Exchequer, 88, 97
Exeter, 41, 47, 62, 69, 85–86, 97, 109, 146, 148
Exeter Book, 33
Eye Priory, 89, 153

Faritius, abbot of Abingdon, 15, 74, 82, 83, 88, 90, 96, 111, 118, 132, 149, 151, 153
fitzHamon, Robert, 57
fitzHerbert, Geoffrey, 151
Flambard, Ranulf, 59, 79, 87, 88, 97–98, 122, 152, 156
Freeman, Edward Augustus, 23
Fulbert, Bishop of Chartres, 42–43

Gaimar, Geoffrey, 41, 70, 136, 137
Galbraith, V. H., 108
Geoffrey, Dean of Waltham, 100, 158, 159
Gerard, Archbishop of York, 156
Gernon, Robert, 59, 82, 89, 99–100, 118, 120, 154
Gervin, Abbot of St Riquier, 48
Giezi, Biblical royal servant, 131
Giffard, Walter, 157
Giffard, William, Bishop of Winchester, 75, 98
Gilbert, Abbot of Westminster, 159
Gilbert the Sheriff, 109, 110, 114
Godric and Godiva, 73
Godwin, Earl, 44, 45, 46
Goscelin of St Bertin and Canterbury, 18–20, 37, 127–128, 142
Green, Judith, 89

Gregory I, Bishop of Rome, 170
Gregory of Ely, 92
Gregory of Tours, 38
Grimbald the Physician, 74, 153
Gundulph, Bishop of Rochester, 77, 78, 112, 149
Vita Gundulphi, 77, 78, 112
Gunnhilda, member of Matilda of Scotland's household, 101
Gunnhildr, daughter of Harold Godwinson, king of England, 20–25, 28
Guthery (Devonshire), 62, 154

Hadcock, R. N., 19
Hamo dapifer, 96, 154
deHanslope, Michael, 62, 96–97, 154, 155, 156
Hardacnut, King of England, 40, 43, 44
Harold Godwinson, King of England, 21, 49, 77, 126
Harold Harefoot, King of England, 42, 43
leHarpur, William, 142
Helena, St, 169
Henry V, Emperor, 85, 147
Henry I, King of England, 1, 4, 25, 51, 56, 65, 68, 73, 74, 80–83, 84, 86, 88, 89, 90, 92, 97, 99, 101, 102, 107, 108, 115, 117, 118, 120, 122, 125, 130, 145, 146, 147, 148, 154, 156, 157, 158, 159, 160
 Accession, 26–27
 Degree of courtliness in his reign, 134–138
 Dowers Matilda, 70
 Extramarital affairs and illegitimate children, 84–85
 Marries Matilda of Scotland, 27
 Role in Investiture Controversy, 76–78
Henry II, King of England, 6, 60, 61, 85, 106, 147, 148, 149
Henry III, King of England, 63, 148
Henry VI, King of England, 85
Herbert, Abbot of Westminster, 101
Herbert the Chamberlain, 151
Hermann of Tournai, 21–22, 27, 29–30
Hervey, Bishop of Bangor, 98, 155
Heslop, T. A., 138
Hildebert of Lavardin, Bishop of LeMans, 4, 89, 92, 112, 113, 117, 119, 125, 128, 129, 133, 138, 139
Hincmar of Reims, 33, 35
Hinde, Hodgson, 161
Hollister, Charles Warren, 1, 3, 27, 79, 95, 96, 137, 149
Holy Trinity, Aldgate (London), 62, 63, 66, 69, 86, 108, 110, 112, 114, 115, 145, 156, 157
 Aldgate Chronicle, 113, 115
Holy Trinity, Dunfermline, 14, 15, 112, 145
vanHouts, Elisabeth, 133

Hugh, Abbot of Chertsey, 92
Hugh, Prior of Eye, 153
Hugh, Sheriff of Northamptonshire, 156
Hugh the Chanter, 59, 61
Hugh of Leicester, 152
Huntingdonshire, 97
'Hyde Chronicler', 3, 113, 145, 146

Illingworth, R. N., 141
Investiture Controversy, 75–78
Iona, church on, 14
Isabella of Angoulême, Queen of England, 61, 63, 66, 68
Islip, Oxfordshire, 41
Ivo, Bishop of Chartres, 112, 113, 116, 119, 128, 129, 134

Jaeger, C. Stephen, 135
Jerome, St, 131
Job, 173
John, King of England, 61
John, Bishop of Bayeaux, 98, 155
John, Bishop of Sées, 98, 155
John the Evangelist, St, 89, 111, 112, 123
John of Tynemouth, 11, 104, 162
John, Queen's Chaplain, 100, 106
Jones, Robin F., 140–141
Judith, Queen of Wessex, 35

Katherine of Alexandria, St, 115
Kealey, Edward J., 79, 86, 95, 105, 115, 118
Keir, Gillian, 66
Ketton (Rutland), 70
Kilburn Wells, 101
Kirkham Priory, 121
Knowles, David, 19

Lambeth Palace, 90
Lanfranc, Archbishop of Canterbury, 29, 51, 90, 112
Langley Marish (Buckinghamshire), 59, 62, 160
Larson, Lawrence Metellus, 39
Lateran Council of 1215, 12
Laughton-en-le-Moreton (Yorkshire, west riding), 62, 80–81, 155
Laverkerstoke, 99
Lawrence of Canterbury, St, 3, 20
Legge, Mary Dominica, 139, 140
Leland, John, 108
Leo IX, Bishop of Rome, 50
Leprosy, 105–106
Lewknor (Oxfordshire), 88, 151
Liber Eliensis, 36
Lifshitz, Felice, 41, 43
Lifton Hundred (Devonshire), 62, 69, 154
Lillebonne, 86, 155

Lilleburne, 62, 121–122
Lincoln Cathedral, 90, 119
deLisors, William, 152
Liulf the Sheriff, 159
Llanthony Priory, 102, 106, 108
Loch Leven, hermits of, 15
London, 14, 123, 149
Losinga, Herbert, Bishop of Norwich, 87, 92, 111, 112, 113, 114, 120
Louis VI, King of France, 73
deLovetot, Roger, 155
Luffenham (Rutland), 62, 71, 156
Luffield, 91, 93, 108, 152

Malcolm 'Canmore', III, King of Scotland, 2, 9, 12, 13, 14, 21, 105, 122, 127, 130, 131, 133, 136, 148, 159, 165
  As husband and father, 15–16
  Killed in England, 22, 25, 119
  Negotiates daughter Edith's marriage, 21
  Negotiations with William II, King of England, 21
  Present at dedication of Durham Cathedral, 21, 122
Malet, Robert, 96, 154, 155
Malling Abbey, 83
Malmesbury, 66
  Malmesbury Abbey, 62, 64–65, 111, 117, 157
deMandeville, Geoffrey, 151
Manning, Owen, 114
Map, Walter, 147
Marbod, Bishop of Rennes, 4, 112, 125, 138
Margaret, St, Queen of Scotland, 2, 9, 10, 21, 58, 105, 106, 111, 112, 122, 123, 125, 127, 128, 131, 133, 136, 139, 145, 148, 159
  Death of, 22
  Her Gospel Book, 12, 125, 131
  Life of St Margaret, 2, 4, 10–16, 106, 112, 122, 123, 123, 132–33, 139, 146, 161–178
  Miracles of St Margaret, 161
  Piety of, 14–15
  Visits shrine of St Lawrence, 20
Martin of Tours, St, 111, 131
Martinsley Hundred (Rutland), 69, 70
Martock (Somerset), 68
Mary, St, mother of Jesus, 111, 112–113, 119, 173, 174
Mary Magdalen, St, 110, 112, 128
Mary, Countess of Boulogne, Princess of Scotland, 16, 17, 18, 58, 90, 108, 127, 134, 150, 158
Mason, Emma, 100, 101
Matilda, 'Lady of the English', Empress, Countess of Anjou, 30, 61, 65, 74, 85, 87, 146, 147, 150, 159

INDEX

Matilda of Boulogne, Queen of England, 6, 61, 64, 68, 149
Matilda of Flanders, Queen of England, 6, 10, 30, 49–51, 52, 53, 57, 112, 117, 128, 138, 145, 159
Matilda of Scotland, Queen of England, 1–6, 31, 49, 53, 57, 90, 102, 115, 122, 125
   Acta of, 2–3
   Ancestry, 2
   Attests king's charters, 80, 89
   Birth and Baptism, 9–10
   Childhood of, 13–26
   Coronation ceremony, 30
   Criticism of, 116–118
   Death and burial, 145–46
   Degree of 'courtliness' in her patronage, 137–138
   Education of, 18–20, 130–132
   Founds Holy Trinity, Aldgate, 109
   Founds leprosarium, 105–106
   Gives birth to daughter, 74
   Gives birth to son, 77–78
   Her assigned dower lands (*dos*), 61–72
   Her dowry, 58–59
   Her household, 99–102
   Her seal, 89
   Her taste in art, 126–27
   Income from gifts, 59–61
   Intercessory role, 82–84, 86, 89, 108
   Leaves monastery, 22–25
   Life of Matilda, 146
   Marries King Henry I, 28–29
   Modern judgements, 149–150
   Originally named Edith, 2, 5, 26
   Patronage in city of London, 114–115, 123
   Patronage decisions, 128–130
   Patronizes Augustinian order, 106–108
   Political role, 73–78
   Popularly considered a saint, 104, 146–149
   Presides over Exchequer, 88
   Possible illness c. 1113, 89
   Role in Investiture Controversy, 75–78
   Vice-regal authority, 78–79, 85, 91, 93
Mauduit, William, 97
Mauger, prior of Luffield, 91, 93, 152
Merton Priory, 89, 109–110, 126
Meschin, Ranulf, 154
Meyer, Marc, 38, 57
Migne, J. P., 89
deMontchesny, Hugh, 153
deMontchesny, Robert, 89
deMontfichet, William, 59, 99
deMowbray, Robert, 22, 24, 25, 152
Muriel, Anglo-Saxon nun and poet, 19
deMuschamps, Robert, 88, 152

Nazeing (Essex), 62, 159
Nelson, Janet, 38
Nettleham (Lincolnshire), 62, 68, 154
Norman, prior of Holy Trinity Aldgate, 109, 112, 124, 156
Northamptonshire, 97
Norwich Cathedral, 120
Nottingham, 88

Odo Moire/Moricus, 100, 154, 158
Offa, King of Mercia, 147
deOilli, Nigel, 96, 158
deOilli, William, 151
Opus anglicana embroidery, 119, 126, 128
Orderic Vitalis, 3, 18, 21, 23, 24, 26, 51, 48, 58, 73, 80, 91, 96, 98, 137
Osbert of Clare, 46
Osbert the Chaplain, 152
Osbert, Sheriff of Lincoln, 154
Osmund, Bishop of Salisbury, 26, 27
Oswy, King of Northumbria, 34
Ottery (Devonshire), 69
Owin, Northumbrian queen's household official, 34

Papebroch, Daniel, 161
Paris, Matthew, 106, 147
Parsons, John Carmi, 68, 113
Paschal II, Bishop of Rome, 4, 77, 92, 112, 134
Paul, St, 131
dePavilli, Robert, 155
Peterborough Abbey, 48
   Peterborough Chronicle, 48
Peverel, William, 98
Picot, Roger, 154
Pinkerton, John, 161
Pipe Rolls, 4, 119
dePonte de l'Arche, William, 96, 157
dePort, Adam, 95, 151, 153
Portsmouth, 88
Prescott, J. E., 108

Queenhithe, 62, 66–68, 114, 123
Queen's demesne, 57
Queen's Gold, 57, 59–61, 63
Queenship, 5–6
   Accession rituals, 34–36, 39
   Early-medieval, 31–34
   Integral part of monarchy, 93
   Intercessory role of medieval queen, 82–84

Rahere, 142
Ralph of Tew, 153
Ranulf the Chancellor, 95, 157, 158
Reading Abbey, 66
Regesta regum anglo-normannorum, 64, 100

Reginald of Cornwall, 68
Reginald of Durham, 12, 15, 122, 123
Regularis concordia, 36
Reinhelm, Bishop of Hereford, 75, 86, 99, 154
Richard I, King of England, 61
Richard II, Duke of Normandy, 39, 164
Richard of Cornwall, 68
Richard, Abbot of St Albans, 154
Richard son of Gotze, 155
Richardson, H. G., 38, 60, 78
Ridel, Geoffrey, 151
Ritchie, R. L. Graeme, 11, 17, 20, 58, 141
Robert Curthose, Duke of Normandy, 10, 26, 28, 50, 73, 74, 76, 84, 85, 122, 138
Robert, Count of Leicester, 91
Robert, Count of Meulan, 90, 118
Robert of Torigni, 146
Robert, son of Hervey, 62, 82, 154
Robert the Chapberlain, 153
Rockingham, 41, 97, 100, 155, 156
Roger, Bishop of Salisbury, 75, 78, 79, 86, 87, 90, 93, 95, 98, 99, 119, 130, 145, 151, 152, 153, 157, 158
Roger, Sheriff of Worcester, 152
Roger of Hovedon, 12, 61
Romsey abbey, 17–19, 20, 64, 127, 131, 133
Ross (Northumberland), 88
Rouen, 86
Rutland, 41, 57, 69–72, 97, 100, 101

St Albans, 90, 97, 119–120, 126
St Andrew's church (Scotland), 14–15, 165, 172
St Botolph's, Colchester, 107, 109
St Giles' leprosarium, 62, 66, 105–106, 114, 115, 126
St Katherine's by-the-Tower hospital, 68
St Martin's Abbey, Tours, 79
St Mary's, Huntingdon, 160
St Mary's, Northampton, 62
St Mary's, Tavistock, 62, 69, 120, 154
St Paul's, London, 145–46, 156
St Peter's, Gloucester, 62, 89, 99, 120
Saint's lives as historical sources, 4
Salisbury Cathedral, 62, 119
Sampson, Bishop of Worcester, 89
Sayles, G. O., 38, 78
Searle, Eleanor, 24
Seaton (Rutland), 62, 71, 156
Sedulius Scottus, 32
Selby Abbey, 97, 100, 120, 126
Serlo, Bishop of Bayeaux, 19, 137
Sexburga, St, 91
Sherbourne Abbey, 42
Simeon of Durham, 12, 123
Simon the Earl, 155
Song of Roland, 142

Southern, Richard, 24, 30, 75, 76, 97, 136, 137
Stafford, Pauline, 57
Stamford (Lincolnshire), 70, 156
Stenton, Frank M., 69
Stephen of Blois, King of England, 60, 64, 147, 148
Stoke (Buckinghamshire), 62, 120, 160
Stretton (Rutland), 71, 100
Strickland, Agnes, 1, 55
Sutton Courtenay, 74

T, Son of the Count, 156
Tacitus, 32
Theobald of Étampes, 15
Theodore, 162
Thomas, Archbishop of York, 87, 98
Thomas, Prior of Worcester, 88, 152
Thomas the Chaplain, 156
Thomas of St John, 151
Thorpe, 68, 87, 120
Thorpe-by-Water (Rutland), 62, 71, 156
Thurston, Archbishop of York, 98
Tinchebrai, battle of, 85, 86, 88
Tinewell, 48
Tixover (Rutland), 62, 68, 155
Tostig, Earl, 45
Tottenham, 100
deTroyes, Chrétien, 140
Turgot, Bishop of St Andrew's, 161
Turstin the Chaplain, 151
Tynemouth Priory, dependent of Church of St Albans, 25, 59, 119, 121

Vashti, Biblical Queen of Persia, 39
Victoria, Queen of England, 1
Vitalis of Savigny, mortuary roll of, 20, 147
Voyage of St Brendan, 4, 139, 140–142

Wace, 74
Walcher, Bishop of Durham, 156
Waldric, Bishop of Laon, 98, 119, 155
Walter the Lotharingian, Bishop of Hereford, 47
Walter of Gloucester, 95, 151, 152
Walter, Archdeacon of Oxford, 151
Walter, son of Edward, 158
Waltham, 100
  Waltham Abbey, 60, 62, 63, 64, 65, 80, 93, 109, 121, 126, 153, 156, 157, 158, 159
Waltheof, Anglo-Saxon rebel, 19
Waltheow, Queen (in *Beowulf*), 32–33
Warelwast, William, Bishop of Exeter, 97, 154
deWarenne, William II, Earl of Surrey, 26
Warren, W. L., 70
West, Francis, 78, 88
West Ham, 62

INDEX

Westminster, 85, 88, 89
  Palace, 78, 106, 114, 119, 145
  St James leprosarium, 106
  St Peter's Abbey, 29, 42, 49, 51, 62, 66, 83, 106, 110, 111, 112, 119, 120, 128, 145, 146, 147, 148, 159
William I, King of England, 6, 9, 10, 49, 57, 66, 68, 70, 137
William II 'Rufus', King of England, 18, 21, 22–24, 26, 27, 39, 59, 73, 77, 78, 81, 97, 101, 106, 122, 137, 142
William 'Ætheling', Prince of England, 30, 77, 87, 89, 91, 93, 95, 122, 137, 146, 147
William 'the Lion', King of Scotland, 12
William, Count of Mortain, 79
William of Corbeil, Archbishop of Canterbury, 92
William of St Carileph, Bishop of Durham, 97, 152, 153
William of Malmesbury, 3, 25, 27, 42, 45, 56, 58, 64, 73, 74, 78, 81, 85, 106, 111, 114, 116, 117, 120, 125, 126, 128, 132–133, 134, 137, 138, 142, 145

William, monk of Llanthony, 101–102, 106
Wilmart, André, 23
Wilton Abbey, 10, 18–20, 42, 46, 48, 62, 64, 119, 127, 131, 133, 142, 160
Winchecombe Annals, 26
Winchester, 74, 88, 97, 99, 100, 147
  New Minster, 36, 42
  Part of Anglo-Saxon queen's dower, 37, 41, 69
Witchley Hundred (Northamptonshire), 69
Woodstock Palace, 85
Worcester Cathedral, 88, 89, 93
Wraysbury, 99
Wulfhilda, abbess of Barking, 37
Wulfhilde, St, 18, 133
Wulfstan, Archbishop of York, 43
Wulfstan, bishop of Worcester, 15
Wulfthryth, abbess of Wilton, 10
  Life of St Wulfthryth, 18

York, 96, 120, 155
  St Mary's, York, 62, 108, 120, 154
  St Peter's, York, 80–81, 155